The Urban Tree

There is a growing evidence base that documents the social, environmental and economic benefits that urban trees can deliver. Trees are, however, under threat today as never before due to competition for space imposed by development, other hard infrastructures, increased pressure on the availability of financial provision from local authorities and a highly cautious approach to risk management in a modern litigious society.

It is, therefore, incumbent upon all of us in construction and urban design disciplines to pursue a set of goals that not only preserve existing trees where we can, but also ensure that new plantings are appropriately specified and detailed to enable their successful establishment and growth to productive maturity.

Aimed at developers, urban planners, urban designers, landscape architects and arboriculturists, this book takes a candid look at the benefits that trees provide alongside the threats that are eliminating them from our towns and cities. It takes a simple, applied approach that explores a combination of science and practical experience to help ensure a pragmatic and reasoned approach to decision-making in terms of tree selection, specification, placement and establishment. In this way, trees can be successfully incorporated within our urban landscapes, so that we can continue to reap the benefits they provide.

Duncan Goodwin is a horticulturist, arboriculturist and chartered landscape architect. He has over 30 years of horticultural, landscape design and construction experience, working in landscape construction, commercial nurseries, botanical and public gardens and landscape architecture consultancy.

Duncan is an Associate Director of Land Planning at Capita Property and Infrastructure, managing a team of landscape architects on a large multidisciplinary design and construction project based in the south of England. He is also a Senior Lecturer and Technical Co-ordinator for landscape within the Architecture and Landscape Department at the University of Greenwich, UK.

Duncan holds Master's degrees in Public Garden Management from Cornell University in the USA and Landscape Architecture from the University of Greenwich. He is a chartered landscape architect, a member of the Chartered Institute of Horticulture, a Technician member of the Arboricultural Association and a Fellow of the Linnean Society.

Duncan Goodwin

The Urban Tree

Routledge
Taylor & Francis Group

LONDON AND NEW YORK

First published 2017
by Routledge
2 Park Square, Milton Park, Abingdon, Oxon OX14 4RN

and by Routledge
711 Third Avenue, New York, NY 10017

Routledge is an imprint of the Taylor & Francis Group, an informa business

British Library Cataloguing-in-Publication Data
A catalogue record for this book is available from the British Library

Library of Congress Cataloging in Publication Data
Names: Goodwin, Duncan.
Title: The urban tree / Duncan Goodwin.
Description: Abingdon, Oxon; New York, NY : Rochester, 2017. I Includes bibliographical references and index.
Identifiers: LCCN 2016044689 I ISBN 9780415702461 (hardback : alk. paper) I ISBN 9781315266169 (ebook)
Subjects: LCSH: Trees in cities. I Urban forestry.
Classification: LCC SB436. G64 2017 I DDC 635.9/77—dc23
LC record available at https://lccn.loc.gov/2016044689

ISBN: 978-0-415-70246-1 (hbk)
ISBN: 978-1-315-26616-9 (ebk)

Typeset in Frutiger
by Florence Production Ltd, Stoodleigh, Devon, UK

Printed and bound in Great Britain by Ashford Colour Press Ltd

Contents

Foreword

The transition from rural to predominantly urban living by more than half of the world's population places an ever-increasing reliance upon built infrastructures and technology. This places higher emphasis on energy consumption, which brings a risk of increased air pollution, and inevitable increase in built form, leading to greater impact from the urban heat island effect.

There is a rich history of trees providing the ecosystem services essential to urban living. The benefits to our urban societies provided by trees are at last being fully recognised. This is demonstrated by research from around the globe, supporting the benefits provided by Green Infrastructure, and especially, the larger canopy trees, the most important element within Green Infrastructure.

As with most things in life, a balance needs to be struck and an appreciation that a range of ecosystem outputs are produced, some with benefits and some with dis-benefits. It is up to us, the landscape architects, urban designers and other land planning disciplines, to guide and advise developers in the correct and most advantageous ways to use trees.

With climate change making such an impact, especially on urban living, it is important to ensure that we select the best trees for any given location, based on their ability to adapt to climate uncertainty and become established, productive ecosystem service providers. It is not before time that a book covering the production, establishment and management of urban trees is produced by a British author, about urban trees in Britain.

By providing an overview of how trees function biologically and how they interact with their immediate surroundings affords an insight into how we may better provide for their long-term well-being. A thoughtful and careful approach to the right place, right tree is required, evidenced by scientific research. This book provides such an insight and is backed up with many years of practical experience.

R. Martin Kelly
Founder and Chair of the Trees and Design Action Group
and Land Planning Director with Capita Lovejoy

Acknowledgements

This book began life as a series of ideas during my time at Cornell University when I was still a graduate student. Two of my mentors at Cornell, to whom I owe an enormous amount of gratitude, were Professors Nina Bassuk and Tom Whitlow. Both have always been enthusiastic and generous with their critique and support.

Some of the ideas developed further as CPD presentations to built environment and construction practices, and lectures to my landscape architecture and garden design students at Hadlow College and the University of Greenwich. I must, therefore, thank my work colleagues in both construction consultancy and academia for challenging me, but also supporting me when required.

The progression from presentations and lectures to technical book has been an arduous, and sometimes, frustrating journey that would not have been possible without the help of friends and colleagues who tirelessly reviewed various sections of the text, offering much-needed guidance and advice where required. In particular, I would like to thank Christopher Atkinson, Christopher Carter, Roger Cooper, John Heuch, Robert Holden, James Lewis and Joan Webber, with special thanks to Jim Quaife who, over many beers and curries, challenged me and made me justify everything.

Finally, I would like to thank my wife, Katrina Thomas, for her endless support, for producing many of the figures used throughout the book and for helping to keep me focussed. I could not have done this without her.

Chapter 1: So what have urban trees ever done for us?

We are left in awe by the nobility of a tree, its eternal patience, its suffering caused by man and sometimes nature, its witness to thousands of years of earth's history, its creations of fabulous beauty. It does nothing but good, with its prodigious ability to serve, it gives off its bounty of oxygen while absorbing gases harmful to other living things. The tree and its pith live on. Its fruits feed us. Its branches shade and protect us. And finally, when time and weather brings it down, its body offers timber for our houses and boards for our furniture. The tree lives on.

George Nakashima (American architect, woodworker and furniture maker)

1.1 INTRODUCTION

In 2008, the planet reached an important milestone. The world population, as a whole, moved from being predominantly rural to becoming mainly urban (UN Department of Economic and Social Affairs, Population Division, 2008). This trend is set to intensify, and it is predicted that by 2050, two-thirds of the world's population will be city-dwelling (UN Department of Economic and Social Affairs, Population Division, 2014). In Europe, approximately 80 per cent of the population will be living in urban areas by 2020 (European Environment Agency, 2006). Almost 90 per cent of the British population was already living in urban areas by 1991 (Denham & White, 1998), and this propensity for urban living is likely to be matched by seven other European countries by 2020 (European Environment Agency, 2006). The social and environmental implications of this are obviously enormous.

It is true that urban expansion, if adequately planned for, has the potential to improve peoples' access to health care, education, housing and other services. It is also true that we have been exploiting trees within our urban landscapes, for the benefits they provide us, since the sixteenth century. This use of trees within urban centres reached its peak with the garden city movement and workers' colonies of the mid to late nineteenth century (Lawrence, 2006), where pressure from social reformers to increase access to green open space not only helped in urban beautification, but also improved the life of city inhabitants from all social classes. Formal street tree planting formed part of this urban greening and spread rapidly from London into urban development schemes for other UK cities and commercial centres, where it was seen as a symbol of civilisation. The result of this recognition of the importance of providing city populations with street trees and access to green open space means that many of the finest examples of our existing urban trees are a legacy from the Victorian era. It is sometimes sobering to consider that the

Figure 1.1
A busy pedestrian thoroughfare, a food market, a sunny day, dappled shade from trees, what's not to love? The Southbank, London.

longevity of some of these urban trees has proved to be greater than that of the built form around them.

However, the unending development of an increasingly urban society places an ever-mounting reliance upon built infrastructures and technology to provide the services and goods required to enable that society to function efficiently. The urban heat island effect, the expansion of impermeable surfaces, the inevitable increase in the total energy consumption and the concomitant additional air pollution this creates, lead to an ever-increasing decoupling and independence from ecological systems. Somewhat perversely, it is the solar shading, surface water attenuation, air quality improvements and increased physical and mental well-being (ecosystem services) provided by these ecological systems, of which urban trees and other vegetation are part, which play such an important role in making our cities more pleasant places to be.

Designers are readily cognisant of the aesthetic qualities but infrequently of the other physical and environmental benefits and how trees can improve our mental well-being. This chapter provides an overview of how trees can be used to provide a more beautiful, comfortable, productive and liveable urban landscape. It will also investigate why, despite more trees being planted overall, we are finding fewer and fewer large species trees within our cities, typically due to conflicts during construction and the close proximity of hard, grey infrastructures. It is, after all, these larger trees that are better placed to deliver more of the environmental benefits for a greater period of time than smaller, shorter-lived species. Many of the large canopy tree species we plant have the genetic potential to survive for well over 100 years, yet the redevelopment cycle of many urban plots will be significantly less at, perhaps, 60–80 years. To realise this potential for longevity, however, we must ensure that the trees we plant establish within the site selected and are equipped with the necessary resources to grow to productive maturity.

1.2 GREEN INFRASTRUCTURE, A DEFINITION

The concept of 'green infrastructure' has gained political momentum in recent years, with much popularity among the various levels of decision-makers, from parliamentary and local politicians, government departments and agencies, through to land planning, landscape and urban design professionals. It appears to have originated in the United States from a report submitted to the Governor of Florida by the Florida Greenways Commission (Firehook, 2015). The report states that 'The Commission's mission is to create a system of greenways for Florida, a green infrastructure as carefully planned and as well funded as our built infrastructure (like electric power and transportation systems)' (Florida Greenways Commission, 1994). The linking of the two words, green and infrastructure, was intended to raise awareness that the planning of 'natural systems' must be considered on an equal basis with other traditional grey infrastructures (Firehook, 2015). More general circulation of the term followed the May 1999 publication of *Towards a Sustainable America*, produced by the President's Council on Sustainable Development. Here, the term was described thus: 'the network of open space, airsheds, watersheds, woodlands, wildlife habitats, parks, and other natural areas that provides many vital services that sustain life and enrich the quality of life' (1999).

Since then, many different people have used the term in many different ways, but however it is described, the emphasis, as with any description of an infrastructure, must be on the importance of the benefits provided for people. Mark Benedict and Edward McMahon have been instrumental in helping to define what green infrastructure is and in their book *Green Infrastructure: Linking landscapes and Communities*, they offer the following: 'An interconnected network of natural areas and other open spaces that conserves natural ecosystem values and functions, sustains clean air and water, and provides a wide array of benefits to people and wildlife' (Benedict & McMahon, 2006). They go on to emphasise 'that it is planned and managed for its natural resource values and for the associated benefits it confers' (Benedict & McMahon, 2006). A traditional conservation approach is likely to focus on environmental preservation and restoration in isolation, and this often results in conservation being antagonistic or in opposition to development. A green infrastructure approach, while acknowledging the need for residential, commercial and business development, is more strategic and co-operative. It provides a framework which enables the conservation of natural areas and the provision of additional designed green space to be identified and prioritised within planned development. In this way, land use is optimised for physical, utility and ecosystem service provision, for the benefit of all. In line with any other infrastructure, it is important to consider the fact that planning and management are part of the package. In order to safeguard open areas, green spaces, trees and woodlands, and to capitalise on the benefits provided by them, a strategic approach must be adopted with a clear, logical and achievable vision as its intended goal. It is also worth pointing out that green infrastructures should operate at all spatial scales, from urban cores out to the surrounding countryside (URBED, 2004). Without this approach, green and other open spaces can become a collection of isolated and disparate, undeveloped or abandoned sites, rather than an inter-connected system that is planned, protected, managed, and at times, restored.

Although considered fairly new, the concept of green infrastructure planning certainly is not. The American landscape architect, Frederic Law Olmstead's scheme for Boston's famous Emerald Necklace consists of a 445 hectare (1,100 acres) chain of parks and green spaces, linked together by a network of drives, rides and walks. The chain begins in the downtown area of the city and broadly cuts a sweeping arc, linking Boston Common and Boston Public Garden with Back Bay Fens, Olmstead Park, Jamaica Pond and the Arnold Arboretum, to terminate at Franklin Park, south-west of the city. The project originally started life in 1878 with the restoration of The Back Bay Fens for reasons of sanitation. The Back Bay area was originally tidal salt marsh that had become so contaminated with raw sewage and industrial effluent that it posed a significant health risk to residents of surrounding neighbourhoods. Olmstead realised that not only could it be cleaned and restored to its original salt marsh condition, but it could be used as a flood defence wetland, possibly the first of its kind to be constructed (Spirn, 1995). Beyond the restoration work, an interceptor sewer was added, as was a parkway, footpaths and horse rides to provide recreation facilities for visitors. Boston's first tram service was also constructed to service the newly created park. Collectively, these facilities and functions formed a landscape system that managed the removal of sewage, provided safeguard against flooding and accommodated the recreational needs of the people of Boston (Spirn, 1995). Green infrastructure, therefore, refers to more than the natural areas alone; it can also include constructed landscapes and facilities. The importance is that there are some ecological, social and economic benefits associated with its existence.

There is also confusion sometimes between the use of terms green infrastructure and urban forest. In the United Kingdom, the now defunct National Urban Forestry Unit defined the urban forest as: 'all the trees and woods in an urban area: in parks, private gardens, streets, around factories, offices, hospitals and schools, on wasteland and in existing woodland. Urban forestry is the planned approach to the planting and management of trees and woods in towns' (National Urban Forestry Unit, 1999). The Society of American Foresters add a little more detail to the practice of urban forestry, in *The Dictionary of Forestry*, thus: 'the art, science, and technology of managing trees and forest resources in and around urban community ecosystems for the physiological, sociological, economic, and aesthetic benefits trees provide society' (Helms, 1998). The urban forest, therefore, is considered an element within green infrastructure.

1.3   DESIGNERS' TOOLKIT

In design terms, trees have always been seen as one of the urban planner's most useful tools. They can improve urban landscapes by bringing an aesthetic value, helping to soften hard surfaces, guiding and framing views and by providing a setting for buildings, helping the user and viewer to negotiate that transition from tall built forms to ground level. They can be used to help delineate spaces by introducing visual and physical separation between areas, informing a hierarchy of use. They can deflect the eye to aid circulation. They can concentrate the view to guide movement, helping to inform direction, destination and a sense of arrival. They increase visual diversity by introducing shape and form, often bringing a leafy sense of calm to a setting. They can also introduce vibrancy and excitement with some quite spectacular colour displays during otherwise dull times of the year. Despite all these aesthetic qualities they bring to the landscape, urban trees are being threatened as never before due to reduced local authority budgets, increased development pressure, public apathy and a risk-averse insurance industry.

Trees in Towns II was a research project commissioned by the Department of Communities and Local Government, which investigated the condition and management of the urban tree population in England (Britt & Johnston, 2008). The report highlighted that, on average, over 24 per cent of the local authority trees planted in public open space and 23 per cent of the trees planted along highways die before they become established. These findings have been substantiated by other later research studies (Jack-Scott, Piana, Troxel, Murphy-Dunning & Ashton, 2013; Roman, Battles & McBride, 2014) for publicly owned trees, but may even be higher than this for trees in private ownership (Jack-Scott, Piana, Troxel, Murphy-Dunning & Ashton, 2013). A contemporaneous review of London's street trees for the London Assembly, entitled

'Chainsaw Massacre' (GLA, 2007), highlighted a worrying trend in the progressive reduction of the overall tree canopy cover. Despite 48,000 trees being planted and 40,000 being removed, across London as a whole between 2002 and 2007, twelve of the thirty-three boroughs still reported a net loss in publicly owned tree stock for the same period. In many instances, large mature trees are being replaced with smaller, shorter-lived varieties (GLA, 2007). These findings were echoed by *Trees in Towns II*, which found that what is happening in London appears to be common to other urban conurbations throughout the UK (Britt & Johnston, 2008). If these trends continue, our green infrastructure legacy, in contrast to that of our Victorian forebears, will be one of perpetual immaturity, unable to provide the ecosystem benefits we require of it (Sjöman, Hirons & Bassuk, 2015).

1.4   URBAN PLACES CAN BE TREE-HOSTILE

Unlike the natural environments to which trees have adapted, urban locations can be stressful and far from ideal; yet we still expect these hostile environments to provide the resources necessary for healthy tree growth.

A variety of conditions and factors can cause stress to urban trees; they are surrounded by buildings, often planted within a sea of impervious surfaces and subjected to reflected and radiated heat, wind funnelling and shade from sun and rain (Whitlow & Bassuk, 1988).

- Restricted root volume: Concrete kerbs, building foundations and basements, utility infrastructure, construction rubble and engineered build-up all help to restrict the amount of soil available for tree roots to explore for required water and nutrients (Lindsey & Bassuk, 1992).
- Soil compaction: In order to support engineered surfaces and structures, soils are typically required to be compacted far beyond the limit at which root penetration is prevented. Compaction also reduces the amount of pore space within the soil profile, which, in turn, restricts the movement of oxygen to the root zone and can create localised waterlogging (Craul, 1985; Lichter & Lindsey, 1994; Randrup, 1998).

Figure 1.2
The tenacity of London planes has to be admired. Despite appearing to have very little in terms of soil, water and nutrient cycling, this tree is still able to grow, somehow managing to exploit the resources it can access.

- Alkaline soil: The presence of many lime-containing materials causes the soil to become highly alkaline, limiting the amount of some important nutrients, such as iron and manganese, available to plants. The results of such soil can often be seen as yellowing foliage – chlorosis (Craul, 1985).
- Inconsistent access to water: Despite rainfall in cities being typically 5–10 per cent higher than in the rural areas, the majority of surface water, during heavy summer rain events, flows off hard surfaces, with very little being absorbed into the ground (Hoff, 2001).
- High urban temperature: The re-radiated heat from buildings, paving materials and other hard infrastructures all help to elevate the air temperature within urban centres. The higher the temperature, the more water trees lose through transpiration from their leaves (Doll, Ching & Kaneshiro, 1985; Montague & Kjelgren, 2004). This is thought to have a greater implication in the creation of water deficits in trees than a lack of available water within the root zone (Whitlow & Bassuk, 1988; Whitlow, Bassuk & Reichert, 1992).

A recent urban trend is the use of trees in the training of fighting dogs. The owners encourage their dogs to jump up and lock their mouths onto the lower branches of trees as a way to build up strength in the dog's jaws, neck and shoulders. They are also goaded into attacking tree stems and stripping bark, to encourage aggression and sharpen their teeth. It is not an uncommon sight within urban parks and inner city green spaces to see tree stems and branches stripped of their bark where they have been used to train these so-called 'weapon dogs' (Barkham, 2009). In response, local authorities are using a variety of methods to deter these practices, from bamboo, hessian and mesh wrapping to chestnut paling fencing and metal tree guards. Some local authorities are using a non-toxic, bio-degradable, foul-tasting grease, applied to tree stems and branches. Such measures make a visual impact and could be considered 'unsightly'. The London Tree Officers' Association suggests that tree protection is only one element within what should be a multi-faceted approach (LTOA, 2010). They argue that the tree damage caused by these antisocial activities is best dealt with through education and community engagement initiatives, which are run in tandem with multi-agency co-operation and law enforcement. Somewhat perversely, the Royal Society for the Prevention of Cruelty to Animals (RSPCA) reports that there are more pitbull-type dogs seized by the police in the UK now than when they were outlawed by the Dangerous Dogs Act in 1991 (RSPCA, 2011).

1.4.1 Ecosystem services and perceived disservices

There currently is much enthusiasm, both within the academic and political worlds, to foster a greater mutual understanding of the concept of ecosystem services. The term 'ecosystem services' was popularised by the Millennium Ecosystem Assessment (MA), a multi-nation initiative whose objective was to 'assess the consequences of ecosystem change for human well-being and the scientific basis for action needed to enhance the conservation and sustainable use of those systems and their contribution to human well-being' (Millennium Ecosystem Assessment, 2005). The MA defined ecosystem services as 'the benefits people obtain from ecosystems' (Millennium Ecosystem Assessment, 2003). These benefits were grouped under four functional headings:

- **Provisioning services** are the products obtained from ecosystems, such as food, fibre, fuel and fresh water.

- **Regulating services** are the benefits obtained from the regulation of ecosystem processes, such as air quality mitigation, climate regulation (energy reduction), storm water storage and attenuation, carbon sequestration, water treatment, biological control and pollination.
- **Cultural services** are the heritage, spiritual, social, educational, recreational and aesthetic benefits derived from ecosystems.
- **Supporting services** are those necessary for the production of all other ecosystem services and tend to be indirect or occur over a long period of time, such as nutrient recycling, primary production and soil formation (Millennium Ecosystem Assessment, 2003).

However, if suitable management strategies and environmental policy are to be made, an understanding of both the benefits and dis-benefits that urban ecosystems can provide is essential. For instance, it is not uncommon for trees in built-up areas to be perceived as a nuisance (Schroeder, Flannigan & Coles, 2006). Certainly, large trees growing close to inhabited buildings – both housing and office spaces – may cast unwanted shade, and careful consideration needs to be given to the siting of trees in such locations.

Falling leaves may be cited as the cause for blocked drains and gutters. Leaf fall coupled with wet weather may also be implicated in the disruption to the normal running of rail services due to the increase in braking distances. Network Rail claim that in 2013, 4.5 million hours of delays were caused by leaves (Network Rail). The same safety concerns could also be raised about leaves falling on road surfaces, especially if this occurs close to junctions.

Trees planted close to junctions and points of access, if not correctly located, can also interrupt required clear sight lines (visibility splays), impeding visibility, and can be used as defence in the mitigation of road traffic accidents. All roadside trees, with a stem girth of 250 mm or more at maturity, are treated as hazards when planted within the verges of highways carrying fast-moving traffic. They are considered, for risk purposes, alongside other fixed objects, such as lamp columns, road signs and bridge abutments (The Highways Agency, 2006). Colliding at speed with a large tree can cause significant damage to both vehicle and driver and would either require removal, if within 9 m of the carriageway edge, or protection, with a vehicle-restraint system or barrier (The Highways Agency, 2006). For more formal and avenue planting along inter-urban road corridors and at approaches to settlements, large trees should be positioned at least 7.5 m from the edge of the carriageway (The Highways Agency, 2001a). It is interesting to read the range of responses to a Department for Transport funded Rural Road Safety Demonstration Project, where roadside trees have been planted along the approaches to four Norfolk villages, in an effort to reduce vehicle speed (Road Safety GB, 2010; Youde & Pang, 2010).

Problems are not restricted to road and rail transport; falling leaves and fruit can also create messy, slippery conditions on pedestrian routes. Footways and footpaths can be deflected by tree roots growing beneath them, creating uneven surfaces that can cause real concerns for people with mobility problems and the partially sighted. We live in an increasingly litigious society where local authorities are constantly under threat of personal injury law suits against trip and slip hazards. Large paving units used in close proximity to trees can create quite significant trip hazards, even if the root growth is fairly modest, simply due to the size of the paving unit (The Highways Agency, 2006).

Certain trees can release biogenic volatile organic compounds (BVOCs), allergenic pollen and other air-borne irritants, which can cause severe health problems to some susceptible people,

Figure 1.3
Fallen leaves and fruit can become a slip hazard in wet weather, especially in combination with steps or slopes. As with occurrences of snow and ice, management measures may need to be put in place to prevent slips, trips and falls.

especially problems of a respiratory nature, such as asthma. The BVOCs, mainly isoprene and monoterpenes, are produced during normally healthy growing conditions, but tend to increase when plants are subject to stress. Through a chain of atmospheric reactions, BVOCs are able to combine with nitrogen oxides (NO_x) from vehicle exhausts to create a variety of photochemical pollutants, including ozone (O_3). These pollutants and inhalable, air-borne particulate matter of less than 10 μm in diameter (PM_{10}) can cause inflammation of the respiratory tract to predisposed individuals. This size of 10 μm is important as only particles smaller than this are able to penetrate the respiratory tract deep into the alveoli of the lungs, where they can settle and cause irritation. Although pollen grains typically range from 15 to 40 μm, and so tend to be restricted to the upper respiratory tract, the allergens contained within them can be transferred to other air-borne pollutants within the PM_{10} range and less, allowing them to be inhaled deep into the lungs. For this reason, inhabitants of urban areas, subject to elevated levels of air-borne pollution, tend to show a higher incidence of pollen allergies than those resident in suburban and more rural areas (D'Amato, 2000; D'Amato *et al.*, 2007).

Although the actual incidence of crime in woodlands, parks and other green spaces is generally very low, they are often considered to be unsafe. Because of this common perception of being dangerous, such spaces often encourage feelings of anxiety and insecurity, especially among women, who respond by avoiding using them, especially if they are alone and it is dark (Burgess, 1995; Koskela & Pain, 2000; Jorgensen & Anthopoulou, 2007). There is also a perception among some immigrant and ethnic communities that wooded areas and green open spaces are intrinsically dangerous, either due to spaces being subject to low levels of surveillance or the presence of dogs (Rishbeth, 2001; Lyytimäki & Sipilä, 2009) and the concomitant dog excrement not collected by uncaring owners.

The consideration of ecosystem disservices, when assessing the effects of urban green infrastructure, is a fairly recently emerging one. The typical assumption is that urban trees and other green infrastructure benefit society by providing a range of ecosystem 'goods'. Perhaps, a more realistic scenario is that a multiple and wide-ranging set of ecosystem outputs are produced, which can be considered as either beneficial or deleterious. It is important to have regard for both the positive and the negative ecosystem outputs whenever assessments of the quality of life for urban-dwelling communities is being linked to, or measured against, ecosystem structure and function.

1.4.2 Subsidence claims

If the ground on which building foundations are situated moves or sinks, this movement often manifests itself by signs of diagonal cracking, typically wider at the top than at the bottom and especially during prolonged periods of dry weather. In susceptible soils, known as the *shrinkable clays*, the volume of the soil alters in relation to the amount of water it contains. As the water content rises (typically during the winter), the clay swells. As the water content decreases either through evaporation or transpiration by plants, the soil shrinks. This cyclic shrinking and swelling is often the cause of subsidence.

Trees and other vegetation extract water from the soil, causing it to shrink, and so, are often implicated as the cause of structural damage to property, especially on the shrinkable clay soils of London and the south-east. However, outside these areas, the risk is fairly low, and even within London, the London Assembly recorded that only 5 per cent of all the trees felled between 2002 and 2007 were due to subsidence claims (GLA, 2007). The Mayor's *London Tree and Woodland Framework* suggests that the perceived threat of subsidence is far greater than the actual risk and estimates that less than 1 per cent of the total tree population has been proven to actually cause damage to the property (GLA, 2005). That said, it has been estimated that some 60 per cent of the national housing stock is constructed in areas where shrinkable clay soil predominates (O'Callaghan & Kelly, 2005).

Where there is clear and substantial evidence that trees are involved in subsidence cases, however, local authorities often remove the trees concerned or grant permission for removal, rather than risk expensive repair costs being claimed later. Developers have been known to exploit this as has the media in search of a 'good' story.

The National House-Building Council (NHBC) provides guidance for suitable foundations close to trees. It states that 'Foundations shall be capable of accommodating the effects of trees and hedgerows on shrinkable soils without excessive movement' (NHBC, 2014).

Conventional landscape paradigms in our urban environment, and tree planting in particular, are being challenged as never before. As urban planning and landscape practitioners, we need to look beyond the aesthetic and think much more creatively. Our cities need to be multi-functional, they need to be able to adapt to the expected increases in population and the uncertain outcomes of predicted climate change. To help inform our design objectives, there is a wealth of research out there, which supports the benefits of trees.

1.5 THE BENEFITS

Great emphasis is placed on interpreting current scientific thinking around ecosystem services into regular language and assigning economic values to them, as a way to help inform politicians and other decision-makers on current versus future costs and benefits, when comparing ecological with technological approaches. For such purposes, ecosystems can be regarded as capital assets, yielding flows of vital services, such as the production of goods (provisioning services), life-support processes (regulating services) and conditions that make life worthwhile (cultural services). In this way, it should be possible to develop integrated ecological–economic–social approaches to managing ecosystem assets, and so, embody human welfare within local, regional and national environmental, development and climate change adaptation policies.

Some argue that the economic valuation of goods and services provided by ecosystems is not particularly wise and can certainly be risky (Ludwig, 2000). However, we are already making valuation judgements on ecosystems and ecosystem function. Choices are being made about ecological assets all the time, and each must be based on some form of value-based system, whether it is a monetised system or not (Costanza *et al.*, 1997).

The term 'natural capital' is often used to describe the natural ecosystem assets that provide the goods and services for people. The Natural Capital Committee (NCC), chaired by Professor Dieter Helm, was established in 2012 to independently advise the UK government 'on how to ensure England's "natural wealth" is managed efficiently and sustainably, thereby un-locking opportunities for sustained prosperity and well-being' (NCC, 2015). The NCC has provided a framework for developing a strategy and 25-year plan that considers sustainable economic growth alongside health and well-being and identifies potential actions and initiatives that could be taken to help deliver these services while enhancing the natural capital that facilitates them.

1.5.1   Social and health benefits

Frances Kuo and William Sullivan, from the University of Illinois at Urbana-Champaign, found that, contrary to popular belief and many academic studies, the presence of vegetation in urban areas may actually reduce the incidence of crime (Kuo & Sullivan, 2001). They suggest that the connection between trees and social ecosystem health is an extension of Oscar Newman's defensible space theory (Newman, 1972). The presence of trees can be a decisive factor in the extent to which residents take ownership of their local area, encouraging people out of their homes and into public open space, providing opportunities for informal social contact among neighbours. This helps to create a system of informal surveillance, which in turn can discourage potential perpetrators, while at the same time, mitigating some of the psychological precursors to violence.

Research conducted by Roger Ulrich of Texas A&M University showed that hospital patients who have a view of green space and trees recover faster and require less post-operative pain medication (Ulrich, 1984). Views of nature rapidly reduce the physiological stress response. Further studies by Ulrich and many others show that the heart rate, blood pressure and other body function measures return to normal levels more quickly when people view nature after a stressful experience (Ulrich, Simons, Losito, Fiorito, Miles & Zelson 1991). The Marmot Review of health inequalities recognises these benefits and places great emphasis on 'improving the availability of good quality open and green spaces across the social gradient' (Marmot *et al.*, 2010). Poor mental health costs the UK economy an estimated £26.1 billion per year (Faculty of Public Health, 2010). The Faculty of Public Health suggests that access to safe public green space may be as effective as prescription drugs in treating some mental health illnesses (Faculty of Public Health, 2010). There is increasing evidence to support the notion that people who live near trees benefit from living healthier and happier lives. In its report *Our Natural Health Service*, Natural England stated that 'If every household in England were provided with good access to quality green space it could save an estimated £2.1 billion in health care costs' (Natural England, 2009). When compared to the extraordinary sums of money involved with health provision, incorporating gardens in hospitals and other health care facilities and improving access to green space would appear to offer good value for money if such provisions can provide a range of health benefits for all social groups and reduce the overall cost of care.

1.5.2 Urban heat island effect

Today trees, as part of green infrastructure, are being recognised more and more as an important strategic asset. Ninety per cent of the UK residents live in an urban environment as does more than half the world population. Cities are hot, noisy places with poor air quality, prone to flash flooding during rain storms, and they consume vast quantities of energy to cool in summer and heat in winter. The heat island effect typically raises the mean city temperatures by approx 4°C above surrounding rural areas. This will be made worse by climate change. The urban heat island effect is mainly caused by energy from the sun being absorbed by buildings and hard surfaces where it is stored as heat. Most urban surfaces are dark (low albedo) and reflect often less than 10 per cent of this solar energy. This can be even lower in high-rise cities where the energy is reflected down into so-called urban canyons. At night, the stored heat is slowly released from the buildings and other hard infrastructure, keeping the air temperature high. Pollution, which tends to collect in urban canyons, can exacerbate the problem by helping to trap long-wave radiation and preventing it dissipating. Conversely, rural vegetation typically reflects approximately 25 per cent of the incoming radiation from the sun with much of the remainder being used to drive evapo-transpiration, an important component of the hydrologic cycle. Less energy, therefore, remains to heat the air by convection and the ground by conduction. This is nothing new. Trees have been used for centuries to reduce high summer temperatures by providing shade and by absorbing solar energy to evaporate water, and so, cool the air. Susannah Gill and the research team from the University of Manchester have calculated that increasing the tree cover of Manchester city centre by 10 per cent should reduce the maximum surface temperature by approximately 4°C, which they say should effectively 'climate-proof' the city up to, but not including, the UK Climate Impacts Programme (UKCIP) 2080s high-emissions scenario (Gill *et al.*, 2007).

1.5.3 Air quality

It can be shown that vegetation captures gases, aerosols and particulates more effectively than any other urban surface (Fowler *et al.*, 1989) and trees, because of the relatively large surface area of their canopies, are more effective still than ground or short vegetation (Fowler *et al.*, 2004; Powe & Wills, 2004). It should be noted that these studies looked principally at woodland rather than at individual trees. There are many other studies that have investigated the effects on urban air quality by urban street trees, for example, McPherson *et al.*, 1998; Nowak *et al.*, 2006; McDonald *et al.*, 2007; Selmi *et al.*, 2016 (in press).

The House of Commons Environmental Audit Committee, in its 2010 fifth report, acknowledged that premature deaths caused by air pollution in the UK were likely to be in the region of 35,000 for the year of 1998 (*Air Quality Fifth Report of Session 2009–10 Volume I Report, Together with Formal Minutes, 2010*). From the data gathered by the European Environment Agency (EEA), by 2012, the number had increased to over 52,000 (*Air Quality in Europe – 2015 Report, 2015*). The World Health Organization estimated that in 2012 'outdoor pollution was responsible for the deaths of some 3.7 million people under the age of 60' worldwide (WHO, 2014). In addition, health impacts from air pollution are also expressed as an increase in morbidity (European Environment Agency, 2015).

The primary culprits for these adverse effects upon urban air quality are NO_X, O_3, sulphur dioxide (SO_2), air-borne particulate matter with an aerodynamic diameter of less than 10 μm (PM_{10}) and latterly, fine particulate matter with an aerodynamic diameter of less than 2.5 μm ($PM_{2.5}$).

Figure 1.4
Residential streets
with little traffic
movement are good
locations for large
canopy trees.

The larger particles, greater than 10 μm in diameter, tend to fall out of suspension, due to gravity, fairly quickly (a matter of a few hours). Conversely, those less than 10 μm are respirable, and so, small enough to enter the deepest parts of the human lungs, where they can settle and cause a variety of health problems. Urban particulates can contain toxic compounds of heavy metals, traffic exhaust emissions, car tyre materials and brake dust. Trees can intercept and slow air-borne particulate materials causing them to fix to leaves and branches. It has been claimed that a roadside sugar maple of 300-mm stem diameter can remove 60 mg cadmium, 140 mg chromium, 820 mg nickel and 5,200 mg lead from the air in one growing season (Coder, 2011). When it rains, these particulates can be washed onto the ground where they can be bound within the soil matrix. Trees have also been shown to absorb pollutant gases such as O_3, NO_x, SO_2, carbon monoxide and carbon dioxide (Hewitt, Stewart, Donovan & MacKenzie).

There have been many reports that cite the monetised outputs from computer models to provide evidence of effective ecosystem services improvement through the use of urban tree planting (Nowak, Greenfield, Hoehn & Lapoint, 2013). However, some caution needs to be taken when using such models as a lever to influence policy-making and to focus air improvement strategies towards the planting of urban trees. Air quality improvement is only one of the many benefits provided by urban tree planting, but it is a fairly modest gain. Nowak and co-authors modelled $PM_{2.5}$ removal by trees in ten US cities and calculated that air quality improvement, attributable to trees, may be between 0.05 per cent and 0.24 per cent. Calculating the benefits for New York City would provide an increased life expectancy of 0.64 years per capita. Only when this is multiplied by the overall population does a significant monetary value evolve. This, however, should not mask the fact that the effect realised by any single individual within the population is modest (Whitlow *et al.*, 2014).

In a study that looked at the estimated removal of particulate pollution (in this case PM_{10}) by urban trees in London, Tallis, Taylor, Sinnett, and Freer-Smith (2011) found that the resultant decrease in ambient pollution concentrations due to current tree cover to be somewhere in the region of 0.7–1.4 per cent. By increasing that existing tree cover by 50 per cent, the estimated removal of particulate pollution would increase to 1.1–2.6 per cent by the year 2050. They further postulate that specific targeting of tree planting, and especially street tree planting, to the most polluted areas would have the greatest benefit to future air quality. In other studies (Gromke & Ruck, 2007; Gromke & Ruck, 2009; Gromke, 2011; Gromke & Ruck, 2012; Pugh, MacKenzie, Whyatt & Hewitt, 2012; Wania *et al.*, 2012; Vos, Maiheu, Vankerkom & Janssen, 2013), it has been found that tree planting needs to be carefully considered in urban areas, especially if the pollution source is in a street canyon. Closely spaced tall buildings can create street canyons where wind speeds, at ground level, are low and air circulation is limited. If trees are planted within these canyons, airflow can be further obstructed and ventilation reduced, trapping pollutants beneath the tree canopy and causing a fumigation effect, thereby exposing pedestrians to increasing concentrations of street-level pollution. Where traffic is absent from the street canyon or infrequent, trees can provide valuable air filtering.

Vos, Maiheu, Vankerkom and Janssen (2013) suggest that the scale at which a study has been conducted will influence the conclusions that may be drawn, in terms of urban vegetation and urban air quality. When studying the local scale, it can be argued that street trees should be planted away from the pollution source to avoid reducing the ventilation, and so, causing a fumigation effect. For studies concerning an optimal city averaged air quality, Tallis, Taylor, Sinnett and Freer-Smith (2011) recommend that, as removal of pollutants increases with pollution concentration, tree planting should take place as close to the source as possible. These apparently opposing views (what Vos *et al.* refer to as a 'green paradox') are purely due to the different scales of assessment. While planting trees may help in some situations, tree planting alone is unlikely to improve urban air sufficiently when compared to other more direct interventions, such as a reduction in the overall pollution loading (Whitlow *et al.*, 2014). The effects that urban trees have on urban air quality are not currently well-enough understood to enable good mitigation strategies to be defined. More multi-scale approaches are required within a single study (Vos, Maiheu, Vankerkom & Janssen, 2013). With many urban local authorities struggling to meet their air quality standards, some may feel encouraged to invest their already stretched resources into planting trees to counter air quality problems, rather than to focus these resources directly towards strategies aimed at reducing emissions. Urban development has steadily replaced what was previously vegetated land with buildings roads and other hard infrastructure. Trees and other green infrastructure are vital elements within the urban ecosystem, 'but the system has been pushed far beyond its biological capacity to compensate for human disturbances like air pollution' (Whitlow *et al.*, 2014).

1.5.4 Opportunities for community orchards

Until fairly recently, almost every suburban garden had its own fruit trees, and orchards were once widespread throughout the country. Indeed, British apple varieties originate from almost every county in Britain, from Scotland to Cornwall. Brogdale Collections, in Faversham, Kent, is home to the National Fruit Collection and holds 2,200 varieties of apple, 550 varieties of pear, 285 varieties of cherry, 337 varieties of plum, nineteen of culinary quince, forty-two varieties of nut, 318 of currants and four of medlar (Brogdale Collections, 2016). In 2007, traditional orchards were added to the UK Biodiversity Action Plan as a declining, priority habitat. An ever-increasing demand on land for development and cheap, imported fruit from around the world have been partly responsible for the demise of the domestic fruit tree. Orchards in villages and on the edges of towns are particularly vulnerable as prime targets for development. The National Trust claims that over 90 per cent of traditional English orchards have been lost since the 1950s (Cider Apple Collection Saved, 2016).

Common Ground was founded in 1983 by Sue Clifford, Angela King and Roger Deakin, with the aim of encouraging communities to make long-lasting connections with their local environment, through art, education and community gatherings. They started work on creating and conserving local orchards in 1992 and first produced a *Community Orchards Handbook* in 2008. This manual, now in its second edition, written by Angela King and Sue Clifford, provides a lessons-learned history of the philosophy and practicalities of creating orchards for and by the local community (King & Clifford, 2011).

In 2009, Carina Millstone and Rowena Ganguli set up the London Orchard Project, which became the Urban Orchard Project, promoting fruit growing and helping local community groups to establish orchards on housing estates, parks, colleges and other public spaces. Although the charity initially started in London, it is now spreading its programme to Birmingham, Manchester and Glasgow. Their most ambitious project has probably been the restoration of the orchard at Bethlem Royal Hospital in Bromley, Kent. The orchard, which dates from the 1920s, was rescued from a sea of brambles and is used to support occupational therapy and cookery classes for people with mental health problems.

One of the main advantages with fruit trees is that they are generally fairly easy to grow and can be quite productive, once they have established, with very little in the way of maintenance. Watering is required during the first growing season, some pruning will be necessary and mulching will help. Food can be such a good vector for crossing social and cultural barriers, and some existing community orchards have been incredibly successful at encouraging community cohesion through celebratory events, horticultural education, fruit production, harvest, juicing and preserving.

1.5.5 Enhanced property prices

The links between property values or consumer behaviour and the proximity of green space and street trees have been talked about in American research literature for many years. By reviewing the actual sale prices of residential property against a range of other property attributes, using a hedonic pricing model, Morales (1980), Morales *et al.* (1983), Anderson and Cordell (1988) were able to analyse the effect that trees may have on property values. In Athens, Georgia, Anderson and Cordell (1988) estimated the average property value enhancement provided by medium to large front garden trees equated to 3.5–4.5 per cent. Morales (1980), found that in Manchester, Connecticut, 'good tree cover' could attribute between 6 and 9 per cent of the total sales price. More recent American research by Donovan and Butry (2010) looked at estimating the effects of street trees on sale prices of residential properties in Portland, Oregon. They found that the combined effects of number of trees fronting the property and overall crown area within 30.5 m of the house raised the sales price by an average of 3 per cent.

These studies used multiple regression analysis to calculate values between the many elements that contribute to the sales prices of property. This enables individual variations between properties to be factored into the statistical calculations to create a 'level playing field' when making comparisons. That said, the results from any study such as these must be treated with some caution if any definite claims are made. As Anderson and Cordell point out, the regression analysis will

Figure 1.5
The fresh green foliage of these Norway maples provides some welcome dappled shade in the summer and helps to keep the rain off shoppers.

not necessarily differentiate between a causal link and an association. The increase in sale price may not be solely due to the presence of trees, but may be due to other features that are *associated* with trees. An example provided by the authors is that properties with fireplaces were statistically more likely to have higher numbers of trees in their front gardens. In this example, it is difficult to categorically state what proportion of the sale price is attributed to either trees or to fireplaces alone. This is a known limitation of hedonic models and is known as collinearity.

In the UK, the GLA commissioned a report *Valuing Greenness: Green Spaces, House Prices and Londoners' Priorities* (GLA, 2003), which confirmed a link between proximity of urban green space and enhanced property prices in London. It found that within a typical London Ward, a 1 per cent increase in green space could lead to a 0.3–0.5 per cent increase in local property prices. Although the report does not mention trees specifically, its main focus was on urban parks and play areas, where trees invariably form a key element within the space. CABE (Commission for Architecture and the Built Environment) took this and other international studies to develop their own in-depth, case-study approach. Their report suggested property value premiums, for properties close to urban parks, of 3–34 per cent, with typical value lifts being in the region of 5–7 per cent (the highest value of 34 per cent, for Mowbray Park in Sunderland, is also thought to be due to other factors such as proximity to the city centre). As an example, the valuation of properties overlooking the restored Queen Square in Bristol was found to be 16 per cent higher than comparable properties elsewhere.

Another aspect of trees in close proximity to buildings, and which has an effect on values, is what attracts people to and how they behave in retail districts. Most of the available research in this area has been produced by Kathy Wolf of the University of Washington, Seattle, Washington. Initial survey results from shoppers suggested that trees are 'important components of a welcoming, appealing consumer environment' (Wolf, 2003). In addition, shoppers were prepared to travel further to visit retail areas with trees, visit more often, pay more for parking once there and spend longer shopping. The argument that car parking spaces lost to tree planting is an over-extravagant use of space appears not to be supported (Wolf, 2003). Results from a later case study, where visitors to the business district of Athens, Georgia, were interviewed, are consistent with the earlier survey. In addition, large, full canopy trees are preferred over smaller, less significant varieties. Interestingly, modern architecture, visually buffered by trees, was found to be preferable to historic buildings without trees (Wolf, 2004).

Shoppers' attitudes to the broader environment within which they are shopping should not come as any surprise. There is extensive retail and consumer behavioural science to inform retailers' marketing strategies which, in turn, guide marketing decisions such as product packaging, shop layout and décor, ambiance and consumer experience, among other things (e.g., Baker & Grewal, 1994; Donovan & Rossiter, 1994; Grewal & Baker, 1994).

1.5.6 Cultural heritage

Trees form a significant part of Britain's historic, cultural and ecological heritage, with these lands containing a high proportion of the ancient trees present in Northern Europe (Fay, 2002). It has even been claimed that there are more ancient trees in Windsor Great Park alone than in the whole of either France or Germany (Stokes & Rodger, 2004). Some ancient trees especially have been treasured by many generations and may be relics or remnants of ancient woods, so providing a direct, historical link back to a previous age and, as such, help to inform local identity and the particularities of a place. They have always held interest for painters, poets and other aesthetes, for their significant and unique contribution to the landscape. They may also contain an important gene pool and so have the potential to provide an enormous biological resource for modern plant breeding. Many were managed as sources for animal fodder, timber or firewood, with many of these pollards and coppices still visible today.

Veteran trees are not as old as ancient trees, but show some ancient tree characteristics, such as low, squat shape with a wide trunk and a canopy that has reduced in size, compared with other specimens. Sometimes, the trunk will show signs of hollowing but this may not be present or visible. Often the characteristic signs have been caused by weather damage, particular tree management techniques or by the environment in which the tree is growing. Many ancient trees are to be found in current and former parkland, such as Windsor Great Park and Greenwich Park, in south-east London. Some ancient and veterans will be present in old hedgerows as boundary trees.

Although it is unusual, sometimes ancient, but less infrequently veteran, trees are affected by development proposals. In these situations, careful consideration needs to be given to the tree, and specialist advice should be sought. One such advisory body is the Ancient Tree Forum, which was launched in 1993, with the aim of promoting the value and importance of ancient and veteran trees and providing guidance on their management, to secure conservation wherever possible.

Figure 1.6
Some of the magnificent sweet chestnuts (*Castanea sativa*) in Greenwich Park are over 400 years old, making them ancient trees. These are remnants of Charles II's formal French-style park, designed by Le Notre in the early 1660s.

1.5.7 Source of fuel

Over the last decade or so, wood has become an increasingly attractive source of low carbon energy in the UK along with other forms of biomass. Indeed, Policy 5.1 of the London Plan sets a carbon dioxide (CO_2) emissions reduction target of 60 per cent below 1990 levels by 2025. There is an expectation that all new development will contribute to this ambitious target through the application of Policy 5.2, which sets zero carbon targets for buildings within major developments of 2016 for residential buildings and 2019 for non-domestic buildings (GLA, 2016). Development proposals should demonstrate how they intend to use less energy, supply energy efficiently and use renewable energy to achieve these targets. The use of biomass is often seen as a cost-effective way to make a significant impact on CO_2 emissions reduction, either as a source of heating alone or by using combined heat and power (CHP) systems, to provide both heating and electricity.

The London Borough of Croydon and environmental consultants BioRegional established a working relationship in 1995 with the aim of improving tree and woodland management within the borough. In addition to some areas of woodland being returned to coppice management, the Croydon Tree Station was set up as part of the council's green waste recycling initiative. This facility was created to make better use of the arboricultural waste, generated by the council's

Figure 1.7
Pieter Bruegel the Elder: *The Gloomy Day (De sombere dag)*. One of the set of six paintings depicting different times of year. The 1565 scene clearly shows woodsmen collecting brushwood from pollarded trees, thought to be willow switches, in late winter or early spring (Mike Aling).

management of its 35,000 street trees, 400 hectares of woodland, parks and other trees in its ownership. The larger arisings from the management of this green infrastructure resource were redirected for selling as either firewood, raw materials for wood-turning and other crafts or made into charcoal. In 1999, LB Croydon was the first local authority in the world to achieve the Forest Stewardship Council (FSC) certification for the management of its street and park trees (BioRegional, 2006).

The Beddington Zero Energy Development (BedZED) was completed and occupied in 2002 and provided an opportunity for using the low-grade arboricultural arisings from the Croydon Tree Station, not suitable for other higher-value purposes. BedZED is reported as being both the first large-scale and the largest mixed-use, carbon neutral development in the UK. Peabody Trust led the project in partnership with the designer, Bill Dunster Architects, and BioRegional. An important part of its zero carbon strategy was the use of wood chip fuel for the CHP boiler and the 1,100–1,200 tonnes of wood chip required each year would be met by the Croydon Tree Station (BioRegional, 2006). City Suburban Tree Surgeons Limited were contracted to manage the council's trees and became interested in the Tree Station project, first becoming a partner and then later managing and operating the facility.

Currently, the majority of wood chip production at the Croydon Tree Station (now the Croydon Timber Station) is sent to the Slough CHP facility, the UK's largest dedicated biomass plant. With the potential to save the equivalent of 7 mega tonnes of CO_2 emissions each year, biomass as heating fuel is one of the most cost-effective and environmentally sustainable ways to decrease UK greenhouse gas emissions (Read, Freer-Smith, Morison, Hanley, West & Snowden, 2009).

1.5.8 Mitigation against flooding

Throughout history, we have settled low-lying areas, in close contact with rivers, estuaries and coastal enclaves. Europe has seen its fair share of major floods in recent years, and this is raising fears that extreme flood events are likely to be increasing due to climate change. The UK Meteorological Office predictions of a 33 per cent increase in winter precipitation along the western side of the UK, under the medium emissions scenario (Murphy *et al.*, 2009), have tended to focus the mind and helped to push the management of flood risk higher up the political agenda. To make matters worse, the built environment is constantly expanding, increasing the area of hard, impervious surfaces, and so, decreasing the area available for water infiltration. Increased water run-off increases erosion and sediment loading on existing surface water systems, which in turn can cause flooding. Sea-level rise and the predicted increase in rain storm intensity due to climate change will make this more problematic. Sea water is not necessarily restricted to the high-tide line along the shore; it can also be encountered inland, deep within the ground, finding its way below fresh water aquifers. As sea levels rise, this inland salt water can push the fresh water up towards the surface, raising the water table and reducing the soil's ability to absorb heavy and persistent rainfall (Gaines, 2016). If the sea level rises sufficiently in some low-lying coastal areas, the elevated fresh water could actually break the surface, as has already been experienced in Miami, Florida, during spring tides (McKie, 2014; Parker, 2015).

It is well known that trees and other vegetation can be shown to intercept, slow and absorb water in forests and woodland ecosytems (Crockford & Richardson, 2000). Researchers at Ghent University in Belgium found that a single beech tree in an oak–beech forest was found to intercept an average of 21 per cent of the precipitation over a 2-year period (Staelens, De Schrijver, Verheyen & Verhoest, 2008). As rainfall interception is mainly due to foliation, it is reasonable to assume that these results should be consistent with urban tree studies. Indeed, a rainfall interception study in Oakland, California, found that 25 per cent of the gross precipitation could be intercepted by deciduous urban trees (Xiao & McPherson, 2011). This is supported by other studies where similar interception rates for a Callery pear (*Pyrus calleryana*) and a cork oak (*Quercus suber*) in Davis, California, were found to average 15 per cent and 27 per cent, respectively (Xiao, McPherson, Ustin, Grismer & Simpson, 2000). Research at the University of Manchester estimates that increasing the tree cover within the residential areas of Greater Manchester by 10 per cent would reduce local surface water run-off by 5.7 per cent (Gill, Handley, Ennos & Pauleit, 2007).

Armson *et al.* found that tree planting pits within test plots surfaced with sealed asphalt were able to absorb significant amounts of surface water run-off (Armson *et al.*, 2013). Trees also direct rainwater to flow along branches and down stems (stemflow) to the base of the tree, where, ideally, it enters the ground. It has also been shown that the roots of some tree species are able to penetrate saturated, compacted subsoils and alter the drainage properties by increasing soil permeability (Bartens *et al.*, 2008). Highly permeable, engineered rooting media have been used for some time, where trees are grown in paved areas, due to their suitability to be compacted sufficiently to support paving systems, while at the same time, allowing root growth. These media are now finding favour with designers seeking opportunities to store surface water run-off. Although green infrastructure alone cannot be relied upon to moderate the expected volumes of surface water run-off under predicted climate change, it could prove useful, especially if integrated with other Sustainable Drainage System (SuDS) measures. For more information, see the CIRIA *SuDS Manual* (Woods Ballard *et al.*, 2015).

1.5.9   Carbon sequestration

Trees are massive carbon sinks, so they can help combat climate change and global warming. The Read Report estimated that a maximum carbon stock of approximately 790 mega tonnes of carbon (MtC) is stored in UK forests, including the soil in which they are growing. In addition, about 15 $MtCO_2$ (4 MtC) is removed from the atmosphere each year (Read, Freer-Smith, Morison, Hanley, West & Snowden, 2009). Clearly, most forestry plantations are located in rural areas;

■ **So what have urban trees ever done for us?**

Figure 1.8
Rain interception can be clearly seen by the lighter colour of the ground beneath the trees.

however, a 2011 UK study did consider the biological carbon storage within the city of Leicester and estimated that over 230 KtC is stored in above-ground vegetation. Of this, 97.3 per cent (225 KtC) consists of carbon stored in trees (Davies, Edmondson, Heinemeyer, Leake & Gaston, 2011). Due to lower tree density alone, urban forests are likely to store and sequester less carbon than commercial forests per unit area. However, when considering per unit tree cover, urban forests may outperform their commercial cousins. This is due to the higher proportion of larger trees in urban environments and faster growth rates due to more open growing conditions with less competition from other trees. In fact, individual urban trees may contain four times more carbon than individual trees growing in forest stands (Nowak & Crane, 2002).

1.5.10 Biodiversity and wildlife

The importance of enhancing the potential for biodiversity within urban wildlife is more than simply addressing the instinctive bond between humans and other living systems, as developed by E.O. Wilson in his concept of biophilia. Urban green infrastructure can provide important refuges and movement corridors for a variety of species, especially if they connect with open green space, parks or areas of woodland. Esteban Fernández-Juricic investigated the bird populations found in tree-lined streets in Madrid, with a range of different levels of connectivity, vegetation structure and human disturbance (both pedestrian and vehicular). He found that wooded streets contained several bird species and could function as movement corridors (Fernández-Juricic, 2000). Improving the quality of the connected urban parks through the introduction of some fairly low-level enhancements, such as nesting boxes and feeding stations, could be quite easy ways to increase urban bird diversity (Fernández-Juricic & Jokimäki, 2001). The city of Christchurch in New Zealand has been shown to be more floristically diverse than the surrounding pastoral landscape (Stewart, Ignatieva, Meurk & Earl, 2004). High biodiversity was also recorded in urban parks within Flanders, Belgium (Cornelis & Hermy, 2004), supporting the notion that large urban and suburban parks may be considered 'biodiversity hotspots', as concluded by Fernández-Juricic & Jokimäki (2001).

1.6   WELCOME TO THE ANTHROPOCENE AGE

In 2000, Paul Crutzen, from the Max-Planck-Institute for Chemistry, and Eugene Stoermer, of the University of Michigan, proposed that the current geological age be defined under the name 'Anthropocene' (Crutzen & Stoermer, 2000). They argued that this term more accurately reflects the state of change experienced during the post-glacial geological epoch of the past 12,000 years, known as the Holocene (translated as 'recent whole'), and describes the impacts that human activities are placing on the earth and its atmosphere, at all scales.

Prior to the Industrial Revolution of the late eighteenth century, humankind's impact on the earth tended to be fairly insignificant and predominantly local. A new fossil fuel-based system of energy provided the opportunity for the mechanised extraction, manufacture and processing of materials, which in turn created conditions suitable for the exponential growth of the world's population. Such growth, and the prosperity and health that have accompanied it, inevitably place an ever-increasing demand for more and more of the earth's resources, from mineral deposits to fertile land, water and fish stocks (Steffen *et al.*, 2004).

The Anthropocene is characterised by the earth's biosphere being pushed beyond its normal operating range and being subjected to forces that are greater than those exerted by natural cycles. The planet is under pressure from its inhabitants as never before, and all this comes with concomitant land cover transformation, biodiversity loss, pollution and climate change, whose implications are globally significant in magnitude.

There are very few geographical areas over which humans have not had some influence. Even if this is not a direct influence, the effects of climate change can be seen throughout the world. The climate change debate will continue to rumble on with some arguing that there is no doubting the correlation between the burning of fossil fuel, atmospheric CO_2 levels and global temperature rise; the other side arguing that atmospheric changes are due to natural, cyclic phenomena. There is little doubt that change is happening, whatever the cause, and the speed of this change is increasing exponentially, so we need to accept it and plan accordingly. Climate change is often, mistakenly, referred to as global warming. I have had many conversations with students and others who state quite clearly that they look forward to the mild winters, and more predictably, hotter summers, which the term implies. Unfortunately, climate change is unlikely to manifest itself in such ways. An increase in global temperature leads to an overall increase in energy within the atmospheric system, and this energy is more likely to cause disrupted and erratic weather events, rather than predictable and steady patterns. Periods of unseasonal or exceptionally warm weather could quickly be followed by unusually severe cold and intense storms. Therefore, not only does our wildlife need to be able to adapt to the steadily increasing rise in overall temperature, but also to an erratic and unpredictable set of weather conditions, such as heat-waves, droughts and flooding.

1.6.1   *Phenology*

The influence of climatic change on biological systems is fairly easy to see from phenological records that date back to the early eighteenth century. Phenology is the study, through observation and record, of particular natural, seasonal events. For instance, an observer may record the date when they hear the first cuckoo call or when a particular oak tree comes into leaf or a particular hawthorn produces its first blossom. By recording these details over a period of time and making comparisons with previous datasets, changes may be observed.

Robert Marsham is considered to be the founding father of phenology, in Britain, recording his 'Indications of Spring' between 1736 and his death in 1798. Gilbert White was making similar phenological observations in Selborne, Hampshire, which were later supplemented with William

Markwick's own records for Catsfield, near Battle, Sussex, and published collectively in *The Natural History and Antiquities of Selborne*, in 1789 (White, 1789). Marsham's records were added to by successive generations of the family, finally ending with the death of Mary Marsham, in 1958. In addition to the annual variations in seasonal occurrences, these data have allowed the investigation of long-term trends and show an observable, gradual increase in temperature. These trends have been confirmed by later datasets, mainly from amateurs around the country. Since 1947, Jean Combes has been recording the dates when the first oak, ash, horse chestnut and lime leaves appear. These data have been invaluable to phenologists and those interested in tracking climate change, as they cover the post-war period when climate change was beginning to be considered as a major environmental challenge. In the autumn of 2000, the Woodland Trust and the Centre for Ecology and Hydrology came together with the view to provide a repository and research facility, promoting phenology around the country. Some 50,000 phenologists, many of them amateurs, continue to provide their data through the Nature's Calendar survey.

Using phenology data from the Nature's Calendar survey and other UK sources, a team of researchers, led by Tatsuya Amano of the National Institute for Agro-Environmental Sciences in Japan, analysed almost 400,000 'first flowering' records from 405 UK plant species. The records, which date back to 1760, indicate that over the last 25 years, flowers have been blooming between 2.2 and 12.7 days earlier than in any other consecutive 25-year period since 1760. They also show that this advance in 'first flower' date correlates with a mean temperature increase during February to April, with each 1°C rise in the mean temperature advancing flowering by an average of 5 days (Amano *et al.*, 2010).

REFERENCES

Amano, T., Smithers, R. J., Sparks, T. H. & Sutherland, W. J. (2010). A 250-year index of first flowering dates and its response to temperature changes. *Proceedings of the Royal Society B*, 22nd August, *277*(1693), 2451-7. Available at: http://rspb.royalsocietypublishing.org/content/277/1693/2451.full.pdf.

Anderson, L. M. & Cordell, H. K. (1988). Influence of trees on residential property values in Athens, Georgia (USA): A survey based on actual sales prices. *Landscape and Urban Planning, 15*(1–2), 153–64. doi:10.1016/0169-2046(88)90023-0

Armson, D., Stringer, P. & Ennos, A. R. (2013). The effect of street trees and amenity grass on urban surface water runoff in Manchester, UK. *Urban Forestry & Urban Greening, 12*(3), 282–6.

Baker, J. & Grewal, D. (1994). The influence of store environment on quality inferences and store image. *Journal of the Academy of Marketing Science, 22*(4), 328–39. doi:10.1177/0092070394224002

Barkham, P. (2009). *Thousands of urban trees mauled and destroyed as 'weapon dog' owners train animals for fighting.* Retrieved 23 November 2014 from *The Guardian*, News, World News, Animals: www.theguardian.com/world/2009/aug/11/urban-trees-destroyed-fighting-dogs.

Bartens, J., Day, S., Harris, J. R., Dove, J. & Wynn, T. (2008). Can Urban Tree Roots Improve Infiltration through Compacted Subsoils for Stormwater Management?. *Journal of Environmental Quality*, November, *37*(6), 2048–57.

Benedict, M. A. & McMahon, E. T. (2006). *Green Infrastructure: Linking Landscapes and Communities.* Washington, DC: Island Press.

BioRegional (2006). *Wood Chip Production from Tree Surgery Arisings in Croydon.* London: BioRegional Development Group. Retrieved from www.bioregional.com/wp-content/uploads/2015/05/WoodChipProduction_Apr06.pdf.

Britt, C. & Johnston, M. (2008). *Trees in Towns II – A New Survey of Urban Trees in England and their Condition and Management.* London: Department of Communities and Local Government.

Brogdale Collections (2016). *Brogdale Collections: The Home of the National Fruit Collection.* Retrieved 30 July 2016 from www.brogdalecollections.org/the-fruit-collection/.

Burgess, J. (1995). *Growing in Confidence: Understanding People's Perceptions of Urban Fringe Woodlands.* Cheltenham: Countryside Commission.

Coder, K. D. (2011). *WSFNR1101 Identified Benefits of Community Trees & Forests CF.* Retrieved 22 May 2015 from www.warnell.uga.edu/outreach/pubs/pdf/forestry/Community%20Tree%20Benefits%2011-01.pdf.

Cornelis, J. & Hermy, M. (2004). Biodiversity relationships in urban and suburban parks in Flanders. *Landscape and Urban Planning, 69*(4), 385–401. doi:10.1016/j.landurbplan.2003.10.038

Costanza, R., d'Arge, R., de Groot, R., Farber, S., Grasso, M,. Hannon, B., Limburg, K., Naeem, S., O'Neill, R., Paruelo, J., Raskin, R., Sutton, P. & van den Belt, M. (1997). The value of the world's ecosystem services and natural capital. *Nature*, 387(6630), 253-60. doi: 10. 1038/387253a0

Craul, P. J. (1985). A description of urban soils and their desired characteristics. *Journal of Arboriculture, 11*(11), 330–9. Retrieved from http://joa.isa-arbor.com/request.asp?JournalID=1&ArticleID=2052&Type=2.

Crockford, R. H. & Richardson, D. P. (2000). Partitioning of rainfall into throughfall, stemflow and interception: Effect of forest type, ground cover and climate. *Hydrological Processes, 14*(16–17), 2903–20. doi:10.1002/1099-1085(200011/12)14:16/17<2903::AID-HYP126>3.0.CO;2-6

Crutzen, P. J. & Stoermer, E. F. (2000). The 'Anthropocene' (W. Steffen, ed.) *Global Change News Letter No. 41* 17–18. Retrieved from www.igbp.net/download/18.316f18321323470177580001401/1376383088452/NL41.pdf.

D'Amato, G. (2000). Urban air pollution and plant-derived respiratory allergy. *Clinical and Experimental Allergy, 30*(5), 628–36. doi:10.1046/j.1365-2222.2000.00798.x

D'Amato, G., Cecchi, L., Bonini, S., Nunes, C., Annesi-Maesano, I., Behrendt, H., Liccardi, G., Popov, T. & Van Cauwenberge, P. (2007). Allergic pollen and pollen allergy in Europe. *Allergy: European Journal of Allergy and Clinical Immunology, 62*(9), 976-90. doi: 10.1111/j.1398-9995.2007.01440.x

Davies, Z. G., Edmondson, J. L., Heinemeyer, A., Leake, J. R. & Gaston, K. J. (2011). Mapping an urban ecosystem service: Quantifying above-ground carbon storage at a city-wide scale. *Journal of Applied Ecology, 48*(5), 1125–34. doi:10.1111/j.1365-2664.2011.02021.x

Denham, C. & White, I. (1998). Differences in urban and rural Britain. In J. Fox (ed.), *Population Trends 91, Spring 1998*, 23–34. Retrieved from http://webarchive.nationalarchives.gov.uk/20160105160709/http://www.ons.gov.uk/ons/rel/population-trends-rd/population-trends/no--91--spring-1998/difference-in-urban-and-rural-britain.pdf.

Doll, D., Ching, J. K. & Kaneshiro, J. (1985). Parameterization of subsurface heating for soil and concrete using net radiation data. *Boundary-Layer Meteorology, 32*(4), 351–72.

Donovan, G. H. & Butry, D. T. (2010). Trees in the city: Valuing street trees in Portland, Oregon. *Landscape and Urban Planning, 94*, 77–83. doi:10.1016/j.landurbplan.2009.07.019

Donovan, R. J. & Rossiter, J. R. (1994). Store atmosphere and purchasing behavior. *Journal of Retailing, 70*(3), 283–94. doi:10.1016/0022-4359(94)90037-X

European Environment Agency. (2006). *Urban Sprawl in Europe: The Ignored Challenge. EEA Report 10/2006*. Copenhagen: European Environment Agency. Retrieved from www.eea.europa.eu/publications/eea_report_2006_10/eea_report_10_2006.pdf.

European Environment Agency. (2015). *Air Quality in Europe – 2015 Report*. Luxembourg: Publications Office of the European Union. Retrieved from www.eea.europa.eu/publications/air-quality-in-europe-2015/at_download/file.

Faculty of Public Health. (2010). *The Great Outdoors: How our Natural Health Service Uses Green Space to Improve Wellbeing*. London: Faculty of Public Health.

Fay, N. (2002). Environmental arboriculture, tree ecology and veteran tree management. *Journal of Arboriculture, 26*(3), 213–38. doi:10.1080/03071375.2002.9747336

Fernández-Juricic, E. (2000). Avifaunal use of wooded streets in an urban landscape. *Conservation Biology, 14*(2), 513–21. doi:10.1046/j.1523-1739.2000.98600.x

Fernández-Juricic, E. & Jokimäki, J. (2001). A habitat island approach to conserving birds in urban landscapes: Case studies from southern and northern Europe. *Biodiversity & Conservation, 10*(12), 2023–43. doi:10.1023/A:1013133308987

Firehook, K. (2015). *Strategic Green Infrastructure Planning: A Multi-Scale Approach*. Washington, DC: Island Press.

Florida Greenways Commission (1994). *Creating a Statewide Greenways System – For People . . . for Wildlife . . . for Florida*. Tallahassee, FL: Florida Greenways Commission.

Fowler, D., Cape, J., Unsworth, M., Mayer, H., Crowther, J., Jarvis, P., Gardiner, B. & Shuttleworth, W. (1989). Deposition of atmospheric pollutants on forests [and discussion]. *Philosphical Transactions of the Royal Society. Series B, Biological Sciences, 324*(1223), 247-65. Available at: http://rstb.royalsocietypublishing.org/content/324/1223/247.full.pdf.

Fowler, D., Skiba, U., Nemitz, E., Choubedar, F., Branford, D., Donovan, R. & Rowland, P. (2004). Measuring aerosol and heavy metal deposition on urban woodland and grass using inventories of ^{210}Pb and metal concentrations in soil. *Water, Air, and Soil Pollution: Focus, 4*(2), 483-99.

Gaines, J. M. (2016). Flooding: Water potential. *Nature, 531*, S54–S55. doi:10.1038/531S54a

Gill, S. E., Handley, J. F., Ennos, A. R. & Pauleit, S. (2007). Adapting cities for climate change: The role of the green infrastructure. *Built Environment, 33*(1), 115–33. doi:http://dx.doi.org/10.2148/benv.33.1.115

GLA (2003). *Valuing Greenness: Green Spaces, House Prices and Londoners' Priorities*. London: Greater London Authority. Retrieved 19 August 2011 from www.london.gov.uk/sites/default/files/valuing_greenness_report.pdf.

GLA (2005). *Connecting Londoners with Trees and Woodlands: A Tree and Woodland Framework for London*. London: Greater London Authority.

GLA (2007). *Chainsaw Massacre: A Review of London's Street Trees*. London: Greater London Authority.

GLA (2016). *The London Plan – The Spatial Development Strategy for London Consolidated with Alterations since 2011.* London: Greater London Authority. Retrieved 15 July 2016 from www.london.gov.uk/sites/default/files/the_london_plan_malp_final_for_web_0606_0.pdf.

Grewal, D. & Baker, J. (1994). Do retail store environmental factors affect consumers' price acceptability? An empirical examination. *International Journal of Research in Marketing, 11*(2), 107–15. doi:10.1016/0167-8116(94)90022-1

Gromke, C. (2011). A vegetation modeling concept for building and environmental aerodynamics wind tunnel tests and its application in pollutant dispersion studies. *Environmental Pollution, 159*(8–9), 2094–9.

Gromke, C. & Ruck, B. (2007). Influence of trees on the dispersion of pollutants in an urban street canyon – Experimental investigation of the flow and concentration field. *Atmospheric Environment, 41*(16), 3287–514.

Gromke, C. & Ruck, B. (2009). On the impact of trees on dispersion processes of traffic emissions in street canyons. *Boundary-Layer Meteorology, 131*(1), 19–34.

Gromke, C. & Ruck, B. (2012). Pollutant concentrations in street canyons of different aspect ratio with avenues of trees for various wind directions. *Boundary-Layer Meteorology, 144*(1), 41–64.

Helms, J. A. (1998). *The Dictionary of Forestry.* Bethesda, Maryland: Society of American Foresters. Available at: http://www.dictionaryofforestry.org/.

Hewitt, N., Stewart, H., Donovan, R. & MacKenzie, R. (n.d.). *Trees and Sustainable Urban Air Quality, Research Summary from Lancaster University.* Retrieved 26 August 2011 from www.es.lancs.ac.uk/people/cnh/docs/UrbanTrees.htm.

Hoff, H. (2001). Climate change and water availability. In J. L. Lozán, H. Graßl & P. Hupter (eds), *Climate of the 21st Century: Changes and Risks* (pp. 315–21). Hamburg: Wissenschaftliche Auswertungen.

House of Commons Environmental Audit Committee. (2010). *Air Quality Fifth Report of Session 2009–10 Volume I Report, Together with Formal Minutes.* London: The Stationery Office.

Jack-Scott, E., Piana, M., Troxel, B., Murphy-Dunning, C. & Ashton, M. S. (2013). Stewardship success: How community group dynamics affect urban street tree survival and growth. *Arboriculture & Urban Forestry, 39*(4), 189–96.

Jorgensen, A. & Anthopoulou, A. (2007). Enjoyment and fear in urban woodlands – Does age make a difference? *Urban Forestry & Urban Greening, 6*(4), 267–78. doi:10.1016/j.ufug.2007.05.004

King, A. & Clifford, S. (2011). *Community Orchards Handbook* (2nd edn). Cambridge: Green Books.

Koskela, H. & Pain, R. (2000). Revisiting fear and place: Women's fear of attack and the built environment. *Geoforum, 31*(2), 269–80. doi:10.1016/S0016-7185(99)00033-0

Kuo, F. E. & Sullivan, W. C. (2001). Environment and crime in the inner city: Does vegetation reduce crime? *Environment and Behavior, 33*(3), 343–67.

Lawrence, H. W. (2006). *City Trees: A Historical Geography from the Renaissance through the Nineteenth Century.* Charlottesville, VA: University of Virginia Press.

Lichter, J. M. & Lindsey, P. A. (1994). Soil compaction and site construction: Assessment and case studies. In G. W. Watson and D. Neely (eds.), *The Landscape Below Ground. Proceedings of International Workshop on Tree Root Development in Urban Soils* (pp. 126–30). Champaign, IL: International Society of Arboriculture.

Lindsey, P. & Bassuk, N. L. (1992). Redesigning the urban forest from the ground below: A new approach to specifying adequate soil volumes for street trees. *Arboricultural Journal, 16*(1), 25–39. doi:10.1080/03071375.1992.9746896

LTOA (2010). *Bark Better than Bite – Damage to Trees by Dogs. Best Practice Note.* London: London Tree Officers' Association. Retrieved from www.ltoa.org.uk/component/docman/cat_view/103-dog-damage-to-trees.

Ludwig, D. (2000). Limitations of economic valuation of ecosystems. *Ecosystems, 3*(1), 31–5. doi:10.1007/s100210000007

Lyytimäki, J. & Sipilä, M. (2009). Hopping on one leg – The challenge of ecosystem disservices for urban green management. *Urban Forestry and Urban Greening, 8*, 309–15.

Marmot, M., Allen, J., Goldblatt, P., Boyce, T., McNeish, D., Grady, M. & Geddes, I. (2010). *Fair Society, Healthy Lives: The Marmot Review – Strategic Review of Health Inequalities in England post 2010.* London: The Marmot Review. Retrieved from www.instituteofhealthequity.org/projects/fair-society-healthy-lives-the-marmot-review/fair-society-healthy-lives-full-report.

McDonald, A., Bealey, W., Fowler, D., Dragosits, U., Skiba, U., Smith, R., Donovan, R., Brett, H., Hewitt, C. & Nemitz, E. (2007). Quantifying the effect of urban tree planting on concentrations and depositions of PM_{10} in two UK conurbations. *Atmospheric Environment, 41*(38), 8455-67.

McKie, R. (2014). *Miami, the great world city, is drowning while the powers that be look away.* (Guardian News and Media) Retrieved 5 April 2016 from *The Guardian*: www.theguardian.com/world/2014/jul/11/miami-drowning-climate-change-deniers-sea-levels-rising.

McPherson, E. G., Klaus, I. S. & Simpson, J. R. (1998). Estimating cost effectiveness of residential yard trees for improving air quality in Sacramento, California, using existing models. *Atmospheric Environment, 32*(1), 75–84.

Millennium Ecosystem Assessment (2003). *Ecosystems and Human Well-Being: A Framework for Assessment.* Washington, DC: Island Press. Retrieved from www.unep.org/maweb/en/Framework.aspx#download.

Millennium Ecosystem Assessment (2005). *Overview of the Millennium Ecosystem Assessment.* Retrieved 31 March 2016 from Millennium Ecosystem Assessment: www.unep.org/maweb/en/About.aspx.

Montague, T. & Kjelgren, R. (2004). Energy balance of six common landscape surfaces and the influence of surface properties on gas exchange of four containerized tree species. *Scientia Horticulturae, 100*(1–4), 229–49.

Morales, D. J. (1980). The contribution of trees to residential property value. *Journal of Arboriculture, 6*(11), 305–8. Retrieved from http://joa.isa-arbor.com/request.asp?JournalID=1&ArticleID=1694&Type=2.

Morales, D. J., Micha, F. R. & Weber, R. L. (1983). Two methods of valuating trees on residential sites. *Journal of Arboriculture, 9*(1), 21–4. Retrieved from http://joa.isa-arbor.com/request.asp?JournalID=1&ArticleID=1854&Type=2.

Murphy, J., Sexton, D., Jenkins, G., Boorman, P., Booth, B., Brown, K., Clark, R., Collins, M., Harris, G. & Kendon, L. (2009). *UK Climate Projections science report: Climate change projections*. Exeter: Met Office Hadley Centre. Available at: http://ukclimateprojections.defra.gov.uk/media.jsp?mediaid=87851&filetype=pdf.

National Trust (15 April 2016). *Cider Apple Collection Saved*. Retrieved 31 July 2016 from National Trust: www.nationaltrust.org.uk/news/cider-apple-collection-saved.

National Urban Forestry Unit (1999). *Trees and Woods in Towns & Cities: How to develop local strategies for urban forestry - A Guide*, Wolverhampton: National Urban Forestry Unit.

Natural England (2009). *Our Natural Health Service - The role of the natural environment in maintaining healthy lives*, York: Natural England. Available at http://webarchive.nationalarchives.gov.uk/20170205000001/http://publications.naturalengland.org.uk/file/65031.

NCC (2015). *The State of Natural Capital – Protecting and Improving Natural Capital for Prosperity and Wellbeing, Third Report to the Economic Affairs Committee*. London: Defra. Retrieved from www.gov.uk/government/publications/natural-capital-committees-third-state-of-natural-capital-report.

Network Rail (n.d.). *Network Rail, Community Relations, Trees and Plants*. Retrieved 28 March 2016 from Network Rail: www.networkrail.co.uk/community-relations/trees-and-plants/.

Newman, O. (1972). *Defensible Space: Crime Prevention Through Urban Design*. New York: Macmillan.

NHBC (2014). *NHBC Standards: Part 4 – Foundations*. Milton Keynes, Bucks: National House Building Council.

Nowak, D. J. & Crane, D. E. (2002). Carbon storage and sequestration by urban trees in the USA. *Environmental Pollution, 116*(3), 381–9. doi:10.1016/S0269-7491(01)00214-7

Nowak, D. J., Crane, D. E. & Stevens, J. C. (2006). Air pollution removal by urban trees and shrubs in the United States. *Urban Forestry & Urban Greening, 4*(3–4), 115–23.

Nowak, D. J., Greenfield, E. J., Hoehn, R. E. & Lapoint, E. (2013). Carbon storage and sequestration by trees in urban and community areas of the United States. *Environmental Pollution, 178*, 229–36.

O'Callaghan, D. P. & Kelly, O. (2005). Tree-related subsidence: Pruning is not the answer. *Journal of Building Appraisal, 1*(2), 113–29. doi:10.1057/palgrave.jba.2940011

Parker, L. (2015, February). *Climate Change Economics – Treading Water* (National Geographic Partners LLC). Retrieved 5 April 2016 from National Geographic: http://ngm.nationalgeographic.com/2015/02/climate-change-economics/parker-text.

Powe, N. A. & Willis, K. G. (2004). Mortality and morbidity benefits of air pollution (SO_2 and PM_{10}) absorption attributable to woodland in Britain. *Journal of Environmental Management, 70*(2), 119–28.

Pugh, T. A., MacKenzie, A. R., Whyatt, J. D. & Hewitt, C. N. (2012). Effectiveness of green infrastructure for Improvement of air quality in urban street canyons. *Environmental Science and Technology, 46*(14), 7692–9. doi:10.1021/es300826w

Randrup, T. B. (1998). Soil compaction on construction sites. In D. Neely & G. W. Watson (eds), *The Landscape Below Ground II. Proceedings of an International Workshop on Tree Root Development in Urban Soils* (pp. 146–53). Champaign, IL: International Society of Arboriculture.

Read, D. J., Freer-Smith, P. H., Morison, J. I., Hanley, N., West, C. C. & Snowden, P. (2009). *Combating Climate Change – A Role for UK Forests. An Assessment of the Potential of the UK's Trees and Woodlands to Mitigate and Adapt to Climate Change*. Edinburgh: The Stationery Office. Retrieved from www.tsoshop.co.uk/gempdf/Climate_Change_Main_Report.pdf.

Rishbeth, C. (2001). Ethnic minority groups and the design of public open space: An inclusive landscape? *Landscape Research, 26*(4), 351–66. doi:10.1080/01426390120090148

Road Safety GB (2010). *Road Safety News: Tree planting scheme sparks debate*. Retrieved 30 March 2016 from Road Safety GB: www.roadsafetygb.org.uk/news/1144.html.

Roman, L. A., Battles, J. J. & McBride, J. R. (2014). The balance of planting and mortality in a street tree population. *Urban Ecosystems, 17*(2), 387–404.

RSPCA (2011). *The Welfare State: Five Years Measuring Animal Welfare in the UK 2005–2009*. Horsham, West Sussex: Royal Society for the the Prevention of Cruelty to Animals.

Schroeder, H., Flannigan, J. & Coles, R. (2006). Residents' attitudes toward street trees in the UK and US communities. *Arboriculture & Urban Forestry, 32*(5), 236–46. Retrieved from http://joa.isa-arbor.com/request.asp?JournalID=1&ArticleID=2961&Type=2.

Selmi, W., Weber, C., Rivière, E., Blond, N., Mehdi, L. & Nowak, D. (2016). Air pollution removal by trees in public green spaces in Strasbourg city, France. *Urban Forestry & Urban Greening*, 17, 192–201.

Sjöman, H., Hirons, A. D. & Bassuk, N. L. (2015). Urban forest resilience through tree selection – Variation in drought tolerance in Acer. *Urban Forestry & Urban Greening, 14*(4), 858–65. doi:10.1016/j.ufug.2015.08.004

Spirn, A. W. (1995). Constructing Nature: The Legacy of Frederick Law Olmstead. In W. Cronon (ed.), *Uncommon Ground: Rethinking the Human Place in Nature*. New York: W.W. Norton & Company, Inc, 91–113.

Staelens, J., De Schrijver, A., Verheyen, K. & Verhoest, N. E. (2008). Rainfall partitioning into throughfall, stemflow, and interception within a single beech (*Fagus sylvatica* L.) canopy: Influence of foliation, rain event characteristics, and meteorology. *Hydrology Processes, 22*(1), 33–45. doi:10.1002/hyp.6610

Steffen, W., Sanderson, A., Tyson, P., Jäger, J., Matson, P., Moore III, B., Oldfield, F., Richardson, K., Schellnhuber, J., Turner II, B. & Wasson, R. (2004). *Global Change and the Earth System: A Planet under Pressure*. (First ed.). Berlin Heidelberg: Springer-Verlag. Available at: www.activeremedy.org/wp-content/uploads/2015/10/Global_Change_and_the_Earth_System_A_Planet_Under_Pressure-2004.pdf.

Stewart, G. H., Ignatieva, M. E., Meurk, C. D. & Earl, R. D. (2004). The re-emergence of indigenous forest in an urban environment, Christchurch, New Zealand. *Urban Forestry & Urban Greening, 2*(3), 149–58. doi:10.1078/1618-8667-00031

Stokes, J. & Rodger, D. (2004). *The Heritage Trees of Britain and Northern Ireland*. London: Constable and Robinson.

Tallis, M., Taylor, G., Sinnett, D. & Freer-Smith, P. (2011). Estimating the removal of atmospheric particulate pollution by the urban tree canopy of London, under current and future environments. *Landscape and Urban Planning, 103*, 129–38.

The Highways Agency (2001a). *DMRB: Volume 10 Environmental Design and Management, Section 0 Environmental Objectives, Part 2, HA 56/92 New Roads, Planting Vegetation and Soils*. Retrieved 31 March 2016 from *Standards for Highways: Design Manual for Roads and Bridges*: www.standardsforhighways.co.uk/dmrb/vol10/section1/ha5692.pdf.

The Highways Agency (2001b). *DMRB: Volume 7 Pavement Design and Mainenance, Section 4 Pavement Maintenance Methods, Part 3, HD 40/01 Footway Maintenance*. Retrieved 31 March 2016 from *Standards for Highways: Design Manual for Roads and Bridges*: www.standardsforhighways.co.uk/dmrb/vol7/section4/hd4001.pdf.

The Highways Agency (2006). *DMRB: Volume 2 Highway Structures, Section 2 Special Structures, TD19/06 Requirement for Road Restraint Systems*. Retrieved 31 March 2016 from *Standards for Highways – Design Manual for Roads and Bridges*: www.standardsforhighways.co.uk/dmrb/vol2/section2/td1906.pdf.

Ulrich, R. S. (1984). View through a window may influence recovery from surgery. *Science, 224*(4647), 420–1.

Ulrich, R. S., Simons, R. F., Losito, B. D., Fiorito, E., Miles, M. A. & Zelson, M. (1991). Stress recovery during exposure to natural and urban environments. *Journal of Environmenatal Psychology, 11*, 201–30.

UN Department of Economic and Social Affairs, Population Division (2008). *United Nations Expert Group Meeting on Population Distribution, Urbanization, Internal Migration and Development*. New York: United Nations.

UN Department of Economic and Social Affairs, Population Division (2014). *The World Population Situation in 2014*. New York: United Nations.

URBED (2004). *Biodiversity by Design - a guide for sustainable communities*, Manchester: Town and Country Planning Association. Available at : http://www.tcpa.org.uk/data/files/bd_biodiversity.pdf.

Vos, P. E., Maiheu, B., Vankerkom, J. & Janssen, S. (2013). Improving local air quality in cities: To tree or not to tree? *Environmental Pollution, 183*, 113–22.

Wania, A., Bruse, M., Blond, N. & Weber, C. (2012). Analysing the influence of different street vegetation on traffic-induced particle dispersion using microscale simulations. *Journal of Environmental Management, 94*(1), 91–101.

White, G. (1789). *The Natural History and Antiquities of Selborne*. London: B. White and Son. Available at: https://archive.org/download/naturalhistorya04whitgoog/naturalhistorya04whitgoog.pdf.

Whitlow, T. H. & Bassuk, N. L. (1988). Environmental stress in street trees. *Arboricultural Journal, 12*(2), 195–201.

Whitlow, T. H., Bassuk, N. L. & Reichert, D. L. (1992). A 3-year study of water relations of urban street trees. *Journal of Applied Ecology, 29*, 436–50.

Whitlow, T., Pataki, D., Alberti, M., Pincetl, S., Setala, H., Cadenasso, M., Felson, A. & McComas, K. (2014). Comments on Modeled $PM_{2.5}$ removal by trees in ten U.S. cities and associated health effects by Nowak et al. (2013). *Environmental Pollution*, August, *191*, 256.

WHO (2014). *Air Quality Deteriorating in Many of the World's Cities*. Retrieved from World Health Organization: www.who.int/mediacentre/news/releases/2014/air-quality/en/.

Wolf, K. L. (2003). Public response to the urban forest in inner-city business districts. *Journal of Arboriculture, 29*(3), 117–26. Retrieved from http://joa.isa-arbor.com/request.asp?JournalID=1&ArticleID=85&Type=2.

Wolf, K. L. (2004). Trees and business district preferences: A case study of Athens, Georgia, US. *Journal of Arboriculture, 30*(6), 336–46. Retrieved from http://joa.isa-arbor.com/request.asp?JournalID=1&ArticleID=163&Type=2.

Woods Ballard, B., Wilson, S., Udale-Clarke, H., Illman, S., Scott, T., Ashley, R. & Kellagher, R. (2015). *The SuDS Manual*. London: CIRIA. Retrieved from https://ciria.sharefile.com/d-scf5d73d72bf4fc2b.

Xiao, Q. & McPherson, E. G. (2011). Rainfall interception of three trees in Oakland, California. *Urban Ecosystems, 14*(4), 755–69. doi:10.1007/s11252-011-0192-5

Xiao, Q., McPherson, E. G., Ustin, S. L., Grismer, M. E. & Simpson, J. R. (2000). Winter rainfall interception by two mature open-grown trees in Davis, California. *Hydrological Processes, 14*(4), 763–84. doi:10.1002/(SICI)1099-1085(200003)14:4<763::AID-HYP971>3.0.CO;2-7.

Youde, K. & Pang, S. (2010). *Tree Scheme Slows Down Fast Drivers*. Retrieved 30 March 2016 from *Independent*: www.independent.co.uk/life-style/motoring/motoring-news/tree-scheme-slows-down-fast-drivers-2053057.html.

Chapter 2: Tree structures and function – how do trees work?

The tree is a centered creature, for its energies are radial. Its roots and branches spread wide, laying a circular network around the bole. The tree lives at both ends; the trunk and the leaves reach up to light and air; the roots stretch down to earth and water. The roots are essential. Leaves and branches fall, the trunk may be severed, but if the roots are not destroyed there is hope for most trees of continuing life. The power is in the roots – the symbol of life.

Meinrad Craighead (artist and writer)

2.1 INTRODUCTION

This chapter reviews how trees function, what makes them grow and what restricts that growth. It provides an insight into the biological, chemical and physical functions of trees to assist in the recognition of healthy growth, suitable growing conditions and plant problems.

There are several definitions of what a tree is, none of which satisfactorily captures all the tree's attributes. Trees usually grow on a single stem, but can be multi-stemmed, and some larger shrubs can be managed in such a way that they also possess one stem. The division between a tree and shrub, therefore, is not always obvious. Shigo describes a tree as 'a highly compart-mented, compartmentalising, perennial, woody, shedding plant that is usually tall, single stemmed and long lived' (Shigo, 1986a). Whatever practical definition one chooses, functionally, trees are self-optimising, dynamic systems of impulses and responses, photosynthesis and respiration. In harnessing light energy from the sun and transporting it downwards, the tree canopy provides a source of fuel for the rest of the tree. Meanwhile, roots absorb water from the soil and transport it upwards to the furthest reaches of the canopy. Trees could, therefore, be thought of as solar-powered evaporators.

Plants are exquisitely adapted to harnessing radiant energy from the sun in their leaves, converting it to chemical energy and using this to manufacture organic carbon compounds from inorganic raw materials. This conversion produces a source of stored energy, in the form of carbohydrates. Almost all life on earth requires energy for growth and maintenance, and those species that are unable to use the sun directly, as plants do, can access the stored energy plants produce by consuming them as food, or by consuming something else that has consumed plants. Because of this, plants are known as primary producers. Put simply, without them, we would not be here.

As they are able to capture radiant energy from the sun and use this to synthesise a source of energy, plants are, therefore, able to produce their own 'food'. Species that are able to do this are known as autotrophs (from the Greek, autos meaning 'self' and trophe meaning 'nourishing' or 'feeding'). More accurately, they can be described as photoautotrophs, because they use energy from the sun, and to distinguish them from the chemoautotrophs found in deep-sea, hydrothermal vents, which use the oxidation of inorganic compounds as the energy source. An important by-product of this autotrophic metabolism is oxygen, which is released into the air around us, and is, of course, fundamental to all aerobic life on earth.

The 'food' so produced is carbohydrate and takes the form of simple sugars, starch or polymers of cellulose. The former provide the source of energy, which enables the various plant cell activities to function. If plants produce their own food, it is fundamentally incorrect to talk about feeding roots. The root systems of plants do not provide food, the leaves do (see *Root Growth and Function* below) and a more helpful term would be absorptive, rather than feeding roots. Fertiliser is not plant food (Shigo, 1982).

2.2 PHOTOSYNTHESIS AND TRANSPORT

When actively growing, trees, like most green plants, take in carbon dioxide via microscopic pores (stomata) through their leaves from the air around them. Through a series of chemical reactions fuelled by energy generated from sunlight, the carbon dioxide is reduced into simple sugars (carbohydrate) using water, extracted from the ground by the root system, as the reducing agent and energy from the sun to power the process known as photosynthesis. This, in a nutshell, is how they manufacture the building blocks which enable them to grow.

$$CO_2 + H_2O \xrightarrow{\text{sunlight}} CH_2O + O_2$$

carbon dioxide + water $\qquad\qquad$ carbohydrate + oxygen

Carbon dioxide from the air enters the plant through controlled openings, typically found on the underside of leaves, known as *stomata*. Here, the carbon dioxide passes into intercellular spaces or cavities lined with moist cells, where it dissolves in water present within the cell walls. It must go into solution because cell membranes are virtually impervious to carbon dioxide in its gaseous form. Wherever moisture is exposed to unsaturated air, evaporation will occur and this is exactly what happens within the sub-stomatal cavities within the leaf.

2.2.1 *Water movement*
All the time that the stomata are open for carbon dioxide to enter and diffuse through the moist cell walls of the sub-stomatal cavities, moisture is being lost through evaporation. This evaporation causes water from within the lining cells to replace that has been lost through the stomata, to the atmosphere. This effect of a negative pressure, or suction, is propagated throughout the other leaf cells to the water-conducting vessels (e.g., xylem), which are continuous from leaves to root tips.

The suction or pull of water initiated within the leaves creates a negative tension within the water column that is held within the water-conducting cells called *xylem* (from the Ancient Greek xulon meaning wood). Xylem is one of the cell types that form the vascular or transport tissue, from which the vascular plants get their name, the other being phloem (from the Ancient Greek phloos, meaning bark).

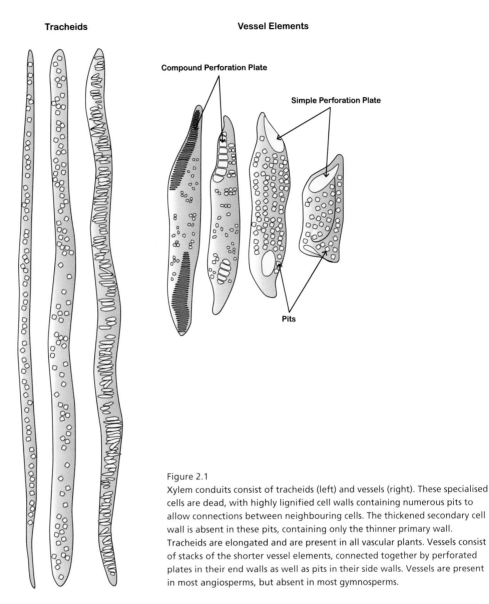

Tracheids

Vessel Elements

Compound Perforation Plate

Simple Perforation Plate

Pits

Figure 2.1
Xylem conduits consist of tracheids (left) and vessels (right). These specialised cells are dead, with highly lignified cell walls containing numerous pits to allow connections between neighbouring cells. The thickened secondary cell wall is absent in these pits, containing only the thinner primary wall. Tracheids are elongated and are present in all vascular plants. Vessels consist of stacks of the shorter vessel elements, connected together by perforated plates in their end walls as well as pits in their side walls. Vessels are present in most angiosperms, but absent in most gymnosperms.

The xylem consists of bundles of very fine, dead, but highly thickened, tubular cells, known as vessels and tracheids. To enable them to withstand the negative suction pressure, the walls of these cells must be reinforced and rigid.

These tiny tubes behave as capillaries, where cohesion (hydrogen bonding) between water molecules and adhesion between the water molecules and the sides of the capillary permits the water to form a continuous column, apparently defying gravity. The finer the capillary, the taller a column of water can be supported. As the xylem is continuous throughout the plant, water lost at the leaves is replaced by water absorbed through the roots from the surrounding soil. Plants use this process of transpiration to cool their leaves as well as the atmosphere around them, ensuring favourable growing conditions, maintaining turgidity within soft tissues and ensuring sufficient availability of water and some soil-derived nutrients are present throughout the plant.

Cells flaccid / Stoma closed   **Cells turgid / Stoma open**

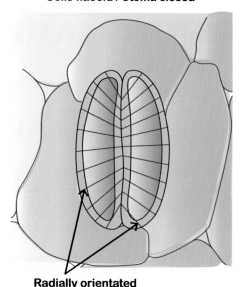 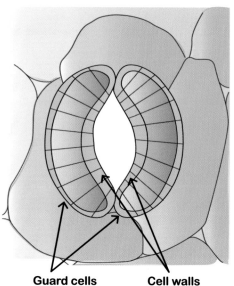

Figure 2.2
In guard cells, cellulose microfibrils fan out radially from the stomatal opening. This results in the inner cell wall being much stronger than the outer. As they engorge with water (right), the cells bow apart and the stomatal pores open.

Radially orientated cellulose microfibrils   **Guard cells**   **Cell walls**

The extent of stomatal opening, and so, the rate of transpiration and availability of carbon dioxide, is determined by a variety of internal and external factors. Externally, the evaporative demand of the local atmosphere will affect leaf water loss, due to humidity, air temperature, wind speed, plant-available soil-borne water and intensity of sunlight. Internally, factors such as response to stress will cause the stomata to close. There are two specialised, elliptical or kidney-shaped cells that control the stomatal opening that lies between them. These are known as guard cells, and they expand or contract due to their turgidity. Their shape coupled with radially orientated thickening on the cell walls cause the cells to bend when they are engorged with water. The greater the volume of water within them, the more they stretch and open the stomata. Conversely, as their water content diminishes, they reduce in size and close the stomata. There is, therefore, a fundamental balance in the relationship between water availability and water loss through transpiration.

This water loss, as a necessary by-product of carbon dioxide uptake, was termed the 'unavoidable evil' of transpiration, by Kramer (1983). Many hundreds of kgs of water are used by plants to produce each kg of dry matter. Of the water used, approximately 97 per cent is simply drawn through the plant and lost through the leaves, to the atmosphere, mostly by transpiration. Approximately 2 per cent is used for volume increases during cell expansion and 1 per cent for photosynthesis and other metabolic processes (Taiz et al., 2015). Some argue that despite a long and successful evolutionary history, plants have been unable to develop a system of maximising carbon dioxide diffusion while minimising water loss (Evert & Eichhorn, 2013). One could respond by pointing out that it is this long and successful evolution that has enabled plants to grow in just about every location on the planet. When water is in plentiful supply, it is advantageous to the plant to trade it for essential photosynthetic products. When the water resource is limiting, the stomata open less or remain closed to avoid dehydration. In some extreme environments, plants have developed a variety of ways to limit the amount of water lost during photosynthesis, but in temperate regions, there is, perhaps, no evolutionary pressure to encourage any change in strategy.

SO WHAT?

Now consider trees growing in conditions where the air is hot, dry and loaded with pollution; the soil provides a fairly sparse supply of water, as it is sealed by impervious surfaces and lacks the physical ability to hold water for any length of time. These are fairly typical site conditions for an urban tree. At the hottest part of the day, when the sun is at, or either side of, its zenith, one would expect the rate of photosynthesis to be at its peak. With high demand for raw materials, the stomata should be fully open to secure maximum carbon dioxide uptake. With the stomata open, the dry air and reflected heat from the concrete, macadam and glass surroundings cause transpiration to run flat out. In response, a tree's water demand on the surrounding soil via its root system is at its greatest and xylem tension is correspondingly high. In these conditions, with a root system able to extract sufficient moisture from the soil, the tree can grow quite unimpeded. When the soil moisture level reduces, however, and the root system is unable to 'suck' sufficient water from the soil to satisfy the evaporative demand from the leaves, the vascular conduits are at their most vulnerable to cavitation, where the water column breaks and loses its continuity. This is where the size and thickness of these vascular cells become important. Those species with finer, thicker-walled vascular cells survive.

Trees may respond to these low soil moisture conditions by reducing the size of their stomata aperture. This will reduce the rate of transpiration, lower the demand on leaf water loss, and so, reduce the xylem tension. However, reducing the size of stomatal opening also inhibits the inflow of carbon dioxide, reducing photosynthetic rate, and so, limiting assimilation of carbon (Ryan & Yoder, 1997).

The tallest living trees in the world are the North American coast redwoods (*Sequoia sempervirens* at 115.6 m (Earle, 2015)) found along the coastal region of north-west California and south-west Oregon, and the mountain ash (*Eucalyptus regnans* at 99.6 m (National Register of Big Trees, 2014)) of South Victoria and Tasmania, south-eastern Australia. Both species, along with Douglas fir (*Pseudotsuga menziesii*) of Washington State, USA, and British Columbia, Canada, have recorded individuals that can exceed 100 m in height. Transporting water to these heights without any mechanical aid would be quite a daunting prospect for any engineer, yet that is exactly what these giant trees manage to do. Studies have shown that Sequoia xylem elements offer very little resistance to the flow of water and solutes even at the enormous tensions experienced in these exceptionally tall trees (Koch *et al.*, 2004). The cell walls are also highly strengthened to prevent collapse. Trees with high tension forces within the xylem tend to produce dense wood to counteract the mechanical stresses imposed (Taiz *et al.*, 2015). The typical working pressure of a UK fire brigade vehicle-mounted pump is between 700 kPa and 2.4 MPa (HM Fire Service Inspectorate, 2001). The pressure difference required to lift water to the top of a 100 m tall tree is in the region of 2 MPa. The next time you are drinking through a straw, suck up some fluid and put your tongue over the end of the straw, so that it prevents the liquid falling back down. The tip of your tongue is drawn into the end of the straw due to the effect of gravity upon the column of liquid suspended within the straw; the longer the straw, the greater the pull due to gravity and the greater the tension within the water column. Now, imagine the tension imposed on a drinking straw 100 m or more in length. Bear in mind also that high pressure fire hoses, or water cannons, are still occasionally used for riot control in certain parts of the world. These are designed to disperse crowds of people and to knock protestors off their feet.

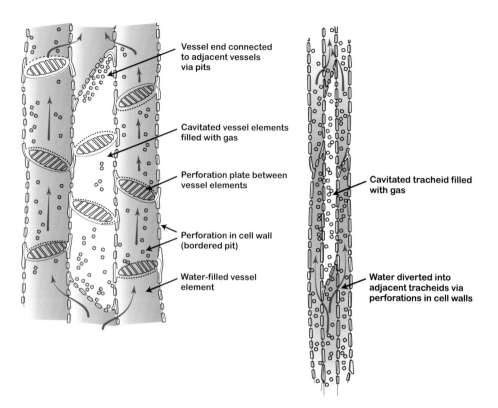

Vessel end connected to adjacent vessels via pits

Cavitated vessel elements filled with gas

Perforation plate between vessel elements

Perforation in cell wall (bordered pit)

Water-filled vessel element

Cavitated tracheid filled with gas

Water diverted into adjacent tracheids via perforations in cell walls

Figure 2.3
Cavitated vessels (left) and tracheids (right) prevent water movement due to gas-filled embolisms filling the conduit. In these circumstances, water is diverted around the embolism into adjacent conduits via the interconnected perforations (bordered pits) in the thickened cell walls.

The major problem associated with high xylem tension is that the tension can be so great that air can be sucked in through a wound or snapped branch or water vapour can come out of solution, forming bubbles within the transport conduits, thereby breaking the water column. This rupture is known as *cavitation*, and generally leads to an embolism, where an entire conduit cell fills with air or water vapour. Such cells are unable to transport water, but as the perforations along the cell walls and ends contain porous membranes, which do not allow bubbles to pass through, these are typically contained within single conduits. Water transport is simply diverted around the cell containing the embolism.

An embolism may also form when water and dissolved materials contained within the xylem capillaries freeze. Dissolved gases are insoluble in ice and will come out of solution to form bubbles. If the bubbles are large enough, they will extend to form an embolism when tension returns at thawing (Sperry & Sullivan, 1992). The new stem (secondary) growth replaces these dysfunctional vessels.

2.2.2 Drought strategies

Niinemets and Valladares (2006) developed a quantitative five-level scale, which ranks a species' tolerance to three important environmental stress factors: shade, drought and waterlogging. They investigated a total of 806 temperate, northern hemisphere, woody taxa, which included conifers, deciduous and evergreen broadleaf species. This ranking (from 1 = very intolerant to 5 = very tolerant), although very attractive as a simple screening tool for urban species selection, made no reference to the strategy employed by the plant subject in response to drought conditions. It can be useful to categorise plant species into those that avoid drought (drought avoiders) and those that are able to tolerate it (drought tolerators). Drought avoiders tend to rely on specific root architectures and/or morphological adaptations (leaf abscission or dormancy) to avoid drought stress, whereas drought tolerators have developed a physiological, or cellular, tolerance to low negative water potential. For urban locations, where soil volumes are typically limiting, drought avoiders are likely to be vulnerable to soil drying (Sjöman *et al.*, 2015). Bassuk *et al.* (2009) also produced a qualitative guide to aid urban tree selection for locations within USDA Plant Hardiness zone 6 or colder. This provides a twelve-point scale for assessing each tree's soil moisture requirements.

The recognised indicator for drought tolerance is cell turgor loss or 'wilting' point (π_{tlp}), the negative water potential at which leaf cells lose turgor, cell expansion stops and eventually the leaf wilts. The turgor loss point also defines the soil water potential (ψ_{SOIL}) at which plants are unable to extract sufficient water to recover from wilting – the *permanent wilting point*. In response to the stress caused by the low negative water potential, plants tend to accumulate the hormone, abscisic acid, which promotes closure of the stomata, reducing gas exchange, limiting photosynthesis and growth (Taiz *et al.*, 2015) and reducing further transpiration loss. Plants with a lower (more negative) turgor loss point are able to maintain open stomata for longer, and so, continue to photosynthesise under drier soil conditions. This trait would be considered a drought toleration strategy, as opposed to an avoidance strategy such as closing stomata and surviving on stored water, shedding leaves, or dying back to below-ground organs (Bartlett *et al.*, 2012). However, by maintaining open stomata for longer, such plants are using more water, and so, if competition from other plants is the reason for scarce water availability, then this strategy may offer a competitive advantage.

Turgor loss point is typically estimated from pressure–volume (p–v) curves, which measure the decline of leaf water potential (ψ_{leaf}) with leaf dehydration. This method is laborious and time-consuming. A meta-analysis of p–v curve data carried out by Bartlett *et al.* (2012) showed that variation in turgor loss point within and across species is virtually entirely due to the changes in osmotic potential at full rehydration (π_0). The main advantage with this approach is that the process of gathering data for π_0 is significantly quicker (Bartlett *et al.* suggest 30 times more rapid) than the standard p–v curve approach. The process involves removing small disks of hydrated leaf material, freezing them in liquid nitrogen to rupture the cells, puncturing the leaf surface, once removed from the liquid nitrogen and sealing in a vapour pressure osmometer. The readings produced by the osmometer are for solute concentration and these can be easily converted to turgor loss point using a simple equation.

2.2.3 Similarity of pathogen symptoms to drought

There are several pathogens that have an effect on plant–water relations and the symptoms present themselves as being very similar to drought. Pathogens that attack roots, tend to interrupt water uptake, decreasing both water and mineral absorption, while many wilt diseases and blights are caused by pathogens that block the xylem and/or phloem conducting tissue, with Dutch elm disease being a very good example. It is thought likely that, once the Dutch elm disease fungal spores have infected the xylem tissue, they can cause vessels to fill with air and cavitate. The response from the tree is to exude gummy substances (tyloses) into the infected vessels, blocking them still further and creating the brown staining within the xylem, indicative of infected branches and stems (Gibbs *et al.*, 1994). Physical, observed symptoms, therefore, closely resemble those associated with severe drought or broken branches; leaves wilt, die and turn brown.

SO WHAT?

Research is currently underway at Cornell University in New York State, USA, in collaboration with the Swedish University of Agricultural Science (SLU), in Sweden and Myerscough College in the UK, where researchers are examining the susceptibility of a variety of temperate tree and shrub species to drought tolerance by predicting leaf turgor loss from leaf osmotic potential at full turgor, using an osmometer. Screening work has already been completed on twenty-seven Acer genotypes growing in the F. R. Newman Arboretum at Cornell University and at the Robert H. Treman State Park, both in Ithaca, New York. The results suggest that substantial differences exist, at both species and cultivar level, in tolerance to water deficits within maples. There are some very interesting aspects of this initial study that set out a methodology for further investigations. Both common urban tree cultivars and more unusual, rarely used species have been selected for screening, and if this encourages a wider diversity in the range of species and cultivars available for urban locations, it should help to address some of the problems associated with a lack of resilience in conventional urban planting. Also, as data were collected during both the spring (19–30 May) and summer (1–10 August), it is anticipated that seasonal variation in turgor loss point, or seasonal osmotic adjustment, can be used as a measure of species plasticity to changing soil water conditions (Bartlett *et al.*, 2014). Thus, species that display a greater osmotic adjustment during the growing season are likely to possess a greater capacity to tolerate a variety of different soil moisture levels (Sjöman *et al.*, 2015). This ability not only broadens the range of suitable planting conditions, in terms of soil water availability, but also becomes important when considering the potential changes in precipitation patterns due to predicted climate change scenarios (Murphy *et al.*, 2009). Some caution does need to be exercised when reviewing these data, however. A low leaf turgor loss point alone is not necessarily a good predictor of drought tolerance throughout the year. As Sjöman *et al.* (2015) point out, even those maple species that showed the lowest summer π_{tlp} may still be sensitive to fairly modest spring drought conditions, requiring irrigation if droughts coincide with leaf emergence.

Further studies, which are examining a variety of tree and shrub species, have adopted the same scientific protocol and may provide much-needed guidance on species selection with respect to drought tolerance. This can be such an important determinant when selecting trees for urban landscapes and becomes an especially significant consideration where soil volumes are restricted. This is an exciting area of research, with the potential to rapidly provide quantitative data for a broad range of tree species. Armed with this, designers, arborists and urban tree managers should be better placed to make more robust decisions when selecting trees for specific urban planting locations.

Figure 2.4
Dr Henrik Sjöman working with the Vapro 5600 osmometer at Cornell University, Ithaca, NY, USA (August 2015).

2.2.4 Photosynthesis

The photosynthetic reaction takes place in organelles within the leaf called chloroplasts. In most trees, these are surrounded by a layer of transparent epidermal tissue within the leaves, typically beneath a waxy cuticle, which both helps to prevent excessive evaporation of water and protects the inner structure from ultraviolet radiation. It is within these chloroplasts that the pigment chlorophyll is found. Chlorophyll absorbs light strongly from either end of the visible spectrum, but not from the middle. This portion of the spectrum is reflected, giving most plant leaves their characteristic green colour (see section 2.6 on Light, below).

The chain of reactions that take place during photosynthesis can be divided into two categories: the light reactions, which require light energy for the photosynthesis to occur and the carbon-fixing reactions, which convert carbon dioxide into more complex, organic carbon compounds. In the light reactions, water is split into oxygen and hydrogen ions, with most of the oxygen being released as gas. In the carbon-fixing reactions, the hydrogen ions, from the light reactions, combine with carbon dioxide to synthesise sugars through a process known as the Calvin cycle.

$$3CO_2 + 6H_2O \xrightarrow{\text{sunlight}} C_3H_6O_3 + 3O_2 + 3H_2O$$

carbon dioxide + water $\qquad$ three-carbon sugars + oxygen + water

Often, the complete equation shows the six-carbon–sugar–glucose ($C_6H_{12}O_6$) as being the primary carbohydrate product of photosynthesis. Actually, very little glucose is produced by photosynthesis directly, with most of the carbohydrate products generated being more simple three-carbon sugars, as shown above. These trioses are later polymerised into more complex sugars such as glucose, fructose (both *monosaccharides*) and sucrose (*disaccharide*) or long-chain *polysaccharides* such as starch and cellulose. Sucrose is the main form of sugar that is transported around the plant, and starch is the main tissue storage form of carbohydrate. Water is shown on both sides of the equation because during a series of reactions where the water and carbon dioxide molecules on the left-hand side are split and recombined to create the three-carbon sugar and oxygen on the right-hand side, some of the hydrogen atoms from disassociated water molecules remove some of the oxygen atoms of the carbon dioxide, forming water (Evert & Eichhorn, 2013).

The dissolved carbohydrates move throughout the plant as an aqueous solution known as sap. The production of carbohydrates within the leaves creates a local increase in pressure, forcing the sap along a network of specialised plant tissue known as phloem to where it is consumed by respiration to provide energy for other biochemical processes of maintenance and growth (see below).

As discussed, the main photosynthetic material (*photosynthate*) that is loaded into the phloem system and transported around the plant is predominately sucrose. This is synthesised from a combination of the monosaccharides glucose and fructose and is the sugar we use to sweeten our food and drinks. Within the plant, it is unloaded from the phloem at various points of biological activity, such as developing leaves, apical buds and organs such as flowers, fruits, seeds and roots. Some of the glucose molecules, rather than being used in sucrose synthesis, are joined together in long chains to form the polysaccharide starch. Unlike glucose, fructose and sucrose, starch does not dissolve in water, so is not osmotically active and has low chemical reactivity. It is the most common form of stored carbohydrate in plants and serves as an energy source (for respiration) during the night, when photosynthesis has ceased. As plants come towards the end of their growing season, starch accumulates near the areas of spring activity, such as twig and root buds. Here, it provides the energy required to facilitate active growth when conditions are suitable in the spring. It also protects vulnerable tissues during the cold temperatures experienced in winter by acting as antifreeze.

2.2.5 Respiration

As photosynthesis produces simple sugars that are further manipulated and joined together to form complex carbohydrates such as starch, the reverse, which splits the starch back into simple sugars and uses these as a form of energy fuel, is known as respiration. All living cells respire to produce energy, and plants, like animals, produce carbon dioxide as a by-product of respiration.

$$C_6H_{12}O_6 + 6O_2 \longrightarrow 6CO_2 + 6H_2O + Energy$$
glucose + oxygen   carbon dioxide + water + Energy

In most organisms, the energy yielded from respiration is used to drive other biological processes, such as biosynthesis, active transport and growth. In trees, energy is especially important in the fight against infection. If energy levels are low, defence is reduced and attack from opportunistic pathogens is more likely (Shigo, 1982; Shigo, 1986; Shigo, 1986).

2.2.6 Cellulose, lignin and other biochemical products

Two plant polymers that should be discussed are cellulose and lignin. Cellulose and lignin are laid down in various tissues and organs and together help to form the physically rigid structure of the plant. Cellulose is synthesised at the cell wall from many glucose-building blocks, joined together to form long, linear chains. These bind to each other, side-by-side, to produce immensely strong *microfibrils*, which provide cells with tensile strength. Cellulose is the most abundant organic polymer found on earth and has been used in the manufacture of paper and paper products since the Chinese first made paper pulp in the early second century AD.

Unlike cellulose, lignin is not synthesised directly from the glucose-building blocks, but from aromatic phenol units (6-carbon phenyl-propane monomers). Lignin acts as a binding or cementing compound within the cell wall, which connects cells together and provides stiffness and a waterproof layer to xylem tissues. A useful analogy is that of glass fibre or GRP manufacture, where the lignin behaves as epoxy resin and the cellulose microfibrils behave like glass fibres. The fibres are the primary load-bearing elements, and resin or lignin provides the rigidity. Without lignin, trees would not be able to reach the immense heights they can and remain upright (Schmidt, 2006). Lignin is very difficult to digest and provides a physical barrier to invading pathogens and insect pests. However, some fungi are able to biodegrade it using particular enzymes known as *ligninases*. As brown lignin is degraded by the fungus, effectively bleaching the white cellulose that is left behind, such fungi are known as *white rots* (see Chapter 7, Disorders, pests and diseases).

Much effort is being placed on the production of cellulosic ethanol fuel from agricultural residues and wood waste. Up until recently, lignin was treated as a waste product in the production of plant-derived biomass, but future perspectives are looking at a range of possible uses from high energy-content fuels to nanotechnology elements, lithium-ion battery electrodes and pharmaceutical hydrogels.

A proportion of the simple sugars created through photosynthesis is used to provide some of the raw materials for the synthesis of proteins, oils and fats. In addition to carbon, hydrogen and oxygen provided by sugars, proteins also contain nitrogen. This makes up approximately

Figure 2.5 Harvesting willow biomass in New York State, USA, to produce biofuels. A breeding programme conducted by the College of Environmental Science and Forestry at the State University of New York (SUNY-ESF) in Syracuse, NY, has resulted in reliable and cost-efficient crops of feedstock being available for harvesting every 3 years (Tim Volk, SUNY-ESF).

78 per cent of the air around us, but is not available directly to plants in this form. First, it is captured by a few soil-borne bacteria, and these convert it into forms, such as ammonium and nitrate compounds, which are accessible to plants. The nitrogen is incorporated into the plant biochemistry to form amino acids, and these provide the building blocks for protein synthesis. Although animals can manufacture some of their own amino acids, by reprocessing those consumed in their diet, some cannot be manufactured and must be obtained either directly from plants or from other animals that have consumed them. These are known as essential amino acids.

The proteins not only provide nutrition for secondary feeders, such as grazing animals, but some are found as hormones and enzymes, which form vital functions in other plant processes and biochemical pathways (Evert & Eichhorn, 2013). The oils, fats and waxes contained in plants have been used by many human cultures for millennia, their uses ranging from culinary and medicinal to spiritual and ritualistic. Plant-derived oil has become headline news in the modern age for its potential as a fuel source. It is claimed that biodiesel from large-scale, terrestrial plantations or from algal photo-bioreactors, could provide a long-term, sustainable alternative to mineral oil.

One waxy substance that does need to be discussed is *suberin*. Suberin is the substance that renders the cork within outer bark of trees waterproof. The chains of carbon and hydrogen in suberin are highly complex and variable, making it difficult for microorganisms to access it as a source of energy. Corky bark from *Quercus suber* (from which suberin acquires its name) has been used to seal bottled liquids for millennia due to its characteristic stability and resistance to attack by microorganisms. This also makes outer bark a good material for mulching. Because it is not easily broken down, its aesthetic qualities last for some time, and it does not release significant quantities of nutrients back to the soil. Suberin is also found within roots, where it plays important roles in the control of water and dissolved nutrients (see 'Root Growth and Function' below).

2.3 GROWTH

As discussed, during photosynthesis, carbon dioxide from the air is reduced to form simple sugars. These are further processed into more complex, long-chain carbohydrates, which in turn are used to provide a source of energy and build the tissues and fibres that form the structure of the plant. This process is responsible for the sequestration of some 100–115 thousand million tonnes of carbon into biomass each year by all the world's photosynthesising organisms (Field *et al.*, 1998; Evert & Eichhorn, 2013; Hall & Rao, 1999).

To provide an urban tree context, Nowak *et al.* calculated that urban tree carbon storage densities average 7.69 kg for every square metre of tree cover and sequestration densities average 0.28 kg for every square metre of tree cover per year. These calculations rely on urban tree field data gathered from 28 cities within the USA and were analysed using the i-Tree Eco model (Nowak *et al.*, 2013). American studies, although useful, do not necessarily accurately reflect the UK or European condition. Urbanisation patterns in the USA tend to rely on what would be considered in the UK as low-density suburban sprawl, facilitated by cheap land and federal subsidies for highway construction and houses (Jackson, 1985). In contrast, UK and western European urban development tends to concentrate on the densification of existing urban and suburban areas through infill development and the reuse of brownfield sites (Greed & Johnson, 2014). In a UK study, Davies *et al.* (2011) found that, within the city of Leicester, an estimated 231,521 t of carbon is stored in above-ground biomass, with 97.3 per cent (225,217 t) being attributable to trees.

Trees are self-optimising structures, and as such, they respond to mechanical stress by adding wood at points of weakness. This ensures that growth is initiated in such a way that the stresses caused from weight, wind or snow-loading are evenly distributed throughout the structure. The outcome of such a strategy is efficient use of materials, where no point within the structure has too much or too little support material, but is only as strong as necessary (Mattheck & Breloer, 2010). The work of Mattheck in developing the *uniform stress axiom*, where trees mechanically optimise themselves, has proved to be invaluable when considering tree hazard evaluation.

2.3.1 Stem growth
As discussed earlier, wood comprises lignin and cellulose. Lignin is not very flexible, making it very good at resisting compressive stress. Cellulose, on the other hand, is much more flexible, and so, responsive to tensile stresses.

PLANT METABOLITES AND HUMANS

Sucrose is the main form of table sugar, extracted from sugar beet (swollen roots) and sugar cane (stems) where it accumulates after being manufactured within the photosynthetic parts of plant.

Starch is the most common form of carbohydrate found in the human diet and is typically sourced from grains, such as rice or maize, and from root vegetables, such as potatoes or cassava.

Secondary metabolites:
Alkaloids: These naturally occurring plant compounds can be purified to extract a range of pharmacological drugs, such as morphine, quinine and ephedrine. Some provide stimulant effects, such as cocaine, caffeine and nicotine, while others, such as atropine, are toxic. All tend to have a bitter taste.

Terpenoids (isoprenoids): They tend to be aromatic compounds and are found in many essential oils, herbs and spices. Isoprene is emitted by tree leaves and is responsible for the bluish haze that can be observed in wooded areas, during the summer. It is also a component of urban smog. The pharmacological drug taxol (generic name paclitaxel) has been used in treatments to fight cancerous tumours, while the cardiac glycoside digoxin has been used to treat various heart conditions for many years. Rubber is probably the best known and most widely available of the plant terpenoids.

Phenolics: These include a broad range of compounds such as flavonoids, tannins, lignins and salicylic acid. Flavonoids have been closely investigated recently for their antioxidant properties, as dietary supplements and their claimed ability to lower blood cholesterol. Tannin was used in the tanning process of leather, being used to confer bacterial resistance to the animal skin. Salicylic acid is the active ingredient in aspirin.

Annual shoot elongation or extension growth is a good way to assess the overall tree health and vigour. On deciduous trees, each increment of growth is marked by the terminal bud scars from previous years. On most conifers, it is marked with each whorl of branches. Starting from the terminal bud, the annual extension growth can be compared to previous years by looking along a single stem and determining the previous increments.

The terminal bud contains a mass of rapidly dividing and expanding cells known as the apical meristem. This is protected during dormancy by bud scales, which are highly modified leaves formed at the end of the previous season and which are loaded with sugars. Within the apical meristem, the leaves, flowers and axillary buds for the new shoot are all formed, ready for growth. Once initiated, the shoot elongates by cell division and expansion. The extending shoot may form side branches at axillary buds, so called because they are formed within leaf axils, at nodes along the stem. In many species, the terminal bud has dominance over these axillary buds, which are kept suppressed by the growth hormone (auxin) produced by the terminal bud. If the terminal bud is removed due to damage or pruning, the axillary bud closest to the site of injury will be free from hormone suppression and will come into active growth. As it will now effectively be the terminal bud, the growth hormone it produces will keep the buds below it suppressed. This phenomenon is known as apical dominance and tends to range from very strong (complete dominance of axillary buds) to weak (axillary buds do grow).

Sometimes, vigorous shoots develop from dormant buds near the base of a tree or from below the ground. Such growths are known as epicormic or water shoots when they arise from above the ground, and suckers if from below. Some tree species are particularly prone to such behaviour such as *Tilia* x *europaea* and many oaks are well known for producing epicormic shoots and suckers from their bases. Sometimes, as a result of stress such as drought, severe crown thinning, heavy pruning and crown dieback, these dormant buds are stimulated into growth, producing many low-vigour epicormic shoots anywhere within the canopy. Growth regulators and herbicides have all been tried as methods of control, but no chemical treatment appears to

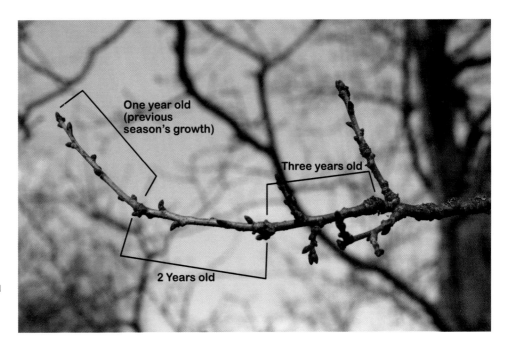

Figure 2.6
Three years of annual growth increments indicated on an oak stem.

be particularly effective for any length of time. Manual removal is probably the surest way to manage any unwanted growth.

2.3.2 Secondary thickening

The stems of all woody plants expand in circumference, so that they are able to support the weight of an ever-increasing size of plant. To facilitate this stem expansion, secondary thickening occurs within a band, one cell thick, known as the *vascular cambium*.

The vascular cambium forms a continuous, or near continuous, single band of dividing cells around the circumference of the stem. As the cambium cells divide, the stem expands. The multiplying vascular cambium cells differentiate into two types of cells, depending on in which direction they are produced. To the inside of the cambium, they differentiate into secondary xylem cells, which then develop into mature primary xylem cells and xylem tissue. To the outside, they differentiate into secondary phloem cells, which develop into mature primary phloem cells and phloem tissue. They also divide sideways to enable the cambium to expand in circumference and to produce ray cells, which provide radial vascular communication. As the tree grows ever larger, it requires greater mechanical strength. As it is the lignified xylem that provides this strength, more xylem is present within the stem than phloem. Much of this xylem will be in the form of heartwood, which is older, dysfunctional transport tissue, stained from the accumulation of stored waste products and mainly providing support and rigidity. The expanding tree has increased demands for the circulation of food metabolites. As the stem girth increases, the phloem also increases in size, providing a larger sap transport volume.

The cambium receives hormonal signals from the shoot and root tips, and these signals help to control how the cells divide. Therefore, we can see that each growth increment is a product of leaf, shoot and root growth, the whole system working as a series of signals and responses, one to another.

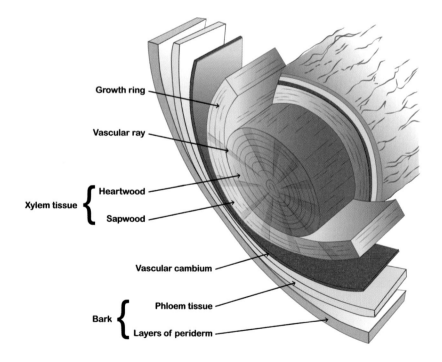

Growth ring

Vascular ray

Heartwood

Xylem tissue {

Sapwood

Vascular cambium

Phloem tissue

Bark {

Layers of periderm

Figure 2.7
Section through a typical tree stem showing the arrangement of vascular tissues: xylem, phloem and vascular cambium.

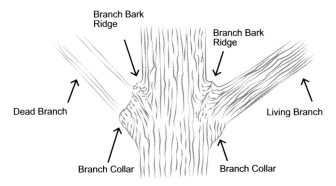

Figure 2.8
Branch connection, showing branch collar and branch bark ridge.

2.4 PRUNING

When wounded, rather than repair and replace damaged tissue as humans do, trees recover by sealing off the damaged area and growing over the site of the wound; thus, once injured, forever injured. To prevent infection and spread of diseases, trees respond to injury by producing a series of barriers to close the damage or infection off from surrounding healthy tissue by a process known as *compartmentalisation*. Vascular tissues above and below the wound are plugged with tyloses, gums and other products to limit vertical spread, the previous vascular rings are also plugged to limit inward spread, vertical ray cells limit lateral spread and new growth forms outside the wound, thus effectively sealing the wound in all directions, within a compartment. The outer barrier would appear to be the strongest of the four and may help to explain why many trees can continue into healthy maturity despite possessing a hollow or decayed interior. Every year, new compartments (secondary thickening) grow over older ones as the tree stem, branches and twigs expand. This ensures that a constant source of protection barriers is always present, should damage occur and infection threaten.

The process of compartmentalisation does not work perfectly each and every time. Sometimes, pathogens and wood-digesting organisms are able to enter the tree either before the defence systems have been fully deployed or they may have developed effective ways to overcome or circumvent the defence barriers.

Pruning cuts are, in effect, wounds and trees respond accordingly. The aim of the arborist or tree manager must, therefore, be to ensure that any wound that needs to be inflicted must be done so in such a way that the tree is able to recover as quickly as possible. Shigo tells us that the site of any pruning cut is as important as what is being removed, if the tree is to grow over the wound and recover expediently. Also, the sooner in the tree's life such pruning cuts can be made, the smaller the size of the wound, and so, the faster the recovery. Pruning is one of the most common tree treatments and oldest tree management activities. Incorrect pruning is a worldwide problem that causes serious injury to trees by encouraging decay.

The *branch collar* is a swollen area just beneath the branch connection point, where the tree lays down structural, support tissue. Above the branch connection, this tissue is squeezed by the expanding trunk to form the *branch bark ridge*.

Correct pruning cuts take place immediately outside the branch collar, without removing any of the swelling created by the structural tissue. These branch collar tissues are able to form protective chemical zones that help prevent ingress of pathogens. If the tissues are removed during pruning, this ability is lost and recovery is delayed. The tree responds to wounding by producing new, undifferentiated cells, which divide rapidly to create *callus* tissue around the margins of the wound. As the callus cells proliferate and compress against each other, their growth diminishes and *woundwood* starts to develop. Woundwood contains more lignin than either callus or normal wood, is tougher so adds strength and is typically seen as ribs around the margins of the wound. Once the woundwood has closed the site of the wound, normal wood tissue continues to grow.

Shigo (1982) points out that if trees are over-pruned, through topping or lopping, too much stored energy is removed from the system, resulting in a compromised ability to defend against attack from pathogens. Shigo explains this as an imbalance between the dynamic mass, where a connected system of living cells creates growth and stores reserves of energy, and the static mass, where a network of dead cells provides a system for water transport and a support structure that keeps the tree upright.

2.4.1 Formative pruning

Formative pruning typically starts in the production nursery during the early years of a tree's life in order to produce a balanced branch structure that is appropriate for the tree species. Early onsite tree management may also be considered formative pruning until a permanent scaffold system of structurally sound branches has been produced. The objectives should be restricted to correcting branch formations, which are likely to become hazards later. Such work could include the removal of codominant stems and crossing branches, which are likely to rub together. Early identification of undesirable branching is critical to ensure that corrective work is carried out on young growth, which is more able to recover quickly from wounding. Crown thinning, crown lifting, crown reduction, reshaping and pollarding are all specialist forms of tree crown manipulation, which are typically carried out on more mature trees. As such, they should be carried out by suitably trained and certified arboricultural operatives. All pruning works should be conducted in accordance with *BS 3998 Tree Work–Recommendations* and all other current industry guidance.

2.5 ROOT GROWTH AND FUNCTION

Roots perform several vital functions: they provide access to water and mineral nutrients dissolved within the soil water and transport them to the stem; they store carbohydrate in the form of starch, which is used as a source of energy to allow re-growth following a period of dormancy; they are responsible for the production of hormones or plant growth regulators that help to determine shoot growth; and they physically anchor the tree in the ground, providing stability. To enable all of this to function efficiently, the root system must be able to exploit the below-ground environment and maintain a sufficient level of health and functionality. As discussed in the following chapter, the rooting environment in urban settings is often suboptimal. Urban trees are often subjected to inhospitable conditions, which are restrictive to tree root growth, and insufficient volumes of soil to enable them to achieve their full potential.

Historically, there has been little study of the root systems of established and mature trees, even within woodlands where such experimentation would be thought to be fairly simple. Much of the work conducted by David Cutler and others focussed on the trees that were uprooted during the 'great storm' of 15 and 16 October 1987. Within urban landscapes, where trees are surrounded by buildings, paved surfaces and other hard infrastructure, our knowledge is even less. It is not difficult to see why. Up until fairly recently, excavation and scientific observation would have meant, at the very least, severe damage to the tree and more usually, death. This would not be possible in accessible urban settings unless the tree was removed completely. As no one with responsibility for the risk management of trees would deliberately create a situation that increases the exposure of the public to any tree hazard, most of the experimental work has been carried out on young trees in very controlled environments, such as forestry research institutions and universities. The results and findings are then extrapolated to surmise likely effects on more mature specimens growing in completely uncontrolled and heterogeneous environments, such as our urban centres.

However, over the last 10 years or so, some recent innovations in research methodology and techniques (ground penetrating radar, compressed air and vacuum soil extraction, non-invasive, laser pulse heat-tracing sap flow measurement, detection and analysis of stable isotopes of carbon, oxygen and nitrogen and neutron probes, to name a few) have resulted in a greater understanding of root function. First, back to basics. For roots to extract water from their growing environment, they must have intimate contact with the soil, and more importantly, with the water associated with that soil (water movement through soil will be discussed in more detail in Chapter 3, Urban soils and functional trees). This contact is extended by the production of tiny, filamentous root hairs, which are extensions of epidermal cells, growing just behind the actively growing root tips. The root hairs greatly increase the surface area of the root system, and so its potential to absorb water and nutrients from the soil. Most of the water taken up by the plant is absorbed through the root tips and the root hairs, as the cells in these areas are permeable. As roots age, the outer surface tends to thicken with a corky bark (suberin) and becomes impermeable to water and the mass flow of chemical ions. This response ensures that the ever-extending root system is able to absorb water at its extremities and is also able to retain that water within the roots, without it leaking back out into the soil. A newly planted tree will quickly produce new roots and root hairs, once the soil reaches a suitable temperature, and these extend out into the planting soil. The contact between root hair and soil can be fairly easily disrupted, and it is vital that trees are well supported for the first few seasons to prevent these delicate associations being broken. Every time this happens, the tree's water uptake is disrupted and energy is expended in producing replacement roots and root hairs.

2.5.1 Root architecture

We have moved on from the view that the tree root system is a mirror image of the above-ground structure of trunk and branching crown. Extensive research does show that, rather than deep root systems, most rooting is fairly superficial, typically concentrated within the top metre of soil and rarely deeper than 2 m (Gasson & Cutler, 1990; Gilman, 1990). A useful mental guide is that of a wine glass atop a dinner plate, where the glass represents the tree stem and crown, and the plate represents the root system (Dobson & Moffat, 1993).

There have been various attempts to classify tree root systems of individual tree species to specific root morphology types, but none appears to have been particularly successful. Significant variability even within species has thwarted any firm categorisation of root form, and so, only generalisations can be made. Three main types of root system shape have been identified by Büsgen et al. (1929) and Köstler et al. (1968).

These ways of describing root systems help to satisfy our inclination to classify the world around us, but the assignment of root morphologies to tree species or stages of growth is not clearly defined, and so, not terribly helpful. Dobson and Moffat (1993) reviewed a range of available research and concluded that soil conditions play a much more important role in influencing the eventual architecture of a mature root system than any predetermined tendency linked to species. There also appears to be little consistency in the research literature when it comes to empirical root spread and depth data linked to species, even when growing in similar conditions (Watson & Himelick, 1982). As Day et al. (2010b) point out, being able to identify tree clones, which display a genetic characteristic for deep rooting, may be very useful when selecting trees for urban settings as they are less likely to interfere with paved surfaces.

(a)

(b)

(c)

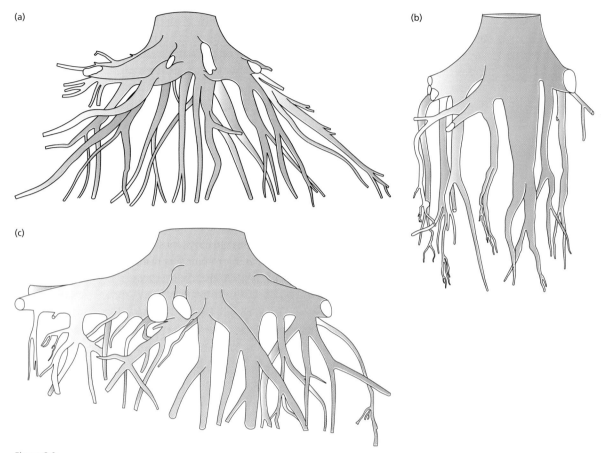

Figure 2.9
Root morphologies redrawn from Köstler *et al.* (1968).
(a) Heart root system – Several small and large roots emanating diagonally, in all directions from the base of the trunk. For example, *Betula* spp., *Fagus* spp., *Larix* spp., *Tilia* spp. and *Acer platanoides*. (b) Tap root system – A main root with a strong tendency to grow vertically downwards. For example, *Quercus robur*, *Pinus sylvestris* and *Abies* spp. (c) Surface or plate root system – Main lateral roots emanating horizontally from the base of the trunk in all directions. Several large and small roots tend to grown downwards at intervals along these strong laterals (droppers). For example, *Fraxinus* spp., *Populus tremula*, *Picea abies*, *Pinus monticola* and *Pinus strobus*.

Unfortunately, despite some evidence for this trait, separating the influence of genetics on root architecture from the influence of those that confer tolerance of soil conditions is likely to be difficult at best.

Roots are opportunistic and tend to grow wherever ground conditions are favourable, proliferating in nutrient-rich or moist pockets of encountered soil (Harris *et al.*, 2004). In urban settings, these conditions may often be facilitated by damaged sewers or ill-fitting pipe seals (Rolf & Stål, 1994; Randrup *et al.*, 2001). Dobson and Moffat (1993) consider and classify the four main constraints imposed on root development by soil conditions. These are mechanical resistance (compaction), aeration, fertility (chemistry) and moisture and are discussed more fully in Chapter 3.

Temperate tree species typically show root dormancy or at least a diminution of growth rate and number of roots during the winter months. Root growth tends to be initiated during the spring, prior to shoot growth, which was observed by the Greek philosopher Theophrastus

2,300 years ago! It would appear that the roots receive transported auxins from the swelling buds, and due to their lower temperature optimum, are able to start growing prior to the buds (Lyr & Hoffman, 1967). During August, growth tends to diminish, and by September, for most species, root growth has ceased.

2.5.2 Mycorrhizae

The acquisition of mineral elements by foraging roots can be greatly enhanced by the presence of mycorrhizal fungi, which interact with the root system to form mycorrhizal networks. This relationship between roots and fungi is especially useful in soils of low fertility and an example of symbiosis. The host plant provides the associated mycorrhizal fungi with a source of carbohydrate, and in return, receives nutrients from the fungi via its extensive hyphal fan of mycelia. The mycorrhizal mycelia are much smaller in diameter than tree roots, so are able to explore microsites that roots cannot access, providing a larger surface area for nutrient absorption. They also extend beyond zones of nutrient depletion close to roots, thus increasing the overall volume of soil explored for nutrient exploitation. Of the macro-nutrients plants require, the most difficult to access in sufficient quantities is phosphorous. This occurs in the soil as phosphate ions, which are very poorly soluble, and so, move through soil very slowly. Once the phosphate resource is used up in the immediate vicinity of an exploratory root, access to more requires further ions to diffuse through the soil solution from other, unexploited soil close by. This happens so slowly that phosphorous uptake can be a severely limiting growth factor in many plants. In soils of high pH, phosphorous becomes extremely insoluble, and so even more difficult for plants to assimilate. Evolution has enabled plants with mycorrhizal associations to gain better access to soil-borne phosphate ions. In fact, hyphae of mycorrhizal fungi can provide up to 80 per cent of the plant's phosphorous requirement (Allen *et al.*, 2003).

Although not nearly as dramatic as the effect on phosphorous uptake, some plants are also thought to be able to benefit from increased drought resistance through mycorrhizal symbioses (Augé, 2001). Most of the mycorrhizal studies that look at water relations use non-woody plants as subjects. The results of these studies, therefore, cannot necessarily be assumed to be indicative of woody plant responses, and much more research needs to be carried out on trees before any firm conclusions can be made.

There are two main types of mycorrhizae that occur in approximately 90 per cent of terrestrial plant species (Taiz *et al.*, 2015), vesicular-arbuscular mycorrhizae (often referred to as VA mycorrhizae or VAM) and ectomycorrhizae (ECM). The most widespread and most ancient are the vesicular-arbuscular mycorrhizae. These are present in the fossil record as early as 400 million years ago, when early Devonian land plants are shown to have arbuscular fungi associated with their roots, which bear a remarkable similarity to modern VAM fungi (Remy *et al.*, 1994). Certainly, fossil plants of the Triassic period (200 million years ago) clearly show VAM associations. Systematically, these fungi are grouped within the newly described fungi phylum, Glomeramycota, and are found associated with an extensive range of both broadleaf and coniferous species. They can only survive in association with the roots of a host plant and are typified by the structures they form within the root tissue of their host. The hyphae penetrate the root epidermis and colonise the root cortex, where they extend through intercellular spaces and occupy individual cortex cells. It is here that they form highly branched structures called *arbuscles*, where transfer of materials between host and fungus occurs, and occasional storage bodies called *vesicles*. It is from these structures that this form of mycorrhiza acquires its name. VAM hyphae have the capacity for fast growth, efficient absorption and rapid translocation and transport of nutrients to the root cells.

The more recent ectomycorrhizae, in contrast, have formed far fewer symbioses with plant species and are commonly found associated with species within the families Pinaceae (pine, fir, spruce, larch, hemlock, Douglas fir), Fagaceae (beech, oak, chestnut), Betulaceae (birch, alder), Salicaceae (willow, poplar) and Myrtaceae (*Eucalyptus*). These fungi are grouped mainly within the Basidiomycota, or less often, the Ascomycota. Several have developed distinctive fruiting bodies such as fly agaric (*Amanita muscaria*), ceps (*Boletus* spp.) and truffles (*Tuber* spp.). Ectomycorrhizae were discovered before VA mycorrhizae simply because their effect on root structure is more visible. Infected roots are typically stubby and highly branched to produce dense clusters of short roots. Each root tip is surrounded by a thick sheath, or mantle, of mycelium with hyphae also radiating out into the surrounding soil. These exploratory hyphal threads are able to collect the immobile phosphate ions and transport them back to the mycelial sheath, where they are stored before being passed on to the root. Other hyphae penetrate the root tissues, creating a network of threads between individual root cells, the *Hartig net*, where mineral nutrients and carbohydrate may be transferred between the symbiotants.

The benefits to the host are fairly obvious. Plant roots are complex organs, with a central conducting structure, surrounded by other layers of tissue. Fine plant roots are typically one-tenth of a millimetre in diameter, while fungal hyphae, in comparison, are typically ten times finer. The cost to build either is proportional to the volume of material required and this depends on the square of the radius. Therefore, in resources alone, hyphae are ten-squared (10 × 10 = 100) times less costly to manufacture than plant roots and plants have evolved to harness the ability of fungi to scavenge for phosphate rather than manufacture their own roots to do the job (Davis *et al.*, 1992).

It is worth reflecting that the benefits of this relationship are not only in one direction. The cost to the host plant may be that 25 per cent of its photosynthetic production is lost to mycorrhizal fungi. Occasionally, negative responses have been observed, where the loss of carbohydrate by the host is excessive and the garnering and supply of nutrients by the fungus is insufficient to satisfy the demand (Taiz *et al.*, 2015), but these are rare occurrences. Rayner (1996) suggests that the coexistence between tree root and fungus provides a more fundamental link between the root systems of adjacent trees of the same species. In addition to increasing the interface between tree root and soil, he postulates that communication may be possible between trees, allowing adult trees to 'nurse' their offspring, reducing competition between species and facilitating an extensive resource harvesting and redistribution network, which can more efficiently provide the nutrient requirements for interconnected trees within populations.

Imported top soils and manufactured soils in particular may be deficient in mycorrhizae and the addition of composted green waste and forestry by-products may help to address this short coming. Mycorrhizae can be reduced or eliminated completely by certain urban conditions and landscape management practices for instance, mycorrhizae are typically killed by flooding, high compaction, extensive soil disturbance caused by excessive cultivation and high levels of fertiliser application.

2.6   LIGHT

The visible spectrum of light, from violet at one end to red at the other, is but a small fraction of the vast overall electromagnetic spectrum that reaches the earth's atmosphere from the sun.

The solar energy that strikes the earth's atmosphere each year is equivalent to approximately 56×10^{23} J of heat (Hall & Rao, 1999), approximately half of which is reflected back or absorbed by the atmosphere. As a comparison, the world primary energy use (as defined by Grubler *et al.*

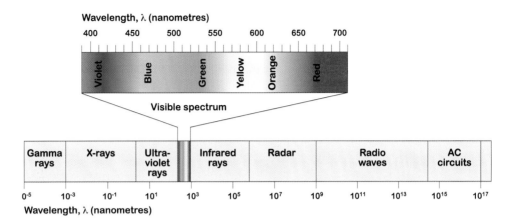

Figure 2.10
The electromagnetic spectrum – gamma rays (10^{-5}) to AC circuits (10^{17}), showing the trend in energy. The electromagnetic spectrum ranges in wavelength from 10^{-5} to 10^{17} nanometres. The light visible to the human eye represents only a small part, from violet light, where the shortest wavelengths are approximately 380 nm, to red light where the longest wavelengths are approximately 750 nm.

(2012)) in 2012 was approximately 55.9×10^{19} J (OECD/IEA, 2014). Most of the high-energy short wavelengths from the sun are screened by oxygen and ozone high in the atmosphere, while much of the infrared radiation is absorbed by water vapour and carbon dioxide. Most of the radiation reaching the earth from the sun, therefore, is within a fairly tight band, which includes the various wavelengths that make up white light. It is, perhaps, no accident that this portion of the entire electromagnetic spectrum includes the wavelengths of light, which are visible to the vast majority of animals, and which are responsible for photoperiodism (the alternation of light and dark periods that affect the physiological activities of many plants), phototropism (the growth of plant shoots towards a light source) and photosynthesis (Bailey, 2006). In fact, George Wald from Harvard University was convinced that life, wherever it exists, must be based on similar conditions to those found on earth. One of his arguments was that it is quite fundamental to the survival of life that such a tight band of solar radiation does reach the planet's surface. Life forms are composed of highly complex molecules that are held together by hydrogen bonds. Short wavelength light within the ultraviolet range is able to break those bonds, denaturing proteins and splitting nucleic acids (DNA molecules being particularly susceptible). For example, wavelengths between 320 nm and 400 nm (UV-A) are not harmful to humans at normal doses and are instrumental in the production of vitamin D. Wavelengths within the 290 nm to 320 nm (UV-B) band can burn the skin and are responsible for tanning. The 230 nm to 290 nm (UV-C) band causes skin cancer. Shorter wavelength light, of 200 nm or less, is known as ionising radiation because it is able to dislodge electrons from atoms, creating ions, and so, is destructive. At the other extreme, longer wavelengths beyond the visible red range are absorbed by water-containing molecules. Most life relies on water as a solvent to carry various dissolved materials throughout their bodies, and these longer wavelengths cause the water molecules to heat up rather than create the various energy states necessary for photochemical reactions to take place (Wald, 1959).

As discussed earlier, chlorophyll is the pigment in leaves which makes them appear green. It absorbs almost 90 per cent of the violet and blue wavelengths that strike it and nearly as much

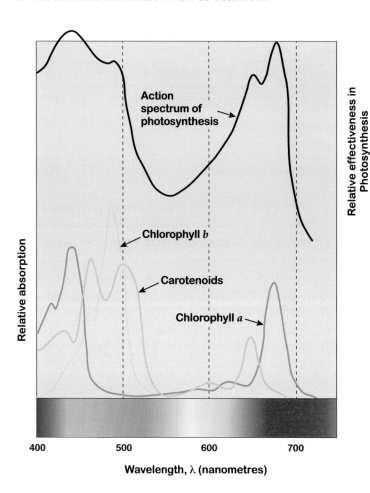

Relative absorption

Relative effectiveness in Photosynthesis

Action spectrum of photosynthesis

Chlorophyll *b*

Carotenoids

Chlorophyll *a*

| 400 | 500 | 600 | 700 |

Wavelength, λ (nanometres)

Figure 2.11
Comparison between photosynthetic activity and wavelengths of light – the action spectrum of photosynthesis. Chlorophyll is much more efficient at absorbing light within the blue and red wavebands of the visible spectrum than within the green and yellow. The photosynthesis action spectrum fairly closely matches the combined absorption spectra for chlorophyll a, chlorophyll b and carotenoids. The combination of the different pigments extends the range of wavelengths of light absorbed by the leaf, increasing the level of photosynthesis.

of the orange and red wavelengths (Salisbury & Ross, 1992). Green light, in the middle of the visible spectrum is not efficiently absorbed and is reflected, giving plants their characteristic green colour. In fact, chlorophyll is not one pigment, but exists in several forms. In higher plants, the important photosynthetic pigments are bluish-green chlorophyll *a*, yellowish-green chlorophyll *b* and the yellow, orange and red carotenoids.

Although the carotenoid pigments do extend the range of light wavelengths collected, their primary function is to protect the chlorophyll molecules against excessive photo-oxidation in high light intensities. If carotenoids were not present within the photosynthesising organs, photo-synthesis would not occur in the presence of oxygen. The carotenoid pigments are usually masked, during the growing season, by the much more abundant chlorophylls. However, during autumn, in temperate regions, the chlorophylls start to break down and in the process lose their green colour to reveal the yellows, oranges and reds of the carotenoids.

Plants are particularly affected by the quality of light – its colour (wavelength), intensity of the light source and duration of exposure. The measurement of light for most environmental and engineering purposes tends not to reflect these qualities, and so, some caution needs to be employed when measuring light, with plants in mind. Architects, interior designers and lighting engineers are interested in the illumination provided by the visible light incident on a given surface (illuminance). Illuminance is measured in lux and is defined with reference to the sensitivity of the human eye. Plants do not use or respond to light in the same way as the human eye, and so, such measurements have no real value unless the light source is identified and defined (Salisbury & Ross, 1992).

Photobiologists are more interested in measuring irradiance, which is a measure of the amount of radiant energy incident on a given surface (i.e., the leaf) and is measured in watts per square metre ($W\ m^{-2}$ or $mW\ m^{-2}$). As plants respond differently to different wavelengths of light, some description of the spectral distribution must be provided or implied by describing the light source. The photochemical reactions that occur during photosynthesis depend on the number of photons incident on the surface, rather than the energy contained by them. When looking scientifically at photosynthesis, therefore, it is more appropriate to consider quantum flux or photosynthetic photon flux density (PPFD), that is, the number of photons (quanta) striking the leaf during a specified length of time. This is expressed as micro moles per square metre, per second ($\mu mol\ m^{-2}\ s^{-1}$) within the photosynthetically active wavelength range, 400–700 nm (Hall & Rao, 1999).

Although there are no exact conversion factors between these various units, an approximation can be obtained from Table 2.1.

Research has shown that forest communities subjected to diffuse light have been observed to increase the rate of photosynthesis compared with the same communities when exposed to direct sunlight. The reason for this appears to be that on cloudy days, assuming that the cloud cover is not so dense as to reflect too much of the sunlight back into the atmosphere, there is more diffuse light being bounced around, and this can reach a greater proportion of the tree canopy, rather than being restricted to the top leaves only. Also, when the sunlight is very intense, the exposed leaves tend to close their stomata to prevent losing too much transpirational water, and as a consequence, experience a midday depression in photosynthesis (Gu et al., 1999; Gu et al., 2002; Urban et al., 2007; Urban et al., 2012).

Table 2.1
Illuminance values from various sources and requirements for plants. Adapted from Helliwell (2013), Harris, Clark and Matheny (2004) and revised using McCree (1972) conversion factors. Sunlight readings are thought to be typical for London at a latitude of 51.5°N

	Illuminance lux	Irradiance $mW\ m^{-2}$	PPFD $\mu mol\ m^{-2}\ s^{-1}$
Full summer sun at noon in London	102,000	408	1,836
Full winter sun at noon in London	22,000	88	396
Cloudy summer day at noon in London	44,000	176	792
Cloudy winter day at noon in London	18,000	72	324
Shady side of a two-storey building (sunny) in summer	21,600	86	386
Shady side of a two-storey building in winter	2,300	9	41
Moonlight	0.22	–	–
Adequate for most plants	54,000	216	972
Shade plants	9,000	36	162
Indoor illuminance suitable for reading	200–300	0.8–1.2	4–6
Incandescent light bulb (100 W with 250 mm reflector at 1.5 m)	240	1	4.8
Fluorescent: Deluxe cool white (150 W at 1.5 m)	1,050	2.8	12.6

Table 2.2
The midday elevations of the sun and average day lengths for the solstices and equinoxes at different latitudes in Britain. From Helliwell (2013). To calculate zenith angle of the sun for the summer solstice at noon: 90° minus latitude plus 23.5° (i.e., London: 90° − 51.5° + 23.5° = 62°). For the winter solstice at noon: 90° minus latitude minus 23.5° (i.e., London: 90° − 51.5° − 23.5° = 15°). For the spring and autumn equinoxes at noon: 90° minus latitude (i.e., London: 90° − 51.5° = 38.5°)

Latitude at British locations	Maximum angle (°) of sun from horizon at mid-day and approximate day length (in hours)		
	20 December	20 March and 20 September	20 June
50° (Land's End)	16.5 (8)	40 (12)	63.5 (16.5)
52.5° (Birmingham)	14.0 (7.5)	37.5 (12)	61.0 (17)
55° (Newcastle)	11.5 (7)	35 (12)	58.5 (17.5)
57.5° (Aberdeen)	9.0 (6.5)	32.5 (12)	56.0 (18.25)
60° (Lerwick)	6.5 (6)	30 (12)	53.8 (19)

SO WHAT?

As the capture of photosynthetic energy provides plants with almost all of their chemical energy requirements, it is an essential process that ensures a plant's ability to survive and compete in its environment. Photosynthetic energy capture, therefore, underpins the ability for trees and other green infrastructure to provide ecosystem services, when all other growth requirements are satisfied (Givnish, 1988). Kjelgren and Clark (1992) found that *Liquidambar styraciflua* (a known shade-intolerant tree species) growing in street canyons, with diminished sunlight, displayed flattened and thinner leaves, which were held horizontally, and decreased shoot and trunk growth. Such responses are all typical of acclimatisation strategies employed by tree species growing in heavy shade of forest understorey. In contrast to forest understorey conditions, however, urban canyons may cause shade-intolerant tree species, such as *L. styraciflua*, to suffer chronic low-radiant-energy stress. In these conditions, photosynthesis is prioritised through the production of fewer, thinner leaves, which increases photosynthetic area and reduces self-shading. This increased specific leaf area and reduced crown density result in less carbohydrate available for trunk growth. In contrast, a more shade-tolerant species, *Acer platanoides* 'Emerald Queen', was also investigated by Kjelgren (1995). It was found to retain both its appearance and utility when planted in deeply shaded urban canyons, but still showed significant, reduced growth responses. Careful species selection would appear to be important when considering planting within deep urban canyons and other urban locations, subject to dense shade and reduced seasonal irradiance. It may be determined that reduced trunk growth rates and lower canopy density may be acceptable responses, but trees growing in heavily shaded landscapes will have lowered photosynthesis, and this could predispose them to additional, endemic urban stresses, pests and disease (Harris & Bassuk, 1993).

Trees have evolved to efficiently capture and harness energy from sunlight. The arrangement of leaves along the stem is so arranged that they maximise exposure to the sun and so are able to photosynthesise to their full potential. To ensure this, it is important that the leaves higher up the stem do not shade those lower down. Leaf arrangement, known as *phyllotaxis*, tends to follow one of the three patterns. The most common is *alternate*, where a single leaf emerges from each node and the leaves are arranged in a spiral along the stem. Examples of this arrangement can be seen in *Carpinus*, *Fagus*, *Morus* and *Quercus*. In some plants with a single leaf present at each node, the leaves are arranged in two rows opposite each other along the stem. This pattern is known as distichous and is most common in the grasses, but is also apparent in some conifers, such as *Cephalotaxus*, *Podocarpus*, *Sequoia*, *Taxodium* and *Torreya*, but also in *Ulmus*. Where two leaves emerge from the same node, the arrangement is said to be *opposite*. If each pair of these opposite leaves is arranged at 90° to its neighbour, they are said to be decussate, as in *Acer*, *Cupressus* and *Thuja*. It may be easy to see how the arrangement of leaves may provide some benefit to various tree species, but the great variety in leaf shapes is not so easily explained. Despite this, the diversity in leaf shapes and their aesthetic qualities are used by designers to create a variety of different visual effects.

2.7 TEMPERATURE

Assuming that the raw materials are in abundance, virtually all chemical and biochemical reactions work faster as temperature increases, up to a point where enzymes are destroyed. The temperature range over which most plants can photosynthesise is considerable, typically 10°–35°C, but exposure to temperatures above and below this range can cause irreversible damage to the photosynthetic system (Berry & Bjorkman, 1980). At higher temperatures, the photosynthetic system is disrupted and photosynthesis declines, but respiration continues to increase until cell death occurs somewhere in the region of 45°–50°C. Similarly, the roots of a number of different woody species were killed by a single 4-hour exposure of temperatures between 40°C and 45°C (Wong *et al.*, 1971).

Paved surfaces are not subject to evaporative cooling and so heat up in the sun, reflecting and re-radiating heat. This is likely to be of most concern to urban tree managers working in the temperate regions of the world, rather than low temperatures. However, frozen ground can be especially important for evergreens, which, on bright winter days, are actively photosynthesising, so using water, but unable to replenish the water used because it is frozen and so unavailable. Soil moisture is often concentrated on the underside of paved surfaces, and root proliferation can be high in these conditions, exploiting the availability of water. As these surfaces are most affected by increased temperatures in the summer months, high root mortality can be quite common.

Whitlow and Bassuk (1988a) found that localised conditions within Columbus Avenue (between 68th and 75th Streets, lat. 40°46′N, long. 73°58′30″W), New York City, a fairly typical urban street, were significantly different to the official weather records. The maximum air temperature reached within the street was 42°C and relative humidity fell to between 10 and 12 per cent. The official weather figures (from the Central Park weather station, situated on 86th Street, a few blocks away) recorded the high temperature as 30°C and the relative humidity as 40 per cent. These conditions of high air temperature and low relative humidity caused a much higher atmospheric evaporative demand on the street trees than would have been expected from the official weather records. The authors suggest that the conditions recorded on the west side of Columbus Avenue would be more consistent with those experienced in the desert regions of south-west USA rather than the north-east Atlantic coast. These results indicate the extreme differences that can be experienced between urban green open spaces and nearby in-street, tree planting sites. It should also be noted that local weather station records cannot necessarily be relied upon to predict planting site conditions (Whitlow & Bassuk, 1988b).

It is generally considered that the optimum soil temperature for the propagating of temperate species stem cuttings is between 18°C and 25°C (Hartmann *et al.*, 1990). There is no reason to assume that this temperature range would not be considered optimal for more mature plants, assuming that all other growth factors are not limited. However, Lyr and Hoffman (1967) summarised the minimum, optimum and maximum temperature values from the literature and showed that optimum temperatures range from 18°C to 32°C and maximum temperatures range from 25°C to 36°C, for a variety of temperate tree species. As this optimum range varies for each species, it is likely that this corresponds to those conditions experienced by the species, or species ecotype, within its native habitat (Harris & Fanelli, 1999; Day *et al.*, 2010a).

Although root growth is dependent on metabolic activity and so is likely to be influenced by soil temperature, it is difficult to make any definitive assertions regarding the direct effects of soil temperature alone. From experimentation, changes in root growth, during the vegetation period, vary markedly more than soil temperature fluctuations. Soil temperature would appear to have much more influence on root growth initiation in the spring and cessation in the autumn than during the summer, when the effects of other limiting factors, such as soil moisture and shoot activity are also evident (Lyr & Hoffman, 1967; Harris & Fanelli, 1999). As the latter is influenced by light quality and duration, air temperature, humidity and root activity, it is difficult to prove simple dependencies between soil temperature alone and root growth.

Soil temperatures in urban landscapes covered with hard paving have been found to be significantly higher than those found in areas of planting. Kjelgren and Montague (1998) measured the surface temperature of an asphalt car park situated within the Utah State University research farm in Logan, Utah (lat. 41°45'N, long. 111°49'W) and found that it could reach over 55°C in mid-July and nearly 60°C in mid-August. In their Columbus Avenue study, Whitlow and Bassuk (1988) measured the surface temperatures of asphalt paving and car roofs to investigate how environmental conditions may be affected by re-radiated heat. They found that car roofs heat up rapidly as they are exposed to the sun, reaching a maximum temperature of 55°C in mid-August and cool rapidly as direct solar radiation is removed. Asphalt, in contrast, heats up more slowly, and due to its greater thermal mass, also loses heat over a longer period of time, in this case long after the sun had passed behind local buildings. The maximum temperature recorded for the asphalt surface was slightly less than for car roofs, but was still 32°C at 8:00 pm. In a later study by Montague and Kjelgren (2004) (again at the Utah State University site in Logan, Utah), temperature measurements were collected for a paved asphalt surface and for the soil immediately below the paving. They found that the soil temperature could be 42°C under the asphalt, while the surface temperature reached 50°C in the height of summer. In each of these research studies, the measured high temperatures are comparable to those found by Wong *et al.* (1971) to kill roots.

In the arid environment of the Logan study, low humidity was found to limit stomatal opening, so reducing water loss, and therefore causing the foliage temperature to rise. If these conditions were to be experienced over any length of time, reduced stomatal opening could have a fundamental impact on photosynthesis, and so lead to reduced growth. In turn, such conditions would impose increased levels of stress on trees growing in these locations, making them susceptible to other urban stresses, pests and disease. Conversely, Whitlow and Bassuk (1987) observed midday stomatal closure only once during their 3-year study. Perhaps, it is possible that more water was available beneath the asphalt-paved surface than is frequently assumed or the trees were benefitting from leaking sewers.

Soil temperature not only affects the physiological function of tree roots, but also other biological activities within the soil biota. High temperature increases biological oxygen demand and microorganisms tend to migrate deeper within the soil profile when temperature is raised.

2.8 WIND

As anyone who uses the quaint old washing line rather than an energy-hungry tumble dryer knows, heat is not needed to dry clothes; air movement alone can provide the right conditions. Similarly, wind has the same effect on leaves; as air flows across the leaf surface, it causes the evaporation of water, and this, in turn, places a high water demand on the tree. This situation is often exacerbated in urban landscapes where the built form can concentrate the movement of air, causing localised wind funnelling. Urban air also tends to be drier and at a higher temperature than rural air, intensifying any effects caused by the wind. Some tree species have characteristics that display possible adaptations to windy conditions, such as possessing long leaf petioles, which allow the leaves to bend and turn, and so, reduce their sail area. Trees exposed to constant or frequent wind tend to respond by directing resources to root elongation and stem diameter growth, rather than overall height (Harris *et al.*, 2004).

Wind rock can be a problem for newly planted trees that are not secure. New roots are likely to be damaged if the root ball is allowed to move within its planting location. In coastal areas, salt-laden air can increase the effects of wind damage by scorching the leaves and even desiccating buds, creating a characteristic witch's broom affect at the ends of branches. It is worth bearing in mind that salt can be carried inland many miles, by the wind.

Contrary to its effect on humans, wind chill tends not to be a problem for plants. In cold weather, wind will affect an object by removing heat from it, if it has been added by radiation, but only if that object is warmer than the air. As long as the plant is sufficiently hardy to withstand the temperature of the air, the wind will not increase any injury due to cold. On the contrary, wind will tend to keep the plant at air temperature, rather than allowing it to cool further due to radiation loss (Harris *et al.*, 2004).

REFERENCES

Allen, M. F., Swenson, W., Querejeta, J. I., Egerton-Warburton, L. M. & Treseder, K. K. (2003). Ecology of Mycorrhizae: A conceptual framework for complex interactions among plants and fungi. *Annual Review of Phytopathology, 41*, 271–303.

Augé, R. M. (2001). Water relations, drought and vesicular–arbuscular mycorrhizal symbiosis. *Mycorrhiza, 11*(1), 3–42.

Bailey, J. (2006). *Collins Dictionary of Botany.* Glasgow: Collins.

Bartlett, M. K., Scoffoni, C. & Sack, L. (2012). The determinants of leaf turgor loss point and prediction of drought tolerance of species and biomes: A global meta-analysis. *Ecology Letters, 15*(5), 393–405.

Bartlett, M. K., Zhang, Y., Kreidler, N., Sun, S., Ardy, R., Cao, K. & Sack, L. (2014). Global analysis of plasticity in turgor loss point, a key drought tolerance trait. *Ecology Letters, 17*(2), 1580–90.

Bassuk, N. L., Curtis, D. F., Marranca, B. Z. & Neal, B. (2009). *Recommended Urban Trees: Site Assessment and Tree Selection for Stress Tolerance.* Ithaca: Urban Horticulture Institute, Department of Horticulture, Cornell University.

Berry, J. & Bjorkman, O. (1980). Photosynthetic response and adaptation to temperature in higher plants. *Annual Review of Plant Physiology, 31*, 491–543.

Büsgen, M., Münch, E. & Thomson, T. (1929). *The Structure and Life of Forest Trees.* London: Chapman & Hall.

Davies, Z. G., Edmondson, J. L., Heinemeyer, A., Leake, J.R. & Gaston, K.J. (2011). Mapping an urban ecosystem service: Quantifying above-ground carbon storage at a city-wide scale. *Journal of Applied Ecology, 48*(5), 1125–34.

Davis, B., Walker, N., Ball, D. & Fitter, A. (1992). *The Soil.* London: Collins.

Day, D. S., Wiseman, P. E., Dickinson, S. B. & Harris, J. R. (2010a). Tree root ecology in the urban environment and implications for a sustainable rhizosphere. *Arboriculture and Urban Forestry, 36*(5), 193–205.

Day, D. S., Wiseman, P. E., Dickinson, S. B. & Harris, J. R. (2010b). Contemporary concepts of root system architecture of urban trees. *Arboriculture & Urban Forestry, 36*(4), 149–59.

Dobson, M. C. & Moffat, A. J. (1993). *The Potential for Woodland Establishment on Landfill Sites*. London: HMSO.

Earle, C. J. (2015). *The Gymnosperm Database* (Online). Retrieved 26 July 2015 from www.conifers.org/cu/Sequoia.php.

Environmental Audit Committee (2010). *Fifth Report: Air Quality*. London: The Stationery Office.

Evert, R. F. & Eichhorn, S. E. (2013). *Biology of Plants* (8th edn). New York: W. H. Freeman and Company.

Field, C. B., Behrenfeld, M. J., Randerson, J. T. & Falkowski, P. (1998). Primary production of the biosphere: Integrating terrestrial and oceanic components. *Science, 281*(5374), 237–40.

Gasson, P. E. & Cutler, D. F. (1990). Tree root plate morphology. *Arboricultural Journal, 14*(3), 193–264.

Gibbs, J., Brasier, C. & Webber, J. (1994). *Dutch Elm Disease in Britain – Research Information Note 252*. Farnham, UK: Research Division of the Forestry Authority (now Forestry Commission Forest Research).

Gilman, E. F. (1990). Tree root growth and development. I. form, spread, depth and periodicity. *Journal of Environmental Horticulture, 8*(4), 215–20.

Givnish, T. J. (1988). Adaption to sun and shade: A whole-plant perspective. *Australian Journal of Plant Physiology, 15*, 63–92.

Greed, C. & Johnson, D. (2014). *Planning in the UK: An Introduction*. Basingstoke, UK: Palgrave Macmillan.

Grubler, A., Johansson, T. B., Mundaca, L., Nakicenovic, N., Pachauri, S., Riahi, K., Rogner, H. H. & Strupeit, L. (2012). Chapter 1 – Energy primer. In *Global Energy Assessment – Toward a Sustainable Future* (pp. 99–150). Cambridge and New York: Cambridge University Press and the International Institute for Applied Systems Analysis, Laxenburg, Austria.

Gu, L., Baldocchi, D., Verma, S. B., Black, T. A., Vesala, T., Falge, E. M. & Dowty, P.R. (2002). Advantages of diffuse radiation for terrestrial ecosystem productivity. *Journal of Geophysical Research (Atmospheres), 107*(D6), ACL 2-1-ACL 2–23.

Gu, L., Fuentes, J. D., Shugart, H. H., Staebler, R. M. & Black, T.A. (1999). Responses of net ecosystem exchanges of carbon dioxide to changes in cloudiness: Results from two North American deciduous forests. *Journal of Geophysical Research (Atmospheres), 104*(D24), 31421–34.

Hall, D. O. & Rao, K. K. (1999). *Photosynthesis* (6th edn). Cambridge: Cambridge University Press.

Harris, J. R. & Fanelli, J. (1999). Root and shoot growth periodicity of pot-in-pot red and sugar maple. *Journal of Environmental Horticulture, 17*(2), 80–3.

Harris, R. J. & Bassuk, N. L. (1993). Adaption of trees to low-light environments: Effect on branching pattern of *Fraxinus americana*. *Journal of Arboriculture, 19*(6), 339–43.

Harris, R. W., Clark, J. R. & Matheny, N. (2004). *Arboriculture: Integrated Management of Landscape Trees, Shrubs, and Vines* (4th edn). Upper Saddle River, NJ: Prentice Hall.

Hartmann, H. T., Kester, D. E. & Davies, F. T. (1990). *Plant Propagation: Principles and Practices* (5th edn). London: Prentice Hall International (UK).

Helliwell, R. (2013). Daylight in relation to plant growth and illumination of buildings. *Arboricultural Journal: The International Journal of Urban Forestry, 35*(4), 202–19.

HM Fire Service Inspectorate. (2001). *Fire Service Manual Volume 1: Fire Service Technology, Equipment and Media – Hydraulics, Pumps and Water Supplies*. London: The Stationery Office.

Jackson, K. T. (1985). *Crabgrass Frontier: The Suburbanization of the United States*. New York, NY: Oxford University Press.

Kjelgren, R. K. (1995). Variable urban irradiance and shade acclimation in Norway maple street trees. *Journal of Arboriculture, 21*(3), 145–9.

Kjelgren, R. K. & Clark, J. R. (1992). Photosynthesis and leaf morphology of *Liquidambar styraciflua* L. under variable urban radiant energy conditions. *International Journal of Biometeorology, 36*(3), 165–71.

Kjelgren, R. K. & Montague, T. (1998). Urban tree transpiration over turf and asphalt surfaces. *Atmospheric Environment, 32*(1), 35–41.

Koch, G. W., Sillett, S. C., Jennings, G. M. & Davis, S. D. (2004). The limits to tree height. *Nature, 428*, 851–4.

Köstler, J. N., Brückner, E. & Bibelriether, H. (1968). *Die Wurzeln der Waldbäume: Untersuchungen zur Morphologie der Waldbäume in Mitteleuropa*. Hamburg: Verlag Paul Parey.

Kramer, P. J. (1983). *Water Relations in Plants*. London: Academic Press.

Lyr, H. & Hoffman, G. (1967). Growth rates and growth periodicity of tree roots. *International Review of Forestry Research, 2*, 181–236.

Mattheck, C. & Breloer, H. (2010). *The Body Language of Trees*. Norwich: The Stationery Office.

McCree, K. J. (1972). Test of current definitions of photosynthetically active radiation against leaf photosynthesis data. *Agricultural Meteorology, 10*, 443–53.

Montague, T. & Kjelgren, R. (2004). Energy balance of six common landscape surfaces and the influence of surface properties on gas exchange of four containerized tree species. *Scientia Horticulturae, 100*(1–4), 229–49.

Murphy, J., Sexton, D. M. H., Jenkins, G. J., Booth, B. B. B., Brown, C. C., Clark, R. T., Collins, M., Harris, G. R., Kendon, E. J., Betts, R. A. & Brown, S.J. (2009). *UK Climate Projections Science Report: Climate Change Projections*. Exeter: Met Office Hadley Centre.

National Register of Big Trees (2014). *National Register of Big Trees*. (Online). Retrieved 26 July 2015 from www.nationalregisterofbigtrees.com.au/height.pdf.

Niinemets, Ü. & Valladares, F., (2006). Tolerance to shade, drought, and waterlogging of temperate northern hemisphere trees and shrubs. *Ecological Monographs, 76*(4), 521–47.

Nowak, D. J., Greenfield, E. J., Hoehn, R. E. & Lapoint, E. (2013). Carbon storage and sequestration by trees in urban and community areas of the United States. *Environmental Pollution, 178*, 229–36.

OECD/IEA (2014). *Key World Energy Statistics 2014*. (Online). Retrieved 3 August 2015 from www.iea.org/ publications/freepublications/publication/KeyWorld2014.pdf.

Randrup, T. B., McPherson, E. G. & Costello, L. R. (2001). Tree root intrusion in sewer systems: Review of extent and costs. *Journal of Infrastructure Systems, 7*(1), 26–31.

Rayner, A. D. M. (1996). The tree as a fungal community. In H. J. Read (ed.), *Pollard and Veteran Tree Management* (pp. 6–9). Slough: Richmond Publishing, on behalf of the Corporation of London.

Remy, W., Taylor, T., Hass, H. & Kerp, H. (1994). Four hundred-million-year-old vesicular arbuscular mycorrhizae. *Proceedings of the National Academy of Sciences of the United States of America, 91*(25), 11841–3.

Rolf, K. & Stål, Ö. (1994). Tree roots in sewer systems in Malmo, Sweden. *Journal of Arboriculture, 20*(6), 329–35.

Ryan, M. G. & Yoder, B. J. (1997). Hydraulic limits to tree height and tree growth. *Bioscience, 47*(4), 235–42.

Salisbury, F. B. & Ross, C. W. (1992). *Plant Physiology* (4th edn). Belmont, CA: Wadsworth Publishing Company.

Schmidt, O. (2006). *Wood and Tree Fungi*. Berlin: Springer-Verlag.

Shigo, A. L. (1982). Tree health. *Journal of Arboriculture, 8*(12), 311–16.

Shigo, A. L. (1986a). *A New Tree Biology: Facts, Photos, and Philosophies on Trees and their Problems and Proper Care*. Durham, New Hampshire: Shigo and Trees, Associates.

Shigo, A. L. (1986b). *How Wounds Injure Trees* (pp. 106–8). East Lansing, MI: Michigan State University.

Sjöman, H., Hirons, A. D. & Bassuk, N. L. (2015). Urban forest resilience through tree selection – Variation in drought tolerance of Acer. *Urban Forestry and Urban Greening, 14*(4), 858–65.

Sperry, J. S. & Sullivan, J. E. M. (1992). Xylem embolism in response to freeze-thaw cycles and water stress in ring porous, diffuse porous and conifer species. *Plant Physiology, 100*(2), 605–13.

Taiz, L., Zeiger, E., Møller, I. M. & Murphy, A. (2015). *Plant Physiology and Development* (6th edn). Sunderland, MA: Sinauer Associates.

Urban, O., Janouš, D., Acosta, M., Czerny, R., Markova, I., Navratil, M., Pavelka, M., Pokorny, R., Šprtová, M., Zhang, R. & Špunda, V. (2007). Ecophysiological controls over the net ecosystem exchange of mountain spruce stand. Comparison of the response in direct vs. diffuse solar radiation. *Global Change Biology, 13*(1), 157–68.

Urban, O., Klem, K., Ač, A., Havránková, K., Holišová, P., Navratil, M., Zitová, M., Kozlová, K., Pokorny, R., Šprtová, M. & Tomášková, I. (2012). Impact of clear and cloudy sky conditions on the vertical distribution of photosynthetic CO_2 uptake within a spruce canopy. *Functional Ecology, 26*(1), 46–55.

Wald, G. (1959). Life and light. *Scientific American, 201*, 92–108.

Watson, G. W. & Himelick, E. B. (1982). Root distribution of nursery trees and its relationship to transplanting success. *Journal of Arboriculture, 8*(9), 225–9.

Whitlow, T. H. & Bassuk, N. L. (1987). Trees in difficult sites. *Journal of Arboriculture, 13*(1), 10–17.

Whitlow, T. H. & Bassuk, N. L. (1988a). Environmental stress in street trees. *Arboricultural Journal, 12*(2), 195–201.

Whitlow, T. H. & Bassuk, N. L. (1988b). Ecophysiology of urban trees and their managment – The North American experience. *HortScience, 23*(3), 542–6.

Wong, T. L., Harris, R. W. & Fissell, R. E. (1971). Influence of high soil temperatures on five woody-plant species. *Journal of American Society of Horticultural Science, 96*, 80–2.

Chapter 3: Urban soils and functional trees

3.1 INTRODUCTION

Beneath our feet, in every urban centre, stretches a complicated underground world of life-supporting infrastructures that rarely cross our minds; that is, until it breaks down and fails to deliver what we have come to expect. We then demand that the problem is expediently resolved and that the water, electricity, gas, surface drainage, foul sewer or communications system is returned to full operation, so that our lives may continue to function as before. Surrounding this network of utility and service infrastructures is another vitally important, life-supporting system, soil. Soil is a dynamic, living material, home to a complex arrangement of physical, chemical and biological processes that are fundamental, not only to healthy plant growth, but also to the health and well-being of us all. Healthy soils provide important ecosystem services, such as storm water mitigation, carbon sequestration and provision for plant growth, while also supporting the myriad of other biological activities upon which life depends. Urbanisation often involves the disturbance, removal, degradation or destruction of existing soils, introducing instead non-soil materials or contamination, and mechanically compacting the soil strata, so that the ground is able to support the various structures and surfaces built upon it. This chapter investigates soil processes, assessment, analysis and amelioration. It provides practical guidance to designers, contractors and managers to facilitate appropriate site and soil management, without which long-term establishment of functional trees is likely to be compromised.

Much of the information available to us is the result of academic research mainly investigating agricultural soils, with some coming from forestry. Very little consideration has been given to the often unique situation found in urban settings. However, for a very thorough investigation of urban soils, one must turn to the work of Phillip J. Craul. As professor of Soil Science at State University of New York, Syracuse, and Lecturer in Landscape Architecture at Harvard University, Boston, Craul wrote the seminal works on urban soils, *Urban Soils in Landscape Architecture* (1992) and *Urban Soils: Applications and Practices* (1999).

First, some definition of terms so that we can be precise in what we mean by 'soil'; the term soil means different things to different people, and it might be useful to consider how various disciplines view soil, as a way to provide some context and look for commonality.

- BS 1377-1:1990 Soils for civil engineering purposes – Part 1: General requirements and sample preparation describes soil thus: An assemblage of discrete particles in the form of a deposit, usually of mineral composition but sometimes of organic origin, which can be separated by gentle mechanical means and which includes variable amounts of water and air (and sometimes other gases). A soil commonly consists of a naturally occurring deposit forming part of the earth's crust, but the term is also applied to made ground consisting of replaced natural soil or manmade materials exhibiting similar behaviour, for example, crushed rock, crushed blast-furnace slag, fly-ash.

- BS EN ISO 14688-2: 2002 Geotechnical investigation and testing – Identification and classification of soil – Part 1: Identification and description and BS 5930: 2015 Code of practice for ground investigations, refer to soil in very similar ways to the above, as does Norbury in *Soil and Rock Description in Engineering Practice* (2010). In addition, Michael Smith warns against any confusion between an engineering description and the geological definition, pointing out that 'topsoil is generally removed before any engineering projects are carried out' (Smith, 1981).

- The UK National Soil Resources Institute at Cranfield University defines soil as: a combination of four constituents: mineral material (sand, silt, clay and rock particles), organic material, air and water. Soil is made from the breaking down of rocks and organic matter by physical, chemical and biological processes. Topsoil is the surface layer of soil containing partly decomposed organic debris, and which is usually high in nutrients, containing many seeds, and is rich in fungal mycorrhizae. Topsoil is usually a dark colour due to the 'organic matter' present. In arable land, 'topsoil' refers to the soil down to plough depth (NSRI Staff, 2011).

Soil, to the Engineer and Geologist, then is completely different to the soil defined by the Agronomist, Horticulturist and Landscape Architect. For trees, soil is the source of water, nutrients and a host of beneficial, antagonistic and hostile biological organisms and is a substrate that allows anchorage and support. It is the fact that soil is a complex assemblage of rock and mineral particles, organic matter, bacteria, fungi, algae, invertebrate and vertebrate populations, which is sometimes forgotten. If soil is treated like an engineering material, it can behave as one to the detriment of the organic, living portion, which is vital to life.

3.2 CHARACTERISTICS

In general terms, soil is the product of biologically, chemically and physically weathered rock material that slowly combines with accumulated organic matter provided by the decomposition of plant and animal remains. It is like a protective and productive skin around the earth, which, in many parts of urban Britain, has been compacted, damaged and stripped, to make way for buildings and transport infrastructure. In a natural and undisturbed state, an idealised soil comprises horizontal layers that exhibit differing functional characteristics. The easiest way to observe this is to excavate a pit, a metre or so in depth, preferably in a place that has not been disturbed by human activity for some time, such as unploughed pasture. On the surface will often be a layer of leaves and other plant debris in various states of decomposition. Immediately below this layer will be a region that is darker than the regions further down the profile, due to the downward migration of organic materials from the surface. Often, this migration will be due to earthworm activity, pulling the organic material down into the soil, causing this darker layer to be riddled with small fissures, burrows and tunnels. The soil particles tend to aggregate together to form crumbs or *peds*, making the surface layers fairly granular, when disturbed. Moving down through the profile, animal activity becomes less and less as soil density increases and the oxygen content of the air decreases. As a result, the soil tends to become progressively lighter

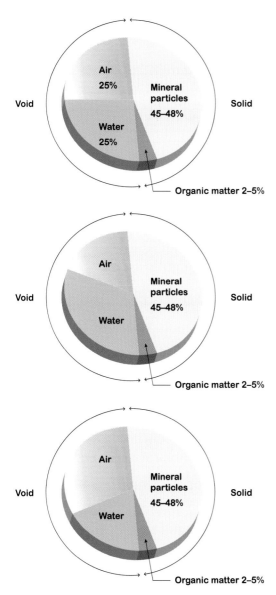

Figure 3.1
The volumetric composition of an ideal soil likely to promote optimum root growth. The solid, mineral fraction constitutes approximately 45–48 per cent, with organic matter making up approximately 2–5 per cent. The remaining 50 per cent consists of air space and water (top). We could say, therefore, that half of a typical unit volume of productive soil is void. Note that the proportions of water and air fluctuate depending upon how hydrated the soil is following rain or irrigation (middle) and how much water has been lost to plants, evaporation or drainage (bottom) (after Brady 2008).

in colour as the organic matter content reduces. This deeper layer tends to be less granular, and if disturbed, the soil aggregates tend to separate into more massive units.

The darker layers we know as topsoil and the lighter layers we refer to as subsoil. This may appear to be ill-defined and it is, by design. We are considering here an *idealised* soil, and the majority of soils do not show well-defined boundaries between the layers. It should be remembered that in an effort to produce a systematic taxonomy for all soils, we have determined the various horizontal layers and the particular chemical and physical qualities associated with them, and unsurprisingly, not all soils are the same. Below those layers, which look like soil to most people, lies the parent material, which, with increased depth, tends to become progressively more massive, harder to penetrate and less structured. Sometimes, solid bedrock will be evident. Soil, then, can be said to form a functional link between the mineral world of the sub-surface, and the biologically active and dynamic world of our surface ecosystems. Later, we will consider how soils within our urban centres differ with those discussed above.

3.2.1 Air/water/mineral fraction/organic matter

We can see that soil is a complex matrix of rock materials that have been weathered and ground down into smaller and smaller fragments. This is the mineral portion of our idealised soil. The fragments cluster together to form discrete grains and are surrounded by an extensive network of channels, tunnels and fissures. This porous matrix is the home of many soil-inhabiting organisms that live, die and shed their skins, as well as eat, digest plant materials and excrete waste products.

This, and the plant debris that falls on the surface of the ground, form the organic portion of our idealised soil. These two types of material collectively form the solid fraction and comprise approximately 50 per cent of the overall volume of a productive, well-granulated soil. The remainder consists of the fissures, tunnels, channels and voids that fluctuate between being occupied by either air or water. As we will see, the air and water contents are intimately linked, and they will vary proportionally.

3.2.2 Particles, particle size distribution and texture

The sizes of the various mineral particles that are found within soils can differ greatly. They can be large boulders, stones, gravels and so on, reducing in size down to particles termed sand, silt and clay.

Soil texture refers to the proportions of sand, silt and clay particles that are contained within the soil sample (i.e., those particles 2 mm and less in size). The vast majority of soils contain

Table 3.1
Soil particle size classes. Those materials that make up soil are 2 mm or less in size (shaded area of table). Data from Soil Survey Division Staff (1993), BSI (2015) and MAFF (1988). ASTM is the acronym for the international standards organisation, the American Society of the International Association for Testing and Materials

Size class	Equivalent particle diameter range		BS 5930: 2015 and MAFF (1988) shaded area
	USDA (1993)		
Large boulders			> 630 mm
Boulders	> 600 mm	(> 24 in.)	630–200 mm
Stones	600–250 mm	(24–10 in.)	
Cobbles	250–75 mm	(10–3 in.)	200–63 mm
Coarse gravel	75–20 mm	(3–0.75 in.)	63–20 mm
Medium gravel	20–5.0 mm	(0.75 in.–ASTM #4)	20–6.3 mm
Fine gravel	5.0–2.0 mm	(ASTM #4–#10)	6.3–2.0 mm
Very coarse sand	2.0–1.0 mm	(ASTM #10–#18)	
Coarse sand	1.0–0.5 mm	(ASTM #18–#35)	2.0–0.6 mm
Medium sand	0.5–0.25 mm	(ASTM #35–#60)	0.6–0.2 mm
Fine sand	0.25–0.10 mm	(ASTM #60–#140)	0.2–0.06 mm
Very fine sand	0.10–0.05 mm	(ASTM #140–#270)	
Silt	0.05–0.002 mm		0.06–0.002 mm
Clay	< 0.002 mm		< 0.002 mm

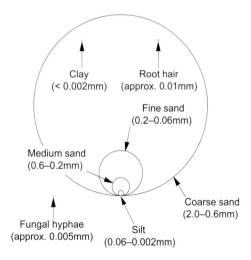

Figure 3.2
Relative soil particle sizes. For comparison, fungal hyphae and a typical root hair are also shown.

a mixture of all three, and the dominant particle tends to influence the name given to the particular soil type. For example, if a soil comprised of 50 per cent sand, 40 per cent clay and 10 per cent silt, it would be called a sandy-clay. Similarly, a soil containing 55 per cent silt, 15 per cent sand and 30 per cent clay would be called a silty-clay-loam. 'Loamy' is a term used to describe soils that contain less than 30–35 per cent clay, with the remainder being a mixture of sand and silt, so that the soil is of an intermediate composition.

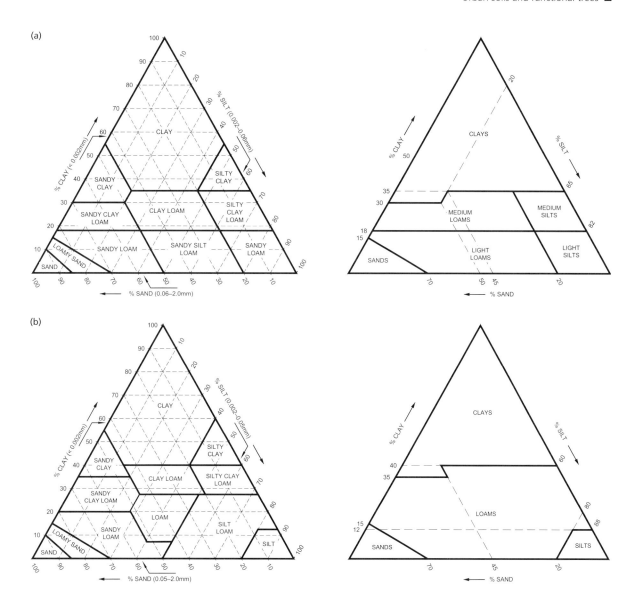

Figure 3.3
Soils texture triangles from Defra-NSRI (top) and USDA-NRCS (bottom). These provide a way to classify soil texture from the relative amounts of sand, silt and clay particles they contain. Note the subtle differences between the UK and USA systems.

Texture is one of the most stable of soil properties. As texture has a fundamental influence over porosity and soil moisture relation, as well as structure and chemical activity, it helps to determine the overall potential of a soil, in terms of its ability to provide a suitable growing medium for plants. Texture will remain stable unless the overall proportions of clay, silt or sand are amended. (See Appendix 4, Simple field test (ADAS method.)

Clay particles are composed of many fine layers, rather like a deck of cards, and consequently, have a very large surface area. This many-layered structure enables clay soils to store large quantities of water, together with the nutrients dissolved within this water. This, coupled with the fact that the layers are interlocking sheets of silica alternating with aluminium oxide, makes them very chemically active. This is why they are so important in the fixing and transfer of plant nutrients contained within the soil water; a process known as cation exchange capacity.

Figure 3.4
Shrinkage cracks can form in fine-grained soils during long periods of dry weather. In some cases, they can cause damage to roots.

As a consequence of being moisture-retentive, the layers within the clay particles are forced apart by water molecules as they hydrate. This causes them to swell, making the soil plastic, sticky and difficult to cultivate. On drying, the reverse happens; they shrink and form hard clods that are difficult to break down, unless they are rewetted. In extended periods of dry weather, deep shrinkage cracks can form, and these can cause root rupture and moisture loss (see Chapter 8 for further details on the swelling and shrinking of clay soils).

There is no quick and easy way to 'improve' this function of heavy clay soils – although very thorough digging, timed to avoid working the soil when it is too wet, incorporating bulky organic matter into the upper layers, and mulching the surface will help. If clay soils are disturbed when too wet, they will easily smear or compact and are difficult to restore. Conversely, sand particles, consisting predominantly of hard quartz grains, have relatively low surface areas. Sandy soils are loose, drain very quickly, have a limited capacity to store water and so do not swell or shrink. Unlike clays, therefore, sandy soils tend not to be naturally very nutrient-rich.

Although the silty soils of the Fens are some of the most productive in the UK, they can exhibit low structural stability and can be very difficult to manage unless they also contain sufficient quantities of organic matter. Particularly, silts in cultivation can quite easily slump into a structureless rooting medium that is prone to surface compaction, lacking aeration and drainage (Mullins, 1991). Mulching with organic materials helps to protect the surface from the compacting effects of heavy rain or irrigation, so preserving the crumb structure and aiding water penetration.

Loam is a term used to describe soils that contain a mixture of clay, sand and silt in varying proportions. Their performance is intermediate between the two extremes of sandy soils and clay soils, with the relative proportions of each, determining how the soil behaves and should be handled. The higher the clay content, the greater the storage capacity for water and nutrients and the more it is susceptible to compaction, and reduced drainage and aeration.

Why then not simply amend clay soils with sand or organic matter to improve the drainage? Unfortunately, it is not as simple as that. Let us consider sand as an amendment first. The difference in size between coarse sand and clay particles is 500-fold and so the pore spaces in sand are comparatively large and those in clay are small. When sand and clay are mixed together, the clay particles fill the pores between the sand grains, resulting in a soil mix that is denser and contains less pore space than either the sand or clay alone. This was shown by Spomer (1983), and has since been verified by others. Spomer showed that adding sand to soil in a range of

Figure 3.5
Badly timed use of machinery can completely destroy soil structure. Access routes would be better managed by stripping all organic soil and replacing it with a freely draining, temporary working platform.

proportions decreased the porosity, drainage, aeration and water retention until the sand occupied approximately 75 per cent of the mix. This level of amendment would make it prohibitively expensive to implement on most landscape schemes, but is sometimes used on higher-value projects, such as golf courses and sports pitches.

3.2.3 Structure

The arrangement of soil mineral solids into aggregated particles, crumbs or peds, and the pore spaces between them is referred to as soil structure. Structure is constantly changing due to the influence of the local climate factors such as freezing/thawing and wetting/drying cycles. Unlike texture, which, as we have seen, can be difficult at best to modify, soil structure can be influenced through the way that it is managed and handled. For example, excessive, inappropriate and/or badly timed cultivation is likely to degrade soil structure.

Even correct cultivation tends to shear and mix the mineral components, upsetting normal biological activities and filling pore spaces with the finer particles, which can lead to compaction.

Because the assessment of structure considers the relationship between the solid fraction and the intervening large pore spaces, it also provides an insight into the movement of water and air through the soil profile via drainage and aeration. These functions, in turn, have a fundamental effect on plant rooting and the activity of soil-borne organisms.

In sandy and silty soils, the particles are not especially prone to clustering together very well and so tend not to have particularly well-defined structures. The individual particles themselves

Figure 3.6
Soil with good structure (a) and compacted, structureless soil (b).

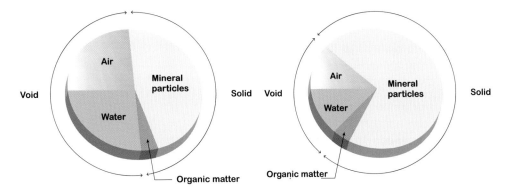

define the structure. Clays and loams, on the other hand, do tend to cluster or aggregate together, into larger units. Somewhat counterintuitively, the number of large pores between peds can actually be greater in well-structured clay soils than in some sands.

A good way to determine soil structure is to look at bulk density. Well-structured soil will consist of many peds, divided by a large number of fissures or macropores. Because the macropores contain mainly air, the same volume of our well-structured soil is likely to weigh less than a less structured, compacted soil. We can, therefore, use this weight-to-volume relationship to calculate the amount of pore space (porosity) within a given soil sample. In soil science, this is known as bulk density and is determined by driving a cylinder of known volume into the ground, so that its top is flush with the soil surface and digging it up in a manner that ensures that no soil is lost. The contents are then removed from the cylinder, dried and weighed. Bulk density can be calculated from the following equation:

$$\text{Bulk density (g/cm}^3) = \text{Mass of soil (g) / Volume of cylinder (cm}^3)$$

Soils with reduced pore space tend not to be well aerated or drained. As such, they have an increased bulk density and mechanical strength, making them difficult to penetrate. Crucially, root growth will be inhibited at bulk densities of 1.75 g cm^{-3} in sandy soil and 1.46–1.63 g cm^{-3} in clay soil (Veihmeyer & Hendrickson, 1948; Daddow & Warrington, 1983; Kozlowski, 1999). Patterson (1976) conducted soil surveys at various points along the Mall in Washington, DC, where he found heavily compacted soils with bulk densities between 1.7 and 2.2 g cm^{-3}. To provide some context, the bulk density found within the surface layer of a forest soil may typically be 1.3 g cm^{-3} or less. The bulk density of concrete paving is typically 2.26 g cm^{-3} (Patterson, 1976; Patterson et al., 1980).

Table 3.2
General relationship of soil bulk density to root growth based on soil texture. From Soil Quality Test Kit Guide (USDA, NRCS, 2001) USDA Soil Quality Institute, Washington, DC

Soil texture	Ideal bulk density (gcm^{-3})	Bulk density that may affect root growth (gcm^{-3})	Bulk density that restricts root growth (gcm^{-3})
Sands, loamy sands	< 1.60	1.69	> 1.80
Sandy loams, loams	< 1.40	1.63	> 1.80
Sandy clay loams, loams, clay loams	< 1.40	1.60	> 1.75
Silts, silt loams	< 1.30	1.60	> 1.75
Silt loams, silty clay loams	< 1.40	1.55	> 1.65
Sandy clays, silty clays, some clay loams (35–45 per cent clay)	< 1.10	1.49	> 1.58
Clays (> 45 per cent clay)	< 1.10	1.39	> 1.47

3.2.4 Organic matter

Soil organic matter (SOM) has a fundamental influence on soil structure. Increased levels of SOM lead to heightened earthworm and microbial activity, and SOM mucilage can help to 'glue' soil aggregates together to create more pore space and stabilise the aggregates. It has been found that organic material worked into the surface, followed by the application of organic mulch is the best way to increase overall SOM content. Our idealised soil contained up to 5 per cent SOM by volume. However, increasing the level far above this optimum can lead to plant health problems.

For example, there can be a tendency to 'improve' planting holes with the addition of organic matter to the bottom of the hole and to amend the backfill material. Organic matter is in the process of decomposing and requires oxygen to complete its transformation into humus. If buried at any great depth, organic matter will not have ready access to oxygen (more on this later); decomposition will continue, but it will become anaerobic. The by products of this type of breakdown are methane (CH_4), carbon dioxide (CO_2) and ammonia (NH_3). All are toxic to plants and will inhibit root growth. Furthermore, as organic matter decomposes, it reduces in volume, so it can lead to settlement.

Amended backfill can, on the face of it, sound like a good idea, but in reality, can also lead to plant health problems. By amending the local soil environment, significant nutritional and structural differences can be created between the planting hole and the surrounding soil. The root zone within the planting hole may be well aerated and full of readily available nutrients, but the surrounding soil is likely to be comparatively low in nutrient, more finely textured and less aerated. In response, plant roots are likely to grow much like they do within containers. They will vigorously explore the immediate root zone, and the above-ground plant growth will appear to be correspondingly extensive and healthy. Root growth responds positively to good aeration and a supply of water and dissolved nutrients. Roots will quickly extend to the limit of the planting hole, and rather than venturing into the more inhospitable soil outside, will tend to follow the perimeter of the hole. This will continue until the readily available moisture and nutrients have been exhausted and the planting hole is full of roots. As the top growth has continued to develop, exceeding the root growth, which has been contained within the planting hole, the tree becomes unstable and prone to windthrow. It would be a far better prospect to improve the topsoil as far beyond the planting hole as possible. This is much more likely to encourage rooting out into the surrounding soil, and so, ensure some long term stability.

3.3 WATER

Water is the most important and impactful essential resource that affects tree survival and growth. Lack of water fundamentally reduces a tree's ability to function effectively and will affect tree health, either by causing physiological damage, or by burdening the tree with stress and so predisposing it to pests and disease. A calculated and measured programme of supplemental irrigation is therefore likely to be necessary for the first few years of establishment, following planting.

The most beneficial time to apply irrigation is at night when plants replenish the water lost during the day. Watering at night also reduces losses due to evaporation. Treegator®, or similar watering bags have proved to be very useful at providing a slow, long-term application of water, immediately around the stem, where the roots are actively growing on recently planted trees.

Plants absorb water from the soil via their roots and lose the majority of it to the atmosphere through *transpiration* of water vapour on the surfaces of their leaves. Some water is also lost directly at the soil surface due to

Figure 3.7
These slow-release watering bags can hold up to 55 lt of water and empty in up to 8 hours. This slow, gentle watering is very useful during the summer of the first one or two growing seasons.

evaporation. The two processes combined are known as *evapotranspiration*. It is this constant movement of water through the tree that keeps its soft tissues turgid. As actively growing plants use large quantities of water, equally large quantities need to be constantly available for them to continue growing. Also, water is the solvent that carries all the dissolved nutrients from the soil, up through the root system, to make essential elements available to the plant.

3.3.1   Movement through soil, drainage and pore space

It is not appropriate to investigate this in too much detail here, and those who are interested should read a more in-depth analysis such as *The Nature and Properties of Soils* by Nyle Brady and Raymond Weil. For our purposes, it is sufficient to say that water moves through and within the soil due to a number of factors and processes, which rely on differing energy states of the water and the materials around it.

We can fairly easily measure the amount of water present in soil by weighing an amount of soil, drying it and weighing it again. The reduction in mass will be due to water loss. This could be represented as a percentage of the overall mass of soil. This approach does not tell us very much about the amount of soil water available to plants, however. If we were to consider a sponge that has been plunged into a bucket of water, allowed to absorb as much water as it can and then held clear of the bucket, water will initially pour out of it and gradually subside. The sponge could then be gently squeezed and more water will be lost. If the sponge is squeezed more tightly, some more water can be made to run out, but eventually a point will be reached where no more water can be released. The sponge is still not dry, but the remaining water is held so tightly within its pores that more effort is required to squeeze the water out than we are able to provide with our hands alone.

If soil is thoroughly drenched, from rainfall or irrigation, to the point where it is completely saturated, and therefore unable to absorb any more water, and then allowed to drain under gravity, it is said to be at field capacity. Following wetting, water will percolate down through the cracks, worm channels and spaces between soil particles, as demonstrated by the sponge held above the bucket. In the process, air will be displaced. Some water will adhere to soil particles, some will remain lodged within the matrix of small channels and fissures, held in place by trapped air and some will be absorbed into the soil granules, drawn up through the network of tiny pores within each soil ped, by capillary action. The pores, then, are fundamentally linked to water storage and movement within the soil.

The various pore spaces can, perhaps, be usefully sub-divided by size, as this determines how they affect soil water. The largest, known as macropores, are those greater than 50 μm in size (Ashman & Puri, 2002). These pores are typically caused by structural cracking, worm tunnelling or division between the soil peds. They are important in the rapid drainage of water under gravity, and ready movement of air within the soil. They are also large enough to allow roots to penetrate and provide accommodation for the wide range of subterranean animal life that inhabits the soil. The next smallest, the mesopores, are between 0.5 μm and 50 μm in size (Ashman & Puri, 2002) and can be considered as the water storage pores. After drainage, water is held within these against the force of gravity, by surface tension, and it is this soil water that is available for plant roots to extract. The smallest, less than 0.5 μm in size (Ashman & Puri, 2002), can be considered as residual water pores. They are found within the peds and are known as micropores. Although the water held within these micropores is important for chemical reactions and for holding the soil particles together, it is typically held too tightly to be accessible to plants.

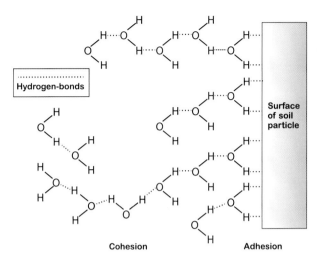

Figure 3.8
Cohesive forces attract water molecules to other water molecules. These are what cause water to form drops or beads. Adhesive forces attract water molecules to other substances, and if those other substance are negatively charged, like soil particles, water sticks to them really well. The closer the water molecules are to the soil particles, the stronger are the forces of adhesion. Sand particles have relatively large spaces between them or pores, compared to clay particles. In sands, the water is held tightly to the immediate surface of the sand grain, but within the remainder of the pores, the water is held only to more water, by weaker cohesive forces. In clays, the pores between the clay particles are so small that the water is held incredible tightly.

Therefore, the size of the pore determines how tightly the soil water is held. Soil particles attract water molecules due to strong adhesive forces, and water molecules attract other water molecules by weaker cohesive forces. The smaller the pore, the closer the water is to the soil solid, the greater the adhesion and the more tightly the water is held. As the pores increase in size, the further water can be held from the soil solid, and so the weaker the adhesive forces. The tightness that the water is held within the soil is referred to as tension.

Plants require a continuous supply of water to replace that lost through transpiration and will continue to 'suck' it up until the forces of tension attracting the water to the soil particles are greater than the osmotic force of suction that can be exerted by the roots. At the point where no more water can be extracted by the roots and the plant starts to wilt, the soil is said to be at permanent wilting point. As with the tightly wrung sponge earlier, some water remains within the soil matrix as thin, hygroscopic films within and around soil particles, but it is too tightly held to be accessible to root hairs.

The soil water between field capacity and the permanent wilting point is known as the plant-available water, and is typically expressed as a percentage of overall soil volume. The greater the plant-available water, the higher-performing the soil will be during periods of drought. Soils of differing textures and structures will have varying proportions of macro-, meso- and micropores, and as we have seen, the quantities, arrangement and connectivity of these different pores determines the way that water moves through, and is stored within, the soil. Ideally, there should be a balance between the aeration provided by the large macropores and the water storage provided by the smaller pores. Many urban soils have been highly compacted and lack structure. As a consequence, the larger pores are crushed, reducing aeration and drainage, and creating waterlogged and anaerobic conditions.

In sandy soils, due to their open texture and comparative abundance of large pores, water tends to drain through them fairly quickly. Some water is retained only on the surfaces of the soil particles as thin, hygroscopic films, but not much is easily obtainable by plant roots. Conversely, in soils with a high clay content, the pores are so small that water is held tightly within them, resisting the effect of gravity. We should be able to observe, then, that sands will drain more freely than clays and clays will retain water better than sands. This is generally true, but, in the summer, clay soils can crack if they are not kept hydrated. As a consequence, they will drain quickly at first, but, as they absorb water through capillary action, the clay particles swell, closing the cracks and impeding drainage through the soil profile.

Hall *et al.* (1977) determined that the major factors affecting the amount of soil water available to plants are texture, structure and organic matter. The following table (Table 3.3), originally produced by the Ministry of Agriculture Fisheries and Food, takes this into consideration by stratifying the measurements according to whether they are for topsoils or subsoils and whether

Table 3.3
Estimation of available water (%) related to textural class, horizon and structural conditions. Good structural development refers to a granular, friable structure, and poor structure would cover more massive and clod-forming structures. Source: MAFF (now Defra) Agricultural Land Classification of England and Wales (1988) (* represents rare occurrences for which there are no data)

Texture class	Estimation of plant-available water (%)			
	Topsoil	Subsoil structural development		
		Good	Moderate	Poor
Coarse sand	*	5	5	*
Medium sand	12	7	7	*
Fine sand	*	14	14	*
Loamy coarse sand	11	11	8	*
Loamy medium sand	13	12	9	*
Loamy fine sand	18	15	15	*
Coarse sandy loam	17	22	16	11
Medium sandy loam	17	17	15	11
Fine sandy loam	18	22	18	17
Coarse sandy silt loam	19	23	19	15
Medium sandy silt loam	19	19	17	15
Fine sandy silt loam	22	22	21	15
Silt loam	23	23	22	15
Silty clay loam	19	21	17	12
Clay loam	18	21	16	12
Sandy clay loam	17	19	15	13
Sandy clay	17	19	15	13
Silty clay	17	21	15	12
Clay	17	21	16	13

the subsoils are of good, moderate or poor structure. It must be remembered that these measurements are for use in the classification of agricultural land, and assumptions are made that good land management has been practised. Therefore, only one value, representing a moderate structure, is provided for topsoil in each category. The values shown are based on a dataset collected by staff of the Soil Survey and Land Research Centre and represent approximately 3,600 plant-available soil water measurements from over 1,000 soil profiles found in England and Wales. The data are available through the LandIS (Land Information System) Soil Portal, operated by Cranfield University (2015).

The values for poor structural conditions are based on measurements taken from undisturbed soils. Where soil has been compacted mechanically, these values may overestimate the available water. It is worth pointing out that these values are less than those provided by Kays and Patterson (1982) and shown by Craul (1992). These are shown below for comparison. The differences are partly due to there being inconsistencies between North American and British soil classifications, making casual comparisons a little troublesome.

Changes in the soil properties listed below are given as soil texture changes from sandy to clayey (i.e., as soil particle size decreases). (See Table 3.5.)

Table 3.4
Figures derived from the Soil and Water Assessment Tool (SOILWAT) computer modelling package and not from actual field tests. The data do, however, provide a good relational overview of different soil types.
Source: Saxton and Rawls (2006)

USDA textural class	Sand (%)	Clay (%)	Field capacity (33 KPa)	Wilting point (1,500 KPa)	Plant available water (% volume)
Sand	88	5	10	5	5
Loamy sand	80	5	12	5	7
Sandy loam	65	10	18	8	10
Loam	40	20	28	14	14
Silt loam	20	15	31	11	20
Silt	10	5	30	6	25
Sandy clay loam	60	25	27	17	10
Clay loam	30	35	36	22	14
Silty clay loam	10	35	38	22	17
Silty clay	10	45	41	27	14
Sandy clay	50	40	36	25	11
Clay	25	50	42	30	12

Table 3.5
Changes in soil characteristics are given as soil texture changes from sandy to clayey (i.e., as soil particle size decreases (from Hawver & Bassuk, 2000)

Soil characteristic	Sandy soils	Clayey soils
Soil surface area	Less	Greater
Pore space	Less	Greater
Aggregation potential	Less	Greater
Bulk density	Higher	Lower
Moisture retention	Less	Greater
Particle density	Same	Same

Saturated hydraulic conductivity provides a quantitative measurement of a soil's ability to transmit water through it, when in a saturated condition. In essence, it is the ease with which the soil pores of a saturated soil allow water movement. In this context, it provides an indication of permeability.

To give some perspective, a saturated hydraulic conductivity of 180 mm hr^{-1} would be typical of a very sandy soil. Between 10 mm hr^{-1} and 150 mm hr^{-1} is typical of moderately drained soils, suitable for most planting sites requiring good drainage. Between 1.8 mm hr^{-1} and 0.7 mm hr^{-1} is typically found in fine-textured, compacted or poorly structured soils, which are difficult to use for planting (Brady & Weil, 2008).

3.3.2 Stratified soil and saturated flow
It is certainly not uncommon to find stratified soils in urban situations, often due to extensive interference. It is also not uncommon to find deliberately stratified soils in tree pits where a gravel layer has been added to the base of the pit in an effort to improve drainage. Water tends to move

from a wet area to a drier area until the forces acting upon it become equal. We know that the forces of attraction are greater within smaller pores than within larger pores. We also know that a clay soil will tend to attract water more aggressively than a sandy soil, if they both contain the same percentage of moisture. If the two are brought together, soil water will be drawn out of the sand and into the clay. We can, therefore, see that where there is a distinct separation between layers of differing texture and/or structure, water flow from rainfall or irrigation can be inhibited or perched. It will not flow from a fine-textured soil to an open soil until the fine-textured soil is fully saturated and water is draining through gravity. If improved surface drainage is the aim, it would be far better to ensure that the soil used within the planting site is well structured and of a suitable texture to enable good drainage, rather than install a layer of gravel at the base.

As previously discussed, it is quite common for tree planting pits to be surrounded by highly compacted soils, or to be excavated from clay or other fine-grained, low-porosity soils. In these circumstances, the tree pit is likely to function as a sump, collecting water that flows into it and only releasing this very slowly to the surrounding soil. When this happens, the tree rooting zone can quickly become waterlogged and anaerobic. Drainage at the bottom of the pit will be required to remove the trapped water, but this will only function if the soil above is well structured and able to drain well. Sub-surface drainage is very good at lowering high water tables and water trapped in tree pits, but not good at dealing with surface water drainage problems. Details on drainage systems and materials are covered in Chapter 6, Tree planting and establishment: technical design.

3.4   GASEOUS EXCHANGE – O_2, CO_2 AND SO ON

As water drains or is removed from the soil, the spaces previously containing water will become occupied by air. There is an inextricable link, therefore, between drainage and aeration. Atmospheric air is composed of approximately 78 per cent nitrogen, 21 per cent O_2, 0.04 per cent CO_2, with the remainder being made up of other gases. In soil, air near the surface has a different composition, with the CO fraction elevated to approximately 0.25 per cent. This may not appear to be a significant change, but it is a sixfold increase. Even in well-drained soils, the O_2 level can decrease and the CO_2 level increase quite rapidly, relative to depth.

The soil fauna and flora are using O_2 and releasing CO_2 as part of the normal process of respiration, and unless there is a constant turnover of air to flush out the accumulated CO_2 and replenish O_2, conditions within the soil will become anaerobic and respiration will eventually cease. It is clear that the more open the soil, the better will be the movement of air. Little movement occurs in waterlogged soils or soils that have been compacted, which is why these exhibit the foetid smell of anaerobic. Conversely, open, coarse-grained soils are well drained and aerated, allowing O_2 to penetrate deep within the profile and so encourage deep rooting. The passage of water through the soil profile draws fresh air into the macropores, channels, fissures and tunnels, to replace the drained water. Drainage and aeration are, therefore, inextricably linked.

Grey or blue mottling, or gleying, is evidence of soil zones that lack O_2, and so are anaerobic, usually due to waterlogging. Iron products formed in conditions without oxygen are said to be reduced ferrous compounds and tend to be green or blue in colour. Iron products formed in well-aerated conditions are said to be oxidised ferric compounds and tend to be red or brown in colour. Gleyed soils often show both colourations where well-aerated pathways and fissures, such as root channels and earthworm tunnels, show up as rusty brown lines within a mainly grey or blue-grey mass.

3.5   CHEMICAL PROPERTIES

Other than carbon, hydrogen and O_2, which are provided from the air or water, soil is the primary source of plant nutrients, essential for growth. These nutrients are termed macro-nutrients, those that are required by the plant in large amounts, and micro-nutrients, those required in very small quantities. The macro-nutrients are phosphorus, potassium, nitrogen, sulphur, calcium and magnesium and tend to be referred to in percentages. The micro-nutrients are iron, manganese, copper, zinc, molybdenum, boron and chlorine and tend to be referred to in milligrams per litre (mgl^{-1}) or parts per million (ppm). All minerals and nutrients must be broken down into forms that are soluble in water before they are taken up by the roots, in the soil water. In addition, specialised root cells are selective in which nutrients they absorb into the transport system, only allowing those required to pass through the semi-permeable membrane and into the xylem tissue.

As these plant nutrients are available in soluble form, within the soil water, they exist as ions. Many are positively charged and are known as cations. These cations are especially held by soils with a high negative charge, such as those rich in clay or humus from organic matter. This relationship helps to prevent the cations from being washed away by rainfall or irrigation, ensuring that there is a reserve available for absorption by roots. Sandy soils and those low in clay or organic matter tend to be free-draining and with a low ability to retain cations, making them susceptible to nutrient leaching. The ability for soil to hold onto the positively charged cations is known as its Cation Exchange Capacity (CEC). The greater the CEC, the greater the fertility of the soil. Sandy soils are best improved through the addition of organic matter to the upper soil horizons. This is generally the easiest way to increase the CEC, rather than consider adding clay.

3.5.1   Soil pH
Soil acidity or alkalinity can have a marked effect on the solubility of plant nutrients, which in turn affects availability to the plant roots. As many urban soils are likely to be alkaline, due to the presence of concrete and other alkaline materials, some nutrient availability problems are likely to exist unless a thoughtful approach to appropriate species selection is adopted.

Acidity and alkalinity are measured in units of pH, on a fourteen-point scale from 0 to 14.0. That part of the scale from 7.0 to 0 is acidic, with 1.0 being strongly acidic, the part from 7.0 to 14.0 is alkaline or basic, with 14.0 being strongly alkaline and the mid-point, 7.0, being considered neutral. Most UK soils are found to be within the range of 4.0 and 8.5, with the widest range of nutrients available between 6.5 and 7.5. In some highly contaminated sites and colliery spoil heaps, pH readings below 3.0 may be encountered. As pH decreases, the levels of calcium and magnesium also decrease while aluminium becomes increasingly more soluble. In highly acidic conditions, the aluminium reaches toxic levels, inhibiting cell division and root elongation. This toxicity can be observed as stubby, brown, stunted root growth, confined to the upper soil horizons.

The pH scale is logarithmic to base 10, which means that a soil with a pH of 6 is ten times more acidic (or less alkaline) than a soil with a pH of 7 and 100 times more acidic than a soil with a pH of 8.0. For this reason, when measuring soil pH, it is important to ensure accuracy and record the result to one decimal place. It is fairly meaningless to refer to a soil with 'a pH of about 7'. (See Table 3.6.)

As soil pH affects the solubility of nutrients, and so their availability to plants, it is important to gain a good understanding of the soil's chemical properties. This is best achieved through soil analysis. A procedure for collecting soil samples and a typical suite of soil analysis requirements is shown in Appendix 2.

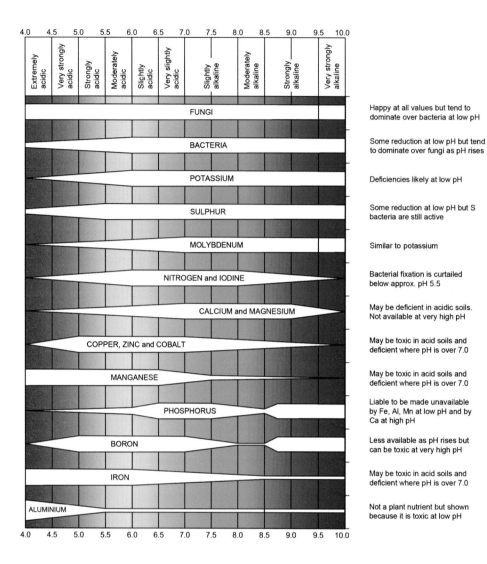

Figure 3.9
Effect of soil pH on availability of plant nutrients and other soil chemicals. The width of the white band denotes availability of different nutrients (from Landon (1991)).

3.6 AGRICULTURAL AND URBAN SOILS COMPARED

In the introduction to this chapter, we looked at different definitions for soil from different viewpoints – the engineer, the geologist and the grower. How then do we define urban soil? Craul (1985) considers that Bockheim (1974) provides an 'appropriate and useful definition of urban soil' as 'soil material having a non-agricultural, man-made surface layer more than 50 cm thick, that has been produced by mixing, filling, or by contamination of land surface in urban and suburban areas'.

Agricultural soil has developed over millennia and continues to be produced. As a consequence, there tends to be a gradual change between layers (or horizons) as one excavates down through the soil profile. In contrast, urban soils, due to the disturbances and modifications that have been applied to them, tend not to show such gradual changes, either vertically or horizontally. Typically, there are abrupt changes between the horizons (known as lithologic discontinuities), where material has been excavated, existing horizons have been buried beneath

Table 3.6
The pH scale is actually measuring the negative logarithm (to base ten) of the activity of hydronium (H$^+$) ions in aqueous solution. The scale is illustrated with some common household substances

Examples concentration (activity)	pH	H$^+$
Caustic drain cleaners (pH 14.0)	14	10^{-14}
Bleach (pH 13.5)	13	10^{-13}
	12	10^{-12}
Milk of magnesia (pH 10.5)	11	10^{-11}
	10	10^{-10}
Baking soda (pH 9.5)	9	10^{-9}
Sea water (pH 8.0)	8	10^{-8}
Blood (pH 7.4)	7	10^{-7}
Milk, urine, saliva (pH 6.3–6.6)	6	10^{-6}
Black coffee (pH 5.0)	5	10^{-5}
Tomatoes (pH 4.5)	4	10^{-4}
Soft drinks (pH 3.0)	3	10^{-3}
Lemon juice, vinegar (pH 2.0)	2	10^{-2}
	1	10^{-1}
Battery acid (pH 0)	0	10^{0}

imported fill or new topsoil has been placed over a sculpted or re-formed sub-base. In urban areas, holes are being dug and refilled continuously, either as part of development projects or to gain access to existing buried infrastructures. This activity causes vertical and spatial variability and creates distinct interfaces between neighbouring zones, especially if the layers differ significantly in their texture, structure or chemical composition. In addition, sub-bases and subsoils tend to be highly compacted to increase their strength, and so their ability to support the structures and surfaces that are built upon them. Another consideration must be the use of machinery and equipment during construction. It is not uncommon for the following sequence of events to take place on a development site: first, the topsoil is stripped and either stored for reuse or sold, regrading then takes place, followed by compaction of the subsoil oversite to allow construction to occur, and finally, the original or imported topsoil is placed where planting is to be carried out. The duration of the preparation and construction phases on large development sites will typically last for many months, sometimes requiring hundreds or even thousands of vehicle and machinery movements. A single pass of a heavy vehicle over soil can irreparably destroy its structure, and unless the movement of vehicles and machinery is managed in a controlled way, it is likely to be very difficult to establish trees and other plants later. Randrup (1997) investigated ground compaction in seventeen different Danish construction sites, where development had taken place on land formerly used for agriculture. He found that the subsoil was consistently compacted more within the construction sites than outside, where the land remained as agricultural. The bulk densities at depths of 0.4 of a metre down to 1 m were typically at levels that would restrict root growth and drainage. In such situations, it is not unusual for perched water tables to exist, the concomitant areas of saturated soil further inhibiting plant root growth. Randrup suggests that urban designers should always assume subsoils and/or topsoils within developments are compacted. It is better practice to control traffic movements, concentrating the compaction to managed zones and preventing vehicle access to areas designated for future planting. Targeted, intensive decompaction of the controlled vehicular routes can be carried out once heavy machinery is no longer required. This advice has since been adopted within BS 5837: *Trees in relation to design, demolition and construction – recommendations*. In practice, this can be very difficult to control, especially on tight sites or where there is little understanding of the requirements of retained trees and proposed new planting. Site training through toolbox talks, and regular arboricultural site supervision can certainly help, but require the engagement of the developer or builder to enable.

The potential for compaction does not end there. Surface and nearby traffic can cause vibrations, which may also have an effect on the settlement of soil. Vibration is likely to lead to the closer packing of aggregates, where finer particles are encouraged to settle and compact within the void spaces and pores, leading to an overall increase in soil bulk density. This phenomenon is well known to engineers and contractors, who will use vibrating rollers or plate compactors to enhance the compacting performance of machinery.

To compound the problem still further, non-soil materials, such as construction wastes and other contaminants, tend to be present within the soil profile. These can have a marked effect on the performance of the root zones of plants. Concrete, mortar and other cementitious materials are notoriously alkaline and can fundamentally raise the pH of soil to a point where very few plant species will be able to grow. Although the impact from such materials is mostly felt when they are present within the root zone, weathering and run-off from surfaces and structures containing cement will also steadily increase the soil pH.

3.6.1 Soil heterogeneity

Craul (1985) warns about the spatial variability of urban soils, stating that 'it is not uncommon to find a drastic contrast in profiles from one tree planting pit to another on the same street within the same block'. When looking at land reclamation in cities, Bradshaw and Dutton (1982) go further, suggesting that the physical qualities of urban soils, even within the same site, are so variable as to make quantifying them somewhat pointless. Such variability can create real problems when dealing with the establishment of trees and other urban planting. Knowledge of site history can be useful, and sometimes, comprehensive local soil mapping can assist in helping to understand how the various textural and structural classes are spatially arranged. In any event, detailed soil sampling will be essential to ensure that any localised drainage, aeration, chemical and contamination problems are identified early, so that remedial action can be carried out prior to planting.

Figure 3.10
This planting trench was supposed to be home to a line of three large, fastigiate shrubs. The concrete haunch supporting the perimeter kerbs has been installed as one large mass, leaving no possibility of drainage or providing adequate soil volume.

Where made ground is known about, it can be useful if the following criteria can be identified and recorded:

- origin of material
- presence of large lumps of concrete/masonry/old cars/voids
- chemical waste and other pollutants
- organic matter and level of decomposition
- unpleasant smell
- striking colour tints
- visible dates on buried papers
- signs of heat or combustion (including steam emerging)
- structure, variability and method of placement
- areas of filled and made-up ground.

It is worth pointing out that sites known to be contaminated should be surveyed by contamination consultants and soil scientists prior to any works taking place. In highly contaminated sites and where buildings may contain asbestos, even demolition works should be delayed until a full contamination survey is carried out (see later).

3.6.2 Organic matter

The cycling of organic matter and any related nutrient activity tends to be lacking in urban soils, as most fallen organic materials, such as leaves, are considered waste and removed as they fall. This interrupts what could provide a useful amount of soil organic matter and a source of energy for soil-inhabiting organisms. This, in turn, will often lead to low populations of invertebrate species, such as earthworms, and other beneficial organisms, such as fungal consumers and nitrifying and nitrogen-fixing bacteria. A consequence of such biodiversity-poor environments is that fallen organic matter is not harvested, taken into the root zone or broken down further, leading to low levels of both nutrient cycling and soil aeration. Without the benefit of earthworm burrows and organic matter mixing, poorly structured soils will remain so, potentially resulting in anaerobic conditions caused by high moisture and low aeration.

Surface mulch will help to mimic the natural organic layer found in woodlands and forests, but it is typically restricted to the extent of openings in paved surfaces, to accommodate the planting of the tree. While this may be beneficial in the early years of tree establishment, such benefits are lost as the tree matures and the zone of active root growth extends beyond the tree pit opening. Some promising initial results have been observed on using pure mulches, derived solely from one tree species, on the establishment and survival rates of *Fagus sylvatica* transplants. The survival rate for this notorious transplant-sensitive tree species was found to increase from 10 to 70 per cent by using *Crataegus monogyna* as the mulch source (Percival *et al.*, 2009). Another field trial is investigating the use of pure Salix mulch in an effort to reduce the incidence of Chalara ash dieback (Percival, 2013). It has been shown that salicylic acid is a potent plant defence activator, and it is hoped that as the mulch breaks down, salicylic acid is released into the soil, causing the plant to activate the production of antibodies, defensive enzymes and other defence strategies.

3.6.3 Rooting volume

To ensure that trees become functionally useful within an extensive urban development and to reduce interference with paving or other infrastructure, they need to be provided with adequate rootable soil volumes for the tree at maturity, with sufficient access to resources such as water, oxygen and nutrients. As discussed earlier, root growth and stem growth are linked, and if any of the required resources are lacking, overall tree growth suffers. Trees can be grown in nurseries with very restricted access to rootable soil volumes, but they are supplemented quite extensively with irrigation water and fertiliser nutrients. Urban situations typically provide the complete antithesis of nursery conditions (Clark & Kjelgren, 1989), and the most important of these appears to be inconsistent access to suitable soil (Bühler *et al.*, 2007) and water (Nielsen *et al.*, 2007).

3.7 CONTAMINATION

Craul describes soil contamination as 'the condition when the content of a natural or synthetic substance is above that of background, natural content' (Craul, 1992). This description, therefore, would include all naturally occurring materials, if they are present in quantities above expected thresholds or what would be considered a 'normal' level. This section will only consider those unnatural or manmade materials that are sometimes present in site soils and which pose some risk to plant and/or animal health. Brownfield sites are the most likely candidates for containing some form of contamination as the majority are former industrial, manufacturing and processing complexes. The range of possible contaminants, from a considerable legacy of industrialisation

SO WHAT?

Lyndsey and Bassuk (1992) reviewed the many attempts to quantify appropriate soil volumes for trees (e.g., Bakker, 1983; Vrecenak & Herrington, 1984; Kopinga, 1985; Helliwell, 1986; Moll & Urban, 1989; Perry, 1980). Some, if used to guide urban tree planting policy, would result in very few trees being planted due to insufficient soil ever being available in most urban street locations. As discussed in Chapter 2, Tree structures and function, tree water use responds to atmospheric demand – duration and intensity of sunlight, air temperature, wind speed and relative humidity. Assuming that water availability is not a constraint, these external factors affect the amount of water evaporated from the leaf surface through transpiration, which in turn determines the amount of water extracted from the soil by the roots. However, if accessible water was not to be limitless, at what point would growth be restricted? The Lyndsey and Bassuk research looked at this question, with the intention of determining a suitable soil volume, which would contain sufficient plant-available water, to avoid tree water stress from occurring between expected rainfall or planned irrigation events. A comparison was made between the water lost through evaporation from a local standard US Weather Bureau Class A evaporation pan and the water lost through transpiration from a variety of tree species. Data were collected over two growing seasons and from these a significant relationship between the two could be shown. In this project, the tree species used were: *Amelanchier* 'Robin Hill Pink', *Fraxinus americana*, *Styphnolobium japonicum* and *Tilia americana*. Such a range of subjects represented a gradient of individual leaf areas from 5 cm^2 to 46 cm^2. Typically, daily tree transpiration averaged 30 per cent of the water evaporated from the pan, across a range of different atmospheric conditions, without much variation between tree species being evident. Whole tree water loss through transpiration only increased as the canopy size increased. This observation would prove very useful when trying to predict suitable soil volumes, as variability between species can, effectively, be removed from the calculation. It should be pointed out that as the tree matures and the canopy increases in size, the ratio of leaf transpiration to pan evaporation rapidly decreases to approximately 20 per cent and this figure is used in the calculations below. This reduction is likely to be due to an increase in leaf shading as the canopy enlarges, resulting in a reduced water demand. Larger trees may, overall, lose more water than smaller ones, but they actually lose less per unit leaf area.

To make the project relevant to the UK, 10 years of evaporation data from the weather station at the Royal Botanic Gardens (RBG), Kew were used. This may require some refinement to the calculation, as the evaporation characteristics of a US Weather Bureau evaporation pan are subtly different to those of a Symons tank, used by the UK Meteorological Office (Holland, 1967). The relationship between tree leaf transpiration and evaporation from a Met Office Symons tank needs to be empirically established, but relationships between Symons tank and USWB Class A pans have been established. For the RBG Kew Observatory site, evaporation data from the Class A pan was shown to average 130 per cent greater than that of a Symons tank. Interestingly, the nearby Kempton site showed the difference rising to 153 per cent (Holland, 1967).

From the Lyndsey and Bassuk model, an approximation of daily tree water use can be calculated by collecting the following data:

- Crown projection (CP) – simply the area under the tree canopy, to the dripline. For simplicity, this is usually regarded as a circle and is calculated using: Area of circle = πr^2 (where r is the radius of the circle).

- Leaf area index (LAI) – is an approximation of the area of leaves, within the tree canopy, above a unit area of ground. If you were to stand under a tree canopy and look up, only the nearest leaves will be visible. We know that there are many layers of leaves within the canopy, not only the layer visible from the ground. LAI allows us to factor this in to our calculation. LAI will depend on tree species, age and condition and a figure of 4 has been used by Lindsey and Bassuk. From UK data collected by the Oak Ridge National Laboratory (ORNL) in USA (Iio & Ito, 2014), a figure of 5 may be used as typical for many healthy, deciduous species of various age classes.
- Evaporation rate – is an indication of atmospheric demand and is determined from the local mean monthly evaporation records. From the RBG Kew data, for a standard UK Symons tank, the month with the highest mean evaporation was July and the evaporation value was 120 mm. This divided by the number of days (31) in the month gives a daily evaporation rate of:

    120 mm ÷ 31 days = 3.87 mm per day.

    Crown projection × leaf area index × evaporation rate × correction factor = daily tree water use

(The correction factor allows Met Office evaporation data to be converted to leaf transpiration. It makes an allowance for the greater resistance to evaporation from the surface of the leaf than from an open body of water. In the Lindsey and Bassuk project, a factor of 20 per cent was used.)

From this calculation, an approximation of soil requirements, based on mature tree canopy size can be made, as follows:

    Daily water use × length of rain-free period ÷ available water-holding capacity of the soil = a realistic soil volume

For the south-east of England, based on the RBG Kew Met data and a leaf area index of 4, Lindsey and Bassuk determined a minimum of 0.15 cu. m soil volume per sq. m mature canopy area. From their calculations, a fairly modest *Tilia cordata* 'Greenspire' of 6 m canopy diameter would require approximately 4.4 cu. m of soil volume (2 m × 4.4 m × 0.5 m approximate tree pit dimensions). This assumes no irrigation or rainfall for a period of 10 days and with the tree growing in a good, medium-loam topsoil of 20 per cent available water-holding capacity. If the difference between the UK Symons tanks and the USWB Class A pan evaporation data is taken into account, the July evaporation figure would first be multiplied by 130 per cent, then divided by the number of days (31) in the month to give an equivalent USWB Class A pan daily evaporation rate as follows:

    120 mm × 130 per cent = 156 mm, then 156 mm ÷ 31 days = 5 mm.

This increases the root volume requirement to 5.65 cu. m (2 m × 5.6 m × 0.5 m approximate tree pit dimensions).

If the LAI is increased to match the ORNL data, the difference between Symonds tank and USWB Class A pan evaporation data is addressed, a 20-day irrigation-free period were to be determined as being more realistic and a typical loamy sand used, with a 12 per cent AWHC, this alters the root volume to 0.83 cu. m soil volume per sq. m of canopy area. Our 6-m diameter lime tree would now require a pit volume of 23.57 cu. m (2 m × 23.5 m × 0.5 m approximate tree pit dimensions). If a structural tree sand were to be used, with a 11 per cent AWHC, then the required soil volume increases to 25.71 cu. m (approx. 0.9 cu. m/sq. m canopy spread) say a pit size of 2 m × 26 m × 0.5 m. If the rain or irrigation-free period could be reduced to 10 days, then the volume can be reduced by half to 12.85 cu. m (approx. 0.45 cu. m/sq. m canopy spread) say a 2 m × 13 m × 0.5 m tree pit.

This, of course, assumes that all the rooting will be within the tree pit. Now we know that is not always the case; London planes, for instance, will invariable root beyond the confines of any tree pit, deflecting paving, but some species are much less inclined to do so.

These calculations also assume that transpiration from the leaves is the only water loss, and there is no evaporation from the soil surface. In many urban situations, this is quite likely as the majority of the root area is typically covered with impermeable paving materials, but not always; urban trees can also be planted in beds or areas of grass. Evaporative losses can often be halved if the surface is covered with an organic mulch (Greenly & Rakow, 1995). Rainfall periods need some further consideration, as not all precipitation events are effective at providing roots with water, especially in urban locations. Knowledge of precipitation intensity and duration will be useful but more importantly, perhaps, is that much summer rainfall may evaporate before it reaches the soil, it may be intercepted within the tree canopy or it may simply be diverted away as surface run-off. Not all precipitation, therefore, results in an increase in soil moisture.

Some ways to achieve the rooting volumes discussed above, using a variety of technical solutions are discussed in Chapter 6.

Figure 3.11
These London plane tree roots extend far beyond the planting site and out into the road build-up.

in many parts of the British Isles, is both varied and complex, but is becoming a progressively less inhibiting issue for land redevelopment. The traditional approach was to excavate the soil and remove it to controlled landfill. The current approach, however, is to treat contamination *in situ*, where possible, thus avoiding expensive excavation and transport, limiting social and ecological disturbance and preventing the transfer of the problem from one location to another.

UK legislation has evolved that helps to address the, sometimes considerable, *in situ* remediation works required to bring parcels of blighted land back into use and to establish a legal framework for dealing with contaminated land. UK government guidance requires that, as a starting point, land is not considered contaminated unless evidence suggests otherwise. Only following a risk assessment that clearly identifies unacceptable risks to its current use is the land classified as being contaminated. The Environmental Protection Act 1990 (as amended by section 57 of the Environment Act 1995) requires that any unacceptable risk to human health and the environment, posed by land contamination, must be removed. Local authorities have an obligation to identify contaminated land, and once land has been determined as contaminated, the local authority or the Environment Agency, as enforcing authority, considers how the land is to be remediated and issues a remediation notice as set out in the Contaminated Land (England) Regulations 2006 (HM Govt, 2006).

Section 78A(2) of the Act defines contaminated land thus:

> . . . any land which appears to the local authority in whose area it is situated to be in such a condition, by reason of substances in, on or under the land, that –
>
> (a) significant harm is being caused or there is a significant possibility of such harm being caused; or
>
> (b) pollution of controlled waters is being, or is likely to be, caused.

Harm, in this context, is defined in section 78A(4) as:

> harm to the health of living organisms or other interference with the ecological systems of which they form part, and in the case of man, includes harm to his property.
>
> (HM Govt, 1990)

In many cases, the current uses of brownfield sites are classified as B1 business, B2 general industrial or B3 storage or distribution. As none of these classifications allows for any residential use, under classes C1 to C3, any change in use would require planning permission. Remediation of contamination and the prevention of problems that may be caused by contamination can be dealt with by attaching planning conditions or obligations to planning permissions (HM Govt, 2012). See Case Study *Olympic Park compared with the Greenwich Peninsula* below for additional information on how remediation can be approached.

3.7.1 De-icing salts

One way that water moves, and which interests us here, is known as osmotic potential. This refers to the movement of water due to differing concentration of solutes and is more relevant to plant water uptake through its roots than movement through soils. Consider two bodies of water separated by a semi-permeable membrane, which allows the free movement of water molecules across it, but prevents the movement of dissolved compounds. If one side of the membrane has a higher concentration of these dissolved compounds than the other, water will migrate from the side of low solute concentration to the side of high concentration until equilibrium is reached. One can see, therefore, that if plant roots are growing within a soil that has a high concentration of dissolved salts, such as sodium chloride from de-icing salt, water uptake by the roots will be severely hampered. In extreme conditions, there may tend to be movement of water from within the root out to the soil, leading to desiccation and scorching.

In coastal areas of the UK, some soil and plant contamination by salt is likely from the constant flow of salt-laden air inland. Some of this salt will be carried on winds much further inland than the immediate coast, but its effect on vegetation is fairly minimal. Although some careful consideration needs to be exercised when considering new coastal plantings, damage caused from the application of de-icing salt to highways is much more of a concern. As could be expected, trees growing close to roads are typically more affected than those growing further away, with damage being most severe within 5 m of the treated road (Dobson, 1991).

Under section 41(1A) of the Highways Act 1980 (England and Wales), the highway authority has 'a duty to ensure, so far as is reasonably practicable, that safe passage along a highway is not endangered by snow or ice' (HM Govt, 1980). Of the 360,000 km (225,000 miles) of roads under the responsibility of UK highway authorities, approximately 128,000 km (80,000 miles) have de-icing salt applied during the winter months (Local Government Association, 2015). Rock salt (occasionally some other forms of de-icing agent) is applied by highway authorities to parts of the road network, to lower the freezing point of moisture on the surface of the road. The quantity of salt applied depends heavily on the severity of the winter weather. For example, the winter of 2014/15 was very mild, requiring 700,000 tonnes, yet during the severe winter of 2010/11 approximately 1.2 million tonnes was applied (Local Government Association, 2015). For it to work effectively, rock salt requires the tyres of moving traffic to grind it up and spread it across the road surface. The main problem to urban trees is salt-contaminated soil in root zones, either where it has been washed from the highway or salt-laden snow has been dumped and piled. Trees positioned downhill of the road and those growing in depressions or hollows are likely to be more affected (Dobson, 1991). Along high-speed roads, turbulent mists of salt spray can drift considerable distances, perhaps landing on leaves and buds, leading to scorching and dieback, mainly on the side facing the road. Where damage occurs frequently, apical buds are repeatedly killed, allowing lateral buds, on wood more than 1-year old, to be released and causing a telltale 'witches broom' appearance to branches (Trowbridge & Bassuk, 2004; Rose & Webber, 2011). Trees growing downwind of the treated road tend to be more affected and show the greatest injury (Dobson, 1991).

The severe winter of 1990/91 provided an opportunity to survey trees in London for damage by de-icing salt applied to the road network and pedestrian routes. By extrapolating from the 1,500 roadside trees surveyed between late July and mid-September 1991, Gibbs and Palmer estimated that some 21,900 roadside trees in London were likely to show symptoms of damage, from salt applied during the previous winter (Gibbs & Palmer, 1994). It is important to note that this research considered the effects on trees planted on main roads and side streets only and did not include traffic-free, pedestrianised areas. Although highway authority applications to roads were the main source of de-icing salt contamination, manual applications close to shops and other buildings used by the public significantly affected the trees in these locations. Indeed, as the salt was likely applied by hand, rather than by machine, the effects on trees in these areas could reasonably be expected to be worse.

In deciduous tree species, salt damage symptoms are typically visible when growth commences during the following spring. Depending on tree species, either buds fail to open, resulting in bare branches, or leaves begin to expand and then wither and die. The latter is known as 'post flushing dieback' (Gibbs & Burdekin, 1983). It is important that salt damage to London plane trees is not responded to prematurely as recovery may take many months. Gibbs and Palmer suggest no definitive decisions are taken for salt-damaged trees before the September following appearance of symptoms. This timing will also minimise any confusion between salt damage and plane anthracnose (*Apiognomonia veneta*). They also suggest that the use of alternative de-icing materials, such as urea or calcium magnesium acetate (CMA), are used in such locations, where their greater cost can, perhaps, be justified. Other than being harmful to plants, sodium chloride salt is also highly corrosive, making its use problematic in places such as airports. The alternative CMA is currently manufactured from petrochemicals, but researchers at Wageningen University, in Holland, are investigating the production of CMA from biomass, such as roadside grass or kitchen waste. It is uncertain what effect this is likely to have on its overall cost (Claasen, 2012).

3.7.2   Industrial pollutants – hydrocarbons

Petroleum hydrocarbons are one of the most widespread sources of organic contamination. Most are persistent in the soil, often lasting for many decades and are extremely toxic due to their mutagenic and carcinogenic properties. Hydrocarbon contamination of soil is often due to leaking storage tanks at fuel-filling stations, garages and fuel depots or from spillages. On construction sites, it is especially important to ensure that all fuel is stored in bunded tanks, and drip trays or plant nappies are used when refuelling plant and machinery. Spill kits must be available and deployed immediately if spills do occur, so that contamination can be contained at source. The major construction companies all have safety, health, environment and quality (SHEQ) teams, whose role is to ensure that their SHEQ policies are adhered to.

In North America and Australia, soil contamination has been removed from around tree roots using a compressed air lance to loosen the soil and a suction or vacuum excavation unit to remove the contaminated soil, replacing it with new topsoil. The main advantage of this method is that the contaminated material is collected directly into a sealed container, reducing exposure and handling. It is likely that best results would be achieved during the dormant period, when the exposed tree is not actively transpiring.

3.7.3   Industrial pollutants – heavy metals

Former industrial sites used for metal smelting, treating and finishing, mining, textile production, timber treatment and paper mills can all have potential for contamination by heavy metals and arsenic. The metals tend to be more soluble at low pH and can reach toxic levels in acidic soils. As most urban soils are more alkaline than acidic, due to the presence of building materials, heavy metal contamination is often not as problematic as it can be in some other restoration sites. It has also been found that the incorporation of organic matter can help to reduce the mobility and plant availability of some contaminants, although its effectiveness appears to vary according to the type of organic matter, soil and metal contamination (van Herwijnen *et al.*, 2007; van Herwijnen *et al.*, 2009). van Herwijnen *et al.* found that the addition of composted green waste to PAS 100 (BSI, 2005) is a suitable remediation measure for metal-contaminated soils, but recommend that plant and leaching tests are carried out before any site-scale remediation of brownfield sites is carried out.

3.7.4   Japanese knotweed – Fallopia japonica *var.* japonica *(but the regulations also include giant knotweed,* Fallopia sachalinensis *and the hybrid between these two species,* Fallopia x bohemica*)*

Japanese knotweed was introduced to Europe by Philipp von Siebold, from its native Japan, in the mid-nineteenth century. According to the Von Siebold and Company's 1848 catalogue, it was awarded a gold medal in 1847 for the most interesting new ornamental plant of the year, by the Society of Agriculture and Horticulture at Utrecht. At this time, it was considered to be the most desirable of ornamental plants (Bailey & Conolly, 2000). William Robinson described Japanese knotweed thus: 'If, instead of the formal character of much of our gardening, plants of bold types similar to the above were introduced along the sides of woodland walks and shrubbery borders, how much more enjoyable such places would be, as at almost every step there would be something fresh to attract notice and gratify the eye, instead of which such parts are generally bare, or given up to weeds and monotonous rubbish' (Robinson, 1870). He went on to recommend it as a plant 'with fine foliage or graceful habit suitable for naturalization' (Robinson, 1870). Robinson, his lifelong friend, Gertrude Jekyll, Canon Ellacombe, Edward Bowles and Ellen Willmott were all highly influential writers and garden makers, among the middle-class gardening set of the Victorian era. If they promoted this fast-growing, graceful and hardy plant among their clients and readers, it was sure to become sought after and very soon the plant had been spread throughout gardens in the UK. Although there had been warning of its ability to spread during the first half of the twentieth century, it was not until the early 1970s that the plant's aggressive invasiveness was really acted upon. By then, it had become established along railway and highway corridors, watercourses and coal mining spoil heaps, either due to the movement of contaminated material or by deliberate planting, in an effort to stabilise slopes (Bailey, 2010; Macfarlane, 2010). Its spread was somewhat inevitable, when one considers that even as little as a 0.8 g piece of rhizome (an underground stem rather than a root) can produce a new plant (Bailey, 2010), and from this, a new colony can soon develop. Benefitting from a comfortable climate in temperate regions and the absence of competition from invertebrate predators and pathogens, Japanese knotweed is able to express the vigour and aggression that elude it in its native habitats. It is sometimes claimed that Japanese knotweed can grow through concrete foundations, yet current advice recommends that it can be contained by a geotextile membrane a few millimetres thick (Jay, 2010). It will certainly grow in the joints between concrete slabs and between structures and slabs, but other pioneer species such as buddleia and betula will also colonise waste land in that way. The difference with the knotweeds is that they are controlled by law.

3.7.4.1 Legislation

Japanese knotweed was one of two land plants that appeared in Schedule 9 of the Wildlife and Countryside Act 1981 (the other being giant hogweed, *Heracleum mantegazzianum*), making it an offence to plant it or otherwise cause it to grow in 'the wild' (HM Govt, 1981). Although the Act contains no definition of 'wild', any area not under active management could be considered a useful and logical assumption (Macfarlane, 2010). Anyone successfully convicted under this legislation could face a fine of £5,000 and/or 6 months' imprisonment, or 2 years' imprisonment and/or an unlimited fine on indictment. Under Part 2 of the Environmental Protection Act 1990, all parts of the plant and any knotweed-contaminated soil are considered to be controlled waste. This requires that any removal must be carried out by licensed organisations and the material can only be taken to appropriately licensed waste facilities. Although it is not an offence to have knotweed growing on your property, if it spreads to neighbouring property, it could be regarded as a nuisance under common law, and so would be a civil matter. Section 215 of the Town and Country Planning Act 1990 empowers local authorities to serve notices on landowners and occupiers, requiring them to remediate land that has become infested with knotweed. If the owner fails to respond, s.219 of the Act provides powers for the local authority to carry out the works themselves and recover costs from the landowner (Office of the Deputy Prime Minister, 2005). All this legislation has led to the new industry of knotweed control and eradication. Developers, fearful of litigation claims against them, tend to look towards the use of various control measures, implemented by specialist companies. A few words of caution:

- Knotweed should be included in any contamination screening survey.
- If discovered, it is essential that a knotweed management plan is set up by an appropriately qualified and/or experienced person or company. RICS suggest accredited members of an industry-recognised trade body such as the Property Care Association

(www.property-care.org/invasive-species) and the Invasive Non-Native Specialists Association (www.innsa.org/).

- The knotweed management plan should identify key responsibilities, and its objectives should be clearly communicated to all contractors and site operatives. This document is important as it could provide evidence of appropriate management, if any re-growth leads to litigation against the contractor.
- Any eradication procedure must comply with Environment Agency guidelines.
- Be cautious of any treatment contractor offering a guaranteed eradication within one growing season.

3.7.4.2 Recognition, treatment and management

The Environment Agency guidance (Environment Agency, 2013) has moved away from a generic 7 m × 7 m × 3 m deep excavation for each knotweed plant encountered. This approach produced enormous amounts of controlled waste, costing huge sums of money and did not always remove all of the problem material. A much more intelligent risk-based approach of dealing with any knotweed contamination must be the way forward. The costs associated with knotweed control on development sites within Great Britain have been estimated at £150.5 million (Williams et al., 2010). To reduce this financial burden and provide an effective response to control, the EA guidance is measured, advising early site investigation to determine the existence of knotweed, emphasising the importance of a knotweed management plan and favouring in situ treatment where possible, rather than excavation and relocation to a licensed landfill site.

Figure 3.12
Japanese knotweed: re-growth from a previously treated stand (left). It can be difficult to completely eradicate established colonies, and regular ongoing monitoring should be carried out to ensure repeat treatments can be made appropriately. New growth from rhizomes imported within loads of topsoil (right). Even the smallest of root fragments can be sufficient to allow this persistent weed onto site. This example was growing from a rhizome 50 mm long and 5 mm in diameter (Right hand image Amber Haigh.)

It is advisable that all employees involved with development, site operations, construction and design are all able to identify the knotweeds covered by the Wildlife and Countryside Act 1981 as amended by the variation to Schedule 9 (HM Govt, 2010). There is good information available in the Environment Agency's knotweed code of practice (Environment Agency, 2013) and on the Japanese Knotweed Alliance website, hosted by CABI (www.cabi.org/japanese knotweedalliance/).

CASE STUDY: OLYMPIC PARK COMPARED WITH THE GREENWICH PENINSULA

Initial site investigations for the 2.5 sq. km, London 2012 Olympic Park at Stratford confirmed the extent of contamination expected to be generated within the site, which had been a mixed industrial development for more than 150 years. As had been found on the nearby Greenwich Peninsula prior to its redevelopment in 1998, a suite of contaminants was also found to be present in the surface and underlying soils of the Stratford site. These ranged from heavy metals (such as lead, arsenic and chromium) to petroleum hydrocarbons (such as fuel oils), ammonia, polycyclic aromatic hydrocarbons (such as coal tar and bitumen), localised chlorinated hydrocarbons and combinations of these. A series of approximately 3,500 investigation boreholes and trial pits were excavated at approximately 25 m intervals across the site. All the excavated material was analysed using an onsite laboratory to assess its suitability for reuse or treatment. Only material that was classified as geotechnically or chemically unsuitable for reuse or could not be treated in such a way as to make it suitable for reuse was taken away for disposal in offsite landfill. Consequently, of the 2.2 million cu. m or more of material, which was excavated as part of the enabling works, 80 per cent was reused in the redevelopment.

Within the Olympic Park, onsite treatment of excavation material was seen to be a more sustainable model and more in-line with the overarching Olympic Development Agency (ODA) ethos of sustainability. Treatment techniques included soil washing in so-called 'soil hospitals', bioremediation and chemical stabilisation. This was in contrast to the more traditional approach used on the Greenwich Peninsula remediation works. There, all contaminated material was excavated and transported to landfill, replacing it with clean, imported bulk fill material.

At Stratford most of the granular excavation arisings were first screened to sort biodegradable and oversized materials from those that were suitable for reuse. Approximately 700,000 cu. m of contaminated soils were washed using physiochemical technologies to remove the heavy metals, arsenic, cyanide, petroleum hydrocarbons, polycyclic aromatic hydrocarbons and other contaminants. Of the screened and washed granular materials excavated, approximately 40 per cent of the sands (greater than 2 mm diameter) and between 40 per cent and 50 per cent of the gravels (less than 50 mm diameter) were deemed suitable for reuse. These were blended with other arisings from site clearance works and the demolition of existing buildings, to produce the various engineering classes of civil engineering bulk fill material, used to create the topographic landforms that became the recognisable landscape features of the park. A minimum 600-mm thick separation layer was formed on top of this sculpted sub-base, from imported subsoil and manufactured topsoil, to produce the final finished site levels. The separation layer was required to provide a human health barrier of clean material between what contamination remained in the ground and the surface finish. Although a minimum cover layer thickness of 600 mm was identified as providing adequate protection for later use, 800 mm was typically used to allow an additional 200 mm for construction tolerance. The interface between the sub-base and the separation layer was identified throughout the site with a bright orange, geotextile fabric marker layer.

Figure 3.13
The bright orange maker layer is clearly visible, beneath the sandy subsoil layer, to the right of the image. Washed excavation material was used as civil engineering bulk fill to create the various landforms. The benching is being formed to allow the planting of large, semi-mature trees (Image Capita Lovejoy.)

Of the other materials, which were separated during the washing and grading processes, the fine silt and clay fractions, the organic matter and the ash and coke materials (approximately 15–18 per cent in total) were all extracted as filter cake or sludge and sent to landfill.

Soft and cohesive soils are not as suitable for washing as the more granular materials, and alternative techniques were employed to remediate them. Those containing predominantly organic, hydrocarbon contaminants were treated in bioremediation beds or biopiles. This technology requires the material to be heaped into cells or piles where it is aerated and its temperature is controlled to stimulate enhanced aerobic microbial activity, which degrades petroleum products. The material was treated in batches, each taking 6–8 weeks. In the Olympic Park, 30,000 cu. m of material (1.5 per cent of the total earthworks volume) was treated using this technique to make it suitable for reuse.

These remediation approaches have been shown to maximise the reuse of existing onsite materials within a highly contaminated urban brownfield development site. The significant reductions in both the amount of contaminated material destined for landfill and the importation of clean bulk fill have not only helped reduce the overall carbon footprint of the project, but have meant that a large number of lorry movements were prevented from disrupting the local road network.

None of the existing site soils were found to be suitable for reuse as topsoil or subsoil above the human health layer. All site-won material, despite being processed through the range of remediation measures discussed above, still retained levels of chemical and biological contaminants above those considered permissible for surface soils, accessible by people. One of the most troublesome biological contaminants was Japanese knotweed. At the outset of the works, approximately 4 ha of the site contained established colonies of Japanese knotweed. This had to be controlled to prevent it spreading and causing later disruption to infrastructure. As a result, a range of site-specific treatments were developed in consultation with the Environment Agency (EA), the London Development Agency (LDA) and the ODA. Control measures included onsite spraying with the herbicides Picloram and glyphosate, to screening and manual removal for controlled incineration or deep burial.

Figure 3.14
Approximately 4 ha of established knotweed colonies were identified within the park site and had to be treated to prevent it spreading.

Initially, excavation of the contaminated areas, sometimes several metres deep, followed herbicide treatment with glyphosate carried out several days earlier. The material was translocated to a burial site, which would not be disturbed by later construction works, where it was encapsulated within an approved knotweed membrane and buried under 2 m of clean fill material. Later, control measures reduced the likelihood of later re-emergence of the knotweed by introducing hand-sorting of the excavation material to remove all visible rhizomes. All these, the crowns and above-ground plant parts were incinerated. The remainder of the excavation arisings were then buried as before.

In 2001, the HM Revenue and Customs (HMRC) introduced Land Remediation Relief (LRR) to encourage the redevelopment of blighted land. LRR creates a mechanism where relief from corporation tax is possible for companies required to clean up land purchased from third parties, that is, in a contaminated state as a result of former industrial activity and at the point of purchase. From April 2009, Japanese knotweed was added to the list of contaminants, which qualified for such relief, to assist with the cost of removal. Additionally, the land does not necessarily need to be acquired in a contaminated state to qualify. If contamination occurred due to fly-tipping, for instance, and the landowner took all reasonable measures to prevent its spread, in a timely manner and preferably under the guidance of an appropriate specialist, they would be able to claim LRR. Treatment methods involving the removal of contaminated material to landfill (often referred to as 'dig and dump') are excluded from relief. To qualify, treatment methods must be *in situ* or involve decontamination in an offsite facility before being returned to site for reuse (HMRC, 2009).

The enabling works project has received the following awards:

- Remediation Innovation Awards: *Best use of a combination of techniques* (2008)
- Regeneration and Renewal Awards 2009: *Environmentally sustainable regeneration scheme of the year*
- Institution of Civil Engineers London Civil Engineering Awards: *Greatest Contribution to London Award* (2010)

- British Construction Industry Awards: *Major Project Category – Enabling works*
- Institution of Civil Engineers: *Edmund Hambly Medal – Enabling works.*

In addition to biopiles as used at the Olympic Park, much research work has been carried out with phytoremediation and the techniques have improved enormously over the last decade or so, but for many urban locations, they are not always possible. For more information, see Fox and Moore (2010): *Restoration and Recovery: Regenerating Land and Communities* and Kennen and Kirkwood (2015): *Phyto: Principles and Resources for Site Remediation and Landscape Design.*

REFERENCES

Ashman, M. R. & Puri, G. (2002). *Essential Soil Science: A Clear and Concise Introduction to Soil Science*. Oxford: Blackwell Science.

Bailey, J. P. (2010). Opening Pandora's seed packet. *The Horticulturist,* 21–4.

Bailey, J. P. & Conolly, A. P. (2000). Prize-winners to pariahs – A history of Japanese knotweed s.l. (Polygonaceae) in the British Isles. *Watsonia, 23*, 93–110.

Bakker, J. W. (1983). Growing site and water supply of street trees. *Groen, 39*(6), 205–7.

Bockheim, J. G. (1974). *Nature and Properties of Highly Disturbed Soils, Philadelphia, Pennsylvania*. Chicago, IL.

Bradshaw, A. D. & Dutton, R. A. (1982). *Land Reclamation in Cities: A Guide to Methods of Establishment of Vegetation on Urban Waste Land*. London: HMSO.

Brady, N. C. & Weil, R. C. (2008). *The Nature and Properties of Soils* (14th edn). Upper Saddle River, NJ: Prentice Hall.

BSI 2005. *PAS 100: 2005; Specification for Composted Materials*. London: British Standards Institution.

BSI 2015. *BS 5930: 2015; Code of Practice for Ground Investigations* (4th edn). London: British Standards Institution.

Bühler, O., Kristoffersen, P. & Larsen, S. U. (2007). Growth of street trees in Copenhagen with emphasis on the effect of different establishment concepts. *Arboriculture & Urban Forestry, 33*(5), 330–7.

Claasen, P. (2012). *De-icing salt made from grass or kitchen waste.* (Online). Retrieved 22 December 2015 from www.wageningenur.nl/en/show/Deicing-salt-made-from-grass-or-kitchen-waste.htm.

Clark, J. R. & Kjelgren, R. K. (1989). Conceptual and management considerations for the development of urban tree plantings. *Journal of Arboriculture, 15*(10), 229–36.

Cranfield University, 2015. *LandIS land Information System.* (Online). Retrieved 9 November 2015 from www.landis.org.uk.

Craul, P. J. (1985). A description of urban soils and their desired characteristics. *Journal of Arboriculture, 11*(11), 330–9.

Craul, P. J. (1992). *Urban Soil in Landscape Design*. New York: John Wiley and Sons.

Craul, P. J. (1999). *Urban Soils: Applications and Practices*. New York: John Wiley and Sons.

Daddow, R. L. & Warrington, G. E. (1983). *Growth-Limiting Soil Bulk Densities as Influenced by Soil Texture*. Fort Collins, CO: Watershed Systems Development Group, USDA Forest Service.

Dobson, M. C. (1991). *De-icing Salt Damage to Trees and Shrubs. Forestry Commission Bulletin 101*. London: HMSO.

Environment Agency, 2013. *Managing Japanese Knotweed on Development Sites (version 3): The Knotweed Code of Practice*. Bristol: Environment Agency.

Fox, H. R. & Moore, H. M. (2010). *Restoration and Recovery: Regenerating Land and Communities*. Dunbeath, Caithness, Scotland: Whittles Publishing.

Gibbs, J. N. & Burdekin, D. A. (1983). De-icing salt and crown damage to London plane. *Arboricultural Journal, 7*(3), 227–37.

Gibbs, J. N. & Palmer, C. A. (1994). A survey of damage to roadside trees in London caused by the application of de-icing salt during the 1990/91 winter. *Arboricultural Journal, 18*(3), 321–43.

Greenly, K. M. & Rakow, D. A. (1995). The effect of wood mulch type and depth on weed and tree growth and certain soil parameters. *Journal of Arboriculture, 21*(5), 225–32.

Hall, D. G. M., Reeve, M. J., Thomasson, A. J. & Wright, V. F. (1977). *Water Retention, Porosity and Density of Field Soils: Technical Monograph No. 9*. Harpenden, Herts: Soil Survey.

Hawver, G. A. & Bassuk, N. L. (2000). Soils: The keys to successful establishment of urban vegetation. In J. E. Kuser (ed.), *Handbook of Urban and Community Forestry in the Northeast* (pp. 137–52). New York: Kluwer Academic/Plenum Publishers.

Helliwell, D. R. (1986). The extent of tree roots. *Arboricultural Journal, 10*(4), 341–7.

HM Govt (1980). Highways Act 198. s. 41(1A). London: HMSO.

HM Govt (1981). Wildlife and Countryside Act 1981. London: HMSO.

HM Govt (1990). *Environmental Protection Act 1990 s. 78A.* London: HMSO.

HM Govt (2006). *The Contaminated Land (England) Regulations 2006.* London: HMSO.

HM Govt (2010). *The Wildlife and Countryside Act 1981 (Variation of Schedule 9) (England and Wales) Order 2010.* London: HMSO.

HM Govt (2012). *Environmental Protection Act 1990: Part 2A – Contaminated Land Statutory Guidance.* London: HMSO.

HMRC (2009). *CIRD61430 – Land Remediation Relief: What is 'land in a contaminated state'? Natural contaminants: Japanese Knotweed – expenditure from 1 April 2009.* (Online). Retrieved 7 July 2015 from www.hmrc.gov.uk/manuals/cirdmanual/CIRD61430.htm.

Holland, D. J. (1967). Evaporation. In M. Office (ed.), *British Rainfall 1961* (pp. 3–5 to 3–34). London: HMSO.

Iio, A. & Ito, A. (2014). *A Global Database of Field-Observed Leaf Area Index in Woody Plant Species, 1932–2011. Data set.* Oak Ridge, Tenn.: Oak Ridge National Laboratory Distributed Active Archive Center.

Jay, M. (2010). Japanese knotweed – the myth untangled. In *Restoration and Recovery: Regenerating Land and Communities* (pp. 178–84). Dunbeath, Caithness, Scotland: Whittles Publishing.

Kays, B. L. & Patterson, J. C. (1982). Soil drainage and infiltration. In P. J. Craul (ed.), *Urban Forest Soils: A Reference Workbook* (pp. 5–1 to 5–25). Syracuse, NY: SUNY College of Environmental Science and Forestry.

Kennen, K. & Kirkwood, N. (2015). *Phyto: Principles and Resources for Site Remediation and Landscape Design* (1st edn). Abingdon, Oxford: Routledge.

Kopinga, J., (1985). *Research on Street Tree Planting Practices in the Netherlands.* University Park, Penn. METRIA, 72–84.

Kozlowski, T. T. (1999). Soil compaction and growth of woody plants. *Scandinavian Journal of Forest Research, 14,* 596–619.

Landon, J. R. (1991). *Booker Tropical Soil Manual: A Handbook for Soil Survey and Agricultural Land Evaluation in the Tropics and Subtropics.* Harlow, Essex: Longman Scientific and Technical Group.

Lindsey, P. & Bassuk, N. L. (1992). Redesigning the urban forest from the ground below: A new approach to specifying adequate soil volumes for street trees. *Arboricultural Journal, 16*(1), 25–39.

Local Government Association (2015). *Your winter watch questions answered.* (Online). Retrieved 22 December 2015 from www.local.gov.uk/community-safety/-/journal_content/56/10180/3510492/ARTICLE.

Macfarlane, J. (2010). A consideration of appropriate and cost effective strategies for dealing with *Fallopia japonica* on redevelopment sites and possible legal implications in relation to the operations. In *Restoration and Recovery: Regenerating Land and Communities* (pp. 185–9). Dunbeath, Caithness, Scotland: Whittles Publishing.

MAFF. (1988). *Agricultural Land Classification of England and Wales.* London: MAFF.

Moll, G. & Urban, J. (1989). Giving trees room to grow. *American Forests, 95*(5–6), 61–4.

Mullins, C. E. (1991). Physical properties of soil in urban areas. In P. Bullock & P. J. Gregory (eds), *Soils in the Urban Environment* (pp. 87–118). Oxford: Blackwell Scientific Publications.

Nielsen, C. N., Bühler, O. & Kristoffersen, P. (2007). Soil water dynamics and growth of street and park trees. *Arboriculture & Urban Forestry, 33*(4), 231–45.

Norbury, D. (2010). *Soil and Rock Description in Engineering Practice.* Dunbeath, Caithness, Scotland: Whittles Publishing.

NSRI Staff (2011). *Glossary of Soil-Related Terms.* Cranfield: NSRI, Cranfield University.

Office of the Deputy Prime Minister (2005). *Town and Country Planning Act 1990 Section 215: Best Practice Guidance.* London: Office of the Deputy Prime Minister.

Patterson, J. C. (1976). *Soil Compaction and its Effects upon Urban Vegetation* (pp. 91–102). Washington, DC: USDA Forest Service Northeastern Forest Experimental Station.

Patterson, J. C., Murray, J. J. & Short, J. R. (1980). *The Impact of Urban Soils on Vegetation* (pp. 33–56). New Brunswick, NJ: U.S. Forest Service, Northeastern Area.

Percival, G. C. (2013). Science and opinion – mulching for disease control. *The ARB Magazine, 162,* 37–40.

Percival, G. C., Gklavakis, E. & Noviss, K. (2009). Influence of pure mulches on survival, growth and vitality of containerized and field planted trees. *Journal of Environmental Horticulture, 27*(4), 200–6.

Perry, T. O. (1980). *The Size, Design and Management of Planting Sites Required for Healthy Tree Growth* (pp. 1–14). s.l., US Forest Service, North-eastern Area, State and Private Forestry.

Randrup, T. B. (1997). Soil compaction on construction sites. *Journal of Arboriculture, 23*(5), 207–10.

Robinson, W. (1870). *The Wild Garden or Our Groves and Shrubberies Made Beautiful by the Naturalization of Hardy Exotic Plants.* London: John Murray.

Rose, D. R. & Webber, J. (2011). *De-icing Salt Damage to Trees. Pathology Advisory Note (No. 11).* Farnham, UK: Forest Research.

Saxton, K. E. & Rawls, W. J. (2006). Soil water characteristic estimates by texture and organic matter for hydrologic solutions. *Soil Science Society of America Journal, 70*(5), 1569–78.

Smith, M. J. (1981). *Soil Mechanics* (4th edn). Harlow, Essex: Longman Scientific & Technical.

Soil Survey Division Staff. (1993). *Soil Survey Manual – USDA-SCS Agricultural Handbook 18.* Washington, DC: US Govt Printing Office.

Spomer, L. A. (1983). Physical amendments of landscape soils. *Journal of Environmental Horticulture, 1*(3), 77–80.

Trowbridge, P. J. & Bassuk, N. L. (2004). *Trees in the Urban Landscape: Site Assessment, Design and Installation.* Hoboken, NJ: John Wiley and Sons.

USDA, NRCS (2001). *Soil Quality Test Kit Guide,* Washington, DC: USDA Natural Resources Conservation Service.

van Herwijnen, R., Hutchings, T. R., Al-Tabbaa, A., Moffat, A. J., Johns, M. L. & Ouki, S. K. (2007). Remediation of metal contaminated soil with mineral-amended composts. *Environmental Pollution, 150*, 347–54.

van Herwijnen, R.; Sellers, G.; Sinnett, D.; Hutchings, T. R.; Al-Tabbaa, A.; Ouki, S. K. (2009). *Integrated remediation, reclamation and greenspace creation on brownfield land – CL:AIRE SUBR:IM bulletin SUB 11,* London: Contaminated Land: Applications in Real Environments (CL:AIRE).

Veihmeyer, F. J. & Hendrickson, A. H. (1948). Soil density and root penetration. *Soil Science, 65*(6), 487–94.

Vrecenak, A. J. & Herrington, L. P. (1984). Estimation of water use of landscape trees. *Journal of Arboriculture, 10*(12), 313–19.

Williams, F., Eschen, R., Harris, A., Djeddour, D., Pratt, C., Shaw, R.S., Varia, S., Lamontagne-Godwin, J., Thomas, S.E. & Murphy, S.T. (2010). *The Economic Cost of Invasive Non-Native Species on Great Britain.* Wallingford, UK: CAB International.

Chapter 4: Site assessment and analysis

4.1 INTRODUCTION

Chapter 1 discussed the environmental and social benefits of green infrastructure and urban greening, but for trees to become functionally useful within our urban landscapes, they need to establish and reach a state of healthy, productive maturity before any of these benefits can be realised. Unfortunately, tree planting is often seen as a piece of 'window dressing' to assist a development scheme through the planning process, with little thought about the long-term requirements of the planting shown on the drawings and in the promotional visualisations. After all, how difficult can it be? Trees seed themselves and grow naturally in woodlands and forests, with no assistance or intervention from us. However, human-impacted landscapes such as those found in urban areas bear virtually no relationship to those of woodlands and forests. As discussed in Chapter 3, urban soils have invariably been fundamentally altered through excavation, filling, grading and compaction, compounded by contamination from the construction and use of buildings and roads. Planting sites are often surrounded by the hard materials that typify the built environment, and so are subject to high temperatures from reflected and re-radiated energy from the sun. The hard surfacing necessary to facilitate the unimpeded flow of pedestrian and vehicular traffic through our urban centres prevents the even spread of rainfall being absorbed by the soil. As a consequence, water availability for plants tends to be highly erratic. Tall buildings can modify the behaviour of wind, sometimes concentrating or funnelling it through gaps and along roads. These are hostile conditions for the majority of plants and can make tree establishment especially problematic. We can see this from national tree surveys such as *Trees in Towns II – A new survey of urban trees in England and their condition and management* (Britt & Johnston, 2008).

As discussed in Chapter 3, it is obviously true that some of the most important factors to be considered when looking at the establishment and long-term well-being of trees lie in the below-ground environment. It is depressingly all too common to see trees being planted within insufficient rootable spaces, surrounded by highly compacted ground and impervious paving materials. As a consequence, roots are encouraged to explore less compacted and moist materials close to the surface and along utility excavations, resulting in deflected paved surfaces and disruption to other infrastructure. The above-ground constraints can also play an important role, however, in helping to determine the location of trees and the species selected. The location of proposed trees will be in line with agreed offsets from underground infrastructure, but must also be considered alongside proximity to building structures with respect to the size of the selected tree species at maturity.

To ensure that a 'right plant, right place' approach is adopted, a comprehensive site assessment is vital to help identify and understand the limitations and opportunities provided in any design or development project. Once this information has been collected and analysed, it should be possible to ensure that the species selected are adequately adapted to the site conditions, meet the design and functional objectives of the scheme, match the available management limitations and provide the aesthetic qualities required.

Early engagement with landscape architects, arboriculturists and soil scientists as part of any master planning process is essential to ensure retention of existing trees, correct site preparation, suitable species selection and appropriate planting layout. An enormous range of good practice guidance is currently available from recognised, authoritative sources; some of it apparently conflicting, and appropriate consultants, with proven track records, should be employed to help interpret this guidance. As a practising landscape architect, I am bound to say that, but one sees all too often where inadequate consideration has been given to the planting within a scheme, resulting in poorly designed and implemented tree planting provision and inappropriate species selected.

This chapter considers the various clues and evidence that can be gathered during site visits to enable informed decisions to be made about site interventions and appropriate tree selection. It rather goes without saying that all information gathered, all observations made and all measurements taken should be recorded and stored in a manner that allows for easy access and retrieval. If a systematic approach is adopted, perhaps, using a checklist as shown below (see Figure 4.1), everything should be recorded in a logical manner. Most observations and notes can be captured by marking-up and annotating site drawings.

4.2 PLANTING OBJECTIVES AND ECOSYSTEM SERVICES

The most important considerations to long-term plant success are the early determination of the intended plant performance and what functions the planting is intended to provide. As discussed earlier in Chapter 1, green infrastructure and trees especially can provide many aesthetic, social and environmental benefits to our urban centres, in terms of ecosystem services. The counter-argument in terms of ecosystem disservices should also be taken into account, so that a balanced assessment for the site can be made. This should help to guide species selection while also helping to determine the nature, quantum and location of desired planting.

There is a rapidly growing array of empirical data that shows the extent of benefits provided by green infrastructure, and it is possible to evaluate the ecosystem services provided using a quantitative assessment tool such as i-Tree. However, from systematic literature searches of scholarly databases, it has been found that there is much less evidence of study, which looks specifically at ecosystem disservices (Lyytimäki & Sipilä, 2009; Roy, Byrne & Pickering, 2012). By far the most examined of these disservices is related to air quality, in terms of the generation and release of volatile organic compounds (VOCs), allergic reactions to some wind-pollinated species, and less publicised, the potential interruption of wind flow in urban canyons.

Street-level air exchange in heavily built-up areas is often fairly low due to the presence of buildings flanking the street and shielding it from roof-top air movements. From wind tunnel experiments, used to compare the dispersion of traffic exhaust pollution in urban street canyons with and without avenue tree planting (Gromke, Buccolieri, Di Sabatino & Ruck, 2008; Gromke & Ruck, 2009; Gromke, 2011), it has been found that large canopy trees planted in dense avenues

URBAN SITE EVALUATION AND ASSESSMENT CHECKLIST	
Climate information	
Desktop study	
Rainfall – monthly average (mm)	
Sunshine – monthly average (hours)	
Prevailing winds (mark on plan prior to site visit)	
Site study – record observations on plans	
Sun/shade – full sun/partial shade/full shade/reflected light from glass facades/overhead shade	
Rain shadow	
Areas of exposure	
Wind tunnel	
Frost pockets	
Re-reflected heat	
Soil information	
Profile pit to determine the depth of topsoil and subsoil, soil structure, and so on – leave pit open, if possible, to determine drainage/high water table, and so on (Consider H and S requirements of breaking ground and leaving open excavations). Note any mottling, obvious banding/buried topsoil, and so on	
Compaction/soil drainage – percolation test (mm/hour) (< 100 mm/hr, 100–200 mm/hr, > 200 mm/hr)	
Soil texture – feel test – Clay, Loam, Sand content (see Appendix 4 – Simple field test (ADAS method))	
Collect soil sample(s) and send for analysis (see Appendix 2, The collection and analysis of soil samples)	
pH from BDH test kit or similar (mark on drawings)	
Irrigation availability – fully automated – none (and various regimes between). It is useful to have some idea of likely availability (e.g., by hand from bowser); also over what period – indefinitely? Or just for establishment?	
Utilities and services	
Below-ground utility routes marked on ground and checked against plans (ground-truthing is required due to frequent unreliability of plans)	

Figure 4.1
Model site assessment checklist. Such a guide could either be printed out and filled in by hand or loaded on to a computer, tablet or notebook.

URBAN SITE EVALUATION AND ASSESSMENT CHECKLIST – *continued*	
Ground disturbance and surface scarring marked on plans	
Overhead cable routes and heights marked on plans	
CCTV camera positions and fields of view marked on plans	
Existing built environment	
Existing use of site – may affect species selection and specification (e.g., clear stem height, fruit production)	
Building massing and heights (have an impact on shade, rain shadow, wind tunnels, windows struggling for light, and so on)	
Evidence of de-icing salt or likelihood of use (paved public spaces in locations of snow or freezing temperatures)	
Evidence of recent construction works/debris	
Evidence of likely contamination – industrial sites, and so on	
Existing vegetation	
Existence of indicator species – drainage/pH	
Competing vegetation	
Health of existing vegetation – evidence of pest, disease, drought stress, waterlogging, wind shaping, contamination, vandalism, management and maintenance issues, and so on	
Presence of noxious weeds – Japanese knotweed, and so on	

Assessment of existing vegetation – identify and mark on site plan			
Species	Size (stem dia., canopy– N, S, E, W, overall height, etc.)	Extension growth (cm) recording previous season's growth	Overall tree health

Figure 4.1 – *continued*

Figure 4.2
These London plane trees have been allowed to develop fairly natural spreading crowns to provide complete canopy cover along Kelvin Way, Glasgow.

Figure 4.3
These London plane trees have been regularly pollarded to maintain an open canopy along Inchmery Road, Catford, SE London.

can further reduce the already low air circulation between street and upper roof levels, inhibiting any natural ventilation. This fumigation effect can trap the traffic emissions at street level and increase local pollution concentrations.

Some thought must be given to this phenomenon when we are designing or creating trafficked areas that are also accessible to pedestrians and are planted with large species trees that will grow to provide complete canopy cover. We could inadvertently be actively encouraging pedestrians to use spaces where local vehicle pollution is being concentrated, thereby increasing human exposure (see more on air quality in Chapter 1). However, this should not be viewed as cause to remove established trees from pedestrian-accessible street canyons with high traffic pollution loading. If a reduction in traffic density cannot be addressed, then either new dense avenue-type planting of large canopy trees should be avoided or pruning regimes should be adopted, which prevent complete canopy closure (Wania, Bruse, Blond & Weber, 2012).

Other problems that have been identified in academic literature include mainly physical aspects, such as damage to structures from branches and roots, shading, littering from leaves and fruits and some expenditure aspects related to implementation management and main-tenance costs. There is still much to be done in developing our knowledge of the biogeochemical regulating processes in urban green infrastructure if any of the uncertainties are to be resolved and knowledge gaps are to be filled (Pataki *et al.*, 2011).

4.3 STRUCTURAL LIMITATIONS

Demolition of existing structures, new development, building maintenance and access to buried and above-ground utilities all need to be assessed against existing trees and any proposed tree-planting scheme. The document that aims to guide the process is British Standard, BS 5837, *Trees in relation to design, demolition and construction – Recommendations* (BSI, 2012).

4.3.1 Trees in relation to design, demolition and construction – recommendations

Any development proposal that potentially has an impact on existing trees will require a tree survey to be conducted in accordance with British Standard BS 5837: 2012. This document provides guidance on the process for determining protection, removal and successful integration of existing and proposed trees into development.

A topographic survey should be commissioned for the development site which, in addition to the usual suite of topographic features, identifies the location of each tree (preferably to the centre of the stem) with a stem diameter of 75 mm or more (to accord with conservation area requirements see Chapter 8) when measured at 1.5 m above the adjacent ground level. It should also provide a spot level at the base of each tree stem. Any woodlands or significant groups of trees would generally not be surveyed as individual trees; however, the extent of canopy cover would typically be identified, as would all trees with a stem diameter of 150 mm or more. It is important that the survey should also include all trees with a stem diameter of 75 mm or more, which are outside the development site and which may be affected by the proposed works.

All trees that may be affected by the works are identified from the survey plan and quantitatively and qualitatively assessed by an arboriculturist (as defined in BS 5837), in a tree survey. This is a purely objective, baseline survey and does not, at this stage, take into consideration any development proposal. The survey report provides an assessment on tree condition, size and an indication on the tree's arboricultural, landscape and cultural value. Other than above-ground constraints provided by tree canopies, the standard requires that the area of ground deemed necessary to provide sufficient roots and rooting volume to sustain the tree in a healthy condition must be determined. This *root protection area* or RPA is an arithmetic calculation that produces

Figure 4.4
RPA is calculated by first measuring the diameter of the stem at a height of 1.5 m above the ground level, multiplying this by twelve. This figure provides the radius of a circle, with the tree stem at its centre, that represents the RPA.

an area on the ground, equivalent to a circle whose radius is equal to twelve times the stem diameter (for single-stemmed trees), measured at a height of 1.5 m above the ground level. For multi-stemmed trees, the radius of the RPA calculation is slightly more complex, but the principle remains.

Curiously and without any explanation of why, the area is capped at 707 sq. m (an area with a 15 m radius), which equates to a tree with a stem diameter of 1.25 m. With over-mature trees, the stem diameter multiplier does not necessarily relate to the crown and root mass alone. Additional consideration must be given to the vulnerability of the aged root systems of veteran trees and the beneficial fungi associated with them. The standard set out in the handbook *Veteran Trees: A Guide to Good Management*, published by English Nature (now Natural England) provides a minimum root protection area, or exclusion zone, with a radius of fifteen times the trunk diameter at breast height, or 5 m beyond the extent of the canopy, whichever is the greater (English Nature, 2011).

The 2012 revision of BS 5837 also requires a soil assessment to be undertaken by a competent person to determine *its structure, composition, pH and shrinkability* (BSI, 2012). Such an assessment could also determine soil texture and provide material for a full soil assessment as shown in Appendix 2. As soil has such a fundamental effect on rooting and will inform suitable engineered design of foundations, it is a welcome addition. There has been some resistance from the construction industry to include this level of data capture at this stage, but as geotechnical, contamination and other ground investigations are quite likely to be required anyway, the addition of a soil assessment would cause only a very modest addition to any pre-construction costs.

There is some concern that this simple arithmetic calculation has very little in terms of empirical data to support it, except work conducted on fairly young nursery stock (Gilman, 1988; Gerhold & Johnson, 2003), which suggests significantly larger areas are occupied by the roots of the young trees investigated. However, Harris, Clark & Matheny (2004) suggest that as young trees are more adaptable to root disturbance, a 6:1 ratio between RPA radius and stem diameter should be sufficient. As trees age and become more susceptible to damage from root disturbance, a more generous 18:1 ratio may be more appropriate.

When we consider root systems, we know that they are three-dimensional, and so we need to talk in terms of volume rather than area. We also know that roots are opportunistic, growing wherever environmental conditions such as the physical and chemical characteristics of the soil allow (Gilman, Leone & Flower, 1987). Therefore, a simple twelve-times stem diameter calculation is clearly only going to provide an estimation at best. It is not uncommon to survey what appears to be a healthy urban tree, surrounded by impervious paving and in close proximity to a range of large built objects, only to wonder where on earth the roots could possibly be. There is clearly sufficient functional root system somewhere to support tree growth, otherwise the tree would die or at least show signs of stress, but the actual location of roots in the ground often remains a mystery. Unfortunately, there is little academic research to help in determining where the roots might be. There is much to help in determining root volumes (see Chapter 3), but this does little to assist in determining root spread in any particular direction.

Paragraph 4.6.2 of the standard does include a method of adjusting the RPA, where there is evidence of asymmetric root growth, such as building foundations and highway construction. The code suggests simply altering the perimeter while maintaining the area determined arithmetically, which requires a degree of guesswork. Because of this, there is always scope for appealing against a decision based on the RPA calculations, which use the twelve-times multiplier.

Table 4.1

Optimum tree protection area for trees of average to excellent vigour. Modified from BS 5837: 1991 Trees in relation to construction. From Harris, Clark and Matheny (2004)

Species tolerance	Tree age	RPA radius multiplier per cm trunk diameter
Good	Young (< 20 per cent life expectancy)	6 times
	Mature (20–80 per cent life expectancy)	9 times
	Over-mature (> 80 per cent life expectancy)	12 times
Moderate	Young	9 times
	Mature	12 times
	Over-mature	15 times
Poor	Young	12 times
	Mature	15 times
	Over-mature	18 times

That said, the standard is generally viewed as being successful and is currently published in its fourth iteration. It is important that each tree is assessed against a standard set of criteria, and BS 5837 correctly provides this as guidance rather than producing any evidence-based certainty.

Any works that are required to be carried out within the RPA, such as tree management, tree removals, temporary and permanent construction works, are evaluated for their direct and indirect impact on retained trees, in an Arboricultural Impact Assessment and are subject to certain controls on construction activity detailed in the Arboricultural Method Statement. An important assessment when considering encroachments within the RPA concerns any significant reduction to the assimilative and support functions of the root system (Quaife, 2015).

In addition to protection of the below-ground RPA, access to underground utilities and other construction works will also often be subject to above-ground constraints, such as overhanging tree canopies. The tree protection measures may need amendment to include the tree canopy. Access space required during demolition and construction can easily be underestimated, and

Figure 4.5
Using BS 5837: 2012 to calculate the root protection area for this London plane (left) at 300 mm stem diameter would be represented by a circle with a radius of 3.6 m. This tree was more than 6 m from the kerb edge and (right) the substantial roots also extended more than 5 m into the road.

Figure 4.6
Where protected trees are likely to be under pressure from construction activities, BS 5837-compliant tree protection fencing could consist of standard construction site mesh panels mounted to a rigid scaffold frame as shown in the left-hand image. Where the protected area is clearly away from construction pressure, a lighter fence construction can be used. The image to the right shows standard mesh panels fixed to rubber or HD plastic feet. This type of fence is easily moved and so not suitable for the level of construction activity evident in the photo.

Figure 4.7
Beneath our feet is a congested and complicated network of utility and service supply infrastructures.

careful consideration should be given to retained trees at all stages of the design process. There is little point in providing a contractor with a work space that is so constrained that it will either significantly hinder the construction process or the tree-protection measures will simply be ignored.

4.4 SUBTERRANEAN STRUCTURES AND UTILITY INFRASTRUCTURE

Many of our dense, urban centres no longer show any signs of their pre-urban existence. As discussed in the previous chapter, urban and brownfield soils invariably bear little relationship to their distant greenfield and rural cousins. They are typically highly disturbed, compacted and contain many anthropogenic artefacts, including building foundations, utility and service infrastructure, construction waste, basement boxes, and so on. Many sites, in fact, consist of podium decks built on top of subterranean structures. Trench-scarring and linear settlement are good indications that utility runs have been installed or accessed for maintenance. These should be checked against existing tree root zones, as such works can often involve root disturbance, damage or removal, and so are likely to have a negative impact on the overall health of the tree. The effects may not be visible immediately, but will often show later as wilting foliage and branch dieback.

4.4.1 Underground utility detection, verification and location

All of these existing underground structures and utility routes along with those that are proposed must be recorded and plotted to enable correct positioning of tree planting. Drawings showing this information are rarely relied upon to provide safe excavation information and sites are typically scanned prior to breaking ground. Most major contractors have quite rigorous 'permit to dig' protocols in place to prevent underground utilities and services being inadvertently struck. The Cable Avoidance Tool (C.A.T.) and signal generator (Genny) have become the industry standard pipe and cable detection equipment. They have proved to be reliable, rugged and cost-effective. They are fairly limited to detecting metallic cables, pipes and conductors, but with the addition of a flexi-trace or mouse, plastic pipes can also be detected. Optical cables can still be problematic unless they are equipped with tracer wire or cable armouring, and sometimes, the only certain way to locate them is by excavating hand-dug trial holes to expose them.

An exciting research project, led by Chris Rogers of Birmingham University, is investigating ways to minimise utility strikes and abortive excavations, by mapping the underground infrastructure using a range of non-invasive technologies. The project has shown that ground-penetrating radar (GPR), Vibro-Acoustics (V-A), low-frequency electromagnetic fields (LFEMF) and passive magnetic fields (PMF) can all be combined into one multi-sensor platform, without signal distortion.

The data collected from this multiple technology survey are appraised alongside: existing utility records; geotechnical and geophysical data to determine soil condition; physical survey of street furniture and surface typologies; and environmental information on rainfall, temperature and seasonal effects. This fusion of data has allowed the development of specific data processing algorithms, which have provided a much clearer three-dimensional map of buried services than has been possible before. The aim of the project is to develop a means to locate, 3D map and record all buried utility assets to within 50 mm in plan and depth such that each can be located within its environment and returned to, throughout its working life, to this accuracy (Mapping the Underworld, 2012).

The National Joint Utilities Group (NJUG) is the UK trade body that represents utility companies and their contractors on utility-related street works. It provides a forum for self-regulation and dialogue with central and local government and other stakeholders. As part of their aim to promote best practice, they have produced several advisory publications for statutory undertakers. Vol. 4, Issue 2, entitled 'NJUG Guidelines for the Planning, Installation and Maintenance of Utility Apparatus in Proximity to Trees' is especially relevant (NJUG, 2007). This provides guidance on the precautions that should be taken when installing or maintaining utility infrastructure, to minimise the damage to both trees and the utility apparatus and to help ensure

Figure 4.8
Scanning for utilities with a C.A.T.
(Image Capita Lovejoy.)

CASE STUDY – PAS128, SPECIFICATION FOR UNDERGROUND UTILITY DETECTION, VERIFICATION AND LOCATION

In June 2014, the BSI launched the Publicly Accessible Standard, PAS128, entitled *Specification for underground utility detection, verification and location*. Up until this time, the utility survey industry was unregulated, resulting in inconsistencies in scope and quality of the surveys produced. PAS128 was sponsored by the Institution of Civil Engineers, and found widespread support from the civil engineering, sub-surface utility and survey communities. The aim of the specification was to set out a clear framework to ensure that practitioners provide: a clear scope of services; adopt a consistent approach to data capture, confidence classification and format of the deliverables; and are accountable for the survey work conducted. It provides a robust methodology for the delivery of utility surveys by assessing the quality of survey information and so the confidence level of the survey outputs. There are four survey category types that imply levels of accuracy:

Type D involves a desktop utility records search, where utility owners would be identified, contacted and their asset information requested. All the data would then be collated and provided as the survey deliverable.

Type C is a site reconnaissance survey, where onsite visual checks are used to confirm the location of utility routes by checking any utility surface features, such as existing street furniture, cabinets, inspection covers and evidence of previous works, such as reinstatement scars, against utility and service plan information. Any differences between the surface features and the plan information would be recorded. The horizontal and vertical alignments remain undefined.

Type B are detection surveys and are sub-divided into different quality level (QL) categories according to the required location accuracy. For detection, it is required that at least two geophysical techniques are used, such as electromagnetic conductivity (EM) and GPR.

- QL-B4: A utility route is suspected to exist, but has not been detected, so is shown as an assumed route.
- QL-B3: The horizontal position can be detected and the alignment would be accurate to ±500 mm, but no reliable depth measurement would be possible.

Some post-processing of the data could be used to improve confidence in the data, and if this is used, a 'P' suffix is added to the QL (so, QL-B3 with post-processing becomes QL-B3P). Post-processing will usually take place offsite, where the data are processed to isolate signals from the buried utilities identified and analysed in 2D and/or 3D data blocks. Complicated underground arrangements can be modelled on a computer to allow them to be better understood. The data can be exported to CAD where linear patterns can be recognised as possible utility routes.

- QL-B2: As QL-B3 above, but the accuracy is determined by a horizontal accuracy of ±250 mm or ±40 per cent of the detected depth, whichever is the greater and a vertical accuracy of ±40 per cent of the detected depth.

As above, if post-processing of data are used, a 'P' suffix is added to the QL.

- QL-B1: As QL-B2 above, but requires detection by multiple geophysical techniques to ensure a horizontal accuracy of ±150 mm or ±15 per cent of the detected depth, whichever is the greater and a vertical accuracy of ±15 per cent of the detected depth.

As above, if post-processing of data are used, a 'P' suffix is added to the QL.

Type A surveys require visual inspection of the utility, either at access points (such as inspection chambers) and/or through excavation and exposure (such as hand-dug trial pits). In these types of surveys, horizontal and vertical locations of the top and/or bottom of the utility are possible and should be recorded. Horizontal accuracy must be no more than ±50 mm and vertical accuracy no more than ±25 mm.

The specification also sets out the likely detection methods required for different applications. For instance, the quantum of data and quality levels required are likely to be less for an undeveloped area than they are for a congested central city location.

that both may co-exist. The guidelines provide 'Tree Protection Zones', where excavations are either prohibited or carried out, subject to certain precautionary controls. Unfortunately, the protection zones are not completely aligned with the RPA calculation in BS 5837. The 'Prohibited Zone' requires that no excavations of any kind may take place within 1 m of the tree trunk, without full consultation with the local authority Tree Officer. The 'Precautionary Zone' is calculated by multiplying the tree circumference by four to calculate an area where the use of any mechanical excavation plant should be prohibited. This effectively gives a protection zone slightly greater than BS 5837. All excavations beyond this 'Precautionary Zone' fall within the 'Permitted Zone'. The use of mechanical excavation equipment within this zone should be limited, and any roots encountered should be protected with sacking, to prevent desiccation and damage from frost.

Some recent innovations in excavation and installation techniques may help to reduce the impact upon tree roots.

4.4.2 Compressed air and vacuum techniques

Compressed air techniques for trenching, such as 'Air Spade' and 'Soil Pick', fracture, pulverise and displace porous and semi-porous materials within the soil profile, leaving non-porous materials, such as buried utilities and tree roots, unharmed. Compressed air is forced through a fine nozzle at the end of a handheld lance, where it reaches supersonic speeds, typically in the region of 1,200 mph, and enters any available air space between the particles, blasting them apart. Modern compressed air lances are typically manufactured from non-conductive materials to prevent electrocution and also incorporate non-sparking nozzles. The high velocity air stream travels approximately 100 mm from the nozzle before it decompresses to atmospheric pressure, so the loosened material must be continually removed to allow the lance to be lowered into the excavation. For this reason, the technique works well with vacuum extraction, where the loosened material is simply sucked up through a flexible hose and into a debris tank, typically mounted onto a goods vehicle chassis.

The West Midlands Gas Alliance was formed in 2005, when National Grid contracted with Morgan Est to replace several kilometres of gas main within the West Midlands area. As part of a safety initiative to reduce the risk of damage to underground utility infrastructure, a compressed air and vacuum excavation trial was started in 2007. They found that the number of utility strikes approximately halved, less manual effort was required by operatives, excavation holes were reduced in size and the works could be completed quicker. As a result of the trial and in the pursuit of best practice, the West Midlands Gas Alliance increased the number of vacuum extractors within their fleet (NJUG, 2009b).

Figure 4.9
Compressed air and vacuum excavation significantly reduces the risk of damaging tree roots compared with other more traditional mechanical methods and even hand-digging. (Images P.J. Carey (Contractors) Ltd.)

4.4.4.3 Trenchless techniques

Laing O'Rourke were contracted by Yorkshire Water to survey the existing water mains and design a cost-effective programme of refurbishment and replacement. The proposed mix of solutions ranged from simple cleaning, through slip-lining existing pipes, to horizontal directional drilling of replacement pipes (NJUG, 2009a). Slip-lining requires a plastic 'carrier pipe' (most often high-density polyethylene – HDPE is used, but fibreglass reinforced pipe and PVC are fairly common) to be inserted into the existing 'host pipe', which is requiring repair. The process normally takes place in sections, between excavation pits, 100 m apart, or 300 m apart if the host pipe is clean and clear of any obstructions. Obviously, the reduced volume provided by the carrier pipe must be taken into consideration. Horizontal directional drilling also requires pits to be excavated at regular intervals (every 100 m in this example, but distances of up to 700 m or more are said to be possible). An initial pilot borehole is drilled along a carefully predetermined path that is designed to avoid other existing underground structures, and this is incrementally increased in diameter by successive bores until the required size is achieved. The pipe or duct is then drawn through the bore. Although this technique was adopted as a way to make savings on transportation and reinstatement materials, it can also ensure that utility installations may be made under the root systems of existing trees, without interfering with them.

4.4.4 Shared utility corridors

New developments often require completely new local utility networks, rather than incorporating and adapting existing infrastructure and so provide opportunities for utilities to share corridors, trenches or tunnels. Such an arrangement of common utility ducts has been adopted within the Dorchester urban extension at Poundbury in Dorset. Although the tree assets will continue to provide environmental and social benefits in ever-increasing amounts, and so effectively appreciate in value, it is the capital expenditure that developers concentrate on. At Poundbury, with all the utilities contained within a managed corridor, suitable offsets for tree planting can be maintained. This allows maintenance access for utility infrastructure and provides room for trees to develop into productive maturity while minimising disturbance to either.

The NJUG promotes trench sharing in their Guidelines on the Positioning and Colour Coding of Underground Utilities' Apparatus (Issue 8) (NJUG, 2013) as a way to reduce disruption, construction costs and reinstatement liability. This document describes the recommended positioning of utility apparatus in a 2-m footway (see Figure 4.12).

4.4.5 Above-ground utilities and services

Wherever you are in urban Britain, it would appear that you are never that far from a closed-circuit television (CCTV) camera. Since the first permanent, public, street surveillance system was installed in Bournemouth in 1985 (McCahill & Norris, 2002) (following the IRA bombing of the Grand Hotel in Brighton), there has been a steady increase in deployment of CCTV systems in British town centres, resulting in hundreds of millions of pounds being spent on the technology (McCahill & Norris, 2002). There have been some unnerving and perhaps, dubious, claims over the last few years that the average Briton passes 300 cameras each day, but whatever the actual figure, there are many of them (*The Guardian*, 2011; *The Telegraph*, 2013), and they require clear and uncluttered fields of view to operate correctly.

The government-funded urban tree survey, Trees in Towns II, found that conflicts between urban trees and CCTV cameras were raised as being a quite frequent threat to local authority urban tree programmes (Britt & Johnston, 2008). With open-street CCTV now an accepted part of the urban landscape and the perception that it provides an effective response to anti-social behaviour and petty crime, it is not unusual for public opinion to favour the removal of trees where there is a conflict. Existing CCTV cameras should be mapped as part of the site assessment procedure, and the operator contacted to ensure that proposed trees can be planted without conflicting with the camera view-cone.

Outside the dense urban core, some utilities are present above the ground, on support poles, such as telephone lines. Further out, into suburbia, overhead electrical supplies can also occasionally be found. A minimum clearance between overhead electricity infrastructure and trees must be maintained to prevent shorting, so ensuring public safety and continuity of supply. Any required tree management works and required clearances are specified in current standards. For electricity providers, Schedule 4(9) of the Electricity Act 1989 (HM Govt, 1989) enables them to require trees that obstruct or interfere with their equipment to be felled or pruned (it actually refers to felling, 'lopping' and root pruning). For telecommunication providers, Paragraph 19 of the Telecommunications Code (HM Govt, 1984), which is contained within the Telecommunications Act 1984,

Figure 4.10
Directional drilling rig being used to install a new gas main. Boring is complete and the pipe is being drawn back along the bore.

Figure 4.11
Shared underground utilities routes make tree placement much easier to determine and reduce the extent of any later ground disturbance. (Image James Lewis.)

Figure 4.12
Recommended
positioning of utility
apparatus within a
2-m footway.
Reproduced from
NJUG Vol. 1, Issue 8
(NJUG Publications,
2013).

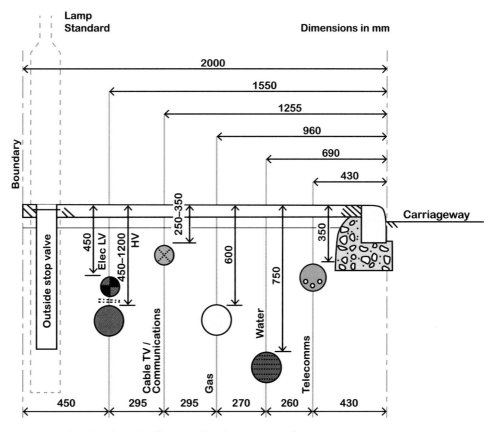

Positioning of utility supplies in two metre footway

under Schedule 2, also allows for trees to be pruned (although it also unfortunately refers to 'lopping'), which obstruct or interfere with the provider's apparatus. It is important to ensure that any tree work is carried out to the highest standard, by competent operatives. In the UK, contractors should be approved by the Arboricultural Association.

4.5 ROOF STRUCTURES AND PODIUM DECKS

The design and construction requirements for planting located on roof structures and podium decks is covered in more detail in Chapter 6. However, in terms of site assessment, the location of structural restrictions and opportunities should be located and recorded. It should be borne in mind that any tree planting in such locations is likely to require some negotiation with a structural engineer to determine what loadings are possible on the structure and what

Figure 4.13
Roadside oak tree pruned around overhead utility lines. Utility providers have the power to prune, lop or even fell trees that interfere with their equipment.

strengthening is required. Most roofs and podium decks are supported on a rectilinear grid of columns. The locations of these columns is likely to be worth determining and recording.

4.6 EXISTING VEGETATION

Existing vegetation can provide clues as to the existing ground conditions, in terms of drainage, soil pH, plant-available nutrients, soil disturbance, and so on. Telltale signs such as yellowing or scorching of the leaves, branch dieback, early autumn colouration and leaf-drop may be observed. Visual inspection of the annual extension growth should be carried out as another indication of vigour and overall health. By looking at successive years of extension growth, from the current terminal bud, a history of plant vigour can be determined. Any worrying signs should be investigated further to establish the cause of the potential problem, so that any remedial action can be taken prior to new planting being implemented.

Existing trees should also be checked for any visible mechanical damage and possible structural problems, such as weak branch forks, co-dominant stems and connections with in-cluded bark. Structural instability, mower and machinery damage to stems and signs of vandalism may be severe enough to recommend that some existing planting is replaced as part of the new planting scheme.

In addition to an overall knowledge of pest and disease prevalence nationally, the incidence of local pests and diseases should be determined from the existing vegetation present (see also Chapter 7, Disorders, pests and diseases).

Existing vegetation can compete with any proposed new planting for water, light and nutrients. The extent of vegetation cover should be recorded and species identified, so that an assessment of the likely impacts can be made. Existing tree cover should be assessed to determine the availability of space to allow crown development of the proposed planting. A tree survey to BS 5837 would provide sufficient data collection to enable these assessments to be made as desktop studies. The existing trees may not be fully mature, so an additional assessment may be required to determine the likely ultimate tree size.

4.6.1 Urban tree diversity

Rather than being restricted to a limited species range, which may already exist locally, a new planting scheme could provide an opportunity to broaden the species palette and encourage greater diversity within the local tree population. Such diversity can be shown to provide resilience to that population in terms of its capacity to recover quickly from stresses caused by perturbations (Bassuk, 1990; Santamour, 1990; Raupp, Cumming & Raupp, 2006; Lacan & McBride, 2008). That said, in natural systems ecology, higher diversity is often attributed to the so-called, mosaic, patchwork communities that are affected by random disturbances, such as windthrow, fire, disease and so on. Typically, diversity increases following disturbance and then settles down, as a few large, long-lived species dominate. Typically, urban landscapes are being constantly disturbed and impacted upon by a variety of stresses, and climate change is likely to exacerbate the intensity of these stresses and disturbances. There is logic, therefore, in treating urban landscapes as disturbed ecosystems under stress.

Studies in ecology show us that several indices for calculating biodiversity have been proposed over many decades. From these, Simpson's index (Simpson, 1949) and Shannon–Wiener's (Shannon–Weaver or Shannon) index (Shannon & Weaver, 1949) appear to be the best known and have proved to be persistent. The diversity of biological communities is a reflection of the overall number of species present (species richness) and their relative abundance (species dominance or evenness). Such diversity indices are useful tools for analysing these attributes. Various benchmarks have been proposed as aids to help manage relative abundance as a proxy for urban tree diversity. Barker (Barker, 1975) suggested that a maximum of 5 per cent of any single tree species be present within any urban tree population. This has proved difficult to achieve in many urban landscapes, and a 'common sense' benchmark, proposed by the late Dr Frank Santamour, Research Geneticist at the US National Arboretum in Washington, DC, has become fairly universally adopted instead (Santamour, 1990). This came to be known as the 10–20–30 rule and requires that any urban tree planting should contain the following:

1   no more than 10 per cent of any single tree species
2   no more than 20 per cent of species in any single tree genus
3   no more than 30 per cent of species in an single tree family.

While it is likely that urban tree diversity has increased as a consequence of adopting the Santamour rule, there appears to be no empirical evidence for it.

An Australian study (Kendal, Dobbs & Lohr, 2014) measured the relative abundance of the most common species, genus and family within urban tree populations from around the world and found this to be a useful indicator of diversity when compared to Shannon index calculations. This suggests that diversity can be fairly simply assessed by urban forest managers, from tree inventory data, without any requirement for complicated statistical analysis. They also found that temperate climate urban forests over areas of differing land use already perform as well or even better than the Santamour 10–20–30 rule and may require a more focussed set of aims, if diversity is to be appreciably increased. Conversely, city streetscapes, especially in continental climates, showed low diversity among their tree populations. A dogmatic application of the 10–20–30 rule in such locations is likely to fail and could, ironically, cause species well-adapted to urban conditions, and so performing well to be replaced by unproven selections of unknown functional success, purely as a way to increase species diversity. It makes more sense to properly assess the site and select trees that are best-suited to the particular conditions – a 'right tree, right place' approach – rather than strive for numerical diversity standards alone (Bassuk, 1990; Richards, 1993).

As tree pests and diseases tend to be fairly selective, such an approach to increase diversity is intended to provide some protection from catastrophic tree loss such as that experienced in Europe and North America with Dutch elm disease in the 1960s and 1970s (see Chapter 7, Disorders, pests and diseases). In addition, there are other good reasons to promote an increase in diversity within urban tree planting. If an increase in diversity provides a corresponding increase in resilience to emerging threats and changing conditions, the predicted effects of climate change on existing urban tree species could be addressed (Forestry Commission, 2011). Biological diversity also appears to enhance the resilience of ecosystem service provision in systems that are subject to change, by buffering the impact that disturbances have on urban ecosystems (Elmqvist *et al.*, 2003; McPhearson, Andersson, Elmqvist & Frantzeskaki, 2015). That said, existing mature tree planting can inform local landscape and townscape character. Some of our urban parks and squares would not provide the same quality of space, were it not for the large London plane sentinels, which grow so well in such situations, but are all produced from a very small number of clones. What we will do if massaria disease becomes more established and plane canker stain makes an appearance in the UK, perhaps, does not bear thinking about. Where possible, existing tree populations should be retained, managed and enhanced with additional and supplementary planting. Informed designers will not only have an appreciation of the identifiable benefits and services provided by green infrastructure, but also an understanding of the local context. Any new planting must respect the relationship between existing planting and the local landscape and heritage character.

4.7 SOIL ANALYSIS

As discussed in Chapter 3, available soils in many urban settings are often not native, but highly disturbed, compacted, sometimes contaminated and often containing construction remnants. Demolition and construction materials containing cement or lime are highly alkaline, and their presence in soil will often cause pH levels to be elevated above those acceptable to many plants. If such materials are found to be present and soil pH is high, it is obviously important to make use of lime-tolerant tree species.

It is likely that a complete suite of tests will be commissioned from a soil consultant or analytical soil laboratory (see Appendix 2). However, a useful assessment can usually be made on site by excavating your own series of trial holes to observe soil texture, structure, compaction, bulk density and drainage. Once clearance to break ground has been given by the site owner or the main contractor and the area scanned for utilities and services, small profile pits can be excavated by machine or by hand as appropriate. Soil samples for analysis can be collected as detailed in Appendix 2 and put to one side. A fairly accurate approximation of soil pH can be determined on site using a British Drug House or similar soil test kit. Throughout the excavation, any unpleasant odours should be noted and the sides of the pit observed for signs of disturbance, defined strata and blue or grey mottling. As we have already seen, a gradual and indistinct transition from dark, organic topsoil to paler subsoil is typical of the brown earths found in many lowland and agricultural areas. In urban locations, it is quite common to observe distinct banding or strata, both horizontal and vertical, showing little sign of gradual transition, due to previous disturbances from excavation and filling. The depth of observable topsoil should be recorded along with any distinct strata, making any assessment of the material that makes up these strata as is possible. It may be, for instance, that existing topsoil has been buried beneath a layer of granular fill and then capped with imported topsoil. Alternatively, a site may have been subject to wholesale excavation and soil stripping, resulting in a reduced final level. If a layer of imported topsoil is spread across an area where the topsoil and some subsoil have been removed, it will take many years for mixing of the materials to take place at their interface. (The soil profile can change rapidly across disturbed areas. See Chapter 3, Urban soils and functional trees, for more information.)

Soil texture can be determined onsite by carrying out a simple *texture by feel* test (see Appendix 4). This involves moulding a small amount of moistened soil in the hand to determine how plastic it is and relies on the fact that the higher the silt and clay content, the more plastic is its behaviour. A palm-full of soil, about the size of a small hen's egg, is gradually moistened with water and kneaded in the hand until it becomes fairly smooth and malleable, like moist putty. Any organic matter and large fragments, such as stones and roots, will need to be removed and discarded. The soil should be first moulded into a ball shape and squeezed tightly, to remove any excess moisture. Appendix 4 shows a method of interpretation devised by ADAS (formerly, the Agricultural Development and Advisory Service, advising the government on agricultural fishery and food matters before becoming a privatised environmental consultancy company in 1997).

4.7.1 Properties of soils at different textures

Table 4.2 shows the general physical properties of typical soils in a given textural class. Note that no one soil provides ideal physical properties in every category; some compromise must be made. A sandy loam (bold) is generally considered to be the best compromise for landscape purposes, as it does not readily compact, it holds moisture and is fairly free-draining.

As discussed in Chapter 3, Urban soils and functional trees, saturated hydraulic conductivity provides a quantitative measurement of the ease with which the pores within a saturated soil allow water movement. In this context, it provides an indication of permeability.

To give some perspective, a saturated hydraulic conductivity of 150 mm/hr could be expected in a very sandy soil and is the minimum requirement for USGA putting green root zones (USGA, 2015). Between 10 mm/hr and 150 mm/hr could be expected in moderately to well-drained soils, suitable for most planting sites requiring good drainage. Between 1.8 mm/hr and 0.7 mm/hr is typically found in fine-textured, compacted or poorly structured soils, which are difficult to use for planting (Brady & Weil, 2008).

The ease and speed at which water passes through soil is quite an important assessment to make for potential planting sites. Blue or grey mottling or banding (usually referred to as gleying), invariably accompanied by a foetid or unpleasant odour, suggests occasional water-logging and poor drainage. An indication of drainage potential can be fairly easily determined onsite by carrying out a simple percolation test. First, excavate a 300-mm square hole, 300–450 mm deep and place the soil to one side, away from the excavation. Fill the hole with water and thoroughly wet a 300 mm strip of ground around the hole. If the ground is very dry, you may need to carry out this stage in the process a couple of times. When you are sure that the ground is virtually saturated, fill the hole with water again, measure and record the depth of water. After 15 min, again measure the depth of water. Subtract the second reading from the first to give the water drained in 15 min. Multiply this by four to give water drained per hour. The soil can be compared to the following drainage rates:

- if less than 100 mm per hour, drainage is poor
- if between 100 mm and 200 mm per hour, drainage is moderate
- if greater than 200 mm per hour, drainage is excessive.

(Trowbridge & Bassuk, 2004)

Table 4.2
Typical indicative soil qualities for different textural classes. A sandy loam is generally considered to be the best 'all-round' compromise for general landscape purposes

Soil texture	Susceptibility to compaction	Nutrient-holding capacity	Plant-available water	Permeability
Sand	Very limited	Limited	Limited	Substantial
Loamy sand	Limited	Limited	Limited to moderate	Substantial
Sandy loam	**Limited to moderate**	**Moderate**	**Moderate**	**Moderate**
Sandy silt-loam	Moderate	Moderate to substantial	Substantial	Moderate
Silt-loam	Substantial	Substantial	Substantial	Moderate
Clay-loam	Substantial	Substantial	Moderate to substantial	Limited
Clay	Substantial	Substantial	Moderate	Very limited

Figure 4.15
A simple approximation of soil bulk density can be made by following one of the procedures referred to above. Here, a small excavated hole has been lined with plastic food wrap film and then filled with water. The volume of water required to fill the hole is recorded.

Figure 4.14
A simple percolation assessment can be carried out onsite by excavating a small hole and following the procedure as set out above.

It is not uncommon, in highly disturbed sites, to encounter layers of granular fill, utility corridors, old drainage pipes and so on. Water will occasionally disappear before the depth can be measured. If this does happen, the test will need to be repeated in another nearby location to determine the extent of any highly porous and free-draining zones. Such incidences must be recorded on a plan to enable further investigation.

Another simple field test can be used to make an assessment of soil bulk density. Bulk density (also known as *soil density* and *dry density*) is defined as the ratio of dry soil mass to bulk soil volume, including pore spaces. We have seen in Chapter 3, Urban soils and functional trees, that root growth is inhibited at particular soil densities, in particular soil texture types. It is, therefore, important to know what the soil texture is to enable correct interpretation of the bulk density results.

The volume extraction technique is often used by soil engineers to make a close approximation of bulk density (Lichter & Costello, 1994), and an adaption of this technique from Trowbridge and Bassuk (Trowbridge & Bassuk, 2004) is shown here. A very similar procedure is also shown in *Soil Quality Test Kit Guide* (USDA, NRCS, 2001), which is downloadable from the USDA Natural Resources Conservation Service website.

A small hole, approximately 150 mm deep and 150 mm diameter, is dug and the soil extracted is placed in a sturdy container (such as a bucket with a lid or an empty food storage container). The excavated hole is carefully lined with a plastic bag or plastic food wrap film and filled to the brim with water. The exact volume of water required to fill the hole must be recorded.

The extracted soil is dried in an oven for a minimum of 8 hrs at 105°C and weighed. Bulk density is calculated by dividing the soil dry weight (in gm) by the extracted soil volume (in cu. cm). Some allowance should be made for any coarse stones and gravel within the extracted sample. The preference is for these to be sieved from the extracted soil sample onsite, if it is sufficiently dry, and simply returned to the excavated hole, on top of the plastic lining, prior to filling the hole with water. Alternatively, they can be sieved from the dried soil sample and their volume subtracted from the water volume, before calculating the bulk density (USDA, NRCS, 2001).

4.8   CONTAMINATION

In this context, contamination is caused by a substance that is in, on or under the ground, and which has the potential to cause harm or to cause pollution of controlled waters (Environment Agency, 2004). Most brownfield sites, especially land previously used for industrial processes, and the treatment and disposal of waste materials, are fairly likely to be affected by some sort of soil contamination and should be assumed to be as such until proven to be otherwise. The typical suite of contaminants tested for by certified soil analysis laboratories is shown in Appendix 2. A study of the site history, the typical suite of site investigations, along with an appropriate risk assessment should identify types and levels of contaminants, the likely receptors (people, systems, property or water bodies likely to be affected), the likely pathways (the means by which a receptor can be exposed to, or affected by, a contaminant), and so, the likely level of risk. From this, an informed decision can be made as to whether the risk is acceptable or whether it is considered to be unacceptable and needs to be treated. If the latter is the case, then the alternatives are either to remove the contamination and send it to controlled landfill (so-called 'dig and dump'), remove it and send it for treatment in an offsite facility, returning it when treated or remediate it onsite (see Olympic Park case study in Chapter 3). Only once the risks have been identified and quantified, can the options be appraised and any removal or remediation measures decided upon and implemented.

4.9   MICROCLIMATE WITHIN THE BUILT ENVIRONMENT

Many of our cities comprise dense assemblages of tall buildings, often arranged within a structured, orthogonal grid. Assessment must be made of the existing built form to establish shading, wind funnelling and rain shadow. Existing land use should be recorded, and where changes are to be made, proposed activities assessed with a view to establishing the most efficacious locations for additional tree planting.

4.9.1   Light and shade

Tall, bulky building masses will cast correspondingly large shadows and can create areas on the ground and at considerable height above it, which remain in shadow for the majority, and sometimes the entirety of the day, even in summer. As there is a linear relationship between the logarithm of light intensity reaching the leaves and net assimilation rate (Blackman & Rutter, 1948) (as a measure of rate of photosynthesis over the mean rate of respiration (Watson & Hayashi, 1965)), plants growing in such positions may not grow as well as expected. Some species will not grow happily at all if kept in constant shade. If building height data are available, shade analysis can be carried out as a desktop study; otherwise, an assessment can often simply be made onsite, recording shadow lengths at different times of day, with allowance made for seasonal variation, which dramatically alters the shade pattern.

Table 4.3
Illuminance values from various sources and requirements for plants. Adapted from Helliwell (2013) and from Harris, Clark and Matheny (2004). Cloudy refers to 50% cloud cover or 100% thin cloud with sun just visible. These figures are approximations and should be treated as such. They do, however, provide a useful comparison

	Value (lux)
Full midsummer sun at noon	
London (51.5°N) the sun is at an elevation of 62°	102,000
Manchester (53.5°N) the sun is at an elevation of 60°	100,000
Edinburgh (56°N) the sun is at an elevation of 57.5°	80,000
Full midwinter sun at noon	
London (51.5°N) the sun is at an elevation of 15°	22,000
Manchester (53.5°N) the sun is at an elevation of 13°	19,000
Edinburgh (56°N) the sun is at an elevation of 10.5°	15,000
Cloudy midsummer day at noon	
London (51.5°N) the sun is at an elevation of 62°	44,000
Manchester (53.5°N) the sun is at an elevation of 60°	44,000
Edinburgh (56°N) the sun is at an elevation of 57.5°	43,600
Cloudy midwinter day at noon	
London (51.5°N) the sun is at an elevation of 15°	18,000
Manchester (53.5°N) the sun is at an elevation of 13°	15,000
Edinburgh (56°N) the sun is at an elevation of 10.5°	12,000
Heavily overcast midwinter day at noon	
London (51.5°N) the sun is at an elevation of 15°	1,800
Manchester (53.5°N) the sun is at an elevation of 13°	1,500
Edinburgh (56°N) the sun is at an elevation of 10.5°	1,200
Shady side of a two-storey building (sunny) in midsummer	
London (51.5°N) the sun is at an elevation of 62°	22,000
Manchester (53.5°N) the sun is at an elevation of 60°	22,000
Edinburgh (56°N) the sun is at an elevation of 57.5°	21,000
Shady side of a two-storey building in midwinter	
London (51.5°N) the sun is at an elevation of 15°	2,300
Manchester (53.5°N) the sun is at an elevation of 13°	1,900
Edinburgh (56°N) the sun is at an elevation of 10.5°	1,500
External illuminance on an 'overcast' winter day – the benchmark for daylight design	5,000
Moonlight	0.22
Adequate for most plants	28,000–56,000
Shade plants	7,000–11,000
Indoor illuminance suitable for reading	200–300
Incandescent light bulb (100 W with 225 mm reflector at 1.5 m)	240
Fluorescent: Deluxe cool white (150 W at 1.5 m)	1,050

SO WHAT?

The use of glass and other reflective surfaces in building construction results in light being bounced around some locations in unexpected ways. An extreme case of this became apparent when it was reported in the summer of 2013 that the curved glass façade of Rafael Viñoly's tower at 20 Fenchurch Street in London, dubbed the Walkie Talkie, reflected energy from the sun so intensely that it melted plastic body parts on a Jaguar car parked nearby. The developer, Land Securities, was required to apply external solar shading to prevent the problem reoccurring (Guardian News and Media Limited, 2013).

Table 4.4
Typical amounts of light permeating a variety of tree canopies. From Helliwell (2013), data collated from Ovington and Madgwick (1955) and other sources

Species	Percentage light under an unbroken canopy, in full leaf
Betula pendula	7
Fraxinus excelsior	5
Quercus petraea	5
Acer pseudoplatanus	3
Fagus sylvatica	2
Pinus sylvestris	4
Pseudotsuga menziesii	5
Picea abies	1
Thuja plicata	1
Abies grandis	1
Tsuga heterophylla	0.5

Light levels can be determined onsite with a light meter, although this is likely to provide results for illuminance, measured in lux rather than give any measure of light quality or adequacy of photosynthetically active radiation (PAR) for plant growth. That said, assuming that the light source being assessed is the sun only, an idea of likely plant response is possible to be determined. As can be seen in Table 4.3, the light requirements for a plant to photosynthesise effectively are significantly less than that available during a clear summer day and has some parity with the light available on overcast days. It should not be forgotten that in all parts of the British Isles the sun is, on average, obscured by cloud more often than it is not. Diffuse light, therefore, is quite common and is the dependable source of energy for many plants. As discussed in Chapter 2, Tree structures and function, diffuse light, by nature of it being scattered rather than directional, is able to be captured by more leaves, and so, enhances the photosynthetic efficiency of the tree canopy.

The shade cast by existing trees will usually be a consideration. Most tree survey computer packages can be used to model shade patterns if required (Keysoft Solutions, 2014; Skellern, 2014).

Shade cast by new trees, as they mature, can sometimes be a consideration when making species selections for particular locations. It is important to be aware of potential conflicts when selecting potential tree positions with provision of shading and protection from wind in mind. If deciduous trees are planted to the south and west of buildings, they can be used to provide summer shading from a full canopy, so assisting in building cooling, while also allowing winter solar gain when the trees are without leaves. Evergreen species may be more appropriate for planting to the north and north-east of buildings, where they can provide protection from cold winter winds, blowing in from Arctic and Scandinavian regions to the north (McPherson et al., 2002).

Helliwell (2013) has helpfully collated data from various sources to provide an indication of the percentage of sunlight that could be expected to pass through the canopies of a variety of trees species. Much of this data comes from the work carried out by Ovington and Madgwick (1955) at the Bedgebury National Pinetum in Kent. These measurements were taken within forestry plantations, and so, will not necessarily reflect typical amounts found beneath single trees. A comparison between species and between deciduous and evergreen, however, is useful.

It should be noted that these figures vary significantly from those shown in Appendix H of the BRE report 209: Site Layout Planning for Daylight and Sunlight (Littlefair, 2011). There have been some questions raised regarding the accuracy of the BRE figures, which show Acer pseudoplatanus, Fagus sylvatica, Quercus robur and Betula pendula all having the same optical transparency of 20 per cent when in full leaf. Most people, with any experience of trees, are unlikely to agree with that observation. Littlefair does concede that the figures are averages from a variety of sources that showed considerable divergence in some of the values, and so, should be treated with caution. It is also worth pointing out that even leafless trees can reduce the amount of light passing through them. This can be as much as 50 per cent to 75 per cent, depending on the density of branches.

4.9.2   Urban security and street lighting

From Chapter 2, we know that day length is implicated in several plant responses such as flowering, branching, dormancy and others. Controlling the duration of exposure to light either by shading or by using supplementary lighting has been a standard commercial horticultural practice for many years, as a way to extend the cropping season of mainly flowering crops. Street lighting is designed and implemented to provide light for human utility, comfort and safety. Some interest and concern have been raised in recent years regarding the possible ecological consequences of growth in the distribution and intensity of artificial night lighting (Longcore & Rich, 2004).

Although the quality (wavelength) of light from street and security illuminations is not likely to be high enough or of sufficient intensity to allow significant photosynthesis, even fairly low-level light can have a locally noticeable effect on tree species that are sensitive to day length. It is not uncommon to see trees growing closest to street lights retaining their leaves longer than others around them, which have lost theirs through normal seasonal leaf fall (Matzke, 1936). Winslow Briggs records observations of *Platanus* trees growing close to street lights on the University of California, Berkeley campus, often keeping their leaves 'into late fall and winter, while branches of trees somewhat further away lose their leaves'.

'Likewise, Liquidambar trees growing on the Stamford University campus show a response to street lighting. One tree had a full complement of leaves (although partially senescent and brightly coloured) in February 2002 on the side of the tree toward a streetlight. Only a few metres away, on the other side of the tree, all the leaves had long since dropped.'

'Thus the effect of the streetlight was highly localised. The light intensity dropped below a threshold value within a couple of metres. Although these examples show the effects of outdoor lighting on tree physiology, it is not possible to know the consequences this influence has for the plant. The light may extend the period during which photosynthesis can take place, if only trivially, or prevent dormancy and expose the tree to the somewhat harsher climate of the winter months while it is still physiologically active' (Briggs, 2006).

It has been shown that night time lighting can inhibit dormancy and promote a continuation in growth or shoot elongation in some tree species, by overriding the more natural environmental triggers for a slowing or cessation in growth, such as a reduction in sunlight hours (Cathey & Campbell, 1975).

Different species vary greatly in their response to light source duration and intensity, but some tree species have been shown to continue growing well into autumn and beyond, preventing typical ripening of shoots, and so exposing them to late season frost injury. Cathey and Campbell report that *Platanus* x *hispanica*, *Acer platanoides*, *Betula*, *Catalpa*, *Ulmus* and *Zelkova* all appear to be highly sensitive to security and street lighting. Continuous access to light can also depress the formation and maintenance of chlorophyll and promote the expansion of leaf area, making trees sensitive to chemical pollution during the growing season. During periods of elevated air pollution levels, leaves subject to supplemental lighting can give the appearance of being coated in oil. The inter-veinal regions will often be pale green or white in colour, and leaf margins can become dry and necrotic before the leaves die and fall (Cathey & Campbell, 1975). To an inexperienced observer, these physical signs could be confused with pest or disease symptoms.

4.9.3 Wind

Where buildings are positioned in close proximity, wind can be funnelled into the gaps between them, increasing speed and energy. Wind can also be deflected down, towards the ground, by tall buildings, creating unusual, concentrated air movements around their bases. Architects will often include canopies and other wind barriers around building entrances where this is likely to be a problem. In March 2011, a tragic accident occurred outside the Bridgewater Place tower in Leeds, when 'extreme winds' picked up a 7.5-t heavy goods vehicle 'like a hot-air balloon', fatally crushing a pedestrian when it came to rest (BBC, 2012). Prior to the accident, pedestrians had already raised concerns about being blown into the path of vehicles by high gusts of wind (Building Design, 2012). It is planned to make alterations to the exterior of the building, such as vertical screens, canopies and pole-mounted baffles, to mitigate the effects of the wind (Building Design, 2014).

Increased wind speeds, especially where the air has been warmed by radiated urban heat, increase the demand on plant-available water by increasing the rate of leaf evapotranspiration. An assessment should be made of the likely impacts on any new tree planting.

Figure 4.16
The use of large canopy species trees planted close to buildings will likely require frequent pruning, as shown in the left-hand image. Sometimes, a more upright form, such as this columnar *Acer platanoides* in the right-hand image, may be a more suitable selection.

Buildings can also have a marked impact on how rain falls on the ground. Tall or closely packed buildings can create quite significant rain shadows, while overhangs and awnings will prevent rainwater landing at or close to tree planters. Where urban trees are surrounded by impermeable hard surfaces and with restricted access to ground water, this can have a fundamental effect on plant-available water, requiring ongoing irrigation to address the balance.

4.9.4 Temperature

The urban heat island effect is caused by shortwave radiation from the sun being absorbed by large building masses and areas of hard surfacing and either reflected or radiated as long-wave radiation or heat. This phenomenon can have fundamental impacts on both users and vegetation, with temperatures being raised typically by 6–8°C, relative to outlying rural areas. Climate change modelling predicts a greater likelihood of more of what are currently considered extreme weather events, and this can only exacerbate the situation.

Roots have been shown to be killed by a single 4-h exposure to temperatures between 40°C and 45°C. Trees growing in raised planters or surrounded by hard, heat absorbing surfaces are likely to be more susceptible than those growing in soft areas. Building façades and hard paving surfaces can reflect and re-radiate stored heat, raising the temperature of the vegetation and causing an increase in water demand. This cannot always be satisfied by the moisture present in the root zone available to the plants.

Low temperatures must also be taken into account. Wind funnelling can exacerbate the cooling effects of winter winds that come in from the north and north-east, bringing with them cold Arctic air from northern Europe, Scandinavia and the Arctic Ocean. The temperature can drop very quickly and cause damage to the plant tissue. Wind will also accelerate the loss of moisture from plants, which can be especially problematic with evergreens. Severe freeze–thaw

SO WHAT?

Trowbridge and Bassuk refer to a row of green ash trees growing alongside a highway in Ithaca, upstate New York, and planted within a short distance of a large, south-facing masonry wall, in a compacted soil. The surface temperature of the wall was measured at 52°C (125°F) on a sunny 22°C (72°F) summer day. The reflected and re-radiated heat from the wall and surrounding hard surfaces placed such a transpiration demand on the trees that they could not take up sufficient water from the soil available to them, causing them to lose their leaves two or three times every summer. In response and as a measure to save the trees, the soil around the tree roots was modified by fracturing to a depth of 30–40 cm with an excavator, allowing them greater access to soil water. As a result, summer defoliation ceased immediately (Trowbridge & Bassuk, 2004). In this example, the soil surface was mulched with shredded bark to retain moisture. Since this work, it has been found that better results can be achieved using an excavator to incorporate bulky, composted green waste through the topsoil profile using the scoop and dump method. A 15-cm thick layer of composted material is placed over the entire surface of the site, and systematically using a mechanical excavator, approximately 45 cm of the resident soil and compost is excavated and dropped from a height to both shatter the soil and mix the compost through the profile. The site is then roughly levelled by hand-raking, and trees and shrubs are planted directly into the remediated soil. Shredded bark mulch is applied after planting and maintained to a depth of 5–7.5 cm each year (Bassuk (e-mail), personal communication, 24 June 2015).

cycles can be particularly damaging during cloudless periods in the winter, when the temperature drops rapidly at night, due to no cloud insulation, and increases during the day due to the sun. Evergreen species can be particularly hard hit in conditions where the soil is frozen for any length of time, especially if the cloud cover is thin or absent. Plants may actively try to transpire, but because the soil water is frozen, and so not available, water uptake by the roots is unable to match demand from transpirational loss. As a result, the foliage may dehydrate and die, having the appearance of being burned. Winds will only exacerbate the situation, by promoting heat loss from the soil and water loss from the leaves. Plants growing in raised planters or containers are likely to be more affected by the cold because they do not benefit from any temperature buffering provided by large volumes of soil. The smaller the soil volume available for rooting, the more pronounced the effects of fluctuating temperature are likely to be.

Frost pockets or traps, although more often considered in rural landscapes, can be a problem in some urban conditions. Cold air is denser than warm air, and so sinks, often moving down slopes and accumulating in low points where there is no means of escape. Such situations can be exacerbated in urban settings if shading from surrounding buildings prevents sunlight reaching the enclosed area. It is, therefore, essential that the correct species is selected for specific planting sites, rather than aiming to provide any form of protective management. Frost pockets can sometimes be avoided or eliminated by careful design of building groups, earth modelling or thick tree groups, enabling cold air to drain away.

4.10 CLIMATE CHANGE

If our planting is intended to mitigate against the effects of climate change, and it should, then we will need to select trees with the potential to adapt to climate change, if the benefits they can provide are to be realised. In addition, we must be choosing plants that are also able to grow well in current conditions, preceding future, predicted climate change effects. It is possible, for example, that the average temperature changes in some climate change models may alter the normal patterns of winter chilling, which could, in turn, affect onset of winter dormancy and emergence in the spring. Many trees species require certain periods of low temperatures to fulfil their chilling needs, only after which buds are able to break when temperatures rise sufficiently. This requirement can be as much as 8 weeks of low temperatures between –4° and 10°C (Harris, Clark & Matheny, 2004).

One prediction is that summer droughts are likely to become more frequent and more severe. This will not only affect the immediate establishment success of new planting, but is also likely to have a fundamental influence on existing planting. The almost inevitable increase in physiological stress experienced by urban trees and other green infrastructure is likely to predispose them to greater incidences of pests and diseases. There is also the likelihood that the expected changes in climate will produce more favourable conditions for some native and exotic pest and disease species (Tubby & Webber, 2010).

Some researchers are turning their attention to the sourcing of plant stock from geographic regions that experience similar conditions to those typically found in urban landscapes (Sjöman, 2012). Selected plants from habitats that share environmental traits common to urban planting sites may be thought likely to possess certain characteristics that allow them to respond best to the local site conditions. This 'right plant, right place' philosophy may well ignore the geographic origin of plant species selected on cultural grounds for use in anthropogenic landscapes, placing more importance on plant performance. Such a *fitness to site* approach should reduce the requirements for resource-intensive site modification and ongoing management in an effort to create and maintain suitable growing conditions (Dunnett, 2008). Ferrini *et al.* (2014) and Roloff, Korn and Gillner (2009) suggest taking this further by investigating places where the conditions are comparable with those experienced under predicted climate change. Their research has provided a range of tree species that may be worth investigating for use in UK urban sites.

4.11   URBAN AIR POLLUTION

Photosynthesis, and so net primary production, depends on the atmospheric concentration of carbon dioxide. Therefore, increases in CO_2 levels, as projected using climate change modelling, are likely to lead to increases in plant growth. This is likely to be true up to a tipping point, when climate effects, such as increased temperature and reduced rainfall, take over and cause a net loss in growth (Saxe, Cannell, Johnsen, Ryan & Vourlitis, 2001). Some research has been conducted that looks at atmospheric CO_2 elevation, using juvenile stock, in growth chambers. Perhaps more interestingly, some experiments have looked at entire forest stands using the free-air carbon dioxide enrichment (FACE) technology (Norby, Todd, Fults & Johnson, 2001). FACE experiments have allowed insights into how terrestrial ecosystems may respond to elevated atmospheric CO_2 levels due to predicted climate change. It has been known for some time that elevated CO_2 increases plant growth, but in the Oak Ridge National Laboratory FACE facility in Tennessee (Oak Ridge National Laboratory, 2014), initial increases in net primary production (NPP) were not sustained. As the experiment progressed, NPP began to decline in response to a steadily increasing nitrogen deficiency (Norby & Zak, 2011; Warren, Jensen, Medlyn, Norby & Tissue, 2014). There is more FACE research being conducted at the University of Western Sydney (University of Western Sydney, 2015), where they are studying what remains of the native eucalypt forest, and the University of Birmingham are in the process of setting up a UK facility, which will study the effects of CO_2 enrichment in a mature woodland ecosystem in Norbury, Staffordshire (University of Birmingham, 2015; Donovan, Hamilton, Holmes, MacKenzie & Hewitt 2015).

Some species are known for their emission of biogenic volatile organic compounds (BVOCs) and allergenic pollens. Some thought should be given to species selection in particularly sensitive locations or if improving air quality is the primary motivation for tree planting, to avoid large numbers of high emitting BVOC species being planted together (Donovan *et al.*, 2005).

4.12   STAKEHOLDERS AND LOCAL INTEREST GROUPS

The principle protection protocols affecting the retention of urban trees are tree preservation orders (TPOs) and trees in conservation areas. Forestry law also includes the provision for requiring a felling licence, where large quantities of trees are proposed to be removed, but this legislation was not put in place to protect trees in towns (see Chapter 8, Trees, regulations and law, for further discussion).

The environmental benefits and ecosystem services provided by urban green infrastructure are now widely understood and generally accepted. However, an appreciation of cost–benefit analysis modelling tools can be beneficial when engaging with stakeholders with an interest in fiscal matters.

Local community groups, especially those with an interest in local planning, history, ecology and wildlife, may be consulted in an effort to engage and establish a sense of ownership towards any new planting. This may prove to be especially beneficial when post-installation care, such as watering, is required and can also be a useful means of reducing vandalism. Further, if locations for planting sites could be extended to include those within private land, but adjacent to the public boundary, coupled with a market-based system of incentivised co-management, perhaps stakeholder engagement could be both broadened and intensified (Hale *et al.*, 2015).

REFERENCES

Barker, P. A. (1975). Ordinance control of street trees. *Journal of Arboriculture, 1*(11), 212-16.

Bassuk, N. L. (1990). Street tree diversity making better choices for the urban landscape. *Proceedings of the 7th METRIA Conference, June 11–12, 1990, Lisle, IL*, June. Available at: http://www.ces.ncsu.edu/fletcher/programs/nursery/metria/metria07/m711.pdf.

Bassuk, N. L. (2015). pers.comm. [email](Personal communication, 24 June 2015).

BBC (2012). *Man crushed to death by 'floating' lorry in Leeds*. (Online) Retrieved 29 November 2014 from www.bbc.co.uk/news/uk-england-leeds-16968325.

Blackman, G. E. & Rutter, A. J. (1948). Physiological and ecological studies in the analysis of plant environment: III. The interaction between light intensity and mineral nutrient supply in leaf development and in the net assimilation rate of the bluebell (*Scilla non-scripta*). *Annals of Botany, 12*(1), 1–26. Retrieved from http://aob.oxfordjournals.org/content/12/1/1.full.pdf+html.

Brady, N. C. & Weil, R. C. (2008). *The Nature and Properties of Soils* (14th edn). Upper Saddle River, NJ: Prentice Hall.

Briggs, W. R. (2006). Physiology of plant responses to artificial lighting. In: C. Rich & T. Longcore, eds. *Ecological Consequences of Artificial Night Lighting*. Washington, DC: Island Press, 389-411.

Britt, C. & Johnston, M. (2008). *Trees in Towns II - A new survey of urban trees in England and their condition and management*. London: Department of Communities and Local Government.

BSI (2012). *BS 5837: 2012; Trees in Relation to Design, Demolition and Construction – Recommendations*. London: British Standards Institution.

Building Design (2012). *Aedas won't face manslaughter charge over Leeds tower.* (Online) Retrieved 29 November 2014 from www.bdonline.co.uk/aedas-wont-face-manslaughter-charge-over-leeds-tower/5034820.article.

Building Design (2014). *Chetwoods and TP Bennett lodge plans to fix 'killer' Leeds tower*. (Online) Retrieved 29 November 2014 from www.bdonline.co.uk/chetwoods-and-tp-bennett-lodge-plans-to-fix-%E2%80%98killer%E2%80%99-leeds-tower/5070214.article.

Cathey, H. M. & Campbell, L. E., (1975). Security lighting and its impact on the landscape. *Journal of Arboriculture, 1*(10), 181-187.

Donovan, R. G., Stewart, H. E., Owen, S. M., MacKenzie, A. R. & Hewitt, C. N. (2005). Development and application of an urban tree air quality score for photochemical pollution episodes using the Birmingham, United Kingdom, area as a case study. *Environmental Science and Technology, 39*, 6730–8.

Donovan, R., Hamilton, L., Holmes, D. & MacKenzie, R. (2015). A wood for the future. *The ARB magazine* (171 Winter), 45–7.

Dunnett, N. P. (2008). The dynamic nature of plant communities – Pattern and process in designed plant communities. In N. P. Dunnett & J. D. Hitchmough (eds), *The Dynamic Landscape* (p. 332). London: Taylor & Francis.

Elmqvist, T., Folke, C., Nyström, M., Peterson, G., Bengtsson, J., Walker, B. & Norberg, J. (2003). Response diversity, ecosystem change, and resilience. *Frontiers in Ecology and the Environment, 1*(9), 488–94.

English Nature (2011). *Veteran Trees: A Guide to Good Management (IN13)*. Retrieved 28 June 2015 from http://publications.naturalengland.org.uk/publication/75035.

Environment Agency (2004). *Environmental Management – Guidance Model Procedures for the Management of Land Contamination (CLR11)*. Retrieved 29 June Monday 2015 from www.gov.uk/government/uploads/system/uploads/attachment_data/file/297401/scho0804bibr-e-e.pdf.

Environmental Audit Committee (2010). *Fifth Report: Air Quality*. London: The Stationery Office.

Ferrini, F., Bussotti, F., Tattini, M. & Fini, A. (2014). Trees in the urban environment: Response mechanisms and benefits for the ecosystem should guide plant selection for future plantings. *Agrochimica, 58*(3), 234–46.

Forestry Commission (2011). *Forests and Climate Change. UK Forestry Standard Guidelines*. Edinburgh: Forestry Commission.

Gerhold, H. D. & Johnson, A. D. (2003). Root dimensions of landscape tree cultivars. *Journal of Arboriculture, 29*(6), 322–6.

Gilman, E. F. (1988). Predicting root spread from trunk diameter and branch spread. *Journal of Arboriculture, 14*(4), 85–9.

Gilman, E. F., Leone, I. A. & Flower, F. B. (1987). Effect of soil compaction and oxygen content on vertical and horizontal root distribution. *Journal of Environmental Horticulture, 5*(1), 33–6.

Gromke, C. (2011). A vegetation modeling concept for building and environmental aerodynamics wind tunnel tests and its application in pollutant dispersion studies. *Environmental Pollution, 159*(8–9), 2094–9.

Gromke, C. & Ruck, B. (2009). On the impact of trees on dispersion processes of traffic emissions in street canyons. *Boundary-Layer Meteorology, 131*(1), 19–34.

Gromke, C., Buccolieri, R., Di Sabatino, S. & Ruck, B. (2008). Dispersion study in a street canyon with tree planting by means of wind tunnel and numerical investigations – Evaluation of CFD data with experimental data. *Atmospheric Environment, 42*(37), 8553–706.

Guardian News and Media (2013). *Walkie Talkie Architect 'Didn't Realise It Was Going to Be So Hot'*. Retrieved 29 November 2014 from www.theguardian.com/artanddesign/2013/sep/06/walkie-talkie-architect-predicted-reflection-sun-rays

Hale, J. D., Pugh, T., Sadler, J. P., Boyko, C. T., Brown, J., Caputo, S., Caserio, M., Coles, R., Farmani, R., Hales, C., Horsey, R., Hunt, D., Leach, J. M., Rogers, C. & MacKenzie, R. (2015). Delivering a Multi-Functional and Resilient Urban Forest. *Sustainability, 7*(4), 4600–24.

Harris, R. W., Clark, J. R. & Matheny, N. (2004). *Arboriculture: Integrated Management of Landscape Trees, Shrubs, and Vines* (4th edn). Upper Saddle River, NJ: Prentice Hall.

Helliwell, R. (2013). Daylight in relation to plant growth and illumination of buildings. *Arboricultural Journal: The International Journal of Urban Forestry, 35*(4), 202–19. Retrieved from http://dx.doi.org/10.1080/03071375.2013.873589.

HM Govt (1984). Telecommunications Act 1984 (c.12). Sch.2 (19). Retrieved 30 March 2015 from www.legislation.gov.uk/ukpga/1984/12/schedule/2

HM Govt (1989). Electricity Act 1989 (c.8). Sch.4 (9). London: HMSO. Retrieved 30 March 2015 from www.legislation.gov.uk/ukpga/1989/29/schedule/4/paragraph/9

Jack-Scott, E., Piana, M., Troxel, B., Murphy-Dunning, C. & Ashton, M. S. (2013). Stewardship success: How community group dynamics affect urban street tree survival and growth. *Arboriculture & Urban Forestry, 39*(4), 189–96.

Kendal, D., Dobbs, C. & Lohr, V. I. (2014). Global patterns of diversity in the urban forest: Is there evidence to support the 10/20/30 rule? *Urban Forestry and Urban Greening, 13*, 411–7.

Keysoft Solutions (2014). *KeyTREE*. Retrieved 29 November 2014 from http://keysoftsolutions.com/landscape/products/keytree/.

Lacan, I. & McBride, J. R. (2008). Pest Vulnerability Matrix (PVM): A graphic model for assessing the interaction between tree species diversity and urban forest susceptibility to insects and diseases. *Urban Forestry & Urban Greening, 7*(4), 291–300. doi:10.1016/j.ufug.2008.06.002

Lichter, J. M. & Costello, L. R. (1994). An evaluation of volume excavation and core sampling tehniques for measuring soil bulk density. *Journal of Arboriculture, 20*(3), 160–4.

Littlefair, P. J. (2011). *Site Layout Planning for Daylight and Sunlight, BR 209*. Watford, UK: IHS BRE Press.

Longcore, T. & Rich, C. (2004). Ecological light pollution. *Frontiers in Ecology and the Environment, 2*(4), 191–8.

Lyytimäki, J. & Sipilä, M. (2009). Hopping on one leg – The challenge of ecosystem disservices for urban green management. *Urban Forestry and Urban Greening, 8*, 309–15.

Mapping the Underworld. (2012). *Mapping the Underworld*. Retrieved 18 July 2015 from www.mappingtheunderworld.ac.uk/MTU Brochure Final Version.pdf.

Matzke, B. E. (1936). The effect of street lights in delaying leaf-fall in certain trees. *American Journal of Botany, 23*(6), 446–52.

McCahill, M. & Norris, C. (2002). *CCTV in Britain, Working Paper Number 3*. Retrieved 29 March 2015 from www.urbaneye.net/results/ue_wp3.pdf.

McPhearson, T., Andersson, E., Elmqvist, T. & Frantzeskaki, N. (2015). Resilience of and through urban ecosystem services. *Ecosystem Services, 12*, 152–6.

McPherson, E. G., Maco, S. E., Simpson, J. R., Peper, P. J., Xiao, Q., VanDerZanden, A. & Bell, N. (2002). *Western Washington and Oregon Community Tree Guide: Benefits, Costs and Strategic Planning*. Silverton, OR: International Society of Arboriculture, Pacific Northwest Chapter.

NJUG (2007). *NJUG Publications*. Retrieved 30 March 2015 from www.njug.org.uk/d/www.njug.org.uk/wp-content/uploads/V4-Trees-Issue-2-16-11-2007.pdf.

NJUG (2009a). *NJUG Case Study 16: Savings through Trenchless Techniques*. Retrieved 30 March 2015 from www.njug.org.uk/wp-content/uploads/145.pdf.

NJUG (2009b). *NJUG Case Study 19 – Vacuum Excavator*. Retrieved 30 March 2015 from www.njug.org.uk/wp-content/uploads/149.pdf.

NJUG (2013). *Volume 1: NJUG Guidelines on the Positioning and Colour Coding of Underground Utilities' Apparatus*. London: National Joint Utilities Group. Retrieved from www.njug.org.uk/document-download/?URL= www.njug.org.uk/wp-content/uploads/V1-Positioning-Colour-Coding-Issue-8.pdf.

Norby, R. J. & Zak, D. R. (2011). Ecological lessons from free-air CO_2 enrichment (FACE) experiments. *The Annual Review of Ecology, Evolution, and Systematics, 42*, 181–203.

Norby, R. J., Todd, D. E., Fults, J. & Johnson, D. W. (2001). Allometric determination of tree growth in a CO_2-enriched sweetgum stand. *New Phytologist, 150*(2), 477–87.

Oak Ridge National Laboratory (2014). *Oak Ridge Experiment on CO_2 Enrichment of Sweetgum*. Retrieved 13 July 2015 from http://face.ornl.gov/index.html.

Ovington, J. D. & Madgwick, H. A. (1955). A comparison of light in different woodlands. *Forestry, 28*(2), 141–6. doi:10.1093/forestry/28.2.141

Pataki, D., Carreiro, M., Cherrier, J., Grulke, N., Jennings, V., Pincetl, S., Pouyat, R., Whitlow, T. & Zipperer, W. (2011). Coupling biogeochemical cycles in urban environments: ecosystem services, green solutions, and misconceptions. *Frontiers in Ecology and the Environment, 9*(1), 27-36.

Quaife, E. J. (14 April 2015), personal communication.

Raupp, M. J., Cumming, A. B. & Raupp, E. C. (2006). Street tree diversity in eastern North America and its potential for tree loss to exotic borers. *Arboriculture & Urban Forestry, 32*(6), 297–304. Retrieved from http://joa.isa-arbor.com/request.asp?JournalID=1&ArticleID=2970&Type=2.

Richards, N. A. (1993). Reasonable guidelines for street tree diversity. *Journal of Arboriculture, 19*(6), 344–50.

Roloff, A., Korn, S. & Gillner, S. (2009). The Climate-Species-Matrix to select tree species fo rurban habitats considering climate change. *Urban Forestry and Urban Greening, 8*, 295–308.

Roman, L. A., Battles, J. J. & McBride, J. R. (2014). The balance of planting and mortality in a street tree population. *Urban Ecosystems, 17*(2), 387–404.

Roy, S., Byrne, J. & Pickering, C. (2012). A systematic quantitative review of urban tree benefits, costs, and assessment methods across cities in different climatic zones. *Urban Forestry & Urban Greening, 11*, 351–63.

Santamour, F. S. (1990). Trees for urban planting: Diversity, uniformity and common sense. *Proceedings of the 7th METRIA Conference, June 11–12, 1990, Lisle, IL*, pp. 57–65.

Saxe, H., Cannell, M. G., Johnsen, Ø., Ryan, M. G. & Vourlitis, G. (2001). Tree and forest functioning in response to global warming. *New Phytologist, 149*(3), 369–99.

Shannon, C. E. & Weaver, W. (1949). *The Mathematical Theory of Communication*. Urbana, IL: University of Illinois Press.

Simpson, E. H. (1949). Measurement of diversity. *Nature, 163*, 688.

Sjöman, H. (2012). *Trees for Tough Urban Sites: Learning from Nature* – Doctoral Thesis. Alnarp, Sweden: Swedish University of Agricultural Sciences.

Skellern, C. (2014). *AxciScape*. Retrieved 29 November 2014 from www.axciscape.com/features.html.

The Guardian (2011). *You're Being Watched: There's One CCTV Camera for Every 32 People in UK*. Retrieved 29 March 2015 from www.theguardian.com/uk/2011/mar/02/cctv-cameras-watching-surveillance.

The Telegraph (2013). *One Surveillance Camera for Every 11 People in Britain, Says CCTV Survey*. Retrieved 29 March 2015 from www.telegraph.co.uk/technology/10172298/One-surveillance-camera-for-every-11-people-in-Britain-says-CCTV-survey.html.

Trowbridge, P. J. & Bassuk, N. L. (2004). *Trees in the Urban Landscape: Site Assessment, Design and Installation*. Hoboken, NJ: John Wiley and Sons.

Tubby, K. V. & Webber, J. F. (2010). Pests and diseases threatening urban trees under a changing climate. *Forestry, 83*(4), 451–9.

University of Birmingham (2015). *The Birmingham Institute of Forest Research (BIFoR)*. Retrieved 13 July 2015 from www.birmingham.ac.uk/research/activity/bifor/index.aspx.

University of Western Sydney (2015). *Hawkesbury Institute for the Environment – EucFACE*. Retrieved 13 July 2015 from www.uws.edu.au/hie/home/facilities/EucFACE.

USDA, NRCS (2001). *Soil Quality Test Kit Guide*. Washington, DC: USDA Natural Resources Conservation Service. Retrieved from www.nrcs.usda.gov/Internet/FSE_DOCUMENTS/nrcs142p2_050956.pdf.

USGA (2015). *Green Section Recommendations for a Method of Putting Green Construction*. Retrieved 2 July 2015 from http://usga.org/course_care/articles/construction/greens/Green-Section-Recommendations-For-A-Method-Of-Putting-Green-Construction/.

Wania, A., Bruse, M., Blond, N. & Weber, C. (2012). Analysing the influence of different street vegetation on traffic-induced particle dispersion using microscale simulations. *Journal of Environmental Management, 94*(1), 91–101.

Warren, J. M., Jensen, A. M., Medlyn, B. E., Norby, R. J. & Tissue, D. T. (2014). Carbon dioxide stimulation of photosynthesis in *Liquidambar styraciflua* is not sustained during a 12-year field experiment. *AOB Plants* – doi:10.1093/aobpla/plu074.

Watson, D. J. & Hayashi, K.-I. (1965). Photosynthetic and respiratory components of the net assimilation rates of sugar beet and barley. *The New Phytologist, 64*(1), 38–47. Retrieved from www.jstor.org/stable/2429975.

Chapter 5: Plant production

5.1 INTRODUCTION

Trees are grown in production nurseries all over the world for purchase. This chapter provides an overview of different growing methods and quality systems to enable buyers, specifiers and contractors to select appropriate trees for their projects.

The two overarching factors that determine the success of the finished trees delivered to site are the quality of the original nursery stock itself and the way it is treated during its production life, packaging and delivery. There are opportunities to inspect, assess and specify any qualitative aspects of the tree stock, prior to it being supplied; yet, the majority of qualitative assessment is carried out onsite following delivery. The recognised available standards work on a minimum specification, and while this may be quite suitable for many mass planting schemes, it may not satisfy the requirements for more intimate public open spaces. A tree planting scheme along a motorway embankment will likely call for mixed species whips planted at 1.5–2.0 m centres, possibly with a smattering of standard or selected standard trees to provide some sense of instant impact. Phased thinning, following establishment, will be required to provide sufficient room for those trees remaining to achieve their potential, in terms of size and shape. This approach is not likely to see favour with a client who is seeking to provide a new tree-lined plaza that provides break-out space for local cafés, bars and restaurants. While the plant stock for the motorway scheme is likely to be determined by price, the plaza planting will typically be selected according to an agreed level of quality. In these instances, it may be decided that the stock is selected and tagged at the nursery, to ensure consistency and quality. In my experience, suppliers welcome such visits and will gladly explain the merits of their production methods and how they ensure a consistent, high quality in the stock available from them.

5.1.1 Clonal stock

By far the vast majority of the nursery stock available has been selected due to some identified aesthetic or functional characteristic that makes it suitable or desirable for planting in gardens, parks or streets. Once selected, such trees are given a unique cultivar name to identify them, and they are propagated vegetatively to ensure that the selected characteristic is maintained within the produced stock. As they are not produced via a seed, but through cuttings or by grafting or budding, they are all identical clones of the donor parent and of each other. This ensures consistency throughout the stock. For most ornamental trees, the popular method of production is through budding. Here a single bud and slither of stem (scion) from the donor cultivar is inserted into a matching wound in the rootstock, approximately 20 cm above the soil level, and the two are tied together until they unite. Generally, the scion and rootstock must be fairly closely related, and quite often, they need to be the same species. For example, Himalayan birch *Betula utilis* cultivars, such as 'Jermyns' or 'Grayswood Ghost' are traditionally budded onto native *Betula pendula* rootstocks. However, the fastigiate oak *Quercus robur* 'Koster' is budded onto *Quercus robur* stocks. The bud is often fitted with a 'bud-clip' to encourage scion growth upwards rather than outwards. These are removed after the scion has produced sufficient growth to maintain itself without support. Budding will typically take place during the growing season, when the rootstock and scion material are in active growth, and so able to recover and unite quickly. The rootstock is cut back to the bud the following autumn and the tree is trained and managed to produce the straight stem and balanced crown required.

5.2   SPECIFICATION

British Standard BS 3936, *Nursery stock – Part 1: Specification for trees and shrubs* (BSI, 1992), provides a specification for trees and shrubs that are suitable for ornamental use. It was produced under the guidance of the Agriculture and Food Standards Policy Committee and was last published in 1992. The document provides clear guidelines on tree forms, acceptable dimensional relationships between tree height, stem circumference (girth) and container size, where appropriate, but little information on requirements placed upon the grower to ensure a quality product. Other than some requirements for the trees to be alive, healthy, free from obvious pests and diseases, show no signs of nutrient deficiency or toxicity and to be free from mechanical damage, there is little else to guide the acceptance or refusal of stock, in terms of quality of the root system, when it is delivered to a site. It is accepted that British Standards certainly contain much useful information, but cannot be expected to keep up with the developments made within the nursery industry, and so can become out-of-date quite quickly. This particular British Standard is in much need of revision, or perhaps, complete withdrawal.

Recently, a new British Standard was released that aims to provide a best practice resource for all those involved in the design, production, procurement, implementation and management of trees in the landscape. BS 8545, *Trees: From Nursery to Independence in the Landscape – Recommendations* (BSI, 2014) considers the time-planning train from production in the nursery through to independent growth on site. Not before time, there is a guidance document that brings together planting objectives, site evaluation and species selection along with nursery production, transport to site, planting and aftercare, under a single umbrella. Too often, constraints due to site conditions and a *right tree, right place* approach are ignored or at least overlooked. There

Figure 5.1
Established nurseries will always accommodate visits from clients, designers and specifiers. For high-value items, it becomes especially important to select individual trees on the nursery and reserve them. (Image Capita Lovejoy.)

is much within this document that is useful, some of which is barely covered, and a couple of niggles that are misleading or incorrect. For instance, a planting pit with a diameter that is 75 mm greater than the extent of the root system will be very difficult to successfully backfill and make the installation of any underground guying or irrigation/aeration system impossible. It is interesting to compare this with BS 4043 *Recommendations for Transplanting Root-Balled Trees* (BSI, 1989), which has since been withdrawn, and the National Plant Specification (CS Design Software Ltd, 2014) where the recommendation is for the diameter of the tree pit to be at least 500 mm greater than that of the root ball.

The National Plant Specification, available through the *www.csdhub.com/national-plant-specification* website, references BS 3936, but in addition, also includes various standards from selected trades bodies, including the Joint Council for Landscape Industries (JCLI), the European Nursery stock Association (ENA), the Horticultural Trades Association (HTA) and the British Container Growers. This is a much more far-reaching form of specification than BS 3936, and being web-based, should be able to respond much more quickly to changes in plant production methods and improvements in grading and specifying plants. That said, the specification has seen little change since November 1995 and is in need of revision. This would appear to be the most appropriate forum for the dissemination of an industry-wide, recognised standard.

5.3 PLANT QUALITY – WHAT TO LOOK FOR

In the introduction above, it is suggested that nurseries supplying tree stock are visited and the stock checked for consistency and quality, to ensure that good, well-grown specimens are delivered. This is especially important if large numbers are required or if unusual species or large specimens are being selected. Ideally, the visit would take place during mid to late summer, when the trees are fully in leaf and any indications of stress are more likely to be visible. Vigorous, healthy

Figure 5.2
Leaves should be free from obvious signs of pests and disease. Growth increments should be quite marked on young trees.

plants should display long growth increments and healthy leaves and will recover from the shock of transplanting quickly.

The specimens should display growth characteristics that are typical of the species. Nursery trees will typically exhibit a prominent, central leader that is fairly straight and continuous to the top of the tree. Some continue to grow in this way, with a noticeable main trunk and subordinate side branches, throughout their lives. Such trees are known as excurrent and examples include most conifers, *Liquidambar styraciflua*, *Liriodendron tulipifera* and *Quercus palustris*. The converse is a tree that loses that apical control and becomes more and more bushy in habit as it matures. Such a habit is known as decurrent and is expressed by the majority of broadleaf trees such as *Quercus robur*, *Fagus sylvatica*, *Gleditsia triacanthos* and *Acer platanoides*. These growth characteristics are difficult to manipulate in the long term. Removal of the central leader from an excurrent tree does not cause it to become decurrent in habit. For this reason, excurrent trees should not be planted under overhead utility lines, where they will need to be repeatedly pruned (Harris, Clark & Matheny, 2004).

Generally, branches should be arranged radially and uniformly spaced, so that there are no gaps within the canopy when the tree is viewed from all directions.

Other than clean pruning wounds, there should be no other signs of mechanical damage, bleeding and evidence of pests or disease. Branch attachment should preferably be wide-angled.

Figure 5.3
As most ornamental trees are clones, there should be consistency in the crop. The arrangement of branches should ensure that the canopy is entire, with no gaps.

Tight forks and signs of included bark should be avoided. Ideally, plants should be inspected at the nursery, tagged and photographs taken to ensure that the selected tree matches the one delivered. A model nursery visit checklist can be found at Appendix 3.

5.3.1 Clear stem height

For most situations where trees are to be planted and allow pedestrian access beneath, a clear stem height is typically specified. The National Plant Specification calls for a minimum of 2.0 m clear stem on selected standard trees of 10–12 cm girth and above. Trees of this specification would have an overall height in the range of 3.0–3.5 m, meaning that they could potentially be top-heavy. Ideally, at least one-half of the side branches should originate from the lower two-thirds of the stem and no more than one-half should originate from the upper third of the stem. With this type of branch distribution, wind loading would be centred on a point approximately two-thirds up the stem, where such a tree is best structured to withstand storm winds (Leiser & Kemper, 1973). This branch arrangement is clearly not possible if trees are specified with a minimum 2.0 m clear stem and are less than 6.0 m in overall height, and so will require some form of staking or underground support during their early life after planting. The idealised one-third–two-thirds distribution of branching could only be achieved as the tree grows and matures, unless much larger stock is planted or the requirement for a clear stem of 2.0 m is revised. Another way of considering the ratio of crown to clear stem is to refer to *live crown ratio*. This is described as the ratio of the height of the crown containing live foliage to the overall height of the tree (Harris, Clark & Matheny, 2004; Gilman & Lilly, 2008).

Table 5.1
Showing the relationship between stem diameter, overall height and recommended tree spacing within the nursery from the National Plant Specification

Stem girth measured at 1.0 m from ground	Overall height range	Minimum space required within the nursery per tree
6 to 8 cm	250–300 cm	0.6 sq. m
8 to 10 cm	250–300 cm	0.6 sq. m
10 to 12 cm	300–350 cm	0.6 sq. m
12 to 14 cm	350–400 cm	0.6–1.0 sq. m
14 to 16 cm	400–450 cm	1.0 sq. m
16 to 18 cm	450–500 cm	1.0–1.5 sq. m
18 to 20 cm	450–500 cm	1.5 sq. m
20 to 25 cm	500–550 cm	1.5–3.0 sq. m
25 to 30 cm	600–650 cm	3.0 sq. m
30 to 35 cm	600–650 cm	3.0 sq. m
35 to 40 cm	700–750 cm	3.0 sq. m
40 to 45 cm	700–750 cm	3.0 sq. m
45 to 50 cm	750–800 cm	6.0 sq. m
Multi-stem	> 2.0 m	2.0–4.0 sq. m

In some roadside situations, where high-sided traffic is expected, a clear stem height of 4.5 m may be required. Here, carefully specified semi-mature trees could be used, which are already at a suitable height and have been pruned. Alternatively, younger trees could be used that will require regular pruning to ensure the required clear stem height is developed and maintained as they mature.

The National Plant Specification suggests nursery bed spacing for trees according to their size at the time of dispatch. If plants are spaced too closely, they will tend to be drawn upward excessively (etiolated) and become over tall. It is important that trees are selected within the height range for each species at a particular stem diameter to ensure the correct tree height to stem diameter relationship.

There is also some evidence to suggest that close spacing in nursery rows can also increase the incidence of included bark within weak, tightly angled forks (Slater, (e-mail) 1 February 2016, personal communication). The closer trees are grown together, the more upright growth is encouraged and wide-angled branching is discouraged. This tight angle is more likely to encourage bark inclusion within the union. Closely spaced nursery rows are also likely to provide wind protection, one row to another, so reducing the amount of stem and branch movement or perturbation. It has been shown that this lack of stem and branch movement in response to wind can prevent the growth of interlocking reaction wood at the apex of the junction (Slater & Ennos, 2016). This lack of strength at the junction apex, coupled with a higher incidence of upright-branching and included bark in closely spaced trees, is much more likely to produce weak branch connections and forks when compared with nursery trees grown at wider spacings.

When growing in a natural environment or within a well-managed nursery, trees will respond to wind stress by producing reaction wood along their stems. More wood is produced at the base and root flare, where the greatest bending moment operates (this is the longest lever arm

Figure 5.4
The stem of this young silver birch is unable to support the weight of its crown, when in full leaf. It is likely that the relationship between the overall height of the tree and the stem girth does not comply with the National Plant Specification, and this tree should have been rejected. A taller tree does not necessarily mean a better tree.

from where the wind acts on the crown) (Mattheck & Breloer, 2010). The tapered trunk enables the tree to bend fairly uniformly along the entire stem. A tree without this taper is inclined to bend closer to the ground (Leiser & Kemper, 1973). It is not uncommon for the central leader of trees to be tied to canes at some point during their production life. Occasionally, the tree spends its entire production life on the nursery tied to stiff supports. Such production methods do not allow the tree stem to flex in response to wind, and so does not thicken. This can cause the stem to be fairly parallel-sided, with no taper or flare at its base, resulting in trees that are not able to support themselves once planted in the landscape and in full leaf.

Once trees grow beyond the extra heavy standard classification, with a stem of 16–18 cm or over, a pronounced root flare should be evident at the base of the stem. It is important that this is visible at the soil or pot surface and not buried. If unsure, a good test is to grasp the stem at chest height and rotate it gently in a circular motion. The stem should pivot at or just below the soil surface and never deeper. If it is planted too deep, it will tend to pivot deep in the soil and a gap will open up around the stem (Watson & Himelick, 1997). Planting too deep can be a problem, and it is worth checking to ensure that this has not happened. Incorrect planting depth can lead to slow growth and poor vigour, which in turn can result in susceptibility to pests and diseases.

Ideally, plants should be inspected at the nursery, tagged with sealed labels and photographs taken to ensure that the selected trees are the ones delivered.

It is also advisable to inspect a selection of trees within each delivery to ensure they conform with the necessary specifications and best practice guidelines. Such a requirement should be included within the softworks specification, forming part of the contract documentation. As the root ball is typically not visible at the time of

Figure 5.5
Locking or tamperproof ties help to ensure that labels do not become unattached or are inadvertently removed. For the Olympic Park project, every tree was assigned a unique reference number, so that it could be tracked from selection in the nursery, through planting and establishment, in its final growing position. (Image Capita Lovejoy.)

delivery, it is especially important that these form part of the inspection, either by knocking a sample out of their containers or by breaking open a selection of root balls (see 5.4.2 below).

5.4   NURSERY PRODUCTION SYSTEMS

Trees for use in urban and other public situations will usually be available in one of the three forms – bare root, root-balled or containerised. Each system has its own merits and draw-backs.

However trees are grown in the nursery, the root system must be well-developed, balanced, without any coiled or girdling roots, moist and free from any physiological damage. Probably, the most important aspect is that the root ball must not be allowed to dry out. Even a short duration of drying will kill delicate roots, reducing the viability of the tree stock. Correct handling from within the nursery right through to final planting and establishment is also essential to get right. Plant stock is a living commodity and does not respond well to rough and thoughtless handling. All too often, one sees trees dropped from delivery vehicles onto their root balls or thrown carelessly onto the ground, causing branches to snap, their containers to crack or their root-protecting bags to tear open, exposing the roots to the threat of desiccation.

All bare root and root-balled trees are grown in the ground and their root systems are managed in such a way as to increase branching of the roots. If the tree was allowed to grow without any intervention, there would be a tendency for the roots to spread out into the surrounding ground, with little branching. As a result, when the tree is lifted from the nursery field, a significant proportion of the root system would be left behind in the soil (Watson & Himelick, 1982). To overcome this, the grower will lift or undercut the tree at specific times during its production lifecycle, thus severing any roots that are tending to grow vigorously away from the tree stem. This process removes the dominant root bud and encourages side and replacement roots to develop. The lifting and replanting takes place during the dormant period and coincides with lifting for sale. If carried out correctly, a more dense and fibrous root system is encouraged, which means that at final lifting, more root is dispatched with the finished tree (Watson & Sydnor, 1987).

That said, a significant proportion of the root system is still left behind when the tree is finally lifted for sale. From eighty-eight trees of seven deciduous species excavated in northern USA, research suggests that up to 98 per cent of the soil volume occupied by roots would be outside standard root ball dimensions, and so left in the nursery if the root ball is not prepared correctly through regular undercutting (Watson & Himelick, 1982). Gilman (Gilman, 1988) also found that 91–95 per cent of the root lengths would remain in the nursery soil if standard root balls were extracted for three popular street tree species. However, Gerhold and Johnson (2003) showed that significantly more root biomass, in terms of its dry weight, is contained within a standard root ball than might be expected from the work of Watson and Himelick and Gilman. It is difficult to see why there should be such disparity between the measurement methods based on biomass and either root length or soil volume occupied by roots (Gerhold & Johnson, 2003). Experience does show, however, that with the correct level of aftercare and maintenance, trees grown and lifted to National Plant Specification standards should establish in correctly created planting sites.

Field-grown trees are typically planted out as young stock, in rows where they are kept weed-free and managed in such a way that they produce a fibrous root system. Most of this management requires the use of some form of machinery, which invariably disturbs the soil

Table 5.2
The relationship between stem size and the recommended number of times trees are undercut/transplanted in the nursery, according to NPS and BS 8545

Stem girth measured at 1.0 m from ground as per NPS	Minimum number of times transplanted/undercut on the nursery to NPS	Minimum number of times transplanted/undercut on the nursery to BS 8545
6 to 8 cm	2	
8 to 10 cm	2	
10 to 12 cm	2	
12 to 14 cm	3	3
14 to 16 cm	3	3
16 to 18 cm	3	3
18 to 20 cm	3	3
20 to 25 cm	4	4
25 to 30 cm	4–5	4
30 to 35 cm	4–5	4
35 to 40 cm	4–5	5
40 to 45 cm	4–5	5
45 to 50 cm	4–5	5
50 to 60 cm	4–5	6

surface, throughout the nursery life of the tree. Cultivation equipment, running up and down between the tree rows, planting, replanting and undercutting are all activities that provide opportunities for the soil level to build up immediately around the tree stem. The progressively rising soil level over the roots essentially buries the root system deeper and deeper into the ground. At harvest time, the tree is lifted in a normal way, but a significant part of the lifted root ball can end up being buried stem and soil containing no roots. Such practices will consistently produce inferior root balls with low numbers of roots contained within the ball.

The National Plant Specification states that 'Root balls must be firm and solid and the roots must penetrate the whole ball' (CS Design Software Ltd, 2016). Root balls where the stem has been buried, are unlikely to conform to this specification, and if encountered, such stock should not be accepted.

Another potential problem with any field-grown production method centres around how the young seedling or whip tree is planted in the field. This process is typically mechanised, and occasionally, a slot is opened in the soil where the root system of the transplant is placed in one direction. The result can be young plant with a wholly one-directional root system, known as 'hockey-stick' roots (RHS, 2005; Sacre, 2015). Once root systems such as this become established and thicken, they are impossible to rectify and should be rejected. The later stability of the maturing tree will always be compromised unless the root system has evenly spaced lateral roots.

In the UK, lifting has historically been carried out from mid-October until the end of March. The last few years have seen mild weather extending into late autumn and early spring, and as a consequence, it may be more appropriate to specify that trees are lifted between mid-November and mid-March. It is important that the ground is moist at the time of lifting, without being waterlogged or frozen. If the root system is moist when it is lifted, it is more likely to retain that moisture once it is out of the ground.

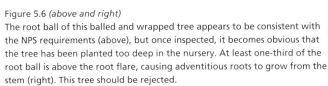

Figure 5.6 *(above and right)*
The root ball of this balled and wrapped tree appears to be consistent with the NPS requirements (above), but once inspected, it becomes obvious that the tree has been planted too deep in the nursery. At least one-third of the root ball is above the root flare, causing adventitious roots to grow from the stem (right). This tree should be rejected.

Trees are self-optimising, dynamic structures that respond to complex hormone pathways and feedback systems. With a reduction in roots comes a corresponding reduction or slowing in top growth. Growers will often use this check in growth to provide an opportunity to shape the canopy and establish a consistent, well-structured and balanced tree crown.

5.4.1 Bare root

Selected trees are lifted, using specialist machinery, in the field and vibrated, so that the soil falls away from the roots. The lack of soil means that the stock is fairly light in weight, reducing the need for mechanical handling and also making transportation cheaper. The amount of root retained tends to be significantly greater than with root-balled trees; it is easy to inspect the root system and correct planting depth is readily determined. It is easy to see why this continues to be a popular method of root preparation for use in many situations.

Despite the apparent ease of handling and reduced cost, it does rely on good planning and site care to ensure correct storage. There is some limit to the size of stock that can be supplied in this form, but experience shows that a diverse range of trees up to 16–18 cm girth can be expected to establish satisfactorily. The key to success is correct management of stock through the nursery-lifting process and during storage onsite to prevent drying out of the roots. By phasing deliveries to ensure that only those trees to be planted within the current working week are onsite at any one time, the site stored stock is kept to a minimum and its moisture requirements are easier to manage.

Some species do not respond favourably to this method of production at all. Experience shows that *Betula*, *Carpinus*, *Eucalyptus*, *Fagus*, *Juglans*, *Liquidambar*, *Liriodendron*, *Quercus*, among others, and all conifers are not suitable for this method of production. For these and any tree stock larger than 16–18 cm girth, root-balled or container-grown stock should be specified.

The root systems of all bare root trees, once lifted and de-soiled, must be immediately placed in thick, co-extruded (black on the inside and white on the outside) polythene bags, which are tied shut around the stem of the tree. These bags prevent light entering, keeping the roots dark. They also maintain a moist atmosphere within and help to reflect sunlight, which could cause damagingly high temperatures to build up without a reflective white exterior. Even so, it is wise not to allow bare root trees to be exposed to direct sunlight, keeping them within a shaded storage facility where possible. Research at Cornell University (Buckstrup & Bassuk, 2009) shows that dipping the root systems of bare root trees in a co-polymer hydrogel slurry before bagging helps to protect the roots from drying and reduces some of the stress inflicted on the trees. In the moist, UK climate, this additional step is generally not considered necessary as long as bagging occurs in the field, as each tree is lifted and de-soiled. If it

Figure 5.7
An advanced nursery stock tree being lifted out of the ground with a special 'U'-shaped blade. Soil is vibrated from the roots, prior to the root ball being placed in a co-extruded, polythene bag. Correct preparation ensures that there are plenty of fibrous roots retained within the root ball and the root flare is at ground level. (Image Hillier Nurseries Limited.)

were decided to include root-dipping as a requirement, it is likely that there would be a cost implication, as this would introduce an additional stage in the lifting process.

5.4.2 Root-balled and wrapped

Often referred to as 'balled and burlapped', this is a very common method of production. The tree is mechanically removed from the field, often using specialist equipment, with the root ball and soil kept intact. The root ball is first wrapped in biodegradable hessian sacking, then tied within a non-galvanised wire cage to ensure that it is adequately supported and the soil is prevented from falling off.

Typically, undisturbed contact between delicate roots and the moist soil surrounding them can be maintained, helping to protect them against fluctuations in temperature and preventing them from drying out. Even so, when storing root-balled plants, they should be kept moist, either by surrounding them with a free-draining, moisture-retentive material such as good quality topsoil, proprietary bark mulch or wood chip material that has finished composting, or by irrigation. In some northern latitudes, the root ball may require protection from exceptionally low temperatures and freezing winds. With the root ball out of the ground, it is possible for frost to access parts of the root system which were previously fairly deep and ill-equipped to deal with such low temperatures.

As the roots are contained within the soil ball, trees tend to be much heavier than those delivered as bare root. This can often require the use of mechanical handling equipment to move them around the site and position them within the prepared planting pit. Each time the tree is moved, the possibility of disturbance to the root ball is increased, causing damage to delicate roots and making successful establishment less likely. Careful handling is always required. When mechanical methods are used, the tree should always be handled and lifted by the root ball only. Sometimes, self-tightening slings or strops are seen being used around the stem. This practice should never be used to move trees. It will invariably bruise, twist or rupture the bark, sometimes completely girdling the tree, leading to eventual death. There was even a procedure, a little while ago, where large root-balled trees had their stems drilled, fairly close to the ground, to take a steel pin that passed through the stem and provided a lifting point. The entire weight of the tree and root ball would be suspended by this pin. Harris, Clark and Matheny (2004) refer to a large *Erythrina caffra* that was moved within the Disneyland site in California. Disney's Director of Landscape Architecture, Morgan 'Bill' Evans devised a method of lifting large trees either saved from other locations outside the park or moved within the park. Steel lifting pins were inserted through the stem or the main scaffolds, above the centre of gravity, and the soil was removed from the root system before the entire tree was lifted and relocated. Once the tree was in its new position, the lifting pins were removed and the holes were filled with epoxy and hardwood dowels.

One aspect of field-grown trees that can cause confusion due to conflicting advice is what are acceptable parameters, in terms of the size of the root ball or the spread of roots when related to stem growth. Even the British Standards are not consistent. BS 4043 *Recommendations for Transplanting Root-Balled Trees* (now withdrawn) suggested that the root ball diameter should be at least ten times the stem diameter of the tree, as measured at 1 m above the ground (BSI, 1989). Using the minimum dimension as being acceptable, it is felt that some of the root ball sizes calculated in such a way, for stock up to what would be considered semi-mature, would be quite modest and not exhibit best practice. BS 8545 *Trees: From Nursery to Independence in the Landscape – Recommendations* provides tables showing the dimensional relationship between tree stem and both root ball diameter and root spread for bare root stock (BSI, 2014). This standard is certainly more generous in its root ball sizes for smaller tree stock and matches those dimensions shown within the European technical and quality standards for nursery stock (ENA, 2010). The American Horticulture Industry Association (formerly the American Nursery and Landscape Association) produces a fairly prescriptive standard, the American Standard for Nursery Stock ANSI Z60.1 (2014), and this is often referred to in texts both sides of the Atlantic, but significantly by Watson and Himelick (1997) and Hartman, Pirone and Sall (2000). This tends to be more generous still in the extent of root ball specified. Hillier Nurseries use their own method of calculating the root ball size, based on their many years of experience and extensive customer feedback (Arshadi, 2014, personal communication). (The American Standard for Nursery Stock ANSI Z60 can be downloaded from: http://americanhort.org/documents/ANSI_Nursery_Stock_Standards_AmericanHort_2014.pdf.)

Figure 5.8
A semi-mature tree lifted out of the ground by a tree spade, prior to being wrapped in hessian and a wire cage. Careful preparation of the root system is essential to ensure that sufficient roots remain within the root ball. (Image Hillier Nurseries Limited.)

Figure 5.9
Root-balled trees lifted, wrapped in hessian and a wire cage, being held prior to dispatch. Notice the drip irrigation to keep the root ball moist. (Image Capita Lovejoy.)

Table 5.3
A comparison between North American ANSI, British Standard, ENA and Hillier Nurseries root ball and bare root specifications. Bear in mind that the North American stem caliper measurement is taken at 6 in (150 mm) above soil level for trees up to 4 in (100 mm) caliper and then at 12 in (300 mm) above the soil for larger caliper trees. The UK and European stem girth measurement is taken at 1 m above soil level. The dimensions required by each of the specifications have all been determined from a combination of academic research and many years of experience

Stem caliper (ins) to ANSI	UK stem girth equivalent (cm) to NPS	Minimum root spread equivalent (mm) to ANSI	Diameter root spread to BS 8545	Minimum ball diameter equivalent (mm) to ANSI	Minimum ball diameter (mm) to BS 8545 & (ENA)	Ball diameter to BS 4043 – 10 x stem diameter	Ball diameter to Hillier Nurseries
0.75	4–6	406		356		127	
1.00	6–8	457	450	406		191	
1.25	8–10	508	450	457	300	254	400
1.50	10–12	559	550	508	300	318	500
1.75	12–14	610	550	559	400	381	500
2.00	14–16	711	700	610	450	445	600
2.25	16–18		700		500	508	600
2.50	18–20	813		711	550	572	700
3.00	20–25	965		813	600	635	700–800
3.50	20–25			965		762	
4.00	25–30			1,067	700	889	800–900
4.50	30–35			1,219	800	1,016	900
5.00	35–40			1,372	900	1,143	1,000
5.50	40–45			1,448	1,000	1,270	1,100
6.00	45–50			1,524	1,200	1,397	1,100
7.00	45–50			1,778		1524	
8.00	50–60			2,032	1,300	1,778	1,200

Obviously, the better prepared the stock and the bigger the root ball, the quicker the expected establishment could be. However, bigger root balls are also heavier, so will be more expensive to transport and may require mechanical handling. For example, the root ball of a 20–25 cm girth tree to Hillier specification could weigh 250 kg or more. Obviously, the immediate impact created by the tree planted in the landscape will need to be balanced against transport costs and the ease of handling on site.

There remains something of a controversy over root-balled trees caused by disagreement between the supplier, the contractor, the designer and whoever will be responsible for the management of the completed scheme. The controversy centres around whether to remove the wire basket and hessian wrapping from the root ball once the tree has been planted (Appleton & Floyd, 2004). Certainly, the arboricultural literature and guidance are fairly unanimous; Harris, Clark and Metheny; Gilman; Hartman, Pirone and Sall; Trowbridge and Bassuk; Watson and Himelick, BS 8545 all recommend at least the removal of the top half of the wire basket once the tree has been positioned in its final location and before completely backfilling the planting hole. None would argue the importance of keeping the root ball intact from harvest through to planting and most would agree that one of the simplest ways of achieving that is through the

Figure 5.10
A galvanised wire basket is still evident on this tree of approximately 200 mm stem diameter. It is vital that the material used is able to degrade fairly quickly to prevent later partial girdling and restricted vascular flow occurring.

use of wire baskets. The nursery trade typically insists that the baskets remain in place to reduce root ball damage and post-planting tree instability. In fact, any removal, either fully or even partially, of the wire cage will cause many suppliers to void any guarantee that existed on the tree. Most planting specifications will take their lead from current best practice guidance, and if that advice suggests the removal of the wire cage, the contactor is likely to find themselves in some dilemma over how best to proceed without contravening either the nursery or the specification requirements. The evidence from current, available research is far from conclusive. Putting anecdotal reports from both camps to one side, Appleton and Floyd (2004) and Watson and Himelick (1997) both record root ball excavations that showed wire baskets remaining intact for 15–30 years and retaining sufficient tensile strength to make them 'very difficult to break' (Appleton & Floyd, 2004). The National Plant Specification requires that 'All materials used to support root balls must decompose within eighteen months of planting and not constrict the continuing growth of the tree' (CS Design Software Ltd, 2016). The ENA standards for nursery stock includes a similar requirement (ENA, 2010). There is clearly a duty on the tree production nurseries to ensure that the materials they use degrade sufficiently quickly if their products are to conform with these UK and European standards.

5.4.3 Container-grown – potted/bagged/spring ring

The main advantage claimed for using container-grown stock is that it can be planted at any time of year. There is very little disturbance to the root system, and as a consequence, growth is unlikely to be checked. Weather conditions still play an important part in successful establishment, however. In addition to avoiding waterlogged and frozen ground conditions, a significant increase in the watering burden will be necessary if planted between late spring and early autumn, and irrigation requirements should not be underestimated. The situation is further compounded by the specialist soils used in container-grown systems, which are open and well-drained to ensure sufficient aeration within the container. Once planted onsite, the finer soil used within the planting pit can cause wicking of water away from the root ball, creating a situation where the root system actually has less access to water than it did in the nursery (Watson & Himelick, 1997).

With any container-grown system, there is always the possibility of circling roots, which, because they are contained, grow around the outside of the pot. This is much more likely if the tree is not potted-on regularly and remains within the same pot for too long. If the condition remains unchecked, the circling roots will thicken and eventually become girdling roots. These, through distortion of the root system, typically reduce the stability of the tree and can even cause strangulation later in life.

There are several production methods that fall under the category of container-grown, each with its own merits and disadvantages. Whatever the method, all stock should contain sufficient fibrous root to ensure that the compost holds together once removed from its container. If the root ball and compost start to disintegrate, it suggests that there has been insufficient root development and the tree should be rejected.

5.4.3.1 Rigid pots

This is the traditional method of growing plants in containers. The ubiquitous smooth-sided, plastic pot comes in a variety of shapes and sizes. The larger pots will typically have handles, one on either side, to ease lifting and moving. Circling roots are the biggest potential problem with any container-grown tree, and this type of container probably has the worst track record of any. As the roots grow, they reach the inside edge of the pot and are deflected around the pot perimeter. If these roots are allowed to thicken, they will not be persuaded to grow in any other way and must be removed. Ideally, the tree is potted into a larger pot before this happens, but not always. Any container-grown stock should be checked by knocking a sample out of their pots, and rejected if any circling roots have become thickened and established. Any that still remain pliable and do not show signs of kinking can be straightened out at planting. Wider, shorter pots tend to be less of a problem, as any circling roots are further from the main trunk, and so, less likely to girdle or strangle the tree stem later in life. That said, it is often difficult to assess the past potting history, and circling roots in particular, without picking the entire root ball apart.

5.4.3.2 Bags

Trees grown in bags are a fairly recent innovation and are manufactured from a flexible material that allows air, water and light to pass through. This is said to discourage waterlogging, encourage fibrous rooting and reduce the formation of circling or spiralling roots. Both black and white woven materials are used in the manufacture of the bags, and each user will vehemently defend the merits of one over the other. Whatever the material, bags are easy to handle due to the addition of carrying handles and are good at keeping the root ball intact. As with any container, circling or spiralling roots will continue to be a problem if stock remains in the same bag for too long. Barcham Trees have introduced the concept of *shelf life*, which ensures that no tree remains in its pot for more than 2 years, without being potted-on. Any unsold tree in its final pot is shredded.

5.4.3.3 Air pots

Through their unusual arrangement of cone shapes, rather like an egg box, the air pot prevents roots from circling

Figure 5.11
These circling or girdling roots once formed are difficult to correct. Trees with these roots should be rejected, rather than planted. Unfortunately, they are seldom noticed at the time of delivery.

Figure 5.12
A fairly typical line of container-grown trees. The trees must be tied to wires or cross bars to prevent them being blown over in the wind. Note the irrigation line fixed to the lower wire and the fine delivery tubes into each container. The rigid pots in the foreground have handles at either side to facilitate easy manual handling. (Image Capita Lovejoy.)

Figure 5.13
Lines of bag-grown trees at Barcham Trees in Ely, Cambridgeshire. The white bags are the trademark 'LightPot' used by Barcham, developed from an Australian system. The irrigation line is again fixed to the lower wire, and delivery tubes take water directly into each bag.

Figure 5.14
Close up of the Spring Ring system, showing the egg box-like appearance of the wrapping. The latest volume of rooting media is visible as a darker band around the outside of the pot.

the outside of the pot. The closed, inward-facing cones direct roots towards the open, outward-facing cones where exposure to the air causes the root tip to dehydrate and die. The base of the pot consists of a circular grille that can be raised off the ground, also creating an air space that exposes the root tips to air pruning. With dominance of the apical root bud removed, the plant responds by initialising growth in root side buds. These create more roots and the process continues, creating a dense, fibrous root system. Once the available rooting volume has been filled with roots, the pot wall is removed, a new larger wall is placed around the root ball and the gap created is filled with fresh compost to allow the new root growth and air pruning to continue.

If this potting-on process is to be used, the grille at the base of the pot will no longer be usable, and another system of keeping the base clear of the ground would be required or a chemically treated ground cover fabric could be used to prevent base rooting.

Directly prior to dispatch, the pot wall should be removed and immediately replaced with a hessian wrapping. On delivery, it is worth checking that the root ball has been adequately irrigated and that the compost around the perimeter of the root ball has not been allowed to dry out.

Figure 5.15
Larger semi-mature stock growing in 'Spring Ring' air pots at Hillier Nurseries' Andlers Ash facility in Liss, Hampshire. The Spring Ring wrapping is removed and replaced with hessian prior to despatch. All handling must be by mechanical means.

5.5   TRANSPORTATION AND STORAGE

These are two areas that require some careful thought, planning and management to avoid causing damage to the stock. Root-balled and containerised trees should only be lifted and handled by the root ball or container rather than by the stem. Bare root stock, being significantly lighter, can often be lifted manually by the stem, but never mechanically, using self-tightening stops. It is likely that the selected trees will be transported at three main points during their journey from their growing location within the nursery to final planting destination, within the scheme. Within the nursery, there is invariably a requirement to relocate the tree from the production line to either a short-term storage or a dispatch area. The tree will either be stored until the remainder of the consignment is lifted and/or collated, or it is loaded onto transport and dispatched directly. Movement within the nursery should be kept to a minimum. Each and every time the stock is handled, there is an opportunity for root balls to be broken apart, branches to be damaged and roots to dry out. If short-term storage is necessary prior to dispatch, the tree should be kept in a sheltered location, free from the buffeting and desiccating effects of the wind and out of direct sunlight. The root ball should be surrounded by and be in contact with freely draining but moisture-retentive material such as composted bark or woodchip. Frequent irrigation may be required to prevent the roots drying out. Some nurseries use dispatch barns or cold stores to provide their storage requirements.

Typically, trees are loaded in such a way that they are laid horizontally onto the flat bed of a lorry or trailer. It is important that damage from stacking one tree on top of another and from security ropes or straps is avoided. Unsupported stems can be protected during transit by placing straw bales or some other soft packing material under them. Any open lorry or trailer used to transport the stock from the nursery to site must be sheeted prior to dispatch and the sheeting must remain securely in place during transit, to prevent exposure to damaging winds. Particular care also needs to be taken to prevent overheating in sunny weather. If the stock is to remain

Figure 5.16
Temporary tree-holding area for the Olympic Park project. Due to the very tight programme, planting had to continue throughout the year. Deliveries were programmed so that trees could be offloaded and planted almost immediately into pre-prepared and checked tree pits. This ensured that stock in the holding area was kept to a minimum. (Image Capita Lovejoy.)

on the vehicle, while stationary for long periods, ventilation may be required. All of these lifting, handling, storage and transport aspects can be checked by visiting the nursery and observing their processes in action.

Delivery arrangements should always be agreed prior to dispatch from the nursery. Such arrangements will include timing of the delivery, access arrangements and handling requirements for offloading. The consignment should be checked at delivery to ensure that it meets the required specification. A delivery checklist can be very useful. Any damage should be reported immediately, and any stock that is considered to be defective or sub-standard should be returned. Any rejected stock should be removed from site free-of-charge.

Offloading should ideally take place as close to the planting site or storage area as possible. Particular care must be taken to ensure that the root system is not subject to physical damage or drying. Stock destined for short-term site storage must have their roots surrounded by free-draining and moisture-retentive material as soon as they have been offloaded and inspected. It is important to keep the roots fully irrigated at all times. The storage area should be protected from vehicular movements, sheltered from wind, out of direct sunlight and away from potential sources of contamination.

Temporary shade netting and webbing materials can be useful when creating an onsite temporary storage facility to provide protection from the elements. Further information on the handling, transportation and storage of tree stock can be found in the *National Plant Specification – Handling and Establishment* download (CS Design Software Ltd, 1995), from the NPS website and section 9, *Handling and storage* of *BS 8545: 2014, Trees: From Nursery to Independence in the Landscape – Recommendations* (BSI, 2014).

REFERENCES

American Horticulture Industry Association (2014). *ANSI Z60.1 American Standard for Nursery Stock*. Columbus, Ohio: American Horticulture Industry Association.

Appleton, B. & Floyd, S. (2004). Wire baskets – Current products and their handling at planting. *Journal of Arboriculture, 30*(4), 261–5.

Arshadi, H. (2014). Personal communication, 30 April 2014.

Briggs, W. R. (2006). Physiology of plant responses to artificial lighting. In C. Rich, & T. Longcore (eds), *Ecological Consequences of Artificial Night Lighting* (pp. 389–411). Washington, DC: Island Press.

BSI (1989). *BS 4043: Recommendations for Transplanting Root-Balled Trees*. London: British Standards Institution.

BSI (1992). *BS 3936–1: Nursery stock – Part 1: Specification for Trees and Shrubs*. London: British Standards Institution.

BSI (2014). *BS 8545: Trees: From Nursery to Independence in the Landscape – Recommendations*. London: British Standards Institution.

Buckstrup, M. & Bassuk, N. L. (2009). *Creating the Urban Forest: The Bare Root Method*. Ithaca, NY: Urban Horticulture Institute, Department of Horticulture, Cornell University.

CS Design Software (1995). *The NPS Handling and Establishment*. Retrieved 21 December 2015 from www.csdhub.com/wp-content/uploads/2014/12/The-National-Plant-Specification-Handling-and-Establishment.pdf.

CS Design Software (2014). *NPS General Information – The NPS Rootballed Trees*. Retrieved 26 December 2015 from www.csdhub.com/wp-content/uploads/2014/12/The-National-Plant-Specification-Rootballed-Trees.pdf.

CS Design Software (2016). *National Plant Specification: Trees – Root Protection*. Retrieved 26 December 2015 from www.csdhub.com/national-plant-specification/trees/nps-trees-root-protection/.

ENA (2010). *European Technical & Quality Standards for Nurserystock*. Cambridge, UK: European Nurserystock Association.

Gerhold, H. D. & Johnson, A. D. (2003). Root dimensions of landscape tree cultivars. *Journal of Arboriculture*, *29*(6), 322–26.

Gilman, E. F. (1988). Tree root spread in relation to branch dripline and harvestable rootball. *HortScience*, *23*(2), 351–3.

Gilman, E. F. & Lilly, S. J. (2008). *Best Management Practices: Tree Pruning* (2nd edn). Champaign, IL: International Society of Arboriculture.

Harris, R. W., Clark, J. R. & Matheny, N. (2004). *Arboriculture: Integrated Management of Landscape Trees, Shrubs, and Vines* (4th edn). Upper Saddle River, NJ: Prentice Hall.

Hartman, J. R., Pirone, T. P. & Sall, M. A. (2000). *Pirone's Tree Maintenance* (7th edn). New York: Oxford University Press.

Leiser, A. T. & Kemper, J. D. (1973). Analysis of stress distribution in the sapling tree trunk. *Journal of the American Society for Horticultural Science*, *98*(2), 164–70.

Mattheck, C. & Breloer, H. (2010). *The Body Language of Trees*. Norwich: The Stationery Office.

RHS (2005). *Royal Horticultural Society, Advice. Trees: Buying and Planting Specimens*. Retrieved 26 December 2015 from www.rhs.org.uk/advice/profile?PID=630.

Sacre, K. (2015). *5. Root System Development and Management*. Retrieved 26 December 2015 from www.barchampro.co.uk/5-root-system-development-and-management.

Slater, D. (2016). (e-mail) Personal communication, 1 February 2016.

Slater, D. & Ennos, A. R. (in press). An assessment of the remodelling of bifurcations in hazel (*Corylus avellana* L.) in response to bracing, drilling and splitting. *Arboriculture and Urban Forestry*.

Watson, G. W. & Himelick, E. B. (1982). Root distribution of nursery trees and its relationship to transplanting success. *Journal of Arboriculture*, *8*(9), 225–9.

Watson, G. W. & Himelick, E. B. (1997). *Principles and Practice of Planting Trees and Shrubs*. Savoy, IL: International Society of Arboriculture.

Watson, G. W. & Sydnor, T. D. (1987). The effect of root pruning on the root system of nursery trees. *Journal of Arboriculture*, *13*(5): 126–30.

Chapter 6: Tree planting and establishment: technical design

6.1 INTRODUCTION

This chapter provides guidance to designers, specifiers and contractors, through investigation of technical design details and specifications, to help ensure that the completed project matches the expectations in terms of trees growing independently in the urban environment.

Chapter 3 looks at the importance of a suitable volume of growing media, selected to suit the needs of the tree. Chapter 4 discusses the range and variety of other infrastructures competing for space and the other constraints imposed on trees in an urban context. The task of ensuring that some of our urban trees establish to a point of maturity sometimes seems overwhelming. The initial planting can be the easy part! It should be remembered from Chapter 1 however that, as they get larger, the benefits they provide increase in terms of ecosystem services. Therefore, unlike other infrastructures, the value of trees increases as they age. Many will, or at least will have the potential to, outlive the built form around them. Also, as they age, their requirements change. The requirements for above-ground space and underground rooting volume for a recently planted street tree will be completely different to those later in life. It is vital, therefore, that the long-term aims and objectives of the tree(s) are addressed early in the design phase, so that sufficient resources are able to be made available. Chapter 3 considers the rooting volume requirements for different size trees growing in different soils and substrates. This chapter looks at methods to achieve increased root volumes using structural media and other load-bearing materials. Perhaps, for particular locations where appropriate space is not possible, a short-term tree replacement policy can be adopted, rather than a longer-term establishment to maturity approach.

For these requirements to be communicated to the design or project team, and ultimately to the person on the ground who is responsible for planning and implementing the planting, good quality information must be provided.

6.2 PRODUCTION INFORMATION

Suitably complete, correct, co-ordinated and realistic detailing, specification writing and accompanying schedules of work/bills of quantities are an essential skill to ensure accurate and comprehensive communication of design intent for scheme implementation and promotion of the desired quality of delivery. Tender and contract drawings, sometimes augmented by illustrations, show the relationship of designed elements to each other and to the surroundings; text is written as specifications to describe what and how to plant; and figures are provided in the form of costed measured quantities either in a schedule or a bill of quantities. This documentation is the vital communication link between design and construction. Drawings are a time-honoured method of conveying design intent and have been used successfully for many generations. Specifications, on the other hand, have not performed so well and continue to be the weak link in the contract information chain. Disputes between bidding contractors, design consultants and clients can sometimes occur when estimators take a very strict line in interpreting the information presented, to ensure a competitive tender submission. It is, therefore, vital that all specification documents, drawings, schedules and bills of quantity are cross-checked to ensure consistent information is shown. Often standard specifications, such as those produced by NBS (National Building Specification), are used, given that these are readily accessible and follow a standardised

Figure 6.1
To ensure that all parts of a scheme are implemented correctly, information between design disciplines and between designers and contractors must be fully co-ordinated. If not, situations like this can easily occur. The all-weather pitch requires access for maintenance vehicles, but the gate position has not been co-ordinated with the dropped kerb. Also, the bollards, installed to prevent delivery vehicles mounting the kerb, restrict access for the maintenance vehicles.

format that is understood throughout the industry. Even so, there is still scope to create a non-standard, bespoke set of documentation, which has both distinct benefits and disadvantages. There are also national or international standards that define processes (e.g., tree transplanting), goods (e.g., trees) and services (e.g., topsoil supply or reuse). In addition, there are industry guidance documents (e.g., NJUG Guidelines for the Planning, Installation and Maintenance of Utility Apparatus in Proximity to Trees), codes of practice (e.g., Defra Construction Code of Practice for the Sustainable Use of Soils on Construction Sites) and other best practice guidance (e.g., CIRIA C753 *The SuDS Manual*). These can all be referred to in contract documents, as necessary and used as a sort of shorthand to save reproducing their entire contents.

Manufacturers and distributors of materials will also provide their own technical information, in terms of drawings, specifications and application and installation guidance, sometimes providing an onsite presence to oversee the installation.

6.2.1 Drawings

Drawings consist principally of graphic information, using lines, graphic symbols and dimensions, to define the size, shape, location and construction of the works. They are, quite understandably, by far the most common form of communication within the construction industry. Drawings should usually be site-specific, but standard drawings are available (both commercially and from trade organisations) and can be useful as a guide, when creating particular details. All too often, however, a standard set of details from a practice or local authority detail library is rolled out with little or no attention to local site conditions. This can result in the contractor being left scratching their head, wondering how on earth they are going to reconcile what is shown on the drawing with what appears onsite.

Tree and other plant schedules, with plant specifications, are often included within planting plans. Information shown on drawings should be carefully co-ordinated, so that it matches that shown in specifications and bills of quantities. There are several software packages available that provide co-ordinated materials schedules in tandem with layout drawings. Often, a document reference will be added to the drawing, rather than a text extract, to avoid inconsistencies like this occurring. That does then require the contractor to have not only the necessary drawings with them when they carry out the works onsite, but also the specification document and plant schedules. That might not be an unreasonable expectation, but when the weather is inclement, paper drawings and documents can quickly become unreadable and useless.

6.2.2   Specifications

The written, technical part of the works, which detail the quality of materials, workmanship and any performance requirements and the conditions under which the work is executed, are contained within the specification document. There are standard specification models that are frequently used to ensure a common arrangement of clauses. In this way, all parties should be familiar as to where each particular element of the works is located within the document. The main systems for landscaping and tree planting are the National Plant Specification (NPS), the National Building Specification (NBS) or the Manual of Contract Documents for Highway Works (MCHW): Specification for Highway Works.

Many landscape schemes will follow the NBS *Classic* system, which contains information related to topsoil and ameliorants in section Q28, seeding and turfing in Q30 and external planting in Q31. The NBS *Classic* conforms to the Common Arrangement of Work Sections (CAWS), and so establishes a consistent arrangement for specifications and bills of quantities. A new and completely revised release of NBS, NBS *Create*, is compatible with the modern construction industry practice of Building Information Modelling (BIM) and uses a new *Uniclass* classification system. Here, amenity and ornamental planting systems are found under section 40-35-00. NBS *Create* will see more revisions as it evolves and responds to the new, comprehensive *Uniclass 2015* classification system, which has been re-structured to be in accordance with BS ISO 12006-2: 2015 Building construction – Organization of information about construction works (BSI, 2015b).

The National Plant Specification is a free, online service that provides recognised industry standards for the quality and size of plant material and a code of practice for plant handling, from the nursery to establishment within the landscape. The NPS is already discussed further in Chapter 5, Plant production, and can be accessed online here: www.csdhub.com. There is a short and simple registration process.

Tree planting as part of a highway scheme could be specified under Series 3000 of the MCHW Specification for Highway Works. Planting is specified in Clause 3006 and refers to both British Standards and the National Plant Specification for the quality of works and plant material. The Specification for Highway Works is also available online here: www.standardsforhighways. co.uk/mchw/vol1/pdfs/series_3000.pdf.

As with drawings, there is a temptation to simply copy text from previous project specification into new documents, with little or no checking. This can lead to obvious discrepancies between documents and errors such as out-of-date or inappropriate information being included. As a consequence, there is still a tendency within some sectors of the industry to largely ignore written specifications and rely solely on the information shown on drawings. Thankfully, this attitude is changing, and it is an obligation on all designers to ensure that the specifications they produce are thorough and correct if they are to be taken seriously and the trend is to be continued. Ideally, items should not be specified as 'to be approved'; a decision has to be made at some point, so no time is saved in the long run. The tenderer will also not be able to price such an item without making a guess as to what may or may not be approved and unnecessary disputes can be caused by such uncertainty.

6.2.3   Bills of quantity

Items of work identified within the drawings and specifications are recorded within a bill of quantities (BoQ) prepared by the client or their consultant. The quantities are typically measured in number, length, area, volume, weight or time and are used by tenderers to assist in preparing a price for carrying out the works. As the BoQ would be provided to each tenderer, the need to calculate (take-off) quantities from drawings and specifications is removed from the process. Each tenderer would be pricing the same quantity for each item of work, so ensuring a comparable and accurate tendering process. It is important to ensure that the information shown within a BoQ and that shown on drawings or in specifications is consistent. Inconsistency can be the cause of contention and dispute later. In such instances where an item is shown in drawings and/or specifications, but not in the BoQ, or if arithmetical errors exist, the BoQ will typically take precedence over the other tender documentation and the client will be responsible for their own errors or omissions. Time spent ensuring that the information within the tender and construction packages is correct and consistent will certainly help the contractor better understand the requirements of the project, This, in turn, should ensure that the quality of the finished works reflects the expectations of the designer. Any risk perceived by a contractor due to inconsistent or poorly structured information is likely to be reflected in the tender sum. Risk, after all, costs money.

In order to promote a common method of measurement for quantities among the various disciplines within the construction industry, the Standard Method of Measurement (SMM) was first published by the Royal Institution of Chartered Surveyors (RICS) in 1922. The final seventh edition (SMM7) was published in 1988 and revised in 1998. It was developed through a set of clearly defined rules that not only ensures consistency in the measurement of construction works, but also encourages the adoption of best practice, and so helps to reduce the incidence of possible disputes. The categorisation of work sections within SMM7 was arranged in such a way that it conformed to CAWS. On 1 January 2013, the RICS released a new standard to replace SMM7, the New Rules of Measurement (NRM) and as a consequence SMM7 should no longer be used. The main obvious difference is that the arrangement of work sections have changed from the previous alphabetic (A to Y) system in SMM7 to a numerical (1 to 41) system in NRM. Soft landscaping works, which were previously under section Q, are now found under section 37. In general, the rules may have changed to encompass revisions to standards and codes of practice, but overall, the changes to content have been fairly modest, and for all soft landscaping works, they remain unaltered.

6.3   NATIONAL AND INTERNATIONAL STANDARDS

Standards are documents that provide requirements, specifications, guidelines and qualities that can be used consistently to ensure that products, materials, processes and services are fit for purpose. On their own, standards are voluntary and carry no obligation for compliance. However, laws and regulations may cite standards, and thereby make compliance compulsory. Certainly, specification by reference to recognised standards is fairly commonplace. It is, therefore, important to ensure that the standard referred to is current and easily available. Certainly, any competent contractor would be expected to be aware of, and fairly well-versed with, most of the British and

European standards relevant to the field of their expertise, such as tree protection, planting and management. Copies of British and European standards are available for purchase through the British Standards Institution (BSI) online shop (http://shop.bsigroup.com) or by subscription through British Standards Online (BSOL). The online subscription platform also allows access to American Society for Testing and Materials (ASTM), European (EN) and International Organization for Standardization (ISO) documents.

All ratified European standards carry the EN reference (e.g., BS EN 14199:2015 *Execution of special geotechnical works – micropiles*) and an obligation to be implemented at a national level. International standards are designated with the ISO reference (e.g., BS EN ISO 11091:1999 *Construction drawings – Landscape drawing practice*). ISO was set up to facilitate world trade by providing common standards among trading nations. As with EN standards, national adoption of ISO standards requires there to be a consistency in available information. This will necessitate the withdrawal of any existing national standards that contain information that conflicts with the ISO standard to be adopted.

The British Standards Institution also produces Publicly Available Specifications (PAS) as a fast-track process of developing and delivering guidelines, benchmarks, management systems or codes of practice, collaboratively with industry organisations, for example, BSI PAS 100:2011 Specification for composted materials was prepared and published by BSI, sponsored by the Waste and Resources Action Programme (WRAP) and developed in partnership with the Association for Organics Recycling (AFOR). These BSI-endorsed PASs share the structure, format and functionality of a formal British Standard. Similarly, the ISO develops international PASs.

In the United States, the American National Standards Institute (ANSI) oversees the creation, endorsement and use of norms, guidelines and standards, rather than developing them itself. The American Standard for Nursery Stock, for example, was developed by the American Nursery and Landscape Association and submitted to ANSI for approval. The latest revision was approved and released in April 2014. It provides a North American counterpoint to the UK National Plant Specification. For comparisons between the two, see Chapter 5, Plant production.

The American Standard for Nursery Stock is available for free download here: http://americanhort.org/documents/ANSI_Nursery_Stock_Standards_AmericanHort_2014.pdf.

6.4 WORKS SPECIFICATIONS AND DETAILS

The production documents (drawings, specifications, bills of quantity, and so on) describe the nature and quality of work that is expected and that the contractor is required to provide. The layout of the scheme, showing the locations for all trees to be planted, will be shown on a layout drawing or set of drawings. The species, sizes, quantities and specification of all the trees will be listed in a plant schedule. The details of all planting materials and accessories, references to codes of practice and standards and explanations on how the work is to be conducted are shown in the specification. Guidance on material selection, processes and requirements can be found from a variety of sources, some of which is contradictory. It is, therefore, important that appropriate arboricultural expertise is included within any design or project team.

6.4.1 *Planting*

The planting requirements should be determined through assessment and analysis of the planting site and selection of the tree species to be planted. Series 3000 of the Specification for Highway Works (SHW 3000) provides dimensions for tree pits, based on the size of the planted tree, which, on the face of it, seems to be quite sensible. However, on close observation, there appear to be a few odd dimensions. Root-balled selected standard nursery shade trees are typically 10–12 cm girth with a root ball of 300 mm (BS 8545 and ENA) to 500 mm (Hillier) diameter and a depth of 350 mm. The planting pit dimensions from SHW 3000 are 1000 × 1000 × 600 mm, with an additional 200 mm decompaction at the base of the pit. Although the lateral dimensions are fine, the root ball would be sitting atop 450 mm of decompacted and reasonably loose soil, which will almost undoubtedly lead to settlement. While breaking up the base of a planting pit is often considered good practice where machinery may have smeared and compacted the bottom of the hole, any disturbed soil beneath the root ball must be thoroughly recompacted, by hand (or rather foot) to prevent later settlement. In fact, British Standard BS 8545 (BSI, 2014) specifically advises against disturbing any soil in the base of the pit. Most rooting will occur in the top 400–500 mm of soil anyway, and if the intention is to provide better rooting conditions, it is unlikely to provide them. If waterlogging in the planting pit is the concern, no amount of disturbance to the bottom of the planting hole is likely to provide a long-term solution to the problem; some form of positive drainage is likely to be required.

6.4.2 Soil

If the excavated material can be reused for planting, even if requiring some amendment and amelioration, that must be the preferred option, rather than transporting it to landfill and importing replacement soil. Problems associated with over-use of organic matter within planting holes and use at depth have been dealt with in Chapter 3. Well-composted organic matter will invariably improve soil, but it should be worked into the surface throughout the planting area and not restricted to the planting pit only.

Sometimes, reusing the existing soil is not possible and alternative sources must be found. For example, approximately 42,000 cu. m of topsoil and 36,000 cu. m of subsoil were imported to the 2012 Olympic Park, much of it by train. In addition, 4,000 cu. m of high-permeability turf rooting media and 1,900 cu. m of specialist root zone material, for trees planted in paved areas, were used. The topsoil was manufactured offsite by blending various combinations of mineral

Figure 6.2
The demand for a consistent topsoil on a project the size of the Olympic Park was so great that most of it had to be manufactured. No existing site soils were reused as topsoil due to contamination and horticultural unsuitability, although it was used as civil engineering bulk fill material. Here, multipurpose topsoil has been spread 300–400 mm deep to create one of the wooded hillocks. (Image Capita Lovejoy.)

Figure 6.3
Low-value quarry
overburden was used
as a suitable
landscape subsoil. It
also provided a good
temporary working
platform for
machinery due to its
ability to drain freely
and resistance to
compaction. (Image
Capita Lovejoy.)

and organic materials, depending on the eventual required use of the soil. The mineral portion was sourced from low-value quarry overburden, screened and processed to remove large stones and ensure a consistent composition. The organic matter was provided by composted green waste.

The quarry overburden also provided the material used as subsoil. Its high sand and stone content resisted compaction and allowed free drainage of water. As a consequence, it provided an ideal temporary working platform during the winter, requiring only surface ripping prior to the placement and grading of topsoil (O'Hare, 2011).

The British Standard *Code of practice for general landscape operations (excluding hard surfaces)* BS 4428-4: 1989 suggests a depth of topsoil for tree planting of 600 mm. Such practice has now been shown to be ill-advised. The use of topsoil at such depths can be subject to anaerobic conditions and should be restricted to the top 300–400 mm only. The British Standard *Specification for topsoil* BS 3882 (BSI, 2015a) and the Defra *Construction Code of Practice for the Sustainable Use of Soils on Construction Sites* (Defra, 2009) both support this approach. Any soil used at any depth below 300–400 mm should be subsoil, containing much less organic matter and soil microbes than the topsoil above it. At planting, smaller tree root balls should sit on top of this subsoil and larger root balls should sit partly below the top of the subsoil level.

6.4.3 Drainage

The vertical drainage within the planting area relies upon the structure and texture of the soil. If the soil is not over compacted, but is well-structured and does not contain too much clay, it should drain quite satisfactorily. In constructed landscapes, however, it is not uncommon for the lower layers, beneath the topsoil, to be highly compacted, due to machinery movements or other construction activity. In these situations, tree planting pits can easily become sumps into which surface water flows and cannot escape, causing the rooting zone to become waterlogged. Some system of sub-surface drainage will be necessary to overcome this problem, but will still require a freely draining topsoil to function correctly. No amount of sub-surface drainage will solve a surface water problem if the soil is so fine-textured and dense that it cannot allow water to drain vertically through it.

Sub-surface drainage systems typically fall into two basic types: piped systems, which can convey excess water fairly rapidly from where it is unwanted to a collection point or sewer, and gravel-filled trench systems, which tend to convey water much more slowly, allowing a certain amount of storage or attenuation within the system. Both will require a fall along their length to ensure a consistent flow of water. The lower end of the pipe or trench must connect either to a surface or storm water sewer or could empty into a pond, if the topography allows.

Occasionally, gravel is specified in the bases of planting pits to 'aid drainage'. As discussed in Chapter 3, the finer the pores within the soil, the tighter water is held. A gravel drainage layer will only work when the soil above the gravel is completely saturated and water is draining through gravity. In other conditions, the gravel layer will be causing a perched water table and takes up space that could be better used to provide a rootable, but free-draining subsoil.

Figure 6.4
The topsoil is a sandy loam, yet the planting pit is filling with water. The preceding summer and autumn had been exceptionally wet and the subsoil, although sandy, was unable to drain quickly enough. In these situations, it is worth checking for compaction and to determine the texture and structure of underlying soil. Here, tree planting was postponed until the surface water had subsided. Later in the season, the trees were able to be planted without a problem.

6.5 DECOMPACTION

If soil within the root zone has been compacted, it should be treated, if possible, to alleviate the problem. There are many methods to achieve decompaction, and selection generally is made according to circumstances.

6.5.1 Subsoiling and ripping

Large landscape schemes can sometimes be treated through ripping or subsoiling, where a long single tine or group of tines is dragged through the soil, up to a metre deep. The power requirements are enormous and these tines are invariably pulled with a tracked machine to both avoid further compaction and provide sufficient traction. Obviously, any utility services, sub-surface drainage and any existing planting would be damaged by such a process, and so its applicability tends to be fairly restricted to new, large developments. Less intrusive ripping was used on the Olympic Park to decompact the subsoil temporary working platform prior to spreading topsoil.

6.5.2 Compressed air excavation tools – Air Spade®/Soil Pick©/Air Knife

These tools operate by directing compressed air along a handheld lance and through a special nozzle that concentrates the air stream into a very narrow jet. The air is travelling at supersonic speed on leaving the nozzle, and when aimed at soil, it blasts the soil particles apart. Originally, this tool was developed for use by utility companies as a way to safely expose service ducts, pipes and cables, without having to use mechanical excavators and risk utility strikes or damaging tree roots. The main advantage with this approach to decompaction is that it can be used on existing trees. The high-velocity air stream does not directly damage non-friable materials such as tree roots, but coarse sand and stone, moving at a high speed can strip the bark off roots. This is especially more of a problem during the growing season, but certainly less extensive than using hand tools.

There are three main techniques that are used to decompact soil within tree root zones: radial trenching, vertical mulching and 'air tilling' surface decompaction.

Figure 6.5
Here, an Air Spade® is being used to decompact segments within the root zone of a park tree (left). The high-speed jet of air fractures the soil, relieving the compaction and leaving it 'fluffed up'. The process can also be used to incorporate organic matter through the topsoil profile. Once the ground compaction has been relieved (right), the entire root zone, at least to the canopy drip line, can be mulched with bulky organic matter. (Images David Humphries.)

6.5.2.1   Radial trenching

Starting from the base of the tree stem, trenches are excavated, working radially away from the stem to the canopy drip line and preferably beyond. The trenches can then be backfilled with the loosened soil amended with organic matter or refilled with new, high-quality topsoil. Sometimes, a series of concentric, circular trenches are also excavated, in addition to the radial trenches, as a way to increase access to good rooting media.

6.5.2.2   Vertical mulching

The compressed air excavation tool can also be used to dig vertical holes arranged in a grid across the root zone of the tree to be treated (also known as potholing). Power-driven augers can also be used to drill a grid of holes, but can cause smearing to the sides of the hole if carried out in moist, fine soils. As above, an ameliorated soil mix can be used to backfill the excavated holes.

6.5.2.3   Air tilling surface decompaction

In parks, public gardens and green open spaces, surface compaction from pedestrians or maintenance vehicles can be a significant problem. Here, the compressed air excavation tool can be used to shatter the soil surface to a depth of 150–250 mm. If organic matter is spread over the ground, it can also be worked through the soil.

6.5.3   Compressed gas injection

Another way to alleviate compaction is to rupture the soil from below by injecting a blast of compressed gas at depth. This causes the ground to lift around the injection point, and if materials are injected with the air blast, such as calcified seaweed, expanded polystyrene beads or vermiculite, it is claimed that the fissures created are kept open.

A variety of trials have been conducted, making comparisons between the various methods of decompaction of root zones, especially between the compressed air excavation method and the compressed gas injection method. There have been some concerns that supersonic air tools can blast mycorrhizae hyphae and fine roots to pieces and can 'sand-blast' roots, stripping them of their protective bark. Others have concentrated on the ineffectiveness of compressed gas injection, claiming that the soil bulk density remains virtually unaltered. However, rather than changing the overall bulk density, this technique creates fissures through the compacted zone, with the intention of allowing water and air to move through the soil profile, and so provide more suitable conditions for roots to grow. Whatever method is used, as long as the compaction is treated and damage to existing roots is reduced as far as possible, evidence would appear to show that the benefits of creating a decompacted root zone more than compensate for the limitations or drawbacks of the system used.

Research has been carried out and continues to investigate the possible benefits of incorporating biochar into the root zones of established trees, especially those showing signs of stress. The methods above can be used to incorporate biochar into the root zone.

6.6 STORM WATER ATTENUATION

Figure 6.6 Compressed gas injection being used to decompact the root zone around a Liriodendron at the RHS Gardens, Wisley. Here, the hollow spike has been driven into the ground, and a high pressure blast of air is being discharged through the end of the spike. The grey cylinders contain the charge of air and are pressurised by the compressor at the front of the machine. (Image Terrain Aeration.)

Increases in urbanisation affect land cover, converting what may have been predominantly permeable surfaces into impervious buildings, roads and other sealed surfaces. In turn, increases in hard surfaces effectively constrain the availability of tree planting sites in places where they are most desirable, providing respite from the hard, urban landscape. Moreover, as tree planting provides more than just an amenity resource, there are other practical advantages in delivering a whole range of ecosystem services. Hard infrastructures also fundamentally change urban hydrology, reducing opportunities for local infiltration, and so causing an overall increase in surface water run-off. The run-off from roads and car parks is also likely to contain significant levels of contamination, with a risk of adding pollutants to receiving water bodies. Not only is there an environmental impact associated with this scenario, but there are also financial implications due to increased costs incurred in maintaining the surface water conveyance and treatment systems.

The aims of any surface water treatment approach that employs green infrastructure must be to reduce peak water flow, reduce overall water volume and remove pollutants. Traditional SuDS features, such as bioswales, detention basins and retention ponds, require significant investments in space and where high land values drive development densities in city centres; competition for space is always going to be fierce. However, in less central urban locations, they can be and have been used very successfully to increase species diversity and public interest in the natural world. The main benefit from these features is that they are above ground, so easy to monitor and maintain and can fairly simply be integrated within the green infrastructure component delivery for the development scheme. Some good examples of where this has been applied in the UK are the Upton Sustainable Development Extension in Northampton (HCA, 2013), the Queen Elizabeth Olympic Park in east London (Hopkins, Askew & Neal, 2011), Beam Parklands in Dagenham, Essex (Beam Parklands, 2016), and Sutcliffe Park in south-east London (The Landscape Institute, 2016).

Trees, and especially large canopy trees, are able to contribute to surface water management through canopy interception, evapotranspiration and infiltration. In addition, they are able to facilitate, through their rooting environment, a certain amount of surface water pollution treatment. Tree canopies are able to intercept and trap water on their leaves and stems during rainfall events, and this can evaporate back into the atmosphere once the rainfall has ceased.

Figure 6.7 The Kidbrooke Village development in south-east London has adopted a SuDS approach to surface storm water management. This links up with the River Quaggy Flood Alleviation Scheme in neighbouring Sutcliffe Park and provides valuable opportunities for increasing tree diversity through the provision of additional habitats.

Figure 6.8
This very narrow bioswale is much more appropriate for tight urban locations. The kerb offlet allows surface water to flow into the swale where it is attenuated and treated prior to discharge into the sewer system.

Canopy interception studies have revealed that effectiveness varies dramatically between tree species, canopy size, climatic conditions and intensity of rainfall. Interception can range between 15 per cent for an isolated 9-year old *Pyrus calleryana* in Davis, California (Xiao *et al.*, 2000) to 60 per cent for a single 15-year old *Ficus benjamina* in Queretaro City, central Mexico (Guevara-Escobara *et al.*, 2007). These figures broadly align with other studies that have looked at both forest stands and urban trees. As could be expected, evergreen species generally contribute more to annual rainfall interception than deciduous species, due to the presence of leaves during the winter and a higher overall leaf area index (LAI) (Xiao *et al.* 1998). It was also found, from water samples collected under trees, that rain falling and dripping through the tree canopy (throughfall) had a lower pH and contained higher concentrations of nutrients and metals (NPK, zinc and chromium) than control sites. This indicates the likely atmospheric deposition of pollutants that occurs within the crowns of trees growing in urban locations. Those with rougher bark and dense branch patterns appear to trap more pollution than smooth bark, open branching species (Xiao & McPherson, 2011).

Much work has been carried out in Australia and the USA, looking at bioretention systems as effective means of managing surface water run-off (Abbott *et al.*, 2013). These features capture and treat stormwater from frequent rainfall events in shallow depressions, typically containing engineered substrates and appropriately selected vegetation, including trees. It is the substrate and the vegetation that carry out the treatment function. The treated water is either passed forward into the wider drainage system or infiltrates the surrounding soil, with a proportion of the water being evaporated from the surface of the feature and transpired through the plant leaves.

In an effort to address the fierce competition for space in urban areas, there is much interest in the use of stormwater reservoirs within tree planting pits, using engineered substrates. Manufacturers and suppliers are able to provide comprehensive data, information from case studies and scientific research to support the use of their product.

6.7 ENGINEERED SUBSTRATES

There is no doubt that trees will generally grow better in conventional topsoil than in an engineered, granular medium. However, in many urban situations, using conventional soil is simply not possible due to the engineering requirement for highly compacted sub-grades and sub-bases to support the paved surfaces required for vehicular or pedestrian movement. Engineered substrates tend to be designed to increase porosity, and so improve permeability below the sealed surfaces. Not only do they provide the structural support demanded by engineers, but they also provide a considerably improved rooting environment for trees. There are two basic approaches: the structural soils approach, where carefully selected aggregates, organic matter and topsoil are combined to create an engineered load-bearing rooting medium (such as tree sands and stone matrix mixes), and those that use soil-filled, prefabricated, structural 'crates' or supports that create a sub-surface 'soil vault' and which provide suitable foundations for the paved surface above. Such approaches to the provision of sub-surface materials create a much less hostile rooting environment and also provide opportunities to absorb surface water run-off, store it and treat it, with the high porosity of the stone matrix materials being of particular interest. Chapter 19 of the revised *SuDS Manual* (Woods Ballard *et al.*, 2015) from the Construction Industry Research and Information Association (CIRIA) provides detailed guidance on the selection, design, implementation, operation and management of structural rooting media within SuDS projects.

6.7.1 Tree sands

The original Amsterdam Tree Sand was developed in Holland during the 1960s and 1970s in response to the poor performance of street trees in Amsterdam. The early research work was conducted by the Amsterdam Highways and Soil Mechanical Research Departments, Omegam laboratories and Wageningen University. It consists of medium coarse sand containing 4–5 per cent (w/w) organic matter and between 2 and 4 per cent (w/w) clay (Couenberg, 1994). The grading of the sand, the clay content and the amount and type or organic matter are very tightly controlled. The organic matter must be well decomposed, to prevent a high oxygen demand, caused by the further decomposition. Organic matter content must be no greater than 5 per cent, to prevent later settling of the mixture and no less than 4 per cent to ensure that trees are adequately provided with nutrients and water. If the clay content rises above 4 per cent or exceeds the organic matter content, the mixture can easily be over-compacted during installation (Couenberg, 1994).

Early Dutch compositions of the rooting media used excavated peat bog topsoils, which are low in clay, to provide the organic matter and clay fractions. Later variations, which are widely available from many suppliers (Heicom/Bourne Amenity/Urban tree sand, and so on), tend to provide the organic matter from composted green waste rather than peat. Tree sands tend to contain a blend of washed, semi-rounded silica sands, with approximately 50% (by weight) in the medium sand (0.5–0.25 mm USDA) fraction. Specifications appear in Appendix 1.

Typical Amsterdam tree pit installations are between 0.8 and 1 m deep. At depths greater than 1 m, oxygen influx has been found to be sufficiently low to inhibit good root growth, despite the relatively high porosity of the material (Couenberg, 1994). In Amsterdam, the ground water table tends to be fairly consistently found at between 1 and 1.2 m in depth, above which is a 100 to 200 mm 'saturation zone', overlain with a compacted layer of non-saturated sand. The Amsterdam tree soil is typically installed above this compacted layer. During installation, the medium is compacted in layers (lifts) of 400–500 mm thickness. Compaction is checked during installation of each lift using a cone penetrometer. Compaction of the media is measured in terms

Figure 6.9 *(left and above)*
One of the tree avenues at the 2012 Olympic Park planted in tree sand (left).
The surfaces in these pedestrian avenues are finished in resin-bonded gravel with
generous unpaved areas being left around each tree, finished in CEDEC® footpath
gravel (above). The CEDEC® should allow the trees to increase in size, without
constricting growth. (left image Capita Lovejoy.)

of its resistance to penetration, measured in mega pascals (MPa), rather than relative to maximum
bulk density determined by the Proctor test. The required penetration resistance of suitably
compacted tree sand is 1.5–2.0 MPa. This equates to a compaction of approximately 70–80 per
cent peak density. While this density has little effect on restricting root growth, it is also not
considered suitable to support highway construction. However, tree sands have been used successfully to provide tree root volumes under pedestrian areas, footways and parking for light
vehicles. A slightly modified Amsterdam tree sand was used extensively for tree planting in hard
areas in the 2012 London Olympics site and during the later legacy transformation to the Queen
Elizabeth Olympic Park.

6.7.2 Stone matrix media

These systems rely on a compacted stone matrix to provide the necessary load-bearing
requirements demanded by engineers while supporting a non-compacted rooting medium within
the voids between the stones. Careful selection of the correct type of stone ensures that imposed
loads are transferred from stone to stone without compacting the soil between them, so
providing a rooting environment that does not impede root growth. Because they are based on
stone aggregates, they can be compacted to much greater densities, making them less prone to
later settlement or movement than the various tree sand mixes. This makes them more suitable
for areas subjected to more intense or a greater volume of use.

CU-Structural Soil®

CU-Structural Soil® was developed at Cornell University in Ithaca, New York, in the mid-1990s.
It is manufactured from crushed stone and soil, blended with a hydrogel co-polymer, which
prevents the stone and soil separating in transit and when mechanically handled during
manufacture and installation.

The stone component is a highly angular, gap-graded (approximately 20–40 mm), crushed aggregate. When compacted, the tightly graded, angular stone ensures that an open lattice structure is created, with approximately 40 per cent porosity. The soil volume is carefully calculated so that it almost fills the voids, without compacting, thus allowing aeration and free root penetration throughout the medium. Research at Cornell revealed that the 'ideal' proportion of stone to soil was approximately 80 per cent stone to 20 per cent soil, by dry weight. It is important that a soil with minimum 20 per cent clay content is used to ensure sufficient water holding and nutrient exchange. In fact, a range between 20 per cent and 40 per cent is acceptable. The organic matter content should be between 2 per cent and 5 per cent, to help maintain nutrient exchange and also to assist beneficial microbial activity

Figure 6.10
CU-Structural Soil® mixed and ready for transportation to site. Mixing is best carried out on a flat, hard surface; a uniform 300-mm layer of stone, followed by hydrogel and topped-off with a layer of moist soil. The layering can be repeated as required, depending on the size of loading shovel used. (Image Nina Bassuk.)

within the root zone. When fully compacted to meet the engineering load-bearing specifications, CU-Structural Soil® has a water-holding capacity between 7 per cent and 12 per cent. Grabosky et al. suggest that a conservative 8 per cent is assumed (2009), a value not too dissimilar to a light, loamy sand soil. As with all aggregate-based rooting media, careful consideration needs to be given, therefore, to the design of an appropriate rooting volume, when considering such a free-draining material.

Because the manufacture of the material needs to be carefully controlled, CU-Structural Soil® has been patented by Cornell University, and to ensure that it conforms to quality control standards, is manufactured only by registered producers. This ensures that all supplied material carrying the CU Structural Soil® or CU-Soil® trademarks has been produced and tested to meet the specification (as shown in Appendix 1).

The structural soil is typically compacted to at least 95 per cent peak bulk density, which should provide a minimum CBR of 50 (Grabosky & Bassuk, 1996). A typical street tree installation would use a minimum depth of 600 mm, with 900 mm depth being preferable. The material is typically installed in 150 mm lifts, and each lift is compacted to an appropriate density to meet the engineering requirements, until the final formation level is reached. Hard surface build-up and finishes would be laid as per normal, ideally with the structural soil providing the sub-base. When fully compacted, voids within the structural soil are only partially filled with soil, allowing aeration and water movement deep into the rooting profile. Observations from excavated trees grown in CU-Structural Soil® have certainly shown that roots tend to grow downwards, rather than close to the surface, therefore overcoming problems of surface deflection caused by tree roots.

Trees are either planted directly into the structural soil or a tree pit containing topsoil, the structural soil then used primarily to extend the accessible rooting volume. The choice really is determined by the chosen surface finish. If a flush-threshold, continuous surface, up to the tree stem is desired, then either some form of support chamber, filled with soil is required or structural soil will be used throughout the installation. Whatever the design, it is advised that the tree root ball is placed on compacted structural soil to provide a firm base and prevent the root ball from

Figure 6.11
A continuous trench filled with structural soil has been installed during footway renovation works to provide an improved rooting environment for the existing tree (left) and to allow additional street trees (right) to share a large rooting volume. (Image Nina Bassuk.)

Figure 6.12
Maple root system exposed with an air excavation tool shows predominantly downward direction of root growth in structural soil.
(Images Nina Bassuk.)

sinking. It is also important to consider the provision of a sufficient opening within the finished surface to allow expansion of the buttress roots. This opening should either be paved with removable paving units or mulched. Structural soil is free-draining and where the sub-grade is highly compacted and impermeable, some form of positive drainage at the bottom of the planting areas is likely to be required to prevent saturation of the root zone. This drainage would be connected to the existing surface or storm water system, or if topography allows, could discharge into an attenuation pond, as part of a SuDS scheme (Woods Ballard *et al.*, 2015).

Some research has been carried out at Cornell to look at retrofitting structural soil around existing trees. The existing soil is removed using high-velocity air and vacuum excavation. It is important to keep exposed roots moist until backfilling with structural soil, and this may be achieved by misting and wrapping using moist hessian sacking. The structural soil is then worked in among the exposed root system and compacted. It is important to note that, to avoid damaging roots, the structural soil may need to be raised up above the existing ground level and then compacted to form the sub-base for the paving. If the root zone cover is changing from soft to hard, some form of permeable surface should be used (Bassuk *et al.*, 2015).

Figure 6.13
The parking bays in this car park have been paved with permeable asphalt, with structural soil as a sub-base. The bare root elm trees were planted in 900 mm openings (left), directly into the structural soil during November 2005. Growth is regularly monitored and the trees appear to be performing well in 2016 (right) (Images Nina Bassuk.)

Figure 6.14
This mature *Cercidiphyllum* (left) was destined for removal as the required paving works for a new plaza would have destroyed much of its root system. An alternative approach was adopted using CU Soil as an elevated sub-base for permeable block paving. After the surface soil was removed with an air excavation tool, 300 to 400 mm of CU Soil was worked between the exposed roots (right) and compacted (Images Nina Bassuk.)

Other aggregate/soil mixes have been used elsewhere. Palle Kristoffersen tested three tree species growing in eight different materials and found that lava and crushed brick, mixed with topsoil, performed as well as topsoil alone, in terms of crown growth and crushed brick mixed with topsoil outperformed all other materials, in terms of root growth (Kristoffersen, 1999).

Carolina Stalite Soil (CS Soil) is similar in its make-up to CU Soil, but uses an expanded slate (Stalite) to create the aggregate matrix. Stalite is manufactured by feeding raw, crushed slate into a rotary kiln that reaches temperatures in excess of 1,200°C. The slate becomes almost molten, and in this state, gases are evolved, which create an open network of pores within the material. As it cools, these pores remain. CS Soil comprises 80 per cent 19-mm Stalite Expanded Slate and 20 per cent sandy clay loam, by volume. Another, similar material, Davis Soil (DS), consists of 75 per cent 19-mm lava rock and 25 per cent clay-loam soil, by volume (Xiao & McPherson, 2008). It was developed by the Department of Land, Air and Water Resources at the University of California, Davis and the US Forest Service's Centre for Urban Forest Research, principally as a material to treat parking area stormwater run-off in bioswale SuDS projects, rather than as an engineered sub-base for paving systems. Lava rock, rather than other stone aggregates, is used because it is readily available in California, making it a fairly inexpensive material, and because it has a high surface area to volume ratio. This latter attribute assists in its ability to trap pollutants and provide sites for pollutant-decomposing bacteria to grow (Xiao & McPherson, 2008).

Stockholm skeleton soil

In Stockholm, Sweden, Björn Embrén produced another similar system. Here, a much larger grade of aggregate has been used, within the 100–150 mm range. In a similar manner to the above systems, the aggregate is installed in lifts (250–300 mm), with each being compacted before the next is installed. The main difference with the Stockholm system is that the mixing of aggregate

Figure 6.15
The various layers of build-up in the Stockholm skeleton soil system (left). The large crushed aggregate, containing soil can be seen at the bottom of the image, covered with the 32–63 mm bearing layer. The geotextile is visible between the bearing layer and the build-up for the concrete pavers. A pre-formed concrete planting chamber surrounded with large crushed aggregate (right). (Images Björn Embrén.)

Figure 6.16
Retrofitting Stockholm skeleton soil to an existing row of lime trees (left). The paving has been lifted and the compacted soil has been removed. Note the irrigation bags to keep the root zones hydrated. The recycled, crushed concrete has been installed and compacted (right). An air and water inlet can be clearly seen middle-right of the image. (Images Björn Embrén.)

and soil takes place as each stone layer is installed and compacted. The soil is applied to the surface of the compacted stone skeleton and is washed between the stone interstices, using a high-pressure water hose. Approximately 0.25 cu. m of topsoil is required for each cu. m of crushed stone and is applied in small amounts (approximately 20 mm covering) at a time. The entire stone skeleton installation is then capped with a 200 mm aerated, bearing layer of 32–63 mm crushed stone. This is compacted, covered with a geotextile fabric and the whole finished with a suitable surface-paving material. Trees are either planted into pre-formed, modular concrete or bespoke, *in situ* chambers that sit on top of compacted coarse, crushed stone and should be adjusted to level before the final layers of stone are installed. The chambers are filled with topsoil in preparation for tree planting.

In Stockholm, rain water from adjacent roofs and surface water from paving is directed into the stone matrix to maintain tree irrigation needs. To ensure that the stone layers do not become inundated and anaerobic, a drainage system must be installed to divert excess water to the existing stormwater sewer (The City of Stockholm, 2009).

Further experimental work has been carried out using carefully graded crushed concrete instead of crushed stone. The pH will be initially much higher, but with appropriate selection of tree species, results have been quite encouraging, with little difference evident between crushed concrete and stone installations (Embren, 2015 personal communication). Some early results using biochar within the aggregate profile have also proved encouraging.

As with all of these structural soils, careful site monitoring is essential and should be timed to coincide with materials deliveries and top soil installation, so that quality control can be maintained. Rigorous control of the aggregate grading is probably the most crucial aspect to ensuring success. If the aggregate fractions are inconsistent, it will not be possible to retain essential spaces between each individual particle. The smaller size stones will simply fill the voids, preventing access for roots. For the same reason, it is also vital to ensure that the surface bedding layer is isolated from the coarse aggregate layers below. The city of Stockholm has produced a

Figure 6.17
Topsoil is spread in layers over the compacted stone and is washed through the stone with a high-pressure hose (left). The concrete pavers are re-laid on a stone dust bedding layer (right). (Image Björn Embrén.)

Figure 6.18
Crate systems typically require a firm and level sub-base upon which they are set-out (left). Of the engineered systems, soil vaults provide maximum access to top soil (right).

comprehensive handbook that explains the installation procedure in some detail. It is available as a free download from: http://foretag.stockholm.se/Regler-och-ansvar/Bygga/Handbocker/.

6.7.3 Structural soil vaults

The granular materials discussed above include both patented or proprietary systems and uncontrolled materials, allowing the designer a certain degree of freedom when selecting a technique suitable for the site. To add to that palette of choice, there is a range of purpose-made commercial, modular products that provide the load-bearing for surface treatments, through various methods of structural support. They can be broadly divided into plastic crate and concrete support systems and plastic crate raft systems.

Figure 6.19
Underground guying, aeration-irrigation systems (left) and tree grilles (right) can fairly easily be integrated with whichever soil vault system is being used. Each manufacturer will provide a design service to ensure correct specification and co-ordination (left image Amber Haigh).

Each system requires a structurally sound sub-grade on which to be installed, and this typically will require a layer of compacted stone capping material. An underdrain can also be installed to prevent excess water collecting within the rooting zone of the pit. As before, this can either connect to the existing surface or stormwater network or could discharge into an attenuation pond, if part of a SuDS scheme. It is always preferable to consider the use of permeable final surface treatments for use where tree planting is planned.

The soil vault systems should allow for reuse of the excavated native soil, assuming that it is chemically and physically suitable. The main advantage here is a reduction in transportation of excavated material. It certainly does appear to be somewhat counterintuitive to remove material from site, only to replace it with another imported material. This surely should be avoided if at all possible.

Aeration and irrigation systems can be installed as required. The surface treatments are constructed on typical build-up layers as usual, but details change from product to product.

Each manufacturer provides access to fairly comprehensive drawn details and materials and performance specifications on their website. They should be involved in the design process to ensure compliance, as any warranties and guarantees will be dependent on such compliance.

6.7.3.1 Structural support systems

Of these, the two main plastic crate systems available in the UK are the *StrataCell* and *StrataVault* produced by GreenBlue Urban (www.greenblue.com) and the *Silva Cell*, produced by DeepRoot (www.deeproot.com). These are all high strength, composite (typically glass-reinforced polymer), modular systems that provide an open structure that can be filled with topsoil. The *StrataCells* and *StrataVault* systems each clip together to form an integrated, monolithic framework, whereas the *Silva Cell* consists of a series of free-standing vaults, topped with structural decks.

Both provide trees with access to good rooting environments of lightly compacted topsoil. The cells are built up in layers to provide the required rooting volume and are wrapped within

Figure 6.20
The Deeproot Silva Cell is a free-standing vault system, topped with a structural deck (left). Each cell of GreenBlue Urban's StrataCell clips to its adjoining cell to create one massive unit (right) (right image GreenBlue Urban).

suitable open-grid geotextile to prevent migration of adjacent granular materials into the cell soil. This could otherwise cause localised settlement around the edge of the cell installation.

An alternative to high-strength composite cells is a concrete system that employs pre-cast concrete support modules and bridging slabs and is distributed under the name TreeBox HP by InfraGreen (http://infragreen-solutions.com). The system was introduced in 2003 and has developed and evolved in consultation with the City of Amsterdam. The base components are carefully positioned on a structurally sound base to engineer's requirements and enclosed within a retaining wall of open cell units and geotextile. The internal volume is filled with topsoil and the surrounding area is backfilled with granular material and compacted in the usual way. Aeration and irrigation systems can be installed prior to positioning of the pre-formed, reinforced concrete bridging slabs. The slabs are covered with a permeable geotextile, and the final surface treatments are placed on typical bedding layers as usual. The system is said to have a load capacity of 60 t, which would make it suitable for the majority of load-bearing applications (InfraGreen Solutions, 2015b).

6.7.3.2   Raft systems

InfraGreen also distribute the ArborRaft system, which is a modular, interlocking, geocellular framework that 'floats' between the rooting medium and the finished surface treatment. The interconnected cells distribute the imposed vertical loading laterally, preventing compaction of the rooting medium. The system is said to accommodate vehicle loadings ranging from domestic cars through to heavy goods vehicles (InfraGreen Solutions, 2015a).

Other 'floating' systems rely upon a flexible, three-dimensional, cellular mattress that expands when installed to form a network of interconnected cells, with perforated walls. As above, the system is designed to absorb the vertical loading and transfer it laterally through the network of cells. Geosynthetics have been producing their Cellweb TRP® (Tree Root Protection) system since 1998 (Geosynthetics Ltd, 2012). This is a 'no dig' solution, requiring only surface vegetation, surface rocks, debris and any compressible organic matter to be removed prior to installing. Local low spots are then filled with clean angular stone or sharp sand, but are not mechanically

Figure 6.21
The interlocking, cellular ArborRaft system is designed to spread the imposed load laterally across a wide area. The cells are being filled with soil prior to installation of the surface finish build-up (left). Paving material laid and tree pit furniture installed (right). (Images Green-Tech.)

Figure 6.22
The cellular mattress being filled with clean 20–40 mm stone. Note that the contractor is using the stone-filled mattress to provide a working platform. In this way, compaction of soil beneath the mattress is minimised.

compacted. The mattress is placed upon a geotextile membrane and secured prior to filling with a clean granular material (e.g., 20–40 mm) to ensure adequate aeration and free drainage.

Treated timber boards fixed to treated timber pegs are typically used as edge restraints, rather than any permanent pre-cast concrete kerb system. Many of these products comply with the hard surfacing requirements set out in section 7.4 of BS 5837: 2012 *Trees in relation to design, demolition and construction – Recommendations*, making them suitable solutions where permanent vehicular access is required within tree root protection areas. They are typically available in a variety of different depths, from 50 mm to 200 mm and are selected according to the required design loading.

6.8   ROOF GARDENS, GREEN ROOFS AND PODIUM DECKS

As the built form in urban centres increases in density, opportunities for tree planting and other urban greening are becoming more and more scarce. One way to address that lack of opportunity is to look at roof spaces. In certain parts of Germany, such as Stuttgart, planning regulations are in place that require all new flat-roofed buildings to be green roofs. Similarly, the City of Toronto, in Canada, adopted a Green Roof Bylaw in 2009, whereby all new developments with a gross floor area in excess of 2,000 sq. m require green roofs (City of Toronto, 2015).

There are distinct advantages with installing green roofs on buildings: they can help to mitigate against the effects of the urban heat island effect, attenuate storm water, provide wildlife habitats, reduce building energy consumption and help to protect water-proofing materials against the deleterious effects of exposure to sunlight, weather and temperature fluctuations. A good example of the latter are the roof gardens on the top of the former Derry and Toms building at 99 Kensington High Street, which were designed by the landscape architect Ralph Hancock and completed in May 1938. The waterproofing was found to be 'in near-perfect condition after around fifty years' (Scrivens, 1989). Later investigations revealed that although the breeze-cinder filter layer had thoroughly mixed with the clinker drainage layer below, both the drainage layer and the mastic asphalt waterproofing were both in good condition and free of roots after 60 years (Osmundson, 1999).

Since the Derry and Toms roof garden, the technology has progressed enormously, with a wide range of proprietary products available in what appears to be a growth industry. New products, materials and best practice guidance are continuously evolving, helped, in part by the green roof trade organisations, manufacturers and other key stakeholders coming together to form the Green Roof Organisation (GRO). This promotion and quality compliance body provides best practice guidance in the form of the Green Roof Code for the UK (GRO, 2014), based very much on the German Green-Roofing Guidelines and a result of technical co-operation across the UK green roof industry. Ongoing research and exchange of information is ensured through the Sheffield University Green Roof Centre (www.thegreenroofcentre.co.uk) and the University of Greenwich Green Roofs and Living Walls Centre (https://greenroofslivingwalls.org). For an historical overview of green roofs and roof gardens, the reader is directed towards Theodore 'Ted' Osmundson's 1999 treatise, *Roof Gardens: History, Design and Construction*.

It should be remembered that many urban landscapes are built over underground structures, such as car parks, basements and storage facilities. These podium decks, if they are to be planted, are ostensibly roof gardens, and so, could legitimately be treated in the same manner. A development such as Canary Wharf in London's Docklands has a 'ground level' six storeys up above the Jubilee Line underground station, basement retail areas, services and car parking. Here,

Jubilee Park was designed by Wirtz International, technically detailed by Barry Chin Associates and implemented by Willerby Landscapes Ltd. The park contains approximately 250 semi-mature trees, of which the thirty-eight *Metasequoia glyptostroboides* are the most noticeable.

Extensive use of lightweight materials to create the foundations for the undulating ground form were necessary due to loading constraints, as was the use of expanded clay aggregate in the subsoil and topsoil mixes, to ensure light weight, prevent compaction and provide drainage. Roof gardens are, therefore, not necessarily on high roofs. Indeed, many city centre housing developments have basement services or car parking. So, for the past half century, roof garden planting has become increasingly widespread.

6.8.1   Green roof systems

Green roofs can be broadly categorised into extensive and intensive systems, depending on the intended use and depth of rooting substrate.

The purpose of extensive systems is to provide visual interest and biodiversity habitat, rather than amenity or leisure space. They tend to contain plant species that are tolerant to shallow depths of low nutrient substrate (typically 100–200 mm), are drought-tolerant and require very little in the way of maintenance and irrigation. These roofs may, subject to engineering advice, be post applied to buildings, but while providing suitable conditions for sedums and some grass and wildflower species, they are not suitable for tree planting.

Intensive systems include what would be termed 'roof gardens', where space is designed to be accessible for recreational and amenity use. Such use will require a range of materials, not typically associated with roof construction, to be used to create the recreational and/or amenity space.

6.8.2   Loads

The first requirements of the designer invariably relate to the structural loadings and weight of materials, particularly if trees are to be planted. Structural engineers require superimposed dead loads of the materials specified from the landscape architect, supplier or nursery, including the weight of the plants themselves at planting and at maturity, to enable design calculations to be made. They may also request information on transient live loads such as those created by water contained within the growing media or drainage

Figure 6.23
Jubilee Park is built above Canary Wharf station, so is, essentially, a roof garden. It is not unusual for parks and other green spaces in cities to be constructed on podium decks, above buildings.

Figure 6.24
This intensive green roof is used as break-out and staff amenity space. The depth of substrate has been locally increased in the planters to provide a suitable rooting volume for tree and shrub planting.

Table 6.1

Green tree mass and calculated imposed loads for eight tree species, by stem diameter and overall tree height. From Steinhilb, Arola and Winsauer (1984)

Species and height		Mass and load figures according to the stem diameter									
		100 mm		200 mm		300 mm		400 mm		500 mm	
		kg	kN m^{-2}	kg	kN m^{-2}	kg	kN m^{-2}	kg	kN m^{-2}	kg	kN m^{-2}
Populus tremuloides	6 m	35	0.34	100	0.98	220	2.16	–	–	–	–
(Typical for a fast-	9 m	45	0.44	150	1.47	320	3.14	600	5.88	–	–
growing low-density	12 m	60	0.59	195	1.91	425	4.17	800	7.84	–	–
wood tree)	15 m	70	0.69	240	2.35	530	5.20	1,010	9.90	1,600	15.69
Betula papyrifera	6 m	30	0.29	105	1.03	–	–	–	–	–	–
(Typical for other	9 m	40	0.39	155	1.52	345	3.38	–	–	–	–
birches)	12 m	55	0.54	205	2.01	460	4.51	–	–	–	–
	15 m	70	0.69	255	2.50	570	5.59	–	–	–	–
Quercus rubra	6 m	30	0.29	–	–	–	–	–	–	–	–
(Fairly typical of	9 m	45	0.44	175	1.72	–	–	–	–	–	–
medium density oak)	12 m	60	0.59	235	2.30	520	5.10	925	9.07	–	–
	15 m	75	0.74	290	2.84	650	6.37	1,155	11.33	1,800	17.65
Acer rubrum	6 m	35	0.34	105	1.03	–	–	–	–	–	–
(Fairly typical of other	9 m	45	0.44	155	1.52	330	3.24	–	–	–	–
large maples)	12 m	60	0.59	200	1.96	440	4.31	775	7.60	–	–
	15 m	70	0.69	250	2.45	550	5.39	965	9.46	1,500	14.71
Picea glauca	6 m	95	0.93	165	1.62	–	–	–	–	–	–
(Fairly typical of many	9 m	105	1.03	210	2.06	385	3.76	–	–	–	–
softwoods)	12 m	115	1.13	260	2.55	490	4.80	820	8.04	–	–
	15 m	130	1.27	305	2.99	595	5.83	1,005	9.86	–	–
Pinus resinosa	9 m	45	0.44	160	1.57	360	3.53	–	–	–	–
(Fairly typical of many	12 m	55	0.54	215	2.11	475	4.66	–	–	–	–
pines)	15 m	70	0.69	265	2.60	595	5.84	1,050	10.30	–	–

layers and the predicted movement of people. Some of this information can be difficult to find, and occasionally, supply nurseries are somewhat reticent about providing much detailed information due to liability concerns.

6.8.2.1 Tree loads

It can be difficult to accurately determine the load applied by living trees because the water content varies so much between species and at different times of year. Water content within living xylem and associated tissue can range from 30 per cent to 250 per cent more than the weight of any wood material (Coder, 2011). There are some data from the US Forest Service, which determined green weight tables for eight common North American forestry species, from within a 55 mi radius of Houghton, Michigan. All the measurements were taken between 1966 and 1981 (Steinhilb, Arola & Winsauer, 1984) from felled trees, being careful to limit limb damage and loss. Once felled, the height was measured to the nearest 30 cm and the above-ground portion of each tree was weighed. Extracts from the data are shown in Table 6.1 above.

As can be seen from this table, the loadings become quite substantial once trees reach maturity. The design parameters of a typical accessible roof slab may be assumed to be 7.5 kN m^{-2} to cover high density pedestrian traffic and public assembly areas (BSI, 2002; BSI, 2005), and this would be insufficient for most tree species that could be expected to mature up to 400 mm stem diameter. Careful positioning of trees above supporting columns is typically the answer. Although columns are almost always arranged in a rectilinear grid, by omitting trees from certain locations on the grid, a less formal arrangement can be achieved (Osmundson, 1999).

Once the load has been calculated or derived from other sources, a problem then arises when the area of imposed load needs to be determined. Most structural engineers will wish to assume that the load is concentrated over a 1 sq. m area, whatever the size of tree. As the tree grows, the load is likely to be spread over an ever-increasing area of expanding root system, but the majority is still likely to be concentrated close to where the base of the stem and the soil surface meet. Assuming a constant 1 sq. m area would at least ensure that the calculation errs on the side of caution.

6.8.2.2 Wind loads

Wind-induced moment or load calculations may also be required if large canopy trees are to be planted on exposed roofs or podium decks. The important wind-induced load threshold as far as trees are concerned is when the wind speed exceeds approximately 56 mi per hour (90 km per hour). At this point, the branches have been bent as far as they are able and the tree's drag has been reconfigured to a point where it cannot be reduced any further without tissue loss (Coder, 2014). At this point, twigs and branches are torn from the crown and as the wind speed exceeds 60 mi per hour (97 km per hour), branch failure is likely, followed by uprooting. It must be remembered that trees growing in roof gardens are often more exposed than those on the ground and substrates are often significantly lighter than natural topsoils. There will, therefore, be less mass around the root system to prevent it being torn from the ground and the tree is likely to be more impacted by wind loading in its elevated location. Ice accumulation can also impact on the effect of wind loading.

Ice build-up within the branch structure can increase its weight by twenty to fifty times (Coder, 2014). The frozen conditions will lead to a decrease in the branch flexibility, preventing reconfiguration within the canopy. This can cause an increase in wind-induced canopy damage as branches snap rather than bend (Coder, 2014).

The lateral loads imposed on the tree by wind are spread across the extent of its root system. Where tree roots are not constrained by a tree pit or planter, and are allowed to extend beyond the confines of a limited root volume, the lateral loads imposed on the roof structure are likely to be fairly small compared to the more conventional live and dead loads. Where trees growing in containers with restricted rooting volumes, the root system may not be extensive enough to prevent overturning occurring in high winds.

Table 6.2
List of fairly common tree species and approximation of wood density. Adapted from Coder (2011). These figures broadly correlate with the *Timber Design and Construction Handbook* (1965)

Tree species or type	Approximate wood density (kg m^{-3})
Most hardwoods	1,100
Fraxinus spp.	825
Tilia spp.	650
Fagus spp.	925
Prunus spp.	750
Gleditsia triacanthos	990
Magnolia spp.	900
Acer spp.	900
Quercus spp.	1,100
Liquidambar styraciflua	970
Platanus spp.	1,050
Nyssa sylvatica	945
Juglans spp.	945
Liriodendron tulipifera	780
Taxodium distichum	1,050
Juniperus virginiana	815
Pinus strobus	600
Pinus elliottii	950
Tsuga Canadensis	800

Figure 6.25
For more exposed locations, it may be prudent to select more compact or smaller growing trees such as this dwarf field maple, grafted onto a 2-m stem (left) or large shrubs such as this Amelanchier.

6.8.2.3 Rooting media, materials and other load requirements

Green roof growing media tend to be specially manufactured to ensure a lightweight, wind-, erosion- and fire-resistant material with good water retention and aeration properties. These manufactured soils tend to reduce the weight by removing the stone content, above 2 mm in size, from natural soils and replace it with lighter materials, such as expanded clay aggregates or perlite. Topsoil can contain up to 30 per cent by mass of stones above 2 mm to comply with BS 3882: 2015 *Specification for topsoil* (BSI, 2015a). By replacing this with lighter aggregates of similar size classes, quite significant savings in weight can be made. All load data must assume that the material is saturated with water to provide a worst-case scenario.

It can be seen that a fairly typical 800 mm substrate depth required for tree planting and consisting of 600 mm of green roof growing media above a 200 mm expanded clay aggregate drainage layer could produce an imposed load of 10.6 kN m^{-2} (20 × 0.05 = 1.0 kN m^{-2}, 60 × 0.16 = 9.6 kN m^{-2}).

Craning weights are another consideration. Appropriate crane size will need to be calculated along with loading calculations for craning areas or mats to ensure that trees and other materials can be lifted into their elevated locations.

6.8.2.4 Waterproofing

Waterproofing requires rigorous attention to detail to ensure that quality and installation are not compromised. Any later repair or remediation works will be expensive. By far the most difficult locations and common points of failure tend to be where expansion joints and penetrations are present in the concrete deck slab. It is, therefore, vital that the waterproofing system is procured

Table 6.3
Superimposed dead loads associated with green roofs. Adapted from Johnston and Newton (2004) and Osmundson (1999)

Material	kg m⁻³	kg for 1 sq. m/cm depth	Load kN m⁻²/cm depth
Loam topsoil	1,800–2,000	18–20	0.18–0.20
Sand	1,800–2,200	18–22	0.18–0.22
Gravel	1,600–1,950	16–19.5	0.16–0.19
Green roof substrate	1,200–1,600	12–16	0.12–0.16
Expanded clay aggregate (10–20 mm dia)	500	5	0.05
Expanded shale aggregate	650–730	6.5–7.3	0.64–0.72
Turf	–	5	0.05

Figure 6.26
Much of the material being used on green roof spaces is likely to require craning to where they are needed. Crane requirements and localised loadings will need to be determined and agreed with structural engineers. Working methods to ensure correct handling will need to be agreed with the construction or landscape contractors. Note that lifting is by the root ball and not the tree stem. (Image GreenBlue Urban.)

through a reputable company with a long history of successful installations. The waterproof membrane is protected from root ingress with a root-resistant material, either as an independent membrane laid on top or encapsulated as a monolithic waterproof material. All root-resistant membranes should be tested in accordance with section 7.1.1.5 of the German Forschungs-gesellschaft Landschaftsentwicklung Landschaftsbau e.V. (FFL) standard (Guidelines for the Planning, Construction and Maintenance of Green Roofing, 2008), which is more stringent than the European norm EN 13948: 2007 (adopted as BS EN 13948: 2007). An appropriate British Board of Agrément (BBA) certificate will show to what standard the material complies.

One area of possible contention can be fixing the tree root balls using underground guying systems. Perhaps an obvious solution may be to install strategically placed eye-bolts into the surface of the concrete deck to which could be attached guy cables or straps. These could then run over the root ball as is usual in conventional tree planting pits. The problem is that each of these bolts requires a penetration of the slab, and this may cause a potential conflict with the requirements of the waterproofing manufacturer. If trees are to be installed within raised planters, guy-fixing bolts could be attached to the inside of the retaining walls of the planters, rather than the deck structure itself. Otherwise, conventional dead-man guying would be required, although the lighter and freely flowing growing media may not provide the necessary ballast to prevent windthrow on larger tree specimens. It is vital that the growing media supplier, the waterproofing contractor and the structural engineer are all in agreement over the media build-ups, loadings and type of root ball retention required.

REFERENCES

Abbott, J., Simkins, P., Davies, P., Morgan, C., Levin, D. & Robinson, P. (2013). Creating water sensitive places - scoping the potential for Water Sensitive Urban Design in the UK, CIRIA C724, London: CIRIA.

Bassuk, N., Denig, B., Haffner, T., Grabosky, J. & Trowbridge, P. (2015). *CU-Structural Soil - A Comprehensive Guide*. Ithaca (NY): Cornell University: Urban Horticulture Institute.

Beam Parklands (2016). Beam Parklands. (Online) Retrieved 7 May 2016 from www.beamparklands.co.uk/.

BSI (2002). BS EN 1991-1-1: 2002; Eurocode 1: Actions on structures – Part 1-1: General actions – Densities, self-weight, imposed loads for buildings. London: British Standards Institution.

BSI (2005). NA to BS EN 1991-1-1: 2002; UK National Annex to Eurocode 1: Actions on structures – Part 1-1: General actions – Densities, self-weight, imposed loads for buildings. London: British Standards Institution.

BSI (2014). BS 8545: 2014; Trees: from nursery to independence in the landscape – Recommendations. London: British Standards Institution.

BSI (2015a). BS 3882: 2015; Specification for topsoil. London: British Standards Institution.

BSI (2015b). BS ISO 12006-2: 2015; Building construction – Organization of information about construction works – Part 2: Framework for classification (2nd edn). London: British Standards Institution.

City of Toronto (2015). Green Roofs. (Online) Retrieved 23 May 2015 from www1.toronto.ca/wps/portal/contentonly?vg nextoid=3a7a036318061410VgnVCM10000071d60f89RCRD.

Coder, K. D. (2011). Estimating Tree Stem and Branch Weight – WSFNR11-22. Athens, GA: Warnell School, University of Georgia.

Coder, K. D. (2014). Trees and Storm Wind Loads – WSF&NR14-7. Athens, GA: Warnell School of Forestry and Natural Resources, University of Georgia.

Couenberg, E. A. (1994). Amsterdam Tree Soil. In G. W. Watson & D. Neely (eds). *The Landscape Below Ground, Proceedings of an International Workshop on Root Development in Urban Soils* (pp. 24–33). Savoy, IL: International Society of Arboriculture.

Defra (2009). Construction Code of Practice for the Sustainable Use of Soils on Construction Sites. London: Department for Environment, Food and Rural Affairs.

Embren, B. (2015). (e-mail) Personal communication, 30 March 2015. s.l.:s.n.

FLL (2008). Guidelines for the Planning, Construction and Maintenance of Green Roofing. Bonn: Forschungsgesellschaft Landschaftsentwicklung Landschaftsbau e.V. (FLL).

Geosynthetics (2012). Geosynthetics Downloads, Brochures. (Online) Retrieved 9 March 2016 from www.geosyn.co.uk/wp-content/uploads/2015/08/cellweb-trp-brochure1.pdf.

Grabosky, J. & Bassuk, N. L. (1996). Testing of structural urban tree soil materials for use under pavement to increase street tree rooting volumes. *Journal of Arboriculture*, *22*(6), 225–63.

Grabosky, J., Haffner, E. & Bassuk, N. (2009). Plant available moisture in stone-soil media for use under pavement while allowing urban tree root growth. *Arboriculture & Urban Forestry*, *35*(5), 271–8.

GRO (2014). The GRO Green Roof Code: Green Roof Code of Best Practice for UK. Sheffield: Groundwork Sheffield.

Guevara-Escobara, A., González-Sosa, E., Véliz-Chávez, C., Ventura-Ramos, E. & Ramos-Salinas, M. (2007). Rainfall interception and distribution patterns of gross precipitation around an isolated *Ficus benjamina* tree in an urban area. *Journal of Hydrology*, *333*(2-4), 532-41.

HCA (2013). Upton Park Design and Access Statement, s.l.: Homes and Communities Agency.

Hopkins, J., Askew, P. & Neal, P. (2011). Delivering London 2012: Parklands and waterways, Paper 11-00029. Proceedings of The Institution of Civil Engineers – Civil Engineering, November, *164*(6), 30–6.

InfraGreen Solutions (2015a). ArborRaft. (Online) Retrieved 9 March 2016 from http://infragreen-solutions.com/arborraft/.

InfraGreen Solutions (2015b). TreeBox HP. (Online) Retrieved 16 March 2016 from http://infragreen-solutions.com/tree-box-high-performance/.

Johnston, J. & Newton, J. (2004). *Building Green: A Guide to Using Plants on Roofs, Walls and Pavements*. London: Greater London Authority.

Kristoffersen, P. (1999). Growing trees in road foundations. *Arboricultural Journal*, *23*(1), 57–76.

O'Hare, T. (2011). Lessons learned from the London 2012 games construction project: Olympic Park soil strategy, London: Olympic Delivery Authority.

Osmundson, T. (1999). *Roof Gardens – History Design and Construction*. New York: W. W. Norton and Company.

Scrivens, S. (1989). Landscape Update 3 - Urban Planting. *Architect's Journal*, 59–67.

Steinhilb, H. M., Arola, R. A. & Winsauer, S. A. (1984). Green weight tables for eight tree species in northern Michigan. St Paul, MN: US Dept of Agriculture, Forest Service, North Central Forest Experiment Station.

The City of Stockholm (2009). *Planting Beds in the City of Stockholm: A Handbook*. Stockholm: The City of Stockholm.

The Landscape Institute (2016). Case Studies Library – Sutcliffe Park. (Online) Retrieved 9 April 2016 from www.landscape institute.org/casestudies/casestudy.php?id=1.

Timber Engineering Company (1965). *Timber Design and Construction Handbook*. s.l.:F.W. Dodge Corporation.

Woods Ballard, B. *et al.* (2015). *The SuDS Manual*. London: CIRIA.

Xiao, Q. & McPherson, E. G. (2008). Urban runoff pollutants removal of three engineered soils, Albany, CA: USDA, USFS, Center for Urban Forest Research.

Xiao, Q. & McPherson, E. G. (2011). Rainfall interception of three trees in Oakland, California. *Urban Ecosystems*, *14*(4), 755–69.

Xiao, Q., McPherson, E. G., Simpson, J. R. & Ustin, S. L. (1998). Rainfall interception by Sacramento's urban forest. *Journal of Arboriculture*, *24*(4), 235–44.

Xiao, Q. *et al.* (2000). Winter rainfall interception by two mature open-grown trees in Davis, California. *Hydrological Processes*, *14*(4), 763–84.

Chapter 7: Disorders, pests and diseases

7.1 INTRODUCTION

There are various forms of disorders, pests and diseases affecting trees. Many can be overcome by the host tree and simply form part of an interdependent urban biodiversity, but some are proving to be quite serious. This chapter aims to raise awareness, among those responsible for the selection and management of trees, of some of the important tree pathogens and disorders.

It is virtually impossible to separate human influence from a whole host of abiotic factors that affect the trees around us. Nowhere is this more apparent than within our urban centres, where the conditions are fundamentally altered by anthropogenic impacts. Urban planting sites are typically fairly hostile places, and any tree planted in such locations is likely to be predisposed to stresses caused by a range of abiotic factors such as compacted and anaerobic soil conditions, root and bark damage from construction and utility works, pollution loading, high levels of reflected and radiated heat and wind funnelling.

Climate change is also likely to have a marked effect on both biotic activity and abiotic disturbances, with predictions including milder, wetter winters with increasingly intense rainstorm events at one extreme to hotter, drier summers and more frequent and severe periods of drought at the other (Murphy *et al.*, 2009). Some research has been conducted on what effects these predicted weather pattern changes are likely to have on our managed forests (e.g., Forestry Commission, 2011 and Broadmeadow, Morecroft & Morison, 2009), but little has investigated the likely effects on our urban tree populations. However, with many of our urban trees already growing in suboptimal conditions, with restricted access to suitable soil volumes, and with exposure to the urban heat island effect, additional stresses caused by climate change are likely to be more intensely experienced (Tubby & Webber, 2010).

Since time began, perturbations and pathogenic outbreaks have been responsible for the decline, loss and adaption of species throughout the world. Occasionally, such as the intensification and spread of our urban settlements, humans have been responsible for some of these changes. Some researchers are now concerned that the international trade in living plants and timber, combined with an ever-increasing freedom in population movement, could be creating opportunities for the inadvertent introduction of pathogens and that such opportunities have increased greatly in recent decades (Webber, 2010; Brasier, 2008; Defra & FC, 2014). Chris Bright, ex-senior researcher at the Worldwatch Institute, referred to this international trade as a system that 'leaks' exotic species (Campbell, 2001). Of these, the *Phytophthora* species are especially suited to being spread on nursery stock and are likely to be the most dangerous (Brasier, 2008). Even since the Dutch elm disease (*Ophiostoma novo-ulmi*) pandemic of the mid to late 1900s, we are continuing to see how destructive introduced, aggressive pathogens and pests can be to both European and UK natural areas, plantations and gardens.

In ecosystems around the world, pathogenic organisms have been co-evolving with plant communities over millennia. Through natural selection, a balance has been reached whereby native plant species are able to co-exist with the pathogens around them, without suffering catastrophic damage, either by developing resistance strategies or by relying upon other organisms that compete with the pathogen. This situation changes completely when an exotic pest or pathogen is introduced to a different geographical region where there has been no co-evolution and there are no natural enemies (Desprez-Loustau *et al.*, 2007). Native plant species have little or no defence; the exotic introduction is not checked by competition nor is it preyed upon. It is fairly easy to see how aggressive pathogens such as the second Dutch elm disease pandemic, alder dieback (*Phytophthora alni*), box blight (*Cylindrocladium buxicola*) and sudden oak death (*Phytophthora ramorum*, and the similar *Phytophthora kernoviae*) are able to spread so rapidly and with such devastating effects, not only to our horticultural heritage and native ecosystems, but also in terms of the economic costs (Pimentel *et al.*, 2001).

7.2 GLOBALISATION AND THE IMPORTATION OF PLANTS – BIOSECURITY

All of these pathogenic organisms listed above were previously unknown to science before they caused major outbreaks in the UK (Brasier, 2008). It is possible that, through importation, we have inadvertently allowed a range of similar exotic organisms, which ordinarily would be biogeographically separated, to be brought together and to hybridise, both with each other and with endemic species. What were fairly innocuous and weak pathogens on entry to the UK can quickly become highly aggressive hybrids (Webber & Brasier, 2005), which Brasier refers to as 'an uncontrolled, potentially dangerous, open-ended experiment in evolution' (2008). This is certainly what appears to have caused the highly aggressive outbreaks of the *Ophiostoma novo-ulmi* strain of Dutch elm disease and alder dieback (*Phytophthora alni*), (Brasier, 2011).

Previous international biosecurity protocols were created under the International Plant Protection Convention (IPPC) of the FOA and World Trade Organization (WTO), which were written and put in place during the 1950s, when the UK plant trade was largely contained within its own borders. These rules were revised in 1995, under the Sanitary and Phytosanitary Agreement of the WTO, but still have two distinct drawbacks: they favour international trade over the protection of natural or managed ecosystems, and they require that a pest must be identified as such. This becomes especially difficult if the organism is either previously unknown to science or is an exotic introduction and is not known as being a pest in its native range. We are now in a much more globalised market and the protocols controlling international plant trade require revision to address that change. Unfortunately, should these global trade rules, which are enforced by the WTO, pose too high a risk of introduction of pests to a nation, any change would require treaties to be changed and adopted by all of the 160 WTO member states. As Faith Campbell points out, this would be a 'daunting challenge' (2001).

In November 2012, Defra set up the Tree Health and Plant Biosecurity Expert Taskforce, an independent expert panel consisting of academics with plant biosecurity experience, tasked with assessing the current threat to UK plant health from pests, pathogens and syndromes. Their eight recommendations appeared in the joint report published in May 2013 (Defra, 2013).

1   Develop a prioritised UK Plant Health Risk Register.
2   Appoint a Chief Plant Health Officer to own the UK Plant Health Risk Register and to provide strategic and tactical leadership for managing those risks.

3   Develop and implement procedures for preparedness and contingency planning to predict, monitor and control the spread of pests and pathogens.

4   Review, simplify and strengthen governance and legislation.

5   Improve the use of epidemiological intelligence from EU/other regions and work to improve the EU regulations concerned with tree health and plant biosecurity.

6   Strengthen biosecurity to reduce risks at the border and within the UK.

7   Develop a modern, user-friendly system to provide quick and intelligent access to information about tree health and plant biosecurity.

8   Address key skills shortages.

Of these, the Plant Health Risk Register has been set up and is available online and a Chief Plant Health Officer was appointed to lead the operational response and provide leadership and accountability in the event of a disease outbreak.

The report made no reference to the effects that climate change may have on plant health and pathogen impact, neither was there any mention of tighter control on international live plant trade, especially large specimens. Both were highlighted in the 2011 Action Plan for tree health and plant biosecurity, and the workshops that fed into that report, as being key causes of increased risk to plant health. Rather, there is greater emphasis on risk-based approaches to tree health, using the internationally agreed Pest Risk Analysis (PRA) methodologies that set out risks posed by and actions being taken in response to, specific pests and pathogens (Defra & FC, 2014). The PRA process is useful for facilitating the garnering of known information about a particular pest and can, therefore, be very useful at highlighting knowledge gaps to encourage more targeted research. It can also be vital in guiding suitable approaches to control the spread of known invasive pathogens, but it is a reactive tool and will provide very little information and guidance on how to deal with new and previously unknown pathogens. An interesting addition will be the proposed emphasis on commodity or pathway assessments. This approach has worked fairly well for wood packaging materials, by requiring their heat or chemical treatment (FAO, 2002), and so addressing both the known and unknown pathogens, but it waits to be seen how effective such an approach will be with live plants for planting.

The import and export of certain 'controlled' plant species within the EU must be covered by a plant passport, those outside, by a phytosanitary certificate. The current and proposed EU plant health regimes rely upon the producer, providing an assurance that plant material is free from pests and diseases. Providing this sort of guarantee is likely to be very challenging. Phytosanitary certificates are typically issued following a fairly cursory visual inspection of a limited (typically around 2 per cent), and sometimes, unrepresentative sample of plant stock. Clive Brasier points out that most EU nurseries do not even know what *Phytophthoras* are present within their nurseries or on their stock (Brasier, 2010). Records from the Royal Botanic Gardens at Kew also show that imported plant material that comes with a phytosanitary certificate is not guaranteed to be free of pests and diseases. Interceptions of both listed and unlisted pathogens have been made on several occasions, where the plant has required incineration (Redstone, 2014).

There are inherent problems with the current measures that are in place to prevent the introduction and spread of harmful plant pests and diseases. As we have seen, some of the most devastating outbreaks have been caused by organisms that were previously unknown in the UK. Many more are not recorded as causing any problems within their natural ecosystems and only act pathogenically when introduced to new geographical locations and are exposed to exotic plant species. There is a reliance upon the plant producer or grower to ensure that the material supplied is free from pests and disease; yet, it has been known for imported consignments of *Viburnum* plants, labelled as 'pest-free', to arrive from the EU with visible signs of *P. ramorum* infection. One of the problems may be that the current pest control measures can often employ the use of chemicals that suppress the symptoms, but do not kill the pathogen, making any positive identification very difficult. In addition, the emphasis on the importation of mature and semi-mature pot-grown stock brings its own problems. Large container-grown specimens are typically growing in original soil and cannot possibly be inspected adequately at the point of import (Brasier, 2008). The port of Dover, for instance, rarely has a plant health inspector present (Heuch, 2015, personal communication).

Brasier talks of the tension experienced by horticulturists, foresters, garden designers and landscape architects caused by their conservation and environmental protection responsibilities on one side and a desire for novel, instant and cheap plant material on the other. In addition, I would suggest another tension exists, which is an understandable desire to extend the range of suitable plant species available for use in our urban landscapes. In most instances, these will be exotic species, especially if one factors-in the likely impacts of climate change. There must be some onus on the landscape architects, garden designers, arborists, tree managers and specifiers to ensure that all steps are taken to reduce the likelihood of inadvertent pathogen spread. We need to be especially vigilant when it comes to sourcing and selecting plant material to ensure that its production history, and if necessary, a suitable period of quarantine, can be accurately tracked. These measures are likely to come at some cost, but there must be a much greater emphasis placed on the qualitative value of the product, rather than price alone.

It took the well-publicised Chalara ash dieback outbreak in 2012 to raise public and political awareness of the vulnerability of our natural environment to exotic pests and diseases to the point where existing biosecurity measures were able to be challenged (Defra & FC, 2014). Better education highlighting the risks associated with accidental introduction of pathogens is un-doubtedly required, along with revised attitudes towards biosecurity. Many well-documented examples exist of pathogens that have affected commercial and food crops around the world. The Irish potato blight famine of the 1840s is one tragic example. It is because they cause such economic and social strife that they are so well-described and detailed. Over the last 100 years, however, other threats have emerged, which bring with them not only economic, but also environmental and ecological consequences. On both the European and American continents, tree plantations and natural areas alike have been forever altered by the inadvertent introduction of plant pathogens by humans.

In North America, chestnut blight (*Cryphonectia parasitica*) spread rapidly through the widespread American chestnut (*Castanea dentata*) population since its introduction from Asia (most likely China or Japan) during the late 1800s (EPPO, 2005), almost eliminating the species completely. The pathogen has also been detected throughout most of Europe (Robin & Heiniger, 2001), and although both the North American (*Castanea dentata*) and European (*Castanea sativa*) species are susceptible, the pathogenicity of the fungus has been attenuated in many European locations due to the natural occurrence of the *Cryphonectria* hypovirus (Heiniger & Rigling, 1994). Hypovirilence caused by this hypovirus prevents the fungus from producing the virulent form of the disease and has been used as a biological control in Europe (Heiniger & Rigling, 1994). Some European oak species have also been found to be affected, but tend to behave as more tolerant hosts. The European and Mediterranean Plant Protection Organisation also notes that *Castanopsis*, *Acer*, *Rhus typhina* and *Carya ovata* all act as hosts (CABI and EPPO, 1997).

Other examples are numerous and include Cinnamomi root rot (*Phytophthora cinnamomi*), Red band needle blight (*Dothistroma septosporum*), Alder disease (*Phytophthora alni*), sudden oak death (*Phytophthora ramorum*), Kernoviae dieback (*Phytophthora kernoviae*), Plane wilt or canker stain (*Ceratocystis platani*), Horse chestnut bleeding canker (*Pseudomonas syringae* pv *aesculi*) and others. However, a good example, presented here as a case study, and one that amply shows the devastation that can be caused to a landscape by the inadvertent introduction of a pathogen is Dutch elm disease.

CASE STUDY: *OPHIOSTOMA ULMI* AND *O. NOVO-ULMI*, DUTCH ELM DISEASE

Dutch elm disease is caused by the closely related fungal species *Ophiostoma ulmi* and *Ophiostoma novo-ulmi*, and has led to the death of many (perhaps billions) of elms in Europe and North America (Brasier & Buck, 2001). These two ascomycota species are thought to be bio-geographically distinct, from within East Asia, but cannot be traced to specific origins. However, both *O. ulmi* and a subspecies of *O. novo-ulmi* have been found co-existing in Japan, and it is possible that *O. ulmi* is a Japanese endemic and the subspecies of *O. novo-ulmi* is a recent invasive (Masuya, Brasier, Ichihara, Kubono & Kanzaki, 2009). It is hoped that more genetic investigations and field survey work may provide a better understanding of the history of the origins of the two pathogens. They differ mainly in their optimum temperature for growth, *O. novo-ulmi* grows best at 22°C, whereas *O. ulmi* favours 28°C. It is likely that *O. ulmi* is best adapted to a sub-tropical climate and *O. novo-ulmi* to more temperate regions. Both cause a wilt disease in elms, which spreads within the tree's vascular tissues after being introduced from infected trees by boring scolytid beetle vectors or through root contact and grafting. The beetles lay their eggs in weakened or felled elms, where they overwinter as larvae, feeding on the inner bark, and emerge in the spring. *Ophiostoma* spores are picked up within the pupal chambers by the young beetles as they disperse during the spring and summer months. The adult beetles feed in the twig crotches of healthy trees, introducing the fungal spores into the sapwood, which causes the characteristic yellowing and wilting of leaves. Weakened trees then become the target for adult beetles to lay their eggs.

Despite the pathogen being unknown in Europe and North America before 1900, both continents experienced two devastating pandemics in the twentieth century, caused by the two different species.

The first pandemic was caused by the less aggressive *O. ulmi*. It began in northern France in the early 1900s (perhaps 1910) and spread rapidly eastward through western Europe and into south-west Asia. The UK was thought to be initially clear of disease, but it is likely that the pathogen was introduced via beetle-infested elm timber. It was first identified in Hertfordshire in 1927, although is likely to have been already present within the UK for some years prior to that (Peace, 1960). At first, the UK experienced severe losses of elms, but during the 1940s, the virulence declined, with mortality rates rarely exceeding 20 per cent. Despite sporadic localised outbreaks, the Dutch elm disease was treated as a manageable endemic, minor nuisance that did not warrant extensive intervention (Peace, 1960). In fact, Tom Peace's thorough account of the Dutch elm disease concludes with the now infamous, but accurate statement, '. . . but unless it [the pathogen] completely changes its present trend of behaviour it will never bring about the disaster once considered imminent' (Peace, 1960). Unfortunately, he could never have predicted the second and much more virulent pandemic that was about to sweep through the country.

It is likely that the disease entered North America during the early 1900s. The presence of the smaller European scolytid beetle, *Scolytus multistriatus*, was certainly confirmed in elms growing in the College Yard (now Harvard Yard), at Harvard University, Boston, Massachusetts, in October 1909 (Chapman, 1910). Other reports suggest that the disease was introduced via infested timber products, imported from Europe during the 1920s building boom (Webber (e-mail), personal communication, 7 March 2016) or on burr-elm logs imported for the manufacture of veneer (May, 1934). The native American elm (*Ulmus americana*) proved to be much more susceptible to *O. ulmi* than the European species. As a consequence, this first epidemic in North America caused much more widespread devastation than it did in Europe, with no detectable decline in virulence as was seen in Britain.

The second pandemic occurred in Britain during the mid to late 1960s. This was caused by the previously unknown and much more aggressive *O. novo-ulmi* and which has largely displaced the earlier *O. ulmi*. Detection of this later outbreak was initially delayed due to its presence being masked by *O. ulmi*, and the increase in elm deaths was thought to be localised flare-ups of *O. ulmi*, as predicted. However, by 1970, the Forestry Commission Advisory Service at Alice Holt was being swamped with letters and phone calls from farmers, land managers, gardeners and observant walkers, all making reference to sickly looking and dying elms (Potter, Harwood, Knight & Tomlinson, 2011).

This second pandemic began during the 1940s as two separate outbreaks on two different continents: one in the Romania–Moldova–Ukraine region of eastern Europe and the other in the southern Great Lakes region of North America. It transpires that each of these two outbreaks was caused by two distinct strains of *Ophiostoma novo-ulmi*: the Eurasian subspecies in eastern Europe, known as *O. novo-ulmi* subsp. *novo-ulmi* (sometimes referred to as the EAN strain) and the North American subspecies, known as *O. novo-ulmi* subsp. *americana* (sometimes referred to as the NAN strain). Both are considered to be hyper-virulent, aggressive pathogens of European and North American elm species and both spread rapidly from their original centres of appearance. It is likely that the NAN subspecies originated as an introduction into North America of the EAN subspecies and this successively hybridised with *O. ulmi* to create the genetically distinct North American subspecies (Brasier, Kirk, Pipe & Buck, 1998).

Regular shipments of *Ulmus thomasii* (rock elm) logs from the Great Lakes region of Canada were imported into Britain, principally for use in boat building. Rather than being enclosed within containers, these logs tended to be stowed as deck cargo, and any beetle vectors present within the bark of infected logs could emerge and

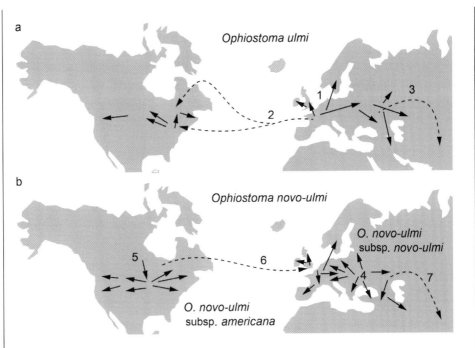

Figure 7.1
Intercontinental spread of *Ophiostoma ulmi* and *O. novo-ulmi* in the two pandemics. Solid arrows = natural migrations from likely sites of initial introduction. Dashed arrows = subsequent spread through importation. (a) shows spread of *O. ulmi*. 1 = initial outbreak in N-W Europe, probably around 1910. 2 = importation of infested timber into North America in 1920s. 3 = introduction into Asian Tashkent from Krasnodar during late 1930s. (b) shows spread of EAN and NAN subspecies of *O. novo-ulmi*. 4 = original appearance of *O. novo-ulmi* subsp. *novo-ulmi* in Eastern Europe. 5 = original appearance of *O. novo-ulmi* subsp. *americana* in North America. 6 = importation of subsp. *americana* via infested timber during the 1960s. 7 = introduction of *O. novo-ulmi* subsp. *novo-ulmi* to Tashkent area of Asia in the 1970s. Adapted from Brasier (1990). Source: Forest Research, Crown Copyright.

migrate to nearby healthy elms, and so initiate infection (Brasier & Gibbs, 1973). Investigations have shown that the known North American vector of the Dutch elm disease, *Hylurgopinus rufipes*, can be present within such shipments. Although this boring beetle vector was successful in spreading the pathogen to other elms in the immediate area, it was not able to establish and died out. The infection, however, was picked up in the breeding galleries of the native scolytid beetle vectors and rapidly spread through the remaining elm population. *O. novo-ulmi* subsp. *novo-ulmi* spread rapidly westwards into western Europe, reaching the Netherlands by the mid-1970s. Likewise, the importation of *O. novo-ulmi* subsp. *americana* into the UK and its subsequent spread into mainland Europe was equally rapid and catastrophic, resulting in the loss of most of the mature elms in Europe. The two subspecies now co-exist at several locations, and this has provided another opportunity for hybridisation and genetic exchange (Brasier & Kirk, 2010). In two of these locations, Limburg in the Netherlands and Orvieto in Italy, intermediate hybrids that are no less aggressive to elms than the parental types are emerging and replacing the parent subspecies. In such conditions, where parents and progeny are

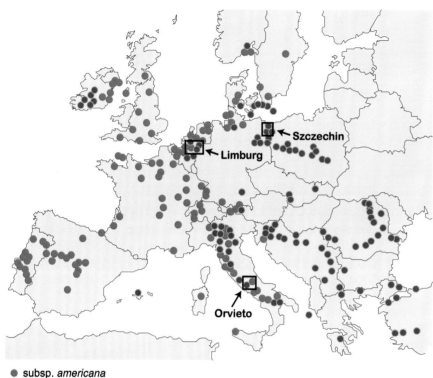

● subsp. *americana*
● subsp. *novo-ulmi*

Figure 7.2
Summary of the known distribution of *Ophiostoma novo-ulmi* subsp. *americana* and subsp. *novo-ulmi* in Europe in 1990, based on > 2500 samples collected by Brasier and Kirk. Subspecies overlap zones included parts of Ireland, Netherlands, Belgium, Norway, Sweden, Denmark and Germany. (Redrawn from Brasier & Kirk (2001) Forest Research, Crown Copyright.)

so promiscuous, it is impossible to predict an outcome. It is possible that, through natural selection, a completely new race or subspecies of the pathogen will emerge (Brasier, 2001). This hypothesis is made more worrisome by the discovery of another elm disease pathogen in northern Himachal Pradesh, western Himalaya, in 1993 (Brasier & Mehrottra, 1995). Potential hybrids between this and the other previously known taxa could pose additional threats to any elm-breeding programmes and disease-control projects (Brasier & Mehrottra, 1995).

Brighton and Hove received the status of UK National Elm Collection from Plant Heritage in 1998 and the collection now consists of over 17,000 trees. This legacy from Victorian and Edwardian civic tree planting was as a result of the species being especially tolerant of the thin soil over chalk and salt-laden winds from the sea. The disease control methods employed include sanitation felling, removal and destruction of infected trees, rapid response to any reports of unhealthy trees and a moratorium on the importation of elm timber and products. Despite continual losses of mature trees, to date, the management plan has been able to limit the damage to the elm stock within the city and retain the collection. However, it is possible that the pressure from relentless and repeated disease cycles will slowly, but steadily compromise mature trees, eventually overcoming any management plan (Harwood, Tomlinson, Potter & Knight, 2011).

Some fairly extensive research, over the last 80 or more years, has been conducted in breeding disease-resistant elms for introduction back into the environment, with much of the breeding work being conducted in North America, Italy and Holland. In Europe, resistance is determined by *Institut Nationale de la Recherche Agronomique* (INRA) in France and the *Istituto per la Protezione Sostenibile delle Piante* (IPSP) in Italy. Testing is carried out by inoculating potential tree cultivars with unnaturally high concentrations of *O. novo-ulmi* and rating the results of wilt, defoliation and dieback.

In 2000, the Hampshire and Isle of Wight branch of Butterfly Conservation initiated trials of elm cultivars, which have been proven to show resistance to the Dutch elm disease (Brookes, 2015). The trial is being conducted at four sites within southern Hampshire and across a range of differing soil conditions. The principle aim of the study is to find suitable host plants for the White-letter Hairstreak (a Defra UK Biodiversity Action Plan 'Priority' butterfly species) that can be planted out to replace the *Ulmus glabra* (wych elm) trees lost to Dutch elm disease. The trial has been able to appraise many elm selections for their tolerance of environmental stress such as exposure, drought and waterlogging, but some focus has also been placed on the growth and appearance of the trees within the landscape. Some of the cultivars differ quite significantly from the European species, either in their overall stature or foliage appearance, and so would probably not be suitable for naturalised planting in the wider British countryside. However, their resistance to the Dutch elm disease would still make them good candidates for urban planting. Some showing promise are:

- *Ulmus* 'Columella'. A vigorous and fastigiate cultivar from the Netherlands, which broadens out later. Can quickly suffer from drought stress.
- *U.* 'New Horizon'. One of the 'Resista' elms raised by the Wisconsin Alumni Research Foundation (WARF) and suitable for fertile, free-draining sites. Can suffer with winter twig dieback.
- *U.* 'Rebona'. Another 'Resista' elm with different parentage from 'New Horizon' and said to have a more pronounced leader. Widely planted in Germany as a street tree.
- *U.* 'San Zanobi'. From IPSP, Italy, where it is widely planted as a street tree, notably in Rome, in and around the Villa Medici. Intolerant of poorly drained soils.
- *U.* 'Sapporo Autumn Gold'. Another WARF-raised cultivar and one of the most resistant to DED. Suitable for fertile, moisture-retentive soils. Has succumbed to Dryad's Saddle in Christchurch.
- *U.* 'Wanoux' = VADA. Another upright form from the Netherlands, providing an alternative to *U.* 'Columella'. Copes well in poor soils, but is not tolerant of bad drainage. May be susceptible to elm yellows (phloem necrosis).

Elm cultivar information compiled from Brookes (2015) and Herling.

Some useful parallels may be drawn from the experiences of Dutch elm disease and current disease outbreaks that are proving to be incredibly difficult to control.

7.3 SENTINEL PLANT SPECIES

The use of sentinel plants, growing both in the UK and abroad, as a way to identify possible unknown risks was identified as a knowledge gap within the Tree Health and Plant Biosecurity Expert Taskforce Final Report (Defra, 2013). Botanic Gardens Conservation International (BGCI) responded by establishing the International Plant Sentinel Network, a global network of botanic gardens and arboreta using sentinel plants to provide early warning of new and emerging plant pests and diseases. The network was launched during the Fifth Global Botanic Gardens Congress, which was held in Dunedin, New Zealand, in October 2013.

Conventional methods of assessing the risks posed by possible plant pest and disease introductions involve the use of Pest Risk Analysis (PRA). This method assesses the potential impact caused by the species considered, if it were to be introduced into a new geographical region. In 2001, the International Plant Protection Convention (IPPC) produced a standard for the process of conducting PRAs to determine whether pests are quarantine pests and adopted the document at its Third Session of the Interim Commission on Phytosanitary measures, in April of that year. Since then, the document has seen several revisions, with the latest being adopted by the Eighth Session of the Commission on Phytosanitary Measures in April 2013 (IPPC, 2013). The limitations of such an approach have already been discussed earlier in this chapter.

7.4 RECOGNISING SIGNS OF DISORDERS, PESTS AND DISEASES

One of the most important skills required by anyone responsible for managing any urban landscape is to correctly recognise when a problem occurs. A key requisite here is recognising what is *normal* and what could be considered *abnormal*. Obviously, the recognition of signs and symptoms of a plant disorder increase with exposure and experience, but sometimes, they are fairly obvious to spot. Typically, trees tend not to fail without first showing some warning signs.

For tree management to be effective, trees must be inspected at certain, specified intervals. These inspections will guide the management approaches taken and the timing of subsequent inspection. Inspections must be recorded, along with the outcomes decided and an appraisal of whether the frequency and intensity are meeting their objectives. The assessment of the tree in its setting records:

- tree species and any predisposition to pests, disease and functional/structural failings
- assessment of overall condition and health, making comparisons with other trees in locality
- history of tree failure and of others nearby
- history of work carried out previously
- age class
- site conditions and history of any changes or disturbances to ground conditions/exposure, and so on.

From this, any health or functional problem should be evaluated, any maintenance or corrective works can be specified and a reasonable and balanced judgement made of any likely structural failure. More information on the management of risk from trees is available from the Health and Safety Executive (HSE, 2013) and the Forestry Commission (Lonsdale, 2000; National Tree Safety Group, 2011). It is important to determine the extent of any problem observed. Is it restricted to a single tree or part of a tree or are many trees affected? Is only one species showing signs of distress or is the problem more widespread, affecting more than one species? Are there any signature symptoms?

It is beyond the remit of this book to cover all the recognised pests, diseases and disorders, which may be encountered, and the reader is directed to the following sources for a deeper and broader understanding:

- Strouts and Winter, 2013. *Diagnosis of Ill-Health in Trees (Research for Amenity Trees No. 2).*
- Lonsdale, 1999. *Principles of Tree Hazard Assessment and Management.*
- Watson and Green, 2011. *Fungi on Trees: An Arborist's Field Guide.*
- Watson, 2013. *Tree Pests and Diseases: An Arborist's Field Guide.*
  Forest Research pest and disease resources can be found at: www.forestry.gov.uk/fr/INFD-9KCEZ7 on the Forestry Commission website.

7.4.1 Biotic and abiotic factors

If we consider all disorders, pests and diseases as tree-damaging agents, it is, perhaps, convenient to divide these into groups, so that each group may be considered in turn. First, there are those where damage is caused by living organisms, and these I have grouped under *biotic agents*. Then, there are those where damage is due to non-living or mechanical causes, and these I have grouped under *abiotic agents*. Included within the biotic agents group are the biting, boring and sucking insects, mammal and bird damage, pathogenic fungi, viruses, bacteria and parasitic plants. Those agents considered as abiotic will include compacted soil, drought, waterlogging, extremes of temperature, root severing and bark abrasion, vandalism, lightning strike, snow and ice loading, chemical damage and so on.

If these two groups are to be further divided and categorised for ease of addressing, such a division may look like Table 7.1.

Table 7.1
The causes of ill-health in trees from Strouts & Winter, *Diagnosis of Ill-Health in Trees (Research for Amenity Trees No. 2)*, 2013

Biotic agents	Abiotic agents	
Insects: • Biting • Boring • Sucking Mammals Birds Fungi: • Macro • Micro Viruses Bacteria Parasitic plants	Soil conditions: • Compaction • Waterlogging and flooding • Mineral deficiencies Weather: • Drought • Severe frosts • Extreme heat • Snow and ice • Lightning strike • Sun scorch • High winds	Chemicals: • De-icing salts • Herbicides • Fuel and oil spillages Others • Vandalism • Construction works • Vehicle impacts • Graft failure • Lack of maintenance such as strangulation from tree ties, abrasion from stakes and cages

7.4.2 Characteristic symptoms

Biotic causes will usually show symptoms and signs progressively, over a period of time, depending on the virulence of the cause. They are typically restricted to displaying signs on one species of tree. Abiotic causes, on the other hand, tend not to be restricted to a single species. They are often location-specific and their affects may be both dramatic and fast acting.

7.4.2.1 Chlorotic leaves

Yellowing of the leaves, which are typically green, is known as chlorosis and is usually due to a reduction in chlorophyll levels within the leaf. It can be caused by a number of factors, such as a deficiency in iron or magnesium, and is symptomatic of poor growth and ill-health. Because of their sensitivity to iron deficiency, *Liquidambar styraciflua* and *Quercus palustris* are both particularly intolerant of soils with a high pH. This manifests itself through a yellowing of the leaf areas between the veins, while the veins remain green. It is caused by a deficiency in iron and is known as interveinal chlorosis.

7.4.2.2 Dieback

This usually starts at the shoot tips and progresses back towards the centre of the tree. It is important to determine progression of the condition, if possible. Sometimes leaves wilt and turn yellow, then die. They may remain on the branch or they may fall. Leaf death is often followed by progressive shoot and/or branch death. Extent of the problem is important to determine. Sometimes, the entire crown is affected, but often it is restricted to an area. Dieback within the upper crown is often a sign of a root disorder, and as these can lead to instability, thorough investigation and assessment are required.

7.4.2.3 Leaf loss

Deciduous species naturally lose their leaves in autumn, and this loss can be hastened by an early frost. Unusual leaf fall before the onset of autumn tends to indicate a stress response, typically water stress. It is important to determine the extent and progression of the defoliation and the presence of any other signs of pest and disease activity, such as leaf necrosis, chlorosis and wilting. Some biting insects can cause significant leaf loss if present in sufficient numbers. The larval stages (caterpillars) of gypsy moth (*Lymantria dispar*) and oak processionary moth (OPM: *Thaumetopoea processionea*) can strip bare large portions of tree crowns, placing trees under stress and making them more vulnerable to attack by other pests and diseases and other stress factors such as drought. The larvae of OPM are especially troublesome due to their tiny, irritating hairs, which can cause itching skin rashes and occasionally breathing problems in humans and their pets.

7.4.2.4 Wilting

Wilting will usually precede leaf loss and dieback. It is caused by the collapse of leaf tissue due to loss of turgor pressure within the cells. This is indicative of lack of water within the leaf and is typically caused by drought, root damage or exposure due to ground level modifications, anaerobis due to flooding, girdling or infection or predation of the water-conducting vessels (the xylem). Many of the wilt-causing diseases produce the symptom due to the tree's response to infection within the xylem tissue. Often, such as with the Dutch elm disease, the tree responds to infection by producing sticky typloses and gums, which block the water-conducting xylem cells and cause the leaves to wilt. The symptom, then, is again indicative of a lack of water within the leaf.

7.4.2.5 Leaf scorch or necrosis

Typically, areas of the leaf turn brown. Sometimes, the entire leaf may dry and shrivel. The position on the leaf and within the crown should be noted as some disorders, pests and diseases leave telltale signs. These symptoms usually denote drought, extreme high or low temperatures, some nutrient deficiencies or de-icing salt damage. Occasionally, as with horse chestnuts (*Aesculus hippocastanum*), brown necrotic patches are caused by the later stages of leaf miner (*cameraria ohridella*) damage and *Guignardia* infection.

7.4.2.6 Epicormic growth

The proliferation of shoots from dormant buds, positioned along the main branches and the main stem, are signs of chronic stress. Epicormic growth is often accompanied by some crown dieback or other leaf disorders.

7.5 THE USE OF CITIZEN SCIENCE

Currently, there are some conditions present within our tree populations, which have the potential to cause similar levels of devastation experienced in the 1960s and 1970s with the Dutch elm disease. Ash dieback (*Hymenoscyphus fraxinea*), sudden oak death (*Phytophthora ramorum*) and its related *Phytophthora kernoviae* are all implicated in rapid and devastating damage to forestry plantings, natural ecosystems and public and private gardens. The Forestry Commission and Forest Research have set up two online tree health monitoring resources that rely on tree professionals and engaged citizens to provide the data.

7.5.1 Tree Alert

This started life as a mobile phone app, but quickly became too complex for use on mobile platforms and is now an online tool for reporting suspected tree pests and diseases that are of concern. Submitted reports are reviewed by the Forest Research Tree Health Diagnostic and Advisory Team for any notifiable or priority pests or diseases. These are sent to the regional Forestry Commission Tree Health Teams to be followed up. Other Tree Alert reports may be forwarded to Observatree volunteers for analysis and verification (Perez-Sierra, 2016).

7.5.2 Observatree

Observatree is a partnership project led by the Forestry Commission Forest Research Agency, funded by the EU Life+ programme, operated in collaboration with the Forestry Commission, Fera Science Ltd and the National Trust and the Woodland Trust, with support from the Department for Environment, Food and Rural Affairs (Defra), the Animal and Plant Health Agency (APHA) and Natural Resources Wales. The aim is to raise awareness, among tree professionals and others actively involved with trees, of pests and diseases that could pose a serious threat to UK trees and to encourage an increase in surveillance and reporting using Tree Alert.

The Woodland Trust provides 230 trained volunteers to undertake monitoring surveys that track the spread of new diseases, such as Chalara disease, and to assist with the spotting and identification of pests and diseases. These volunteers receive annual training from Forest Research and Fera scientists, enabling them to identify signs and symptoms of key priority pests and diseases.

Using a trained body of volunteers to analyse and verify Tree Alert reports has increased the capacity and efficiency of the service provided by the Tree Health Diagnostic and Advisory

Service within Forest Research, allowing them to focus on priority reports and react more quickly to significant findings. Observatree works with other UK and European organisations to collectively share project experiences to establish best practice guidance (Observatree, 2016).

REFERENCES

Brasier, C. M. (1990). China and the origins of Dutch elm disease: An appraisal. *Plant Pathology, 39*(1), 5–16.

Brasier, C. M. (2001). Rapid evolution of introduced plant pathogens via interspecific hybridization. *BioScience, 51*(2), 123–33.

Brasier, C. M. (2008). The biosecurity threat to the UK and global environment from international trade in plants. *Plant Pathology, 57*(5), 792–808. doi:10.1111/j.1365-3059.2008.01886.x

Brasier, C. M. (2010). *Scientific and Operational Flaws in International Protocols for Preventing Entry and Spread of Plant Pathogens via 'Plants for Planting'*. Rome: Fifth Commission on Phytosanitary Measures, International Plant Protection Convention, UN FAO.

Brasier, C. (2011). Rapid evolution of introduced tree pathogens via episodic selection and horizontal gene transfer. In *Proceedings of the Fourth International Workshop on the Genetics of Host–Parasite Interactions in Forestry: Disease and Insect Resistance in Forest Trees.* Eugene, OR: US Department of Agriculture, Forest Service.

Brasier, C. M. & Buck, K. W. (2001). Rapid evolutionary changes in a globally invading fungal pathogen (Dutch elm disease). *Biological Invasions, 3*, 223–233.

Brasier, C. M. & Gibbs, J. N. (1973). Origin of the Dutch elm disease epidemic in Britain. *Nature, 242*(5400), 607–9. doi:10.1038/242607a0

Brasier, C. M. & Kirk, S. A. (2001). Designation of the EAN and NAN races of *Ophiostoma novo-ulmi* as subspecies. *Mycological Research, 105*(5), 547–54.

Brasier, C. M. & Kirk, S. A. (2010). Rapid emergence of hybrids between the two subspecies of *Ophiostoma novo-ulmi* with a high level of pathogenic fitness. *Plant Pathology, 59*(1), 186–99. doi:10.1111/j.1365-3059.2009.02157.x

Brasier, C. M. & Mehrottra, M. D. (1995). *Ophiostoma himal-ulmi* sp. *nov.*, a new species of Dutch elm disease fungus endemic to the Himalayas. *Mycological Research, 99*, 205–15.

Brasier, C. M. Kirk, S. A., Pipe, N. D. & Buck, K. W. (1998). Rare interspecific hybrids in natural populations of the Dutch elm disease pathogens *Ophiostoma ulmi* and *O. novo-ulmi. Mycological Research, 102*(1), 45–57. doi:10.1017/S0953756297004541

Broadmeadow, S. J., Morecroft, M. D. & Morison, J. I. (2009). Observed impacts of climate changes on UK forests to date. In D. Read, P. H. Freer-Smith, J. I. Morison, N. Hanley, C. C. West & P. Snowden (eds), *Combating Climate Change – A Role for UK Forests. An Assessment of the Potential of the UK's Trees and Woodlands to Mitigate and Adapt to Climate Change* (pp. 50–66). Edinburgh: The Stationery Office.

Brookes, A. (2015). *Disease-Resistant Elms – Butterfly Conservation Trials Report 2015.* Butterfly Conservation. Retrieved from www.hantsiow-butterflies.org.uk/downloads/2015%20Elm%20Report.pdf.

CABI and EPPO (1997). *Cryphonectria parasitica.* In *Quarantine Pests for Europe* (pp. 729–32). Wallingford, UK: CAB International.

Campbell, F. T. (2001). The science of risk assessment for phytosanitary regulation and the impact of changing trade regulations. *Bio Science, 51*(2), 148–53. doi:10.1641/0006-3568(2001)051[0148:TSORAF]2.0.CO;2

Chapman, J. W. (1910). The introduction of a European Scolytid (the Smaller Elm Bark-Beetle, *Scolytus multistriatus* Marsh) into Massachusetts. *Psyche, 17*(2), 63–8. doi:10.1155/1910/76129

Defra (2013). *Tree Health and Plant Biosecurity Expert Taskforce: Final Report.* London: Department for Environment, Food and Rural Affairs.

Defra & FC (2014). *Protecting Plant Health A Plant Biosecurity Strategy for Great Britain.* London: Department for the Environment, Food and Rural Affairs and the Forestry Commission.

Desprez-Loustau, M-L., Robin, C., Buee, M., Courtecuisse, R., Garbaye, J., Suffert, F., Sache, I. & Rizzo, D. (2007). The fungal dimension of biological invasions. *Trends in Ecology and Evolution, 22*(9), 472-80.

EPPO (2005). *Cryphonectria parasitica.* EPPO Bulletin, *35*(2), 295–8.

FAO (2002). *International Standards for Phytosanitary Measures (no.15): Guidelines for Regulating Wood Packaging Material in International Trade.* Rome, Italy: Secretariat of the International Plant Protection Convention, Food and Agriculture Organisation.

Forestry Commission (2011). *Forests and Climate Change. UK Forestry Standard Guidelines.* Edinburgh: Forestry Commission.

Harwood, T. D., Tomlinson, I., Potter, C. A. & Knight, J. D. (2011). Dutch elm disease revisited: Past, present and future management in Great Britain. *Plant Pathology, 60*, 545–55.

Heiniger, U. & Rigling, D. (1994). Biological control of chestnut blight in Europe. *Annual Review of Phytopathology, 32*, 581–99.

Herling, D. (n.d.). *Resistant Elms*. Retrieved 8 March 2016 from www.resistantelms.co.uk/.

Heuch, J. (2015). (e-mail) Personal communication, 3 February 2015.

HSE (26 March 2013). *Management of the risk from falling trees or branches – SIM 01/2007/05*. Retrieved 7 February 2016 from Health and Safety Executive: www.hse.gov.uk/foi/internalops/sims/ag_food/010705.htm.

IPPC (2013). *International Standards for Phytosanitary Measures, ISPM 11 – Pest Risk Analysis for Quaranteen Pests*. International Plant Protection Convention. FAO. Retrieved from www.ippc.int/static/media/files/publication/en/2016/01/ISPM_11_2013_En_2015-12-22_PostCPM10_InkAmReformatted.pdf.

Lonsdale, D. (1999). *Principles of Tree Hazard Assessment and Management (Research for Amenity Trees No. 7)*. Norwich: The Stationery Office.

Lonsdale, D. (2000). *Hazards from Trees: A General Guide*. Retrieved 7 February 2016 from Forestry Commission – Publications: www.forestry.gov.uk/pdf/fcpg13.pdf.

Masuya, H., Brasier, C., Ichihara, Y., Kubono, T. & Kanzaki, N. (2009). *First Report of the Dutch Elm Disease Pathogens Ophiostoma ulmi and O. novo-ulmi in Japan*. Retrieved 8 March 2016 from BSPP New Disease Reports: www.ndrs.org.uk/article.php?id=020006.

May, C. (1934). *Outbreaks of the Dutch Elm Disease in the United States. USDA Circular 322*. Washington, DC: United States Department of Agriculture. Retrieved from https://archive.org/details/outbreaksofdutch322mayc.

Murphy, J., Sexton, D., Jenkins, G., Boorman, P., Booth, B., Brown, K., Clark, R., Collins, M., Harris, G. & Kendon, L. (2009). *UK Climate Projections science report: Climate change projections*, Exeter: Met Office Hadley Centre.

National Tree Safety Group (2011). *Common Sense Risk Management of Trees: Guidance on Trees and Public Safety in the UK for Owners, Managers and Advisors*. Edinburgh: Forestry Commission. Retrieved from www.forestry.gov.uk/PDF/FCMS024.pdf/$FILE/FCMS024.pdf.

Observatree (2016). *Observatree*. Retrieved 18 July 2016 from Observatree monitoring tree health: www.observatree.org.uk/.

Peace, T. R. (1960). *Forestry Commission Bulletin No. 33: The Status and Development of Elm Disease in Britain*. London: HMSO.

Perez-Sierra, A. (2016). TreeAlert: A new way to report tree pests and diseases. *Minimising the Impact of New and Future Tree Threats; Tree Health Conference on 11 March 2016, RHS Wisley*. Forestry Commission. Retrieved from www.forestry.gov.uk/pdf/08-AnaPerez-Sierra-TreeAlert.pdf/$file/08-AnaPerez-Sierra-TreeAlert.pdf.

Pimentel, D., McNair, S., Janecka, J., Wightman, J., Simmonds, C., O'Connell, C., Wong, E., Russel, L., Zern, J., Aquino, T. & Tsomondo, T. (2001). Economic and environmental threats of alien plant, animal, and microbe invasions. *Agriculture, Ecosystems and Environment, 84*, 1–20.

Potter, C., Harwood, T., Knight, J. & Tomlinson, I. (2011). Learning from history, predicting the future: The UK Dutch elm disease outbreak in relation to contemporary tree disease threats. *Philosophical Transactions of the Royal Society B, 366*, 1966–74.

Redstone, S. (2014). *Biosecurity at the Royal Botanic Gardens Kew, Presentation to the European Plant Protection Organisation Conference on Contingency Planning, RBG Kew, 18–20 November 2014*. London: EPPO/OEPP.

Robin, C. & Heiniger, U. (2001). Chestnut blight in Europe: Diversity of *Cryphonectria parasitica*, hypovirulence and biocontrol. *Forest Snow and Landscape Research, 76*(3), 361–7.

Strouts, R. G. & Winter, T. G. (2013). *Diagnosis of Ill-Health in Trees (Research for Amenity Trees No. 2)* (2nd edn) Norwich: The Stationery Office.

Tubby, K. V. & Webber, J. F. (2010). Pests and diseases threatening urban trees under a changing climate. *Forestry, 83*(4), 451–9.

Watson, G. (2013). *Tree Pests and Diseases: An Arborist's Field Guide* (1st edn). Stonehouse, Gloucestershire: The Arboricultural Association.

Chapter 8: Trees, regulations and law

8.1 INTRODUCTION

Despite all the benefits that trees are able to bring to the landscape, they are also able to cause harm, and as such, sometimes require control or removal, in order for that harm to be abated. Most reported problems arise where trees are growing on or close to boundaries between properties and are accused of causing damage to the property of a third party (although trees owned by the person suffering the damage can also be implicated). This damage actually or perceived to be caused by trees can either be as a consequence of the tree growing normally, or less likely, due to some structural or physiological defect. In cases of the former, leaf fall, fruit drop, honeydew, bird droppings, slippery surfaces caused by shady conditions have all been cited as problems associated with trips, slips and falls, when people are passing under trees. Another cause of tripping can be uneven and deflected surfaces, caused by root growth. This can be a problem when it occurs on public footways and footpaths and is of particular concern for the elderly, infirm and partially sighted.

Another example of harm caused by trees growing normally is the dropping of limbs or uprooting and toppling caused by severe gales. Trees typically grow adaptively to withstand exceptional weather conditions experienced in their native habitats (Lonsdale, 1999).

To add some context, the Centre for Decision Analysis and Risk Management at Middlesex University identified fifty-four fatalities attributable to tree failure for the 10-year period ending on 31 December 2008, with a further twenty-two cases of serious injury. This equates to less than a one in 10 million risk of dying from falling or fallen trees and branches per annum (Ball & Watt, 2013), meaning that such an exceptionally small risk is considered well within the 'broadly acceptable' category according to the Health and Safety Executive's framework for the tolerability of risk, where the upper limit is considered to be one in 1 million (HSE, 2001).

It should be pointed out that of the fifty-four fatalities and twenty-two cases of serious injury, approximately 64 per cent occurred during episodes of strong wind (i.e., wind speeds in excess of 40 knots or 75 km/h). As Lonsdale points out, these conditions are rare, are extreme and are potentially hazardous with or without trees being present (Lonsdale, 1999). As such, it is not necessarily trees or the way that they are managed where culpability lies.

Conversely, trees may be inherently unstable or in some way defective and may fail without immediate warning and not necessarily during inclement weather. These failures are not particularly frequent. Tree owners and managers, as duty holders, have a responsibility to ensure that all reasonably practicable measures are in place to reduce risk. In situations where a risk is identified, a decision needs to be taken as to whether it is an acceptable risk or not. It is

Figure 8.1
A substantial limb was torn out of this mature oak tree during a storm. The tree is growing in a popular urban park; it is otherwise quite healthy and the loss of this limb could not reasonably have been predicted.

recommended that the principles set out in the National Tree Safety Group guidance – *Common Sense Risk Management of Trees* (NTSG, 2011) and Health and Safety Executive guidance on Tree management SIM 01/2007/05 (HSE, 2013b) are followed. (The legal requirements of landowners and other duty holders are dealt with in sections 8.2 and 8.3 below.)

All these are examples of direct damage caused by trees, either where there is physical contact between the tree and a structure arising from normal growth of roots or aerial parts, or where the tree or parts of the tree collapse and cause damage to property or injure people. Both the longitudinal and radial pressures produced by growing tree roots on below-ground structures are relatively weak. It is true that paving surfaces can be uplifted and utility routes can be disrupted, but it is almost unheard of for massive concrete and masonry structures, such as building foundations, to be disturbed by direct root action alone. Tree roots tend to be distorted or deflected by the presence of immovable

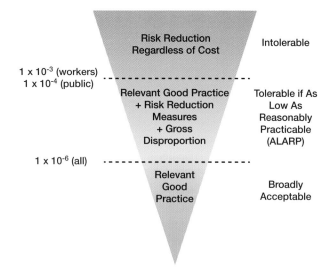

Figure 8.2
HSE framework for the tolerability of risk. A risk falling within the red 'intolerable' zone is regarded as unacceptable, whatever the level of benefits associated with it. In practice, such an activity or method of working would be modified to reduce the risk. Risks falling within the bottom green zone are generally regarded as insignificant and adequately controlled.

Figure 8.3
This mature cedar was 'blown apart' by a lightning strike. Such an impact is very rare, with most strikes causing long scars down the tree stem. This level of damage is caused by an enormous pressure wave that alternately compresses and tensions wood and bark, leading to explosive tissue separation and not the rapid super-heating of water and sap, as is commonly thought (Coder, 2013). Unseen root damage can be a common result of lightning strike. Ongoing monitoring for signs of root damage should be maintained.

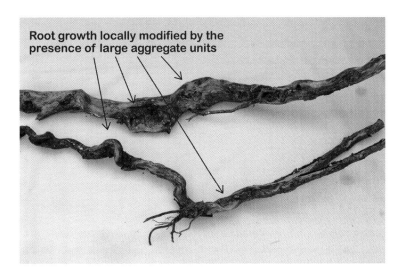

Figure 8.4 Root excavated from within road construction strata. Notice how the root has been flattened and distorted, where it has grown between large aggregate units. More conventional growth resumes where possible. This root distortion does not appear to have any long-term negative effects.

objects, as can be observed where the root systems of trees growing in structural soils have been exposed.

However, where roots are in physical contact with walls and 'non-designed' structures and the tree is subject to wind flexing, the pressure exerted on the structure by the roots can be significant. This is more common where roots are growing under or alongside glazed earthenware underground drainage pipes, and this wind flexing can be enough to crack the pipe seals, allowing a possible site for root ingress.

Indirect damage is more common, and so is perceived as being a greater problem. Indirect damage may arise on a shrinkable clay-dominated soil that changes volume in response to variations of water content. Where such a soil is dried sufficiently, the ground may contract in volume to such an extent that any structure bearing upon it, that is not structurally robust enough to accommodate the movement, may be damaged. The movement of structures caused by soil volume reduction is known as building subsidence and usually becomes apparent through the development of visible cracking on interior plaster and exterior brick or render surfaces. This cracking is typically diagonal, wider at the top of the wall than at the bottom, and occurs at points of least resistance within the building structure, such as around windows and doors. It will usually be more noticeable in the summer, and especially during droughts, often accompanied by sticking or jamming windows and doors. Tree-related subsidence requires three factors to be demonstrated:

(i)   shrinkable soil
(ii)   roots under the foundations
(iii)   seasonal variations in the magnitude of cracks

Figure 8.5
Hazard and risk decision-making. Oaks can hold on to decaying branches, without dropping them, until they crumble away. However, decaying branches overhanging a footpath could also be considered too high a risk to be tolerated in a public space and so should be removed.

In winter, the soil has usually reached maximum saturation, or field capacity, due to autumn rain and lack of transpiring foliage. In the spring, leaves unfurl and transpiration restarts. By the end of summer, with higher temperatures and reduced rainfall, the soil dries, tending to be at its driest in September. Cracking is often first noticed when householders return from their summer holidays.

Movement in clay-dominated soils can be exacerbated by the normal growth of tree roots, which are deeper than most other types of vegetation. As trees grow, they absorb water from the soil and if that water is extracted from beneath the foundation level, the clay is likely to shrink more than if the tree(s) were not present. The movement of structures caused by soil volume changes attributable to tree growth is known as 'tree-related subsidence' and is dealt with in more detail in section 8.4 below. Whereas the applicable legislation sets out the framework of the civil law position, the interpretation is often clouded by specific site circumstances. A very common remedial action is to remove the offending tree(s) to enable soil volume to be stabilised. However, this can be complicated where a tree has statutory protection.

This chapter can only provide a brief overview of the law in relation to trees and the reader is directed towards the encyclopaedic second edition of Charles Mynors (2011), for a more comprehensive investigation into all the legal aspects relevant to trees.

8.2   HOW MUCH IS ENOUGH?

As with many aspects of life, the law requires us all to be observant of what is happening around us and to be aware of the implications of our actions, or lack of action, upon the lives of others. The owner of the land within which the tree is growing and the person responsible for the management of the tree owe a duty of care to those who may be adversely affected by the tree. This principle was set in the famous civil liability case of *Donoghue* v. *Stevenson* (House of Lords) (1932), where a decomposing snail was found in the bottom of a bottle of ginger beer, after the majority of the contents had already been consumed by the claimant. Although the risk associated with death or serious injury from tree failure is exceptionally low, the law does impose a duty on tree owners to consider the risks associated with the trees in their ownership and to employ measures that are reasonable and proportionate to manage that risk. Any approach to tree risk management needs to look at keeping the risk as low as reasonably practicable (ALARP), bearing in mind the level of occupancy by people and property (targets), the magnitude of the hazard if the tree were to fail and the probability of failure occurring. In actuality, the courts often place little value on probability per se, but are rather more interested in foreseeability. If a failure was foreseeable, they will need to know what measures were taken to reduce the risk of failure and whether the action was proportionate. The challenge for tree owners is to take all *reasonable* steps to manage their trees against risk of failure, in a way that the courts will support and not all *possible* steps, which ultimately could lead to wholesale tree removal. This approach reflects case law in establishing what is *reasonably practicable* (*Edwards* v. *National Coal Board* 1949). The principles relating to a landowner's duties were conveniently reviewed and summarised in paragraph 68 of Stagecoach South Western Trains Ltd v Hind and Steel (2014):

- A tree owner owes a duty to act as a reasonable and prudent landowner (*Caminer* v. *Northern Investment Trust Ltd* [1951] AC 88).
- The duty must not amount to an unreasonable burden (*Lambourn* v. *London Brick Co Ltd* [1950] EG 28 July 1950) or force the tree owner to act as an insurer of nature (*Noble* v. *Harrison* [1926] 2 KB 332 (CA)). However, the tree owner (as a layman) does have a duty to act where a danger becomes apparent (*Brown* v. *Harrison* [1947] 177 LT 281).
- A reasonable and prudent landowner should carry out preliminary or informal inspections on a regular basis (*Micklewright* v. *Surrey County Council* [2011] EWCA Civ 922).
- The degree of knowledge and experience required by the landowner to undertake a preliminary or informal inspection will be less than the knowledge of an arboriculturist,

but will be greater than that of an ordinary urban observer of trees or of a countryman not practically concerned with their care (*Caminer* v. *Northern Investment Trust Ltd*).

- Certain circumstances may require the landowner to arrange for a more comprehensive inspection by an arboriculturist (*Caminer* v. *Northern Investment Trust Ltd* and *Quinn* v. *Scott* [1965] 1 WLR 1004). This will usually be because a preliminary or informal inspection has revealed a potential problem (*Micklewright* v. *Surrey County Council*). However, it may also be due to a lack of knowledge or capacity on the part of the landowner to undertake a preliminary or informal inspection (*Caminer* v. *Northern Investment Trust Ltd*).
- The resources available to the landowner may be relevant to the way the duty is discharged, establishing the concept of 'measured duty of care' (*Leakey* v. *National Trust* [1980] 1 QB 485).

The judgement included reference to both the National Tree Safety Group guidance – *Common Sense Risk Management of Trees* (NTSG, 2011) and SIM 01/2007/05 (HSE, 2013) that detail a logical approach to tree inspections, starting with 'informal observations' and progressing to formal inspections and detailed inspections, depending on the nature of any cause for concern and the proximity of the tree to the public. The experts involved in the case agreed that informal observations are a suitable form of inspection for the non-specialist tree owner. However, as determined in Leakey, it does not automatically follow that larger landowners, with greater resources at their disposal, are able to discharge their duty of care requirements in a similar way. Here, a tree safety strategy that assigns tree stock to zones according to access by people and proximity to property, assigns levels of tree inspection according to risk and determines appropriate management, according to the above, would form a reasonable and balanced approach to tree safety management. The typical domestic tree owner, conversely, would be expected to informally observe trees within their ownership and to investigate further anything about the tree that may indicate a change in overall health, well-being or structural integrity. Such an investigation is therefore likely to require the expertise of an arborist, or at least, someone with appropriate experience. If the tree owner feels that they do not have sufficient knowledge or experience to recognise obvious tree defects, they should engage the services of someone who does.

The most effective time of year to inspect for damage and defects is on a clear day, at the beginning of autumn, when premature colouration or shedding of foliage and fungal fruiting bodies are most visible (Lonsdale, 2000).

8.2.1 How often?

The guiding factor in determining the frequency of inspection must surely be proximity and occupancy of a potential target. For some trees in locations that are not visited by people and are not close to property, there is no automatic requirement for them to be checked at all. Conversely, where trees are situated in areas that are frequently visited by the public and within striking distance of property (especially, highways), inspections should be carried frequently (Ellison, 2005). A review of available guidance suggests some inconsistency in the recommended frequency of inspections. The NTSG guidance suggests that for a typical rural local authority, highway trees could be informally inspected each year by non-specialist staff who have received only basic training. Any situation where the surveyor feels that a tree requires further investigation should be referred to specialist arboricultural staff (NTSG, 2011). For many local authorities, this arrangement works well with initial, informal surveys being carried out by tree wardens who have

Figure 8.6
The London Borough of Islington contains within its tree policy a commitment to 'maintain highway trees on at least a three year cyclical basis to ensure its duty of care is maintained and that the Highway remains unobstructed' (Policy 6).

received basic training. For a typical urban local authority, where subsidence is a risk, the usual 3-year inspection and management cycle for street trees in subsidence-prone areas would identify those in poor condition or requiring any remedial work. The NTSG guidance goes on to suggest that trees within schools and public parks are inspected every 2 years and trees within local authority housing estates and gardens are inspected every 4 years (NTSG, 2011). The guidance does also refer to the importance of a tree strategy and record-keeping for local authorities and corporate tree owners to ensure that trees are managed proactively and that inspections and works are recorded (NTSG, 2011).

The UK Roads Liaison Group suggests that most highway trees should have an arboricultural inspection every 5 years, increasing the frequency on the advice of an arboriculturist (UKRLG, 2011). Lonsdale recommends that, for areas where people and property may be at risk, routine inspections are 'carried out frequently enough to detect any hazards that may have recently developed' (Lonsdale, 2000). For large, old trees in highly accessible areas, this may require inspections every year or more and certainly following exceptionally adverse weather conditions, when damage could have occurred (Lonsdale, 2000). Certainly, some highway authorities inspect annually, sometimes as frequently as every 6 months, alternating between drive-by and on-foot inspections (Quaife, personal communication, 2016). Others do less.

8.3   THE TORTS OF NEGLIGENCE AND NUISANCE

In English law, torts are civil wrongs, where one person unfairly causes another to suffer loss or harm, resulting in legal liability. The tort of negligence, therefore, is a wrong caused by a negligent act. As tree owners have a duty to take reasonable care for the safety of others who could be affected by the tree, liability for negligence arises when the tree owner breaches that duty of care. This could either be by causing something to happen to the tree that renders it unsafe, or more likely, not taking action to make the tree safe, despite being aware that there is a problem. If a tree or part of a tree does fail, and in so doing, injures someone or property, it is likely, therefore, that the tree owner and/or the person responsible for the tree's management (the dutyholder) will be on the receiving end of a civil action claim for negligence.

Nuisance is where someone causes *substantial* and *unreasonable* interference with another's land or the use or enjoyment of that land. This was set out in the House of Lords judgement in *Hunter and Others* v. *Canary Wharf Ltd* (1997), where Lord Lloyd of Berwick stated that:

> Private nuisances are of three kinds. They are (1) nuisance by encroachment on a neighbour's land; (2) nuisance by direct physical injury to a neighbour's land; and (3) nuisance by interference with a neighbour's quiet enjoyment of his land.

Under nuisance claims, the effects of trees on another's property or land usually fall under the first category of encroachment, either through the normal extension of their branches or their roots. The position was established in law by *Rylands* v. *Fletcher* (1868), where Mr Fletcher's coal mine was flooded by water from Mr Rylands' mill reservoir. Here, the Lords reaffirmed the judgement that:

> If a person brings, or accumulates, on his land anything which, if it should escape, may cause damage to his neighbour, he does so at his peril. If it does escape, and cause damage, he is responsible, however careful he may have been, and whatever precautions he may have taken to prevent the damage.

Branch and root growth can be cited as causing a nuisance either by causing damage to property or by simply being present, and so, preventing a landowner from carrying out certain works or using their land in a certain way. In *Smith* v. *Giddy* (1904), a nurseryman claimed that a neighbour's overhanging branches interfered with the apple trees growing in his orchard, and so caused damage. He pursued the neighbour for damages and an injunction to prevent the branches overhanging his property. The Court of Appeal held that the neighbour was liable, and so was responsible for keeping the overhanging branches clear. Therefore, for trees overhanging the highway, the tree owner is also liable if the tree constitutes a nuisance to highway users. This can be particularly onerous if high-sided vehicles use the highway (*Hale* v. *Hants & Dorset Motor Services Ltd. and Another*, 1947) (*British Road Services* v. *Slater*, 1964). The fact that overhanging branches can be removed by the neighbour over whose land they are, without providing any notice of his intention to do so, was established in *Lemmon* v. *Webb* (1894). The branches could be removed only from where they hung over the land of the neighbour and without entering the tree owner's property. Although this case was primarily concerned with overhanging branches, it did provide guidance on the right to take a similar course of action to abate a nuisance caused by encroaching roots. However, there is no test case guidance on how the court would respond if irrevocable harm were to be caused to the tree through the action of such pruning. It would seem that it is for the court to determine what would have been reasonable action and whether the harm caused to the tree would have been foreseeable to an ordinary person (Quaife, 2016). If all the roots of a tree were to be severed immediately, the other side of a boundary, for instance, one might reasonably suppose that this action would have some effect upon stability of the tree.

It is no defence to argue that trees (whether naturally seeded or planted), being natural elements within the landscape or being already present prior to the complainant, result in no liability for their owners. This was established by the Court of Appeal in *Leakey* v. *National Trust* (1979). Here, the specific claim centred around a landslip, but the court took the opportunity to consider in detail the duties of landowners to naturally arising hazards on their land. It established that if a landowner is aware of the existence of a hazard, or ought to have been aware, and fails to take reasonable precautions to prevent it interfering with a neighbour's enjoyment of their own land, they have a duty to take *reasonable* steps to prevent or mitigate the risk. Reasonable in this context is determined by a person's resources and ability, thus establishing the concept of *measured duty of care*.

8.4   TREE ROOTS AND DAMAGE TO STRUCTURES

On soils that are subject to shrinking and swelling, such as the firm, plastic clays of south-east England, the volume occupied by the soil is determined by the amount of water present within it (see Chapter 3). As water is removed, the soil volume decreases. As water is added, the soil volume increases. Climatic factors alone can be the cause for such soil volume change, albeit to a limited depth, but it is exacerbated by the influence of vegetation. All green plants transpire, but large woody plants, such as the larger shrubs and trees especially, place the highest water demand on the soil. Unless some recharge from rainfall or irrigation occurs, the soil volume will reduce as the tree roots continue to extract water during the growing season. If buildings are founded upon these shrinkable soils, there is the possibility of movement, and cracking can be observed in the building fabric. Root activity subsides when deciduous trees lose their leaves in autumn, and this generally coincides with soil moisture being recharged by seasonal rainfall. As the soil water content increases, the clay re-swells, the foundations return to their previous positions and the cracks tend to close. If the water demand of the tree is consistently greater than the water available during the year, persistent moisture deficit occurs and the clay never rehydrates to its natural level. In these situations the cracks will not close. Tree-related heave occurs where a structure is built upon a shrinkable soil that has a persistent moisture deficit, caused by a tree and that tree is later removed. With the water demand from the tree removed, the soil moisture deficit will dissipate as the soil gradually rehydrates, and the soil will return to its natural volume. Heave occurs when that natural volume is greater than when the structure was built and the foundations are lifted by the expanding soil.

Typically, however, any adverse interaction between buildings and trees cannot adequately be described in such simple terms. The situation tends to be much more dynamic with the clay fluctuating between various states of hydration and dehydration, contracting and expanding, subsiding and heaving as its water content alters. The result is that, in older housing stock, where shallow strip foundations of mass concrete or corbelled brick have been used, foundations can move up or down, and sometimes, laterally or rotationally, depending on the condition of the material surrounding them. The rates and ranges of change are dependent on the soil type, weather conditions and tree species, and so are highly variable from situation to situation, making any prediction of likely effects, prior to being observed, very difficult to determine.

The Victorians certainly understood that clay soils are shrinkable, and so, problematic when founding buildings upon them. Alfred Bartholomew (1840) said about clay soil that:

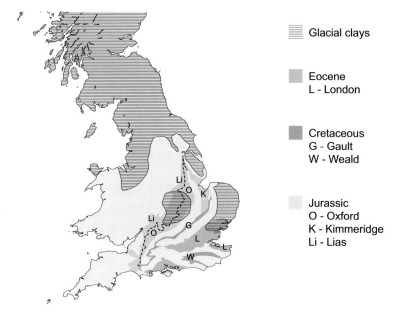

Glacial clays

Eocene
L - London

Cretaceous
G - Gault
W - Weald

Jurassic
O - Oxford
K - Kimmeridge
Li - Lias

Figure 8.7
The distribution of shrinkable clays in the British Isles tends to be concentrated south-east of an imaginary line between Scunthorpe in the north-east and Taunton in the south-west. Other notable occurrences are found around Sunderland and north of Shrewsbury, but the surficial clays found in the north of the country tend to be quite sandy, and so are less prone to shrinkage (BRE, 1993).

in open country situations, during drought, it is apt to split, and cause fracture to the building, unless the foundation be laid below the range of the fissures which occur in it.

Insurance cover for residential building damage caused by subsidence was introduced in 1971 at the request of building societies who wished to protect their investments against loss in equity (subsidence insurance for commercial properties is unusual). Prior to this, the property owner was responsible for any repairs caused by subsidence. Some seasonal damage was accepted as being part of normal building maintenance, and any remedial works would typically be of a fairly minimal extent. As insurers considered such damage to be fairly low risk, the insurance premiums, in many instances, remained unchanged.

In the summer of 1976, the UK experienced a severe drought, which caused some considerable damage to property, and insurance claims rose alarmingly from under 5,000 to nearly 21,500 claims. They peaked again in the mid-1980s and the droughts of 1989 and 1990 saw another massive increase, to 60,000 claims in 1991. Further spikes followed in 1997, 2003 and 2006. Claims have never fallen back to pre-1976 levels, partly fuelled by an increased awareness, partly by changes in attitude to the value of property, but also by, what some have described as, alarmist media coverage, which suggests that any cracking is caused by subsidence and should be claimed for on the property insurance (Biddle, 1998). In addition, one could argue that this heightening of awareness has helped to create a new industry, which employs a raft of both technical and legal consultants and advisors, whose business revolves predominantly around the handling of subsidence claims.

Dr Giles Biddle has spent much of his professional life investigating the practical problems of tree root damage to buildings for insurers, loss adjusters, solicitors and local authorities.

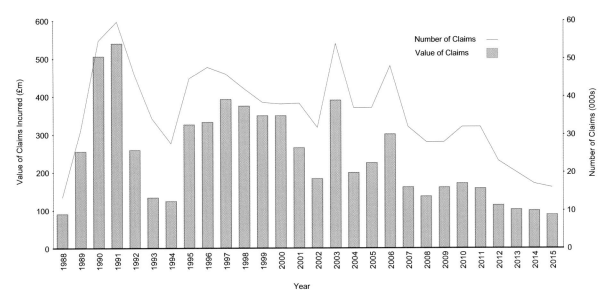

Figure 8.8
The cost of subsidence claims (grey bar) and the number of insurance claims made (red line) from 1988 to 2015.
(Data source: The Association of British Insurers.)

He suggests that because of the increase in emphasis on the duty of care required by professional consultants, in an increasingly litigious environment, a highly cautious approach is often adopted to avoid possible claims for professional negligence. This often encourages such professionals to identify any possible risks, however unlikely they are to occur, leading to an overreaction, with an enormous safety factor, in an effort to prevent any damage (Biddle, 1998). It is true, we are dealing here with living material, which is notorious for behaving in ways that can be very difficult to predict, but armed with a thorough understanding of the nature, cause, diagnosis and remedy of tree-related subsidence, better-informed judgements and swifter responses would be made, which should lead to a more acceptable integration of trees within our urban landscapes.

The work of Dr David Cutler and Dr Ian Richardson, known as the Kew Tree Root Survey, provides data on trees that have been implicated in the movement of buildings. These data were collated and form the body of *Tree Roots and Buildings* (Cutler & Richardson, 1989), which is often referred to in subsidence claims. It is worth emphasising that the survey cards used to conduct the survey contain a range of details, but the individual tree entries in the book only show the number of trees implicated in damage and the distance from that damage. There are no indications of anything about the trees themselves in terms of their condition, vigour, size, pruning history, age or proximity to other trees; no details of the damage caused in terms of severity, extent, or pattern; no description of the buildings or structures involved in terms of size, orientation, location of damage, age, whether original or an extension; and no records of site circumstances in terms of topography, hydrology, other site features, underground impediments, surfacing, exposure or even the soil type, depth, or characteristics.

Furthermore, while the data collected do highlight the problem of buildings founded on shrinkable clay soils, they do not tell us anything about how the number of implicated trees relates to the urban tree population as a whole. It has been estimated that the UK has some 150 million trees growing within its urban conurbations, with a total amenity tree population in excess of

1 billion (O'Callaghan & Kelly, 2005). In 2007, the London Assembly Environment Committee calculated that there were almost 500,000 street trees in London, and despite an increase of 1.7 per cent over the previous 5 years, the total remained broadly the same in 2011 (GLA, 2011). It is true that trees are often implicated in building subsidence cases, but the level of risk remains low and the incidence of tree-related subsidence needs to be considered in this context. It is worth remembering that in locations where trees pre-exist the proposed buildings, foundation construction should comply with NHBC guidelines and best practice. Since the early 1950s, BRE was recommending the use of short-bored piled foundations for buildings on shrinkable clay soils, following work by Ward and Green (1952), yet, the practice is still uncommon. It would appear that the typical response to foundations that fail is guided by capital cost rather than long-term prevention. It is invariably cheaper to remove a tree suspected of being the cause of the problem or repair any damage that does occur, rather than to insist on all foundations being more fit for purpose.

8.4.1   The potential conflict

If cracking is found, the building owner will usually contact their building insurer, who will inspect the damage, and if necessary, arrange for appropriate structural, geotechnical and arboricultural investigations to be carried out. Once the cause of the damage has been identified, it must be removed or rectified and the movement stabilised, only then can the damage be repaired. If a tree is implicated, the tree owner is contacted and put on notice of the potential nuisance claim, and actions to mitigate the nuisance will be requested. Typically, the tree owner will contact their building insurer and the matter is dealt with by the two insurance companies.

Wherever possible, local authorities must show some level of commitment to the retention of what they consider to be important trees within their jurisdictions. Indeed, they are duty-bound to do so by Part VIII, Chapter 1 of the Town and Country Planning Act (HM Govt, 1990), with some trees benefitting from explicit protection by virtue of the Town and Country Planning (Tree Preservation) (England) Regulations 2012 (see section 8.10 below). Many boundary trees are planted alongside the highway and maintained either by the highway authority or the local authority. Such street trees in urban areas can be planted fairly close to buildings, and if the soil is a shrinkable clay, they can be implicated as causing problems with building foundations in subsidence claims.

The London Tree Officers' Association produced a document entitled *A Risk Limitation Strategy for Tree Root Claims* (LTOA, 2008). Running to some ninety-seven pages, it includes not only those owned by the local authority, but includes privately owned trees also. The Risk Limitation Strategy recommends that local authorities implement a regular management strategy that includes cyclical pruning and/or selective removal and replacement of their tree stock, in areas that are predisposed to building movement (LTOA, 2008). In addition, the LTOA, local authority risk managers, the subsidence forum, the property claims forum and the Forestry Commission came together to produce the Joint Mitigation Protocol (JMP). The JMP is an agreed methodology for managing subsidence claims where trees are implicated as being the causal agents. It aims to promote best practice in the processing and investigation of tree root-induced subsidence, provide benchmarking timescales for critical actions and responses and establish standards for the level of evidence required. The JMP should be used to inform critical analysis of the evidence presented by subsidence claimants. Claims must be swiftly and effectively dealt with on a case-by-case basis, but those based on inaccurate or poor investigative evidence must not go unchallenged.

For situations where it is suggested that trees are responsible for building subsidence, it is important that any application for mitigation work or tree removal is supported by appropriate information, demonstrating that the tree is a material cause and other potential influences have been eliminated as far as possible. It is not sufficient to simply identify trees close to buildings and assume that they must be responsible for any building damage incurred (Mynors, 2011). The UK government Planning Practice Guidance website (DCLG, 2014) and section 8 of the guidance notes 'Application for Tree Works: Works to Trees Subject to a Tree Preservation Order (TPO)' (DCLG, 2014) clarify the level of investigative information required in support of an application for tree works to TPO trees and trees in conservation areas:

Reports will usually be provided by a structural engineer and/or a chartered surveyor and be supported by technical analysis from other experts e.g. for root and soil analysis. These reports must include the following information:

- A description of the property, including a description of the damage and the crack pattern, the date that the damage first occurred/was noted, details of any previous underpinning or building work, the geological strata for the site identified from the geological map
- Details of vegetation in the vicinity and its management since discovery of the damage. Include a plan showing the vegetation and affected building
- Measurement of the extent and distribution of vertical movement using level monitoring. Where level monitoring is not possible, state why and provide crack-monitoring data. Data provided must be sufficient to show a pattern of movement consistent with the presence of the implicated tree(s)
- A profile of a trial/bore hole dug to identify foundation type and depth and soil characteristics
- The sub-soil characteristics including soil type (particularly that on which the foundations rest), liquid limit, plastic limit and plasticity index
- The location and identification of roots found. Where identification is inconclusive, DNA testing should be carried out
- Proposals and estimated costs of options to repair the damage.

(DCLG, 2014)

In addition, the application should include a report from an arboriculturist to support the tree work proposals, including arboricultural options for avoidance or remediation of indirect tree-related damage.

Once an application has been made, the LPA will assess the supporting information provided and visit the site to review the tree species, size, location and evidence of any other potential causal agents. From this, an assessment can often be made of the likelihood that the tree is implicated, but sometimes additional investigations are required.

8.4.2   *The legal position*

For damages to be awarded, the risk of damage must be reasonably foreseeable. So declared the Court of Appeal in *Solloway* v. *Hampshire County Council* (1981) 79 LGR 449. Following the two successive dry summers of 1975 and 1976, the claimant's house showed signs of cracking and he claimed that roots from a highway authority-owned horse chestnut tree were responsible for the damage caused. The majority of the house was founded on plateau gravels, but certain sections rested on small pockets of clay, which were not shown on geological maps. The original judgement was given in favour of the claimant, but was overturned by the Court of Appeal, which found that the likelihood of the claimant's house being situated on a pocket of clay was only a '. . . vague possibility, not a real risk . . .', and as such, any reasonable steps taken by the highway authority to eliminate or reduce the risk of damage would be entirely out of proportion to that risk. Sir David Cairns went on: 'To say that a risk of damage is reasonably foreseeable means that it is foreseeable, not merely as a theoretical possibility but as something, the chance of which occurring, is such that a reasonable man would consider it necessary to take account of it. The risk of being struck by lightning when one goes for a walk is not a reasonably foreseeable risk. I should be prepared to hold that the risk in this case was not a reasonably foreseeable risk.'

The Technology and Construction Court, in the first instance, and the Court of Appeal, in *Berent* v. *Family Mosaic Housing and LB Islington* (2012), further emphasised the importance of separating what would be regarded as a 'real risk' from mere possibility while connecting what is reasonably foreseeable damage with what steps could reasonably be taken in light of that risk. The judge found that the defendants could not reasonably be expected to foresee damage to the claimant's property until they had been notified that damage had occurred and been provided with sufficient evidence to show a causal link with the trees. Despite the local subsoil being known to consist of London clay, and so, potentially susceptible to subsidence, there was nothing to suggest that the location was a 'hotspot or problem area' and the judge held that this was insufficient to satisfy the test of 'reasonable foreseeability'.

The arboricultural experts agreed that while it would be possible to show that there was a risk to one or more properties in the locality, due to the soil type and the proximity of street trees, it was not possible to determine which property(ies), if any, may be subject to damage. The only certain way to prevent the risk of any tree-induced subsidence damage to properties in this area was to remove all the trees. Such a response, the judge decided, would be totally out of proportion to the risk; '. . . a responsible local authority mindful of its obligation under Town and Country Planning Acts and the preservation of such amenities as an established treed environment could not reasonably contemplate the desertification of such a neighbourhood by wholesale tree felling to avoid a possible risk of damage'.

The decision in *Berent* means that, in areas that are susceptible to subsidence, it should be unlikely that a local authority or other organisation responsible for tree management will be held liable for damage caused by their trees until they have been notified of the damage. This would appear to be completely contrary to a later judgement from the Technology and Construction Court, in *Khan and Khan* v. *Harrow Council and Kane* (2013). In this case, the defendant (Mrs Kane) was notified of cracks to Mr and Mrs Khan, the claimants' house more than 2 years after they appeared. Once on notice, Mrs Kane acted without delay to remove the implicated cause of the cracking, a section of her 10-m tall Lawson cypress hedge, which was growing on the boundary, half a metre from the wall of the affected building. Following further level survey monitoring, further damage occurred and the Khans' solicitors wrote to Mrs Kane, asking that her oak tree was also removed, following local authority approval, as the tree was protected by a TPO. The tree was felled without delay.

The Khans subsequently submitted a nuisance and negligence claim against Mrs Kane for damages to their property, stating that: 'The risk of damage to the premises by subsidence caused as aforesaid and/or the continuance thereof was or ought to have been reasonably foreseeable to the Defendants'. In her defence, Mrs Kane denied that the subsidence was reasonably foreseeable, and so she was not required to take any pre-emptive, preventative actions to eliminate or reduce the risk.

The judge found in favour of Mr and Mrs Khan stating that damage to the Khans' property, caused by roots of the Lawson cypress hedge, was reasonably foreseeable and so notice to Mrs Kane was not necessary to impose liability on her. It is difficult to understand why the obligations on Mrs Kane, in terms of foreseeability, should be any greater than those upon Islington Council in *Berent*. It is interesting in this case that there was even some initial disagreement between the arboricultural experts as to whether the hedge was, in fact, likely to be the cause of the cracking. If Mrs Kane's arboricultural expert did not initially believe that the hedge materially contributed to the damage, how can a 'reasonably prudent landowner' with no specialist arboricultural knowledge be expected to appreciate that the risk existed? As Muhammed Haque QC pointed out, what if the hedge had been slightly further from the Khans' property? Or not quite as tall? 'How is one supposed to make the judgment about whether vegetation poses a risk' without some specialist knowledge? 'The problem is that to appreciate there is a risk, one must know something about the water-uptake characteristics, spread pattern and depth of the roots in question. Without that, then the risk of damage is only a mere possibility (which would not result in liability). It is difficult to understand why Mrs Kane was deemed to know any of the characteristics of a cypress hedge' (Haque, 2013).

An outcome from this case could be that arboricultural specialists will be flooded with requests for advice from landowners, seeking protection from litigation, on all their trees even if they themselves do not consider them to be a risk.

8.5 HIGH HEDGES AND THE ANTI-SOCIAL BEHAVIOUR ACT

Hedges can be the cause of disputes, where the reasonable enjoyment of a domestic property is adversely affected, predominantly by the height of an adjoining hedge. Problems typically arise between neighbours if the owner of the hedge allows it to grow unchecked, particularly if it comprises fast-growing evergreens such as Leyland cypress.

To qualify, the hedge must be:

- formed by a line of two or more mostly evergreen or semi-evergreen trees or shrubs
- over 2 m in height above the ground level
- affecting the enjoyment of a domestic home or garden because it is considered to be too tall.

Examples of how hedges may affect the enjoyment of a property could be that they block light to main rooms in the house or building, they may deprive property owners of winter sunshine, they may extend across property boundaries, affecting the growth of other plants or crops (see section 8.3 above) or the hedge may be interfering with structures or buildings either directly or indirectly. It should be noted that the high hedges legislation specifically does not apply to complaints involving roots (HM Govt, 2003). Such complaints should be pursued as nuisance.

The government issued a consultation paper in 1999, seeking views on various options for dealing with neighbour disputes regarding high hedges. After some unsuccessful efforts to introduce legislation through the House of Commons, the House of Lords inserted additional provisions within the Anti-social Behaviour Bill 2003, which, largely unaltered, became part 8 of the Anti-social Behaviour Act 2003 (HM Govt, 2003), and which came into force in Wales on 31 December 2004, and in England on 1 June 2005 (Mynors, 2011). In Scotland, the High Hedges (Scotland) Act 2013 (HM Govt, 2013) came into force on 1 April 2014. In Northern Ireland, the High Hedges Act (Northern Ireland) 2011 came into force on 31 March 2012. Both the Scottish and Northern Ireland legislation pretty much mimic that of England and Wales. Rather than preventing the growing of hedges or restricting the height they can be grown to, the 2003 Act provides a procedure whereby domestic property owners are able to take action against the owners of excessively tall hedges that prevent the reasonable enjoyment of their property and where informal negotiation has failed. The Act requires that complainants first 'take all reasonable steps to resolve the matters complained of without proceeding by way of such a complaint to the [local] authority'. Further guidance, available via the DCLG website (www.gov.uk/government/collections/high-hedges), explains the procedure to encourage neighbours to resolve high-hedge disputes through negotiation and mediation prior to submitting any formal complaint. Before the local authority will agree to intervene, they are likely to request evidence to show that approaches to resolve the dispute have been made. Such evidence could be copies of letters, a diary of events, records of mediation and so on.

The complaint is made to the local authority, using a standard complaint form available as a download from the DCLG website. The local authority will invite the hedge owner to submit their case, and once received, they will inspect the hedge. They will decide whether or not it is adversely affecting the reasonable enjoyment of the complainant's property, and if so, what action, if any, should be taken by the hedge owner to remedy the adversity and prevent it reoccurring. If the complaint is upheld, a formal notice, a *remedial notice*, would be served on the hedge owner, setting out what action must be taken and by when. The remedial notice can, therefore, include long-term maintenance requirements. Both the hedge owner and the complainant may appeal against the local authority's decision, within 28 days from when the local authority notified the parties of its decision. Appeals must be made to the Secretary of State or the appropriate devolved authority. Any remedial notice served would be suspended during determination of the appeal. If the hedge owner, in receipt of a remedial notice, fails to appeal or if the appeal is not successful, the works detailed in the remedial notice must be carried out within the time specified. Failure to comply with the requirements of a remedial notice is an offence, and the hedge owner will be liable, on summary conviction, to a fine up to £1,000. The local authority also has power of entry, providing it with the authority to enter the hedge owner's land, carry out the works as detailed in the remedial notice and to recover any expenses reasonably incurred.

There is guidance available on the UK government website, which sets out a procedure for measuring the effect that a hedge is having on a neighbouring property, in terms of blocking sunlight and daylight. The guidance introduces the concept of '*action hedge height*', which is a calculated hedge height, above which a hedge is likely to cause a significant loss of light. It then provides a step-by-step method for homeowners to calculate the action hedge height for their gardens and for windows to main rooms within their homes (Littlefair, 2005). The basic calculation for measuring the extent of garden area affected by the hedge requires the distance from the hedge to the opposite garden boundary to be multiplied by a factor, according to the hedge orientation, and then modified by further correction factors, according to how far the hedge is set back from the boundary and whether it is on a slope. Where a hedge is blocking light to windows, simple calculations can be made, depending on where the hedge is positioned relative to the window. These calculations and worked examples are available in the document *Hedge Height and Light Loss,* which is available from the Department for Communities and Local Government website (www.gov.uk/government/collections/high-hedges) as a free download.

8.6 TREES AND THE HIGHWAY

The Highways Act 1980 requires that the highway is kept clear of obstructions that prevent the public use and enjoyment of the highway (s. 130). Where trees and vegetation overhang the highway, obstructing the passage of vehicles, pedestrians or horse riders, interfering with the lines of sight or interrupting light from a street lamp, the landowner or the occupier of the land may be served with a notice by the local highway authority to remove the obstruction or interference. The landowner or occupier has 14 days to respond (s. 154(1)). The highway authority can also serve a 14-day notice on a landowner or occupier to remove trees, hedges and shrubs that they consider to be dangerous by virtue of being dead, diseased, damaged or insecurely rooted (s. 154(2)a) and may, therefore, fall onto the highway (s. 154(2)b). Also, s. 79 requires unobstructed views at corners, bends and junctions for highway users, and so can require trees, shrubs and other vegetation to be 'altered' to conform with the highway authority's requirements. The landowner or occupier may appeal against the notice to a magistrates' court (s. 154(3)). If the landowner or occupier fails to comply with the order within the 14 days, the highway authority may carry out the works themselves and seek recovery of their costs (s. 154(4)).

The highway authority has the power to plant trees, shrubs and other vegetation within the highway maintained by them at public expense (s. 96). Others require a licence from the highway authority (s. 142). Such a licence will typically include conditions requiring that the tree, shrub or other vegetation planted is suitably maintained to ensure safety to and unobstructed passage for highway users and to prevent interference with statutory undertakers' and utility providers' equipment. No specific guidance on clearance height is given in the 1980 Act, and requirements tend not to be consistent among the authorities. However, the *Landscape Management Handbook* of the *Design Manual for Roads and Bridges* (Highways England, 2004) requires that roadside trees should be crown-lifted to at least 2.5 m above footways and at least 5.2 m above carriageways to allow the safe passage of high-sided vehicles. These heights have been adopted by most highways authorities as an acceptable standard, but as much as 7.0 m clearance above carriageways has been noted as a requirement for one authority. It is advisable, therefore, that the local highway authority is consulted before work is carried out. Bridleways and byways have slightly different requirements, and the British Horse Society (BHS) provides advice on the height clearance for highways used by horse riders and carriage drivers. A tall rider mounted on a large horse may measure 3 m in height, and the BHS suggests that overhanging branches, overgrowth from the sides of the highway and any other obstructions should be cleared to a height of 3.4 m on all equestrian routes (British Horse Society, 2014). Consideration should also be given for wet, foliage-laden branches, which can droop considerably lower than when they are leafless in winter.

When working on trees within or adjacent to a public highway, certain precautions to working practices are essential. Section 174 of the Highways Act 1980, section 60 of the Roads (Scotland) Act 1984 and article 31 of the Road Traffic Regulation (NI) Order 1997 require that any works within the highway must be guarded by barriers, lighting and signs to prevent any

Figure 8.9
Highway authorities must keep the highway clear of obstructions that prevent the public use and enjoyment of the highway. This includes the passage of high-sided vehicles. This leafy urban street will still require access for removals and refuse collection lorries.

danger to highway users. The *Safety at Street Works and Road Works: A Code of Practice* is intended to assist those working on highways (except motorways and dual carriageways with speed limits of 50 mph or more) with signing, lighting and guarding works. All such measures must ensure that road users, including pedestrians, cyclists and horse riders, are not to be put at risk by the works and are able to see the extent and nature of any obstruction well before they reach it. The key questions to ask are 'Will someone using the road or footway from any direction understand exactly what is happening and what is expected of them?' and 'Have I made the site safe to work in and for the general public?' (Department for Transport, 2013). Failure to comply with the code is a criminal offence and may lead to criminal prosecution, in addition to any civil proceedings. Guidance on temporary traffic management is available in Chapter 8 of the *Traffic Signs Manual:* Traffic Safety Measures and Signs for Road Works and Temporary Situations, Part 1: Design (Department for Transport, 2009a) and Part 2: Operations (Department for Transport, 2009b). Although the manual has no statutory force (except under certain situations in Northern Ireland), many of the principles are also contained within the *Safety at Street Works and Road Works: A Code of Practice,* which was issued by the Secretary of State for Transport and Welsh Ministers under section 65 of the New Roads and Street Works Act 1991 and section 174 of the Highways Act 1980, by Scottish Ministers under section 124 of the New Roads and Street Works Act 1991 and by the Department for Regional Development under article 25 of the Street Works (Northern Ireland) Order 1995 and article 31 of the Road Traffic Regulation Order (Northern Ireland) 1997, and so is supported by primary legislation. If a temporary obstruction to the highway or traffic control is required to enable tree works to be carried out safely, the highway authority must be notified (Department for Transport, 2013).

Contractors must hold adequate public liability insurance as required by the local highway authority. There does not appear to be consistency between authorities, some requiring cover to £5 m and others to £10 m. All tree works should be carried out in accordance with industry best practice and to the current British Standard (BS 3998) (BSI, 2010).

8.7 RIGHTS OF STATUTORY UNDERTAKERS

Statutory undertakers have a statutory right to carry out works within the public highway to install, repair and maintain their equipment. This overall right has been provided since the mid-nineteenth century and has been further expanded to include governance on depth and position by the New Roads and Street Works Act 1991 (NRSWA) (HM Govt, 1991), as amended by the Transport Act 2000 and the Traffic Management Act 2004. Most utility companies are statutory undertakers, and so have statutory powers in primary legislation to install, inspect, maintain, repair and replace apparatus in or under the street. The legislation that provides the power is:

- Schedule 4 of the Gas Act 1986 as amended by Schedule 3 of the Gas Act 1995
- Schedule 4 of the Electricity Act 1989
- Section 159 of the Water Resources Act 1991
- Telecommunications Act 1984 as amended by Schedule 3 of the Communications Act 2003.

Under the New Roads and Street Works Act 1991 (NRSWA), street works undertaken by public utilities and other service provision companies must be co-ordinated through the local highway authority (s. 59(3)), and utility and service providers must co-operate with each other and the highway authority (s. 60(2)). This tightens the regulatory framework and gives highway authorities more power to control and direct street works with the aim of minimising traffic disruption (Department for Transport, 2012). The public and organisations who have no statutory right to install apparatus under, over, across, along or upon the public highway, and who wish to do so, must apply for a licence under section 50 of the New Roads and Street Works Act 1991 to enable them to install and maintain their apparatus. The 1991 Act along with associated regulations and codes of practice also introduced new standards for the reinstatement of the highway surface. Utility companies are now fully responsible for all highway reinstatement following installation or maintenance works related to their apparatus. Both temporary and permanent reinstatement works must conform to the third edition of the *Specification for the Reinstatement of Openings in Highways* (Department for Transport, 2010), with permanent reinstatements being guaranteed for a minimum of 2 years (or 3 years for excavations where the depth of cover over the buried apparatus is greater than 1.5 m).

The *Specification for the Reinstatement of Openings in Highways* guides those responsible for underground utilities to Volume 4 of the *National Joint Utilities Group Guidelines for the Planning, Installation and Maintenance of Utility Apparatus in Proximity to Trees* (NJUG, 2007) when working close to trees. This document provides advice on suitable methods of working when installing and maintaining utility infrastructure, so that damage to both trees and utility apparatus can be minimised. See section 4.4 of Chapter 4 for more information.

Schedule 4 of the Electricity Act 1989 (HM Govt, 1989) also provides certain powers to electricity distributors and network operators, enabling them to fell and lop trees and cut back their roots that may obstruct or interfere with the installation, maintenance or operation of electricity lines or apparatus, or where they may 'constitute an unacceptable source of danger' (HM Govt, 1989). The latter follows from the case of a young teenage girl who strayed from an unfenced footpath and climbed a tree, in a field, some 80 m away. By climbing the tree, she was able to access overhead, high voltage electricity cables and was electrocuted (*Buckland* v. *Guildford Gas, Light & Coke Co.*, 1948). The tree was considered to 'constitute an allurement sufficient to make her an implied licensee instead of a trespasser' (W.B.N, 1949).

If works are required to trees and/shrubs, in line with Chapter 9 of Schedule 4 of the 1989 Act, the electricity distributor or network operator must serve notice on the landowner and occupier (if the two are different), requiring the work to be carried out. All reasonably incurred costs for the work are paid for by the distributor. The occupier has 21 days to carry out the works or serve a counter-notice, objecting to the requirements of the notice. If after the 21-day response period, the occupier has neither complied with the notice nor served a counter-notice, the distributor or network operator, or their contractors, can enter the property and carry out the works:

- in accordance with good arboricultural practice and so as to do as little damage as possible to trees, fences, hedges and growing crops;
- in accordance with the directions of the owner or occupier; and
- make good any damage done to the land.

If the occupier does serve a counter-notice, the matter is then referred to the Secretary of State, who may confirm or reject the notice and decide how the relevant expenses are to be paid. If the Secretary of State confirms the original notice, the distributor or network operator can cause the works to be carried out as above.

Health and Safety Executive guidance suggests that if tree works are carried out within 10 m of overhead power lines or if the works are such that equipment or trees could make contact with power lines, specialist advice must be sought from the distributor or network operator to help establish a safe method of working (HSE, n.d., and HSE, 2013). Advice from the Energy Networks Association goes further, advising that the distributor or network operator is contacted if overhead power lines are within two tree heights of felling operations or within two branch lengths of any trimming works (ENA, 2012).

Telecommunications network operators benefit from similar powers under Schedule 2 of the Telecommunications Act 1984 (HM Govt, 1984), except that the notice period runs to 28 days rather than 21 and tree works do not extend to felling or root cutting. Also, a claim for compensation can be made through the court for any loss or damage incurred by the landowner as a consequence of complying with the notice, such as reduction in property value. The other difference is that any counter-claim is either confirmed or rejected by the County Court rather than the Secretary of State. The Act contains two sections; one dealing with provisions to England, Wales and Northern Ireland (where the highway is referred to as 'street') and the other to Scotland only (where the highway is referred to as 'road').

8.8 PROTECTION OF WILDLIFE AND HABITATS

8.8.1 Birds
All wild birds, while actively nest building or otherwise making use of the nest, are protected under the Wildlife and Countryside Act 1981 (as amended) (HM Govt, 2010b). Section 1(1)b

makes it an offence to 'intentionally' damage or destroy an active nest in England and Wales. Additional protection is given to birds that reuse their nests (Schedule ZA1 (amended under the Natural Environment and Rural Communities Act 2006)) and birds protected by special penalties (Schedule 1), where any person who 'intentionally or recklessly' 'disturbs any wild bird included in Schedule 1 while it is building a nest or is in, on or near a nest containing eggs or young; or disturbs dependent young of such a bird, shall be guilty of an offence' (s. 1(5)).

In Scotland, Schedule 6 of the Nature Conservation (Scotland) Act 2004 (HM Govt, 2004a) amended the Wildlife and Countryside Act 1981, making it an offence to either 'intentionally or recklessly' damage, destroy or 'otherwise interfere with' any active nest or if anyone 'prevents any wild bird from using its nest' (s. 1(1)bb). In Northern Ireland, The Wildlife (Northern Ireland) Order 1985 (s. 4(1)b) provides the same protection as the Wildlife and Countryside Act 1981 does in England and Wales, but also introduced the offence of *obstructing or preventing any wild bird from using its nest* (s. 4(1)bb) via an amendment made by the Wildlife and Natural Environment Act (Northern Ireland) 2011.

For any conviction under the 1981 Act to be successful, it would have to be proved that the harm to a bird or damage to a nest was either intentional or reckless. As Mynors points out, it is not likely to be easy for the prosecution to prove where such damage or harm occurs '. . . as an incidental result of works carried out – otherwise perfectly lawfully – to trees' (Mynors, 2011). It could be assumed, however, that those working with trees and hedges should reasonably have some understanding of the nesting of birds at certain times of the year. Information and advice are available on the Arboricultural Association website to guide contractors in complying with the Act. To protect themselves from prosecution, contractors must show that a thorough check has been made of the work area to ensure that no active nest is likely to be affected by the tree works. Including an inspection for birds' nests as part of a tree works risk assessment should suffice.

8.8.2 Animals

As with the protection of wild birds, the Wildlife and Countryside Act 1981 (as amended) also includes similar legislation to help protect wild animals, in section 9. It is an offence to intentionally kill, injure or take any wild animal listed in Schedule 5 of the Act (s. 9(1)). It is also an offence to intentionally or recklessly damage or destroy any structure or place that any wild animal, specified in Schedule 5, uses for shelter or protection; or disturb any specified animal while it is occupying such a structure or place; or obstruct that animal's access to any such structure or place (s. 9(4)). In Scotland, the word 'recklessly' is again added to 'intentionally' in section 9(1). Northern Ireland legislation is similar to that of Scotland, but differs slightly, in that, it is also an offence to intentionally or recklessly damage or destroy

Figure 8.10
Knot holes and cavities in stubs left from naturally shed or removed branches are potential bat roosting features and should be noted in any tree survey to BS 5837. These features should be surveyed more closely by suitably trained individuals to assess the likely presence of bats. If the roost is likely to be impacted by proposed works, any features that cannot be reasonably ruled out as roosts should be subject to a specialist survey, subject to a European Protected Species Licence.

'anything which conceals or protects' any structure or place used by an animal included in Schedule 5 (s.10(4)(b) of The Wildlife (Northern Ireland) Order 1985 (as amended)).

The animals included within Schedule 5 and which are relevant to trees are likely to be restricted predominantly to bats, dormice, red squirrels and some species of beetles, butterflies and moths. Of these, the bats and dormouse are also listed as European protected species in Schedule 2 of the Conservation of Habitats and Species Regulations 2010 (as amended) (HM Govt, 2010a). This makes it an offence to damage or destroy a breeding site or resting place of any Schedule 2 animal. Note that the words 'intentionally' and 'recklessly' are missing. Nor does the legislation make it clear if the protected animal needs to be present, at the time of damage or destruction, for an offence to have occurred.

If there is a reasonable likelihood that protected species are present on a development site, an ecologist must be engaged to carry out species surveys and provide mitigation plans. The survey will need to show whether protected species are present on the site or are nearby and how they use the site. The mitigation plan will show how the adverse effects towards protected species have been avoided or reduced and what compensation measures are to be provided. This is Natural England's standing advice for local planning authorities (LPA), and so, will be expected by the LPA when considering planning applications.

8.8.2.1 Bats

In 2015, the British Standards Institution (BSI) published BS 8596: 2015, *Surveying for Bats in Trees and Woodlands – Guide* (BSI, 2015). In addition, a free micro guide to the standard was made available for download from the BSI website, following a simple registration. This micro guide is aimed at non-specialists to enable them to gain an understanding of the guidance contained within BS 8596 and to assist them in identifying indicators of bat presence and deciding when further expert advice may be required. Before the publication of the British Standard (BS), much disparate guidance was available from a variety of organisations, but none was definitive. The intention of the BS was to collate all the available information into one resource in an effort to standardise how trees and woodlands should be surveyed for bats and bat roosts and how potential bat habitats should be assessed prior to tree works being undertaken.

Suitably trained arborists are well placed to initially scope trees for the likely presence of bats. Quite often, binocular surveys of tree crowns are part of their normal daily duties. Certainly, any tree survey to BS 5837 should include the likely value for bats when assessing the conservation value of the surveyed trees. Both basic bat awareness and more advanced roost survey training are available from the Bat Conservation Trust (www.bats.org.uk/pages/arborists.html).

8.8.2.2 Badgers

Badgers and their setts are protected under the Protection of Badgers Act 1992 (HM Govt, 1992). Section 3 of the Act makes it an offence to either intentionally or recklessly interfere with a badger sett. Interfere in this case is defined within the Act as meaning 'damaging a badger sett or any part of it; destroying a badger sett; obstructing access to, or any entrance of a badger sett; . . . disturbing a badger when it is occupying a badger sett'.

Developments are likely to require excavations and the movement of soil and take place over long periods of time. If badger setts are present and the proposed development will interfere with them, they will need to be closed up and a licence will need to be obtained from Natural England (www.gov.uk/government/publications/badgers-licence-to-interfere-with-setts-for-development-purposes). Failure to obtain the necessary licence when setts are destroyed,

Figure 8.11
Badger sett undermining building foundations. Urban badger populations appear to be rising, possibly due to people feeding them either inadvertently or deliberately. The success rate for closing urban badger setts is lower than for those in rural locations (Defra, 2007).

damaged or entrances are obstructed or badgers are disturbed could result in up to 6 months in prison and an unlimited fine, if found guilty (Natural England and Defra, 2015). Licences are usually only issued between 1 July and 30 November, unless the particular circumstances can be shown to be 'exceptional' (Natural England and Defra, 2015). However, before applying for a licence, an ecologist would need to carry out a protected species survey and provide a mitigation plan, if any are found to be present.

Badger setts can comprise a labyrinth of tunnels typically under 15 m, but exceptionally, up to 20 m in length. They tend to vary in depth, from several metres deep to very close to the surface, depending on the soil and topography. Where large trees are being felled and/or stumps removed, it may, therefore, be possible to inadvertently damage a sett while conducting otherwise perfectly lawful activities. It is wise, therefore, to establish protection zones around sett entrances, thought to be active, with the distance determined by the nature of the work to be carried out. For excavations and works requiring the use of large machinery, a 30-m protection zone should be adequate. For light machinery, 20 m would be more appropriate and for hand operations, 10 m should be sufficient. Trees should be felled away from the sett entrance and clearance works should also be managed, so that operatives work away from sett entrances and badger paths. Loud noises and vibrations, over and above pre-work levels, should be avoided close to active setts to reduce the likelihood of disturbance.

8.8.2.3 Hazel dormice

Hazel dormice numbers and extent of distribution have declined in the last 100 years, contracting southwards and becoming extinct in approximately half of its former distribution range (Bright, Morris & Mitchell-Jones, 2006). Dormice and their nesting places are protected under the Wildlife and Countryside Act 1981 (as amended) and the Conservation of Habitats and Species Regulations 2010 (as amended). They are recognised as a species of *principal importance for the purpose of conserving of biodiversity* under section 41 (England) and section 42 (Wales) of the Natural Environment and Rural Communities (NERC) Act 2006. Dormice are particularly vulnerable to woodland and hedgerow management operations, and so hedge laying, coppicing and tree and scrub thinning works along deciduous woodland edges are likely to be particularly harmful if they are present. Any intentional or reckless disturbance to dormice, their resting places or breeding sites could result in an unlimited fine and up to 6 months' imprisonment if found guilty.

8.9 PLANNING

The UK planning system is 'plan-led', where (under sections 19(2) and 38(6) of the Planning and Compulsory Purchase Act 2004 and Section 70 of the Planning Act 1990) applications for planning permission are determined in accordance with the local plan, unless *material planning considerations* indicate otherwise. The local plan is produced by the LPA in consultation with the community and sets out a vision and a framework for the development of the area for which the LPA is responsible. The development plan includes all current core strategies and planning policies and is referred to as *development plan documents* in the Planning and Compulsory Purchase Act 2004 (HM Govt, 2004b). The National Planning Policy Framework 2012 (NPPF) sets out how local plans and neighbourhood plans must be developed to ensure that they are robust and consistent with national planning policy. Since the introduction of the NPPF, there is a presumption in favour of sustainable development.

In addition to all the environmental and sustainability benefits provided, trees can certainly be a significant factor in the overall character of an area. Where there is a particular historic or architectural presence and interest, '. . . the character or appearance of which is desirable to preserve or enhance . . .' (HM Govt, 1990a), trees are often an important element in creating that desirable character or appearance. Trees, therefore, require careful management and replacement to ensure that their provision in an area is retained. Although planning consent is unlikely to be required for removing a tree, local planning authorities do have specific control over trees protected by tree preservation orders or those growing within conservation areas (see below). If development proposals cause the loss of, or otherwise have an effect on, local trees, the local planning authority will take this into account as a material planning consideration when deciding on a planning application. More specifically, under section 197 of the Planning Act 1990, it is the legal duty of the local planning authority 'to ensure, whenever it is appropriate, that in granting planning permission for any development adequate provision is made, by the imposition of conditions, for the preservation or planting of trees' (HM Govt, 2008). Through development of a tree strategy, the LPA should be able to identify significant individual trees and groups of trees, and these will appear within the core strategy and local plan. Such a strategic approach to trees should provide a robust basis upon which to review existing tree preservation orders and determine new orders (see section 8.10).

Under sections 70(1), 72, 73 and 73A of the Town and Country Planning Act 1990, LPAs have legal powers to attach conditions to planning permissions. Such conditions must be fair, reasonable and practicable (DCLG, 2014d) and should only be imposed where they are necessary to make the development acceptable in planning terms, relevant to planning and to the development to be permitted, enforceable and precise (DCLG, 2012). The online guidance from DCLG advises caution when imposing conditions that prevent any development, permitted by the planning consent, from starting before the condition has been complied with. Such conditions invariably start with 'no development shall take place until . . .' or 'prior to the commencement of development . . .' and are known as 'conditions precedent'. These conditions are generally designed to require the developer to obtain, from the LPA, approvals to certain matters before development commences under the permission. The courts have long agreed that it is quite acceptable to impose such conditions preventing certain activities or matters from proceeding until a specific step has been taken by the developer. However, for a condition to be a true condition precedent, it must be shown that, unlike other conditions, if it is breached, then any development that has occurred in breach of the condition precedent is wholly unlawful.

In *Whitley and Sons Co.* (1992), planning permission had been obtained for mining operations, subject to a condition that 'no working should take place except in accordance with a scheme to be agreed with the LPA'. Details were submitted for approval, but not agreed by the LPA, and because the works had to begin within a specified time, they commenced prior to receiving approval. The question then arises if the works had begun before confirmation that the conditions had been met but within the deadline, were they lawful? The scheme was in the process of being agreed and was eventually agreed, but outside the deadline. In his judgement, Woolf LJ said 'it is only necessary to ask the single question; are the operations (in other situations the question would refer to the development) permitted by the planning permission read together with its conditions? The permission is controlled by and subject to the conditions. If the operations contravene the conditions they cannot properly be described as commencing the development authorised by the permission. If they do not comply with the permission they constitute a breach of planning control and for planning purposes will be unauthorised and thus unlawful.' This then set the 'Whitley Principle', however, Woolf LJ went on to say that the case before him was an exception to the principle. As the condition required that the scheme had to be agreed by the LPA without any indication that agreement had to be reached before the deadline, not that any works could be started prior to that agreement. Therefore, as the scheme was eventually approved, there appeared to be no good reason to pursue enforcement action.

In the case of *R (on the application of Hart Aggregates Ltd)* v. *Hartlepool BC* (2005), the court ruled that the *Whitley* principle does not apply to all conditions, but only those that 'go to the heart of the permission', those that are intended to control the entire development and not just a part of it. The court deemed that it was necessary to draw a distinction between conditions that require something to be done before development takes place and true conditions precedent that contain a prohibitive form of wording. The significance is that if the former is breached, it is a simple breach of condition and can be enforced against. If the latter, then development cannot lawfully be said to have commenced until the condition has been discharged. Therefore, if the development has not lawfully commenced before the commencement period expires, the permission would elapse and the development would be required to be resubmitted for approval, with no guarantee of success.

Careful and specific wording of conditions precedent is, therefore, of utmost importance. A true condition precedent must explicitly prohibit the commencement of the whole development before the condition has been discharged. It must also be able to pass scrutiny when challenged as to its intention to prohibit all development. For instance, in *Bedford Borough Council* v. *The Secretary of State for Communities and Local Government and Aleksander Stanislaw Murzyn* (2008), conditions requiring that a landscaping scheme and details of all boundary treatments be submitted for approval prior to commencement of a barn conversion development were not complied with. The inspector at appeal and the Judge in the High Court both found that neither conditions were true conditions precedent. As such, although the conditions had been breached, the development works that had been carried out could not be considered unlawful. However, in *Greyfort Properties Ltd* v. *The Secretary of State for Communities and Local Government* (2011), the condition that was not discharged prior to commencing development works stated that 'Before any work is commenced on the site the ground floor levels of the building hereby permitted shall be agreed with the Local Planning Authority in writing.' The Court of Appeal upheld the High Court's and the inspector's decision that this was indeed a true condition precedent. It both prohibits development without compliance with it and goes to the heart of the permission, rather than being concerned with some minor detail. The Appellant contested that the wording of the condition was not expressly prohibitive, and although the Court of Appeal dismissed the argument, it does raise the point that careful wording of any pre-commencement conditions is essential.

Another concern with pre-commencement conditions, rather than true conditions precedent, is that they only take effect when the permission is implemented. As Martin Goodall points out in his Planning Law Blog (Goodall, 2011), if a development scheme has permission, subject to a condition that is specifically targeted at retaining and protecting existing trees, but the developer does not implement the development, there is no requirement to comply with any conditions. As such, there is nothing to stop them from clearing the site of vegetation as long as none of the trees are protected with TPOs and the site is not within a conservation area. It is unlikely that such clearance works will be considered to be 'development' as defined in section 55 of the TCPA 1990 nor is it likely to be considered to be a 'material operation' as defined in section 56. As such, the planning permission will not have been implemented, the conditions will not have come into effect and so cannot be enforced. The only sure way to protect trees on potential development sites is to protect them with TPOs. A breach of a planning condition is not in itself an offence, whereas contravention of a TPO is an offence and anyone found guilty is liable to prosecution.

Sample conditions suitable for use with planning permissions are provided by Charles Mynors at Appendix B of *The Law of Trees, Forests and Hedges* (Mynors, 2011).

8.9.1 Ancient woodland

Ancient woodland is defined as an area that has been continuously wooded since at least 1600 AD.

Paragraph 118 of the NPPF states that 'planning permission should be refused for development resulting in the loss or deterioration of irreplaceable habitats, including ancient woodland and the loss of aged or veteran trees found outside ancient woodland, unless the need for, and benefits of, the development in that location clearly outweigh the loss' (DCLG, 2012).

8.9.2 Felling licences

Where 5 cu. m or more of timber is felled in any calendar quarter and where the trees are 80 mm or more in diameter (measured at 1.3 m from the ground), 100 mm or more for thinnings and 150 mm or more for coppice, a felling licence may be required, if planning permission has not already been granted. Trees growing in gardens, orchards, churchyards and designated open spaces, such as village greens, public parks and public gardens, registered under the Commons Act 1899 are exempt. No more than 2 cu. m of felled timber is allowed to be sold in any calendar quarter. Applications for felling licences must be obtained from the Forestry Commission (www.forestry.gov.uk/felling). Under the Forestry Act 1967 (as amended) (HM Govt, 1967a), conditions are typically attached to the licence, requiring restocking. If unauthorised felling takes place without a licence, anyone found guilty will be liable for prosecution, fined up to £2,500 (or twice the value of the felled trees, whichever is the greater). Any offender will also be served with a Restocking Notice, requiring that the trees be replaced and maintained to an 'acceptable standard' for up to 10 years. If the Restocking Notice is not complied with, an Enforcement Notice may be served, demanding that the Restocking Notice is satisfied. Failure to comply can result in a fine of up to £5,000.

8.9.3 The role of the consulting arborist

The process of determining protection, removal and successful integration of existing and proposed trees into development is 'bread and butter' work for many arboricultural consultants. The document that guides this process and provides local authorities with evidence that tree retention and protection have been considered as part of a planning application is the British Standard BS 5837: 2012 *Trees in Relation to Design, Demolition and Construction – Recommendations* (BSI, 2012). This standard provides recommendations on how development may be

RIBA Plan of Work 2013		BS 5837:2012 Recommendations	Site Operations subject to expert monitoring
Preparation	**0** Strategic Definition		
	1 Preparation and Brief	Topographical Survey and Soil Assessment (4.2 & 4.3)	Vegetation clearance if required for survey
		Tree Survey (4.4)	
		Tree Categorisation (4.5)	
		Identification of Tree Constraints and RPAs (4.5, 4.6 & Clause 5)	
Design	**2** Concept Design	Identification and Review of Trees for Retention and Removal (Clause 5)	
	3 Developed Design	Production of Planting and Landscape Proposals (5.6)	
		Production of Tree Protection Plan (5.5)	
		SCHEME DESIGN APPROVALS (from client and regulatory bodies)	– – – – – – – –
Pre-Construction	**4** Technical Design	Resolve Tree Protection Proposals (6.2)	
		Agree Utility Apparatus Location Routes and Arboricultural Methodologies (6.1 & Clause 7)	
		Schedule Trees for Removal and Pre-construction Tree Works (5.4 & 8.8)	
		Identify Tree Protection Measures and include them on all Relevant Documents (6.2)	Physical Barriers Erected (6.2)
			Site Clearance and Demolition (Clause 7)
			Access, Storage & Working Areas Installed (Clause 6)
Construction	**5** Construction	Site Monitoring and Intervention as Required (6.3)	Construction (Clause 7)
		Inspection of Trees and Surrounding Environment (Including relationships to new structures) (8.8)	New Planting (Clause 8)
Use	**6** Handover & Close Out	Recommendations for Post-completion Management (8.8)	Remedial Tree Works if Required
	7 In Use		

Figure 8.12 The new RIBA Plan of Work now comprises eight numeric work stages (0 to 7) compared to the previous eleven alphabetic stages. The stages within the design and construction process and tree care flow diagram have been mapped to the new RIBA work stages above.

integrated with existing trees and sets out to assist those involved to form balanced judgements based on evidence. The standard has been in existence since 1980 and has benefitted from three further revisions, the first in 1991, then 2005 and finally, in 2012. This latest revision includes *design* and *demolition* in the title for the first time in an effort to better reflect the entire development process. The intention is that the approach as set out in the standard is followed whether or not planning permission is required, for example, where structures less than 50 cu. m (Department for Communities and Local Government, 2015) are demolished or where works can be carried out under permitted development.

The standard emphasises the importance of trees as a 'material consideration' in the formal planning process, while accepting that development close to existing trees can be problematic; all decisions taken and advice given, therefore, need to be evidence-based. To assist with this, the standard provides guidance on a systematic and understandable method of deciding: which trees likely to be affected by proposed development, are appropriate for retention; how they should be protected during the demolition and construction phases; and how new trees can be incorporated into the new landscape. The logical process is provided as a flow diagram that has been deliberately aligned with the alphabetic RIBA Outline Plan of Work 2007. This, of course, has now been revised to the numeric RIBA Plan of Work 2013, but can be mapped if required (www.ribaplanofwork.com/PlanOfWork.aspx).

A topographical survey can be specified to include the location of individual trees, with a stem diameter of 75 mm (to accord with conservation area requirements) or more when measured at 1.5 m above the adjacent ground level, within the development site and provides a spot level at the base of the tree stems. Woodlands and substantial groups of trees would not normally be surveyed individually although extent of canopy cover would typically be identified, as would trees with a stem diameter of 150 mm or more. It is important that any trees outside the development site are also considered and surveyed, if it is possible that they may be affected by the proposed development.

The arboricultural survey captures quantitative spatial data and a qualitative assessment of the trees present and any hedges, hedgerows, shrub masses and stumps that may have been missed by the topographical survey. Each tree or group of trees is evaluated against a cascade chart within the standard to reflect the arboricultural, landscape, cultural, heritage and conservation contribution they make, with an assessment of life expectancy. The outcome of the evaluation is to give each tree a category grade as follows:

- 'U' grade trees are those whose existing condition is such that any current value would be lost within 10 years. They are low-quality trees with symptoms of significant, immediate and irreversible decline, either due to untreatable structural defects or serious pathogen infection. They may also be very low-quality trees that are suppressing the growth of much better quality adjacent trees. As such, they are typically removed for sound arboricultural reasons.
- 'A' grade trees are of high quality, with no or few obvious, compromising defects and a safe life expectancy in excess of 40 years. They may be particularly good and/or rare or unusual examples of their species; they may be significant visual features within the landscape; they may provide significant conservation, historical, commemorative or other social or cultural attributes. These trees should be retained as part of the development.

- 'B' grade trees are of moderate quality with a safe life expectancy in excess of 20 years, but unlikely beyond 40 years. These tend to be trees that have been downgraded due to significant but treatable defects.
- Category 'C' trees are of low quality with a safe life expectancy in excess of 10 years or young trees with stem diameters less than 150 mm. Retention of these trees will typically be guided by whether they impose a significant constraint on development or not. Young, good quality trees may be suitable for relocation.

Measurement data are collected and these, along with the qualitative tree evaluation, are made available in the form of a table. Also in the table must be shown the radius of the twelve times stem diameter *Root Protection Area* or RPA (see section 4.3.1 in Chapter 4 for more details). This is shown on drawings, along with the shadow cast by the existing trees, and is used to help inform the site layout design, construction access and utility infrastructure requirements.

A full tree survey is an important part of the evidence base used to influence the design. As such, it must be conducted sufficiently early in the design process to ensure that the results are available to inform feasibility studies and design options rather than specific development proposals. Local planning authorities should not rely upon planning conditions to secure tree surveys. The lack of availability of tree constraints until that late in the formal planning process would mean that the opportunity to control or mitigate against arboricultural impacts would be lost. It is quite possible that some level of site clearance or demolition could take place prior to any planning application being made, and unless there is some safeguard for existing trees, irredeemable damage could easily be done, either in ignorance or maliciously (see under planning conditions below).

The arboricultural consultant uses the information gathered from the tree survey, the proposed tree loss required to realise the design, the proximity of structures and excavations to trees and the proposed site activities through to completion to assess the overall impact likely to be suffered by the retained trees and recommend protection and mitigation measures where necessary. This is presented in an Arboricultural Impact Assessment which, along with an Arboricultural Method Statement that demonstrates how works within the RPA are to be managed, and both written and graphic details of tree protection measures and proposed planting, form part of the planning submission.

8.10   TREE PRESERVATION ORDERS AND CONSERVATION AREAS

The legislation concerning tree preservation orders and trees in conservation areas has changed fairly extensively over the last few years. There is extensive guidance available on the DCLG website, and anyone with an interest in either subject should visit the Planning Practice Guidance pages (http://planningguidance.communities.gov.uk/blog/guidance/tree-preservation-orders/) for current advice.

8.10.1   *Tree protection – a new 'streamlined' system*

Under section 197 and section 198 of the Town and Country Planning Act 1990, local planning authorities, when granting planning consent for development, have a duty to protect trees and woodlands, in the interests of amenity, from wilful damage or removal through the use of planning conditions and TPOs. All trees that benefit from a TPO cannot be cut down, uprooted, topped, lopped or otherwise wilfully damaged or destroyed without consent from the LPA to do so. If consent is given, it may be subject to conditions, and in such circumstances, those conditions must be followed. LPAs have been using this form of protection since the original Town and Country Planning Act made provision for TPOs in 1947. Since then, several pieces of primary and secondary legislation have been implemented, which govern the provision of TPOs: the Town and Country Planning Act 1990, the Town and Country Planning (Trees) Regulations 1999 (SI 1999, No. 1982), the Town and Country Planning (Trees) (Amendment) (England) Regulations 2008 (SI 2008, No. 2260) and the Town and Country Planning (Trees) (Amendment No. 2) (England) Regulations 2008 (SI 2008, No. 3202). TPOs made under such a range of different instruments and the provisions made within the specific order led to inconsistencies within the orders issued, in terms of consented activities, procedure of appealing against an LPA's decision and compensation for any loss or damage arising from any refusal or condition. As each order, once made, was fixed unless the LPA used its powers to vary it or revoke and replace it, the central government decided to simplify and streamline what had become a fairly complex system, through the introduction of new legislation. From 6 April 2012, the tree preservation order system is now governed by new secondary legislation, the Town and Country Planning (Tree Preservation) (England) Regulations 2012 (HM Govt, 2012) – the 2012 Regulations. This approach is intended to reduce the administrative burden on local authorities and to make public understanding of the system easier.

The 2012 Regulations were implemented using powers under sections 192 and 193 of the Planning Act 2008, which omit, amend and insert sections within the Town and Country Planning Act 1990 (TCPA). Section 192 of the Planning Act 2008 amends the TCPA by repealing all previous provisions, other than the information that identifies the order and the protected tree, and replaces them with those contained within the 2012 Regulations. This provided the new provisions for all TPOs made after 6 April 2012, moving forward. Section 193 omits all provisions attached to all existing TPOs, apart from the information that identifies the order and the protected tree, and also replaces them with the provisions contained within the 2012 Regulations, irrespective of when the TPO was made prior to 6 April 2012. This legislation effectively regularises all TPOs, so that they are all subject to the same provisions, in terms of consents, appeals and compensation, as laid out in the 2012 Regulations rather than in the individual order. Therefore, if any of the detailed provisions within the 2012 Regulations change, they will automatically apply to all orders, irrespective of when they were made. New TPOs will principally consist of a schedule of the tree, tree groups or woodlands to be protected and a map showing their position.

8.10.2   The regulations

Typically, TPOs are made 'If it appears to a local planning authority that it is expedient in the interests of amenity to make provision for the preservation of trees or woodlands in their area' (s. 198(1) TCPA 1990). Authorities must, therefore, assess how valuable the tree, group of trees or woodland is to the local environment by considering the significance of public loss were it to be removed, in terms of accessibility and visibility, biological functionality, rarity, contextual, cultural or historical significance and safe life expectancy. The government guidelines stress the importance of tree strategies for identifying individual and groups of trees with potential, and informing an approach to prioritising protection (DCLG, 2014c). Such an approach would help to satisfy the requirement for expediency in making TPOs. A pragmatic response must, therefore, be adopted when determining amenity value of the tree prior to making an order.

8.10.3 Making a tree preservation order

When making a new TPO, the LPA must serve a copy of the order on all persons who have an interest in the land on which the tree is growing and who have a right to prune or fell the tree. This must be accompanied by a notice containing the reasons for making the order, guidance on how to object to the order being made (including a copy of the appropriate Regulation 6 of the 2012 Regulations) and specifying the date by which any objection must be received. A copy of the order must also be made available for free public inspection at all reasonable hours at the offices of the LPA (Reg. 5(3)). The 2012 Regulations also state that the local LPA must inform those with an interest in the tree and provide a copy for public inspection 'as soon as practicable after making the order, and before confirming it' (Reg. 5(1)). With no definition of 'as soon as practicable', that does appear a little open-ended.

The order must be made using the standard form of order as included in the Schedule at the end of the 2012 Regulations, or in a format that is substantially to the same effect. An MS Word version of the standard order is available to download from the government website: (www.gov.uk/government/uploads/system/uploads/attachment_data/file/82790/120405_-_2012_-_Form_of_Tree_Preservation_Order-Arial_FINAL.doc). Details of the trees are specified in the Schedule attached to the order, as individual trees; trees specified by reference to an area; groups of trees; or woodlands. An individual order may contain combinations of each of these categories. Each order must also include, or have attached to it, an appropriate scale map that clearly shows the location of the trees, groups or woodlands. Ideally, maps should not be less than 1:1250, with road names and other landmarks visible, to help identify the location. If there are discrepancies between the map and the schedule, the map takes precedence (Reg. 3(4)).

The individual category is fairly self-explanatory and can be used for any individual tree. The group category is intended to be used where a group of individual trees collectively provides a feature of amenity value and where as individuals they may not. Ideally, the number of each species within the group should be included in the specification. The area category is much less common than it once was. It can be used to cover all trees within a defined geographic area or only those tree species specified, and will only protect those trees present at the time the order is made. It is intended to be used as a short-term measure, where swift action is required to protect trees in imminent danger, to allow authorities to fully assess and reclassify the trees affected. Local authorities are encouraged to revisit the existing area TPOs and reclassify where possible. The intention of woodland orders is to safeguard complete woodland blocks, irrespective of the age of the trees within them (see tree size below). While individual trees within the block may not be of any particular merit, the woodland as a whole collectively commands a high amenity value.

The 2012 Regulations provide immediate provisional protection from the day the TPO is made, allowing local planning authorities a period of 6 months to consider any objections or representations before confirming the order. In practice, most TPOs were made in this way, by making a special direction under the previous system anyway. If 6 months elapse before the TPO is confirmed, the order must be remade (Reg. 4).

8.10.3.1 Tree size

There is no size limit on a tree that can be subject to a TPO. Nor is there any restriction on the species of tree. Fruit trees may be included in a TPO, provided it is in the interests of amenity to do so. There is no definition of 'tree' in the legislation, and so large shrubs can be a little problematic, but as far as TPOs are concerned, the High Court has decided that a 'tree' is 'anything that ordinarily one would call a tree' (Bullock v. Secretary of State for the Environment, 1980). Further, in *Palm Developments* v. *Secretary of State for Communities and Local Government and another*, the developer was refused permission to remove scrub, shrubs, saplings and certain identified trees that were protected under a woodland TPO and appealed that decision. An appeal to the Secretary of State was dismissed on the recommendation of the appointed inspector, following a public enquiry. In her report, the inspector noted that individual trees must not be considered in isolation from scrub, shrubs and saplings as, in the course of natural regeneration, it is the saplings that will replace the mature trees as they die. As such, a tree at all stages of its life is capable of being protected, in a woodland context:

> . . . if the whole purpose of the TPO is to safeguard the woodland as a whole, then there must be some common-sense commitment to regeneration in the form of the trees reproducing themselves or re-growth . . .

Palm applied to the High Court under s. 288 of TCPA 1990 to quash the decision of the Secretary of State. Mr Justice Cranston dismissed the s. 288 application and refused permission to proceed with judicial review, concluding that:

> . . . with tree preservation orders there are no limitations in terms of size for what is to be treated as a tree. In other words, saplings are trees. Moreover, a tree preservation order for a woodland extends to all trees in the woodland, even if not in existence at the time the order is made.

This view was broadly supported by their Lordships in Distinctive Properties (2015), in the Court of Appeal (2015). Sir David Keene noted in his judgement that, although such a definition is appropriate when considering woodland TPOs, it is unlikely that individual seedling trees would be considered suitable for protection under the regulations. It would be a perverse use of an LPA's power and difficult to argue a case for amenity if such an order were to be made.

8.10.4 Special landowners

The Planning and Compulsory Purchase Act 2004 (HM Govt, 2004b) effectively removed Crown immunity from TPO applications for trees on Crown land, without their consent. It is recommended, however, that proposed TPO applications are discussed with the appropriate Crown authority (as defined in Schedule 3 of the Planning and Compulsory Purchase Act 2004). Liaison with the relevant diocese is encouraged when considering the protection of trees within churchyards; with the owner, operator or the Ministry of Defence when considering protecting trees near civil or military aerodromes; and with Historic England for trees close to scheduled monuments.

Under section 200 of the TCPA 1990, TPO regulations will have no effect on trees situated on land owned or managed by the Forestry Commission (the Public Forest Estate), or in which it has an interest for approved forestry purposes. In such situations, the LPA should seek advice from the Forestry Commission as to when or if their interest in the land is likely to cease.

8.10.5 Objections, comments and confirmation

Once an order has been made and served, the tree, trees or woodland benefit from immediate protection, on a provisional basis for a period of 6 months, until the LPA confirms the order or decides not to confirm it, whichever comes first (Reg. 4). In making the order, the LPA invites objections or representations from the public who have 28 days, from the date that the order was made, to make such objections and representations. Once the 28-day consultation period is over, the LPA must duly consider all objections and representations and then decide whether to confirm the order, with or without modifications, or to not confirm the order. Trees, groups or woodlands cannot be added to the original order as modifications. Another consultation period would be required.

When confirming the order, the LPA endorses it to record that it has been confirmed and when that confirmation took place. Copies of the confirmed order are then served to those people previously served with the made order and its details are recorded in the local land charges register, as a charge on the land on which the trees are standing. The order may then only be challenged in the High Court on a point of law, under section 284 of the TCPA 1990.

8.10.6 Works to protected trees

With some exceptions, permission must be sought from the LPA to carry out all work to TPO-protected trees. The exceptions are certain works as follows:

- on dead trees and branches
- to comply with an Act of Parliament
- by or on request of a statutory undertaker (as defined in (Reg. 14(3))
- required for highway operations
- for reasons of national security
- on commercial fruit trees
- required to implement a detailed planning permission
- requested by the Environment Agency or drainage bodies
- to remove an immediate risk of serious harm from dangerous trees and branches
- to prevent or abate a nuisance.

For works to dead trees and branches, at least 5 days' written notice must be given to the LPA prior to commencement of the works (Reg. 14(2)(b)). Where the work is urgently required because there is an immediate risk of serious harm, a written notice must be given as soon as practicable after the works become necessary (Reg. 14(2)(a)). It is still advisable to check with the LPA prior to carrying out any work on protected trees. All other works require consent from the LPA, via an application form available from the LPA or the Planning Portal. The TPO must be identified; a detailed description of the proposed works and why they are deemed to be necessary are also required. The LPA has 8 weeks to determine an application. The applicant has the right to appeal to the Secretary of State, within 28 days, if the LPA fails to determine an application within 8 weeks, if consent is refused or against the conditions imposed as part of a consent, under Regulation 19. The procedure for appealing is set out in Regulations 19 to 23. Schedule 6 to the TCPA 1990 (determination of certain appeals by person appointed by Secretary of State) also applies to appeals heard and determined by a planning inspector, who has been appointed by the Secretary of State.

8.10.7 Conditions

Conditions may be attached to consents (Reg. 17). Each condition must relate to the authorised work, be fairly and reasonably imposed and be precisely worded to ensure that the applicant is quite clear what work is being authorised and the LPA are satisfied that it can be enforced. The decision notice should clearly state the reasons for attaching the conditions. Typical conditions may be:

- To regulate the standard of authorised works (e.g. BS 3998: 2010 *Tree Work – Recommendations*).
- To allow repeated operations or programmes of work to be carried out (unless this condition is attached, the work may only be carried out once). The scope, timing, limit and frequency should be stated.
- To secure replacement planting (see below).
- To vary the default 2-year time limit for the consent (e.g., for repeated operations).

Replacement planting may be required due to a tree being removed, uprooted or destroyed in contravention of the 2012 Regulations. It may also be required because a protected tree has died or needed to be removed to avoid an immediate risk of serious harm. In these situations, section 206 of the TCPA 1990 applies, requiring removed trees to be replaced and that replacement will benefit from the existing TPO. For other consents to fell a protected tree, any replacement would need to be covered by a condition (enforced under a tree replacement notice), and these are not automatically protected under the original TPO. In these circumstances, the LPA may be required to vary the TPO to cover the replacement tree.

Each LPA is responsible for maintaining a public register showing all TPO applications, the LPA's decision, the nature and outcome of any appeal and details of any replanting conditions (Reg. 12).

8.10.8 Compensation

Under Regulation 24, any claimant who can demonstrate that they have suffered loss or damage as a consequence of the LPA either refusing consent or imposing conditions to a consent can submit a claim for compensation. The claim must be made within 12 months of the LPA decision or the determination of an appeal. No compensation is payable:

- for damage or loss incurred before an application for consent to work on a protected tree is made
- for loss of development value in the land
- if, when the consent was refused or granted subject to conditions, the loss or damage claimed for was not reasonably foreseeable from the information submitted
- if it was reasonably foreseeable by the applicant, and no reasonable steps were taken by them to either avert the damage or loss or to mitigate its extent
- any costs incurred making an appeal to the Secretary of State.

Claims for compensation relating to a restriction in forestry operations within protected woodlands are detailed in subsections (3) to (5) of section 11 of the Forestry Act 1967 (HM Govt, 1967b).

8.10.9 Trees in conservation areas

Trees within conservation areas, with a stem diameter of at least 75 mm (100 mm if thinning to aid the growth of other trees), measured at a height of 1.5 m above the ground level, automatically benefit from similar protection, by virtue of their location, under section 211 of the TCPA 1990. The LPA must be consulted before any tree work is carried out using a 'Section 211 notice', unless the work is included in the list of exceptions above. This provides the LPA a period of 6 weeks to determine whether to protect the tree with a TPO, allow the proposed works to proceed or decide to let the 6 weeks elapse without making a decision (non-determination). Although non-determination in planning and TPO applications are deemed refusals, non-determination by the LPA for conservation area applications is deemed consent. There is no option to refuse consent to the works nor to impose any conditions although those options would become available if a TPO was placed on the tree.

8.10.10 Penalties for contravention

8.10.10.1 Tree preservation orders

Anyone who carries out, causes or permits any unauthorised work on a tree protected by a TPO is guilty of an offence under sections 202C, 210(1) or 210(4) of the TCPA 1990. If the tree is cut down, uprooted or wilfully destroyed (s. 210(1)(a)), or wilfully damaged to such a degree that it requires removal or its amenity value is so diminished as to no longer be worth preserving (s. 210(1)(b)), the penalty can be a fine up to £20,000, if convicted in a magistrates' court (s. 210(2)(a)). Particularly, serious cases may be tried in Crown Court where the penalty fine is unlimited (s. 210(2)(b)). The court will consider any financial benefit that has occurred or is likely to occur from the offence (s. 210(3)). For any other contravention of a TPO (s. 210(4)), the case will be heard in a magistrates' court where the fine can be up to £2,500 (for the standard scale of fines for summary offences see section 37(2) of the Criminal Justice Act 1982 (HM Govt, 1982)). Proceedings cannot be brought for an offence committed more than 3 years ago (inserted into s. 210(4B) of the TCPA 1990 by s. 126(3) of the Localism Act 2011 (HM Govt, 2011)). Replacement trees for those that have been removed will be required of an appropriate size and species and to be planted in the same place as soon as reasonably possible (s. 206(1)). The replacement tree will benefit from protection of the original TPO (s. 206(5)).

8.10.10.2 Conservation areas

Trees in conservation areas are protected under section 211 of the TCPA 1990. Anyone who carries out any unauthorised work to a tree within a conservation area, that would if it were protected by a TPO be prohibited, will be committing an offence. The penalty, if convicted, will be the same as for TPO offences. Also if a tree is removed, uprooted or destroyed for whatever reason, the landowner must provide a replacement of appropriate size and species, for planting in a similar location as soon as reasonably possible. This duty is attached to the current and all subsequent landowners, as long as the property remains within a conservation area (s. 213 TCPA 1990).

REFERENCES

Ball, D. J. & Watt, J. (2013). The risk to the public of tree fall. *Journal of Risk Research, 16*(2), 261–9. doi:10.1080/13669877.2012.737827

Bartholomew, A. (1840). *Specifications for Practical Architecture*. London: John Williams, Library of Fine Arts.

Bedford Borough Council v. *The Secretary of State for Communities and Local Government and Aleksander Stanislaw Murzyn*, CO/11416/2007 (High Court of Justice Queen's Bench Division (Administrative Court) 20 August, 2008). Retrieved 4 June 2016 from www.bailii.org/ew/cases/EWHC/Admin/2008/2304.html.

Berent v. *Family Mosaic Housing and London Borough of Islington*, A1/2011/1575 (Court of Appeal (Civil Division) 2012). Retrieved from www.bailii.org/ew/cases/EWCA/Civ/2012/961.html.

Biddle, P. G. (1998). *Tree Root Damage to Buildings*. Wantage, UK: Willowmead Publishing.

BRE (1993). *BRE Digest 240. Low-Rise Buildings on Shrinkable Clay Soils: Part 1*. Watford, UK: Buildings Research Establishment.

Bright, P., Morris, P. & Mitchell-Jones, T. (2006). *The Dormouse Conservation Handbook* (2nd edn). Peterborough: English Nature (now Natural England). Retrieved from https://ptes.org/wp-content/uploads/2014/06/Dormouse-Conservation-Handbook.pdf.

British Horse Society. (2014). *Specifications and Standards Recommended for Equestrian Routes in England and Wales*. Retrieved 3 July 2016 from The British Horse Society – access and bridleways: www.bhs.org.uk/~/media/bhs/files/pdf-documents/access-leaflets/specifications-and-standards-of-bridleways-and-byways.ashx?la=en.

British Road Services v. *Slater* (Court of Appeal 1964).

BSI (2010). *BS 3998: 2010; Tree Work – Recommendations*. London: British Standards Institution.

BSI (2015). *BS 8596: 2015; Surveying for Bats in Trees and Woodland – Guide*. London: British Standards Institution.

Buckland v. *Guildford Gas, Light and Coke Co.* (1948).

Bullock v. *Secretary of State for the Environment* (Queens Bench Division, 15 February 1980).

Caminer v. *Northern and London Investment Trust Ltd*, HT-12-386 (House of Lords, 11 June 1951).

Coder, K. D. (2013). *Trees and Lightning: Principles for Controlling Damage*. Athens, GA: Warnell School of Forestry and Natural Resources. Retrieved from www.warnell.uga.edu/outreach/pubs/pdf/forestry/Lightning Manual Part II Pub 13-8.pdf.

Cutler, D. F. & Richardson, I. B. (1989). *Tree Roots and Buildings*. Harlow, Essex: Longman Scientific and Technical.

DCLG (2012). *National Planning Policy Framework*. London: Department for Communities and Local Government. Retrieved from http://planningguidance.communities.gov.uk/wp-content/themes/planning-guidance/assets/NPPF.pdf.

DCLG (2014a). *Application for Tree Works: Works to Trees Subject to a Tree Preservation Order (TPO)*. Retrieved 25 June 2016 from National Planning Policy Framework: Planning Practice Guidance – Tree Preservation Orders and trees in conservation areas: www.planningportal.gov.uk/uploads/1app/guidance/guidance_note-works_to_trees.pdf.

DCLG (2014b). *Making Applications to Carry Out Work on Trees Protected by a Tree Preservation Order*. Retrieved 25 June 2016 from National Planning Policy Framework: Planning Practice Guidance – Tree Preservation Orders and trees in conservation areas: http://planningguidance.communities.gov.uk/blog/guidance/tree-preservation-orders/making-applications-to-carry-out-work-on-trees-protected-by-a-tree-preservation-order/.

DCLG (2014c). *Tree Preservation Orders and trees in conservation areas, Tree Preservation Orders – general*. Retrieved 8 July 2016 from National Planning Policy Framework: Planning Practice Guidance – Tree Preservation Orders and trees in conservation areas: http://planningguidance.communities.gov.uk/blog/guidance/tree-preservation-orders/tree-preservation-orders-general/#paragraph_007.

DCLG (2014d). *Use of Planning Conditions: Why and how are conditions imposed?* Retrieved 17 July 2016 from Department for Communities & Local Government – Planning Practice Guidance: http://planningguidance.communities.gov.uk/blog/guidance/use-of-planning-conditions/why-and-how-are-conditions-imposed/.

Defra (2007). *Project WM0304. Development of a strategy for resolving urban badger damage problems*. London: Defra. Retrieved from http://sciencesearch.defra.gov.uk/Document.aspx?Document=WM0304_6339_FRP.doc.

Department for Communities and Local Government (2015). *Guidance note – prior notification of proposed demolition*. Retrieved 15 June 2015 from www.planningportal.gov.uk/uploads/1app/guidance/guidance_noteprior_notification_of_proposed_demolition.pdf.

Department for Transport (2009a). *Traffic Signs Manual*: Chapter 8 – Traffic Safety Measures and Signs for Road Works and Temporary Situations, Part 1: Design. Retrieved 4 July 2016 from Government – Publications: www.gov.uk/government/uploads/system/uploads/attachment_data/file/203669/traffic-signs-manual-chapter-08-part-01.pdf.

Department for Transport (2009b). *Traffic Signs Manual*: Chapter 8 – Traffic Safety Measures and Signs for Road Works and Temporary Situations, Part 2: Operations. Retrieved 4 July 2016 from Government – Publications: www.gov.uk/government/uploads/system/uploads/attachment_data/file/203670/traffic-signs-manual-chapter-08-part-02.pdf.

Department for Transport (2010). *New Roads and Street Works Act 1991: Specification for the Reinstatement of Openings in Highways* (3rd edn). Norwich: The Stationery Office. Retrieved from www.gov.uk/government/uploads/system/uploads/attachment_data/file/11042/sroh.pdf.

Department for Transport (2012). *Code of Practice for the Co-Ordination of Street Works and Works for Road Purposes and Related Matters* (4th edn). Retrieved 3 July 2016 from Government – Publications – Guidance: www.gov.uk/government/uploads/system/uploads/attachment_data/file/43578/street-works-code-of-practice.pdf.

Department for Transport (2013). *Safety at Street Works and Road Works: A Code of Practice.* Retrieved 4 July 2016 from Government – Publications: www.gov.uk/government/uploads/system/uploads/attachment_data/file/321056/safety-at-streetworks.pdf.

Distinctive Properties (Ascot) Ltd v. *Secretary of State for Communities & Local Government & Another*, C1/2015/1102 (The Court of Appeal (Civil Division) 17 November 2015).

Donoghue v. *Stevenson* (House of Lords 1932). Retrieved from www.bailii.org/cgi-bin/format.cgi?doc=/uk/cases/UKHL/1932/100.html&query=(donoghue)+AND+(v)+AND+(stevenson).

Edwards v. *National Coal Board* (1949).

Ellison, M. J. (2005). Quantified tree risk assessment used in the management of amenity trees. *Journal of Arboriculture, 31*(2), 57–65. Retrieved from http://joa.isa-arbor.com/request.asp?JournalID=1&ArticleID=178&Type=2.

ENA (2012). *Tree Trimming.* Retrieved 3 July 2016 from Energy Networks Association – Electricity – Public Safety Leaflets: www.energynetworks.org/assets/files/electricity/she/public_safety/leaflets/Updated%20Feb%202014/ena_TreeTrimming_DL.pdf.

FG Whitley & Sons Company Ltd v. *Secretary of State for Wales* (Court of Appeal 1992).

GLA (2011). *Branching Out: The Future of London's Street Trees.* London: Greater London Authority.

Goodall, M. (2011). Pre-commencement Conditions. Retrieved 18 July 2016 from Martin Goodall's Planning Law Blog: http://planninglawblog.blogspot.co.uk/2011/06/pre-commencement-conditions.html.

Greyfort Properties Limited v. *Secretary of State for Communities and Local Government and Torbay Council*, C1/2010/3042 (Court of Appeal (Civil Division) 28 July 2011). Retrieved 3 June 2016 from www.bailii.org/ew/cases/EWCA/Civ/2011/908.html.

Hale v. *Hants & Dorset Motor Services Ltd. and Another* (Court of Appeal 1947).

Haque, M. (2013). Tree root damage: making everyone pay? Retrieved 26 June 2016 from Thomson Reuters Practical Law Construction Blog: http://constructionblog.practicallaw.com/tree-root-damage-making-everyone-pay/.

Highways England (2004). *DMRB:* Volume 10 Environmental Design and Management, Section 3 Landscape Management, Part 2, HA 108/04 *Landscape Management Handbook.* Retrieved 3 July 2016 from Standards for Highways: www.standardsforhighways.co.uk/ha/standards/dmrb/vol10/section3/ha10804.pdf.

HM Govt (1967a). Forestry Act 1967. London: HMSO. Retrieved 19 July 2016 from www.legislation.gov.uk/ukpga/1967/10.

HM Govt (1967b). Forestry Act 1967 (s. 11(3) to (5)). London: HMSO. Retrieved 11 July 2016 from www.legislation.gov.uk/ukpga/1967/10/section/11.

HM Govt (1982). Criminal Justice Act 1982 (Part III s. 37(2)). London: HMSO. Retrieved from www.legislation.gov.uk/ukpga/1982/48/section/37.

HM Govt (1984). Telecommunications Act 1984 ((c.12). Sch.2 (19)). HMSO: London. Retrieved 30 March 2015 from www.legislation.gov.uk/ukpga/1984/12/schedule/2.

HM Govt (1989). Electricity Act 1989 ((c.8). Sch.4 (9)). London: HMSO. Retrieved 30 March 1015 from www.legislation.gov.uk/ukpga/1989/29/schedule/4/paragraph/9.

HM Govt (1990a). Planning (Listed Buildings and Conservation Areas) Act 1990 (Part II). London: HMSO. Retrieved 16 July 2016 from www.legislation.gov.uk/ukpga/1990/9.

HM Govt (1990b). Town and Country Planning Act 1990. London: HMSO. Retrieved 20 June 2016 from www.legislation.gov.uk/ukpga/1990/8/part/VIII/chapter/I.

HM Govt (1991). New Roads and Street Works Act 1991. London: HMSO. Retrieved from www.legislation.gov.uk/ukpga/1991/22.

HM Govt (1992). Protection of Badgers Act 1992. London: HMSO. Retrieved 4 July 2016 from www.legislation.gov.uk/ukpga/1992/51.

HM Govt (2003). Anti-social Behaviour Act 2003. (Pt. 8). London: HMSO. Retrieved 26 June 2016 from www.legislation.gov.uk/ukpga/2003/38/part/8.

HM Govt (2004a) Nature Conservation (Scotland) Act 2004. London: HMSO. Retrieved 4 July 2016 from www.legislation.gov.uk/asp/2004/6/schedule/6.

HM Govt (2004b). Planning and Compulsory Purchase Act 2004. London: HMSO. Retrieved 10 July 2016 from www.legislation.gov.uk/ukpga/2004/5.

HM Govt (2008. Planning Act 2008. London: HMSO. Retrieved 10 July 2016 from www.legislation.gov.uk/ukpga/2008/29.

HM Govt (2010a). The Conservation of Habitats and Species Regulations 2010. London: HMSO. Retrieved 6 July 2016 from www.legislation.gov.uk/uksi/2010/490/made.

HM Govt (2010b). The Wildlife and Countryside Act 1981 (Variation of Schedule 9) (England and Wales) Order 2010. London: HMSO.

HM Govt (2011). Localism Act 2011 (s. 126(3)). London: HMSO. Retrieved from www.legislation.gov.uk/ukpga/2011/20/section/126.

HM Govt (2012). The Town and Country Planning (Tree Preservation) (England) Regulations 2012. London: HMSO. Retrieved 4 July 2016 from www.legislation.gov.uk/uksi/2012/605/made.

HM Govt (2013). High Hedges (Scotland) Act 2013. London: HMSO. Retrieved from www.legislation.gov.uk/asp/2013/6.

HSE (2001). *Reducing Risks, Protecting People: HSE's Decision-Making Process*. Sudbury, UK: HSE Books. Retrieved from www.hse.gov.uk/risk/theory/r2p2.pdf.

HSE (2013a, March). *Avoiding Danger from Overhead Power Lines – Guidance Note GS6 (Fourth edition)*. Retrieved 3 July 2016 from Health and Safety Executive – Electricity – Overhead Power Lines: www.hse.gov.uk/pubns/gs6.htm.

HSE (2013b). Management of the Risk from Falling Trees or Branches – SIM 01/2007/05. Retrieved 7 February 2016 from Health and Safety Executive: www.hse.gov.uk/foi/internalops/sims/ag_food/010705.htm.

HSE (n.d.). Working Near Power Lines and Cables. Retrieved 3 July 2016 from Health and Safety Executive – Guidance: www.hse.gov.uk/treework/safety-topics/power-lines.htm.

Hunter and Others v. *Canary Wharf Ltd.* (House of Lords, 24 April 1997). Retrieved from www.bailii.org/uk/cases/UKHL/1997/14.html.

Khan and Khan v. *Harrow Council and Kane*, HT-11-99 (High Court of Justice; Queens Bench Division; Technology and Construction Court 3 September 2013). Retrieved from www.bailii.org/ew/cases/EWHC/TCC/2013/2687.html.

Leakey v. *National Trust for Places of Historic Interest or Natural Beauty* (The Supreme Court of Judicature, The Court of Appeal (Civil Division) 31 July 1979). Retrieved from www.bailii.org/ew/cases/EWCA/Civ/1979/5.html.

Lemmon v. *Webb* (House of Lords, 27 November 1894). Retrieved from www.bailii.org/uk/cases/UKHL/1894/1.html.

Littlefair, P. J. (2005). *Hedge Height and Light Loss*. Office of the Deputy Prime Minister. London: HMSO. Retrieved from www.gov.uk/government/uploads/system/uploads/attachment_data/file/9408/hedgeheight.pdf.

Lonsdale, D. (1999). *Principles of Tree Hazard Assessment and Management, Research for Amenity Trees No. 7*. London: Department of the Environment, Transport and the Regions.

Lonsdale, D. (2000). *Hazards from Trees: A General Guide*. Retrieved 7 February 2016 from Forestry Commission – Publications: www.forestry.gov.uk/pdf/fcpg13.pdf.

LTOA (2008). *A Risk Limitation Strategy for Tree Root Claims* (3rd edn). London: The London Tree Officers' Association. Retrieved from www.ltoa.org.uk/documents/doc_download/126-the-risk-limitation-strategy-for-tree-root-claims.

Mynors, C. (2011). *The Law of Trees, Forests and Hedges* (2nd edn). London: Sweet and Maxwell.

Natural England and Defra (2015). Environmental Management – Guidance, Badgers: Protection and Licences. Retrieved 4 July 2016 from UK Government – guidance: www.gov.uk/guidance/badgers-protection-surveys-and-licences.

Natural England and Defra (2015). Planning and Development – Guidance, Badgers: Surveys and Mitigation for Development Projects. Retrieved 4 July 2016 from UK Government – guidance: www.gov.uk/guidance/badgers-surveys-and-mitigation-for-development-projects.

NJUG (2007). *Volume 4: NJUG Guidelines for the Planning, Installation and Maintenance of Utility Apparatus in Proximity to Trees (Issue 2)*. Retrieved 30 March 2015 from National Joint Utilities Group – NJUG Publications: www.njug.org.uk/d/www.njug.org.uk/wp-content/uploads/V4-Trees-Issue-2-16-11-2007.pdf.

NTSG (2011). *Common Sense Risk Management of Trees: Guidance on Trees and Public Safety in the UK for Owners, Managers and Advisors*. Edinburgh: Forestry Commission. Retrieved from www.forestry.gov.uk/PDF/FCMS024.pdf/$FILE/FCMS024.pdf.

O'Callaghan, D. P. & Kelly, O. (2005). Tree-related subsidence: Pruning is not the answer. *Journal of Building Appraisal, 1*(2), 113–29.

Quaife, E. J. (20 July 2016). Personal communication.

R (on the application of Hart Aggregates Ltd) v. *Hartlepool Borough Council*, CO/5427/2004 (Queen's Bench Division (Administrative Court, 26 April 2005).

Rylands v. *Fletcher* (House of Lords July 1868). Retrieved from www.bailii.org/uk/cases/UKHL/1868/1.html.

Smith v. *Giddy* (Appeal Court, 1904).

Solloway v. *Hampshire County Council* (Court of Appeal, 1981).

Stagecoach South Western Trains Ltd v *Hind and Steel*, HT-12-386 (High Court of Justice, 2014). Retrieved from www.bailii.org/ew/cases/EWHC/TCC/2014/1891.html.

UKRLG. (2011). *Well-Maintained Highways – Code of Practice*. The UK Roads Liaison Group. London: The Stationery Office. Retrieved from www.ukroadsliaisongroup.org/download.cfm/docid/C7214A5B-66E1-4994-AA7FBAC360DC5CC7.

W.B.N. (1949). Tort – Negligence – Duty to Trespasser on Land of Third Party – Allurement. *The Cambridge Law Journal, 10*(2), 272–3. doi:10.1017/S0008197300012514

Ward, W. H. & Green, H. (1952). House foundations: The short bored pile. Final Report. *Proceedings Public Works and Municipal Services Congress and Exhibition*. London: Institution of Civil Engineers.

Whitley and Sons Co. Ltd v. *Secretary of State for Wales* (1992).

Chapter 9: An integrated approach to green infrastructure

> This is a green world, with animals comparatively few and small, and all dependent on the leaves. By leaves we live. Some people have strange ideas that they live by money. They think energy is generated by the circulation of coins. Whereas the world is mainly a vast leaf colony, growing on and forming a leafy soil, not a mere mineral mass: and we live not by the jingling of our coins, but by the fullness of our harvests.
>
> Patrick Geddes (Scottish sociologist and urban planner)

9.1 INTRODUCTION

As discussed in Chapter 1, we have moved beyond the purely aesthetic, amenity values that trees bring by knocking the hard, stark edges off a sometimes harsh urban landscape and providing a soft, scalar counterpoint to the built form. We recognise, in addition, that green infrastructure is able to provide an enormous, unique and diverse range of environmental, social and economic benefits, or ecosystem services to our communities. Recognition is one thing, but to *realise* the ecosystem services that can be delivered, the green infrastructure resource needs to be managed and funded appropriately. And, to ensure that management, funding and development are targeted most effectively, a strategy is required.

There is now a good understanding that, in terms of *urban* green infrastructure, it is the tree canopy cover that is principally responsible for providing the bulk of ecosystem services over other forms of planting. Trees should be treated as special elements within a broader green infrastructure, therefore, requiring their own strategic approach to implementation, management and development. It is important to point out here that tree and woodland strategies should be distinct from but complementary with other open space or green infrastructure strategies, to prevent conflicts in overall aims. A good starting point for any strategic approach would be to conduct a comprehensive baseline survey of the local tree population to determine its extent, diversity and condition. Without this, there is no opportunity to provide any assessment of the tree stock value, in terms of amenity benefit and ecosystem service provision, nor can one start to set goals and targets, for increases in canopy cover, in any strategic way (Schwab, 2009).

9.2 STRATEGIC GREEN INFRASTRUCTURE MANAGEMENT

The Trees in Towns II survey of local authority tree managers identified a requirement for a more consistent approach to local authority tree management across the country. In particular, it emphasised the importance of local authorities (LAs) producing and adopting comprehensive and long-term tree strategies that establish the requirements for the maintenance, replacement and extension of urban tree cover (Britt & Johnston, 2008). In order for this to be achieved, a good understanding of the existing tree resource, in terms of its extent, composition and quality, must be gained. However, Trees in Towns II found that 'many LAs lacked some basic information about the nature and extent of the trees and woodlands in their district' (Johnston, 2010). Without any tree strategy, it is virtually impossible for local authorities to proactively manage their existing tree stock and integrate it, in any systematic way, with trees in private ownership and any planting within new developments. As a consequence, tree protection and management can quickly become reactive. In addition, there is a tendency to pass responsibility for the quality of new planting to developers or at 'the whim of the arboricultural/tree officer' (DoE, 1993), rather than being targeted to satisfy broader objectives. This is unfortunate as LAs have the power to 'exert a considerable degree of influence' (Britt & Johnston, 2008) over private development proposals, through regulation and planning legislation.

It is somewhat disappointing to note that many of the recommendations highlighted in the first Trees in Towns report, which was published in 1993 (DoE, 1993), were repeated in the later second edition. It would appear that we have learnt little in the intervening 10 years. It would, perhaps, be interesting to travel forward in speculative time and review the outputs from the next, now long overdue, Trees in Towns report. It might make fairly sobering reading.

9.2.1 The London tree and woodland framework

One good example of a successful urban tree and woodland strategy that has been both integrated into and helped to guide local policy, and which, in addition, has attracted funding for active tree management, is the London Tree and Woodland Framework. This policy guidance initiative was implemented through a partnership between the London Woodland Advisory Group and the Mayor of London's office. The London Woodland Advisory Group was formed in 2002, with representation from the following organisations:

Corporation of London
Countryside Agency
English Nature (now Natural England)
English Heritage (Historic England)
Forestry Commission
Government Office for London (GoL)
Greater London Authority (GLA)
Groundwork London
London Development Agency (LDA)
London Tree Officers' Association (LTOA)
Royal Parks
Thames Chase Community Forest
Trees for London
Woodland Trust.

The framework document was subjected to the usual consultation process, was revised accordingly and issued for general release in March 2005. The main objectives of the framework were to provide strategic guidance on how best to manage the trees and woodlands within

London, to safeguard and increase awareness of their value, maximise the contribution they can make and ensure their longevity through regeneration and replanting initiatives (GLA, 2005). One of the key mechanisms identified to deliver these objectives was the production of comprehensive LA tree and woodland strategies (a recommendation that was also repeated in Trees in Towns II). It was recommended that these tree and woodland strategies should approach the management of the borough-wide trees as a single resource, rather than as a fragmented collection of individuals and in a co-ordinated rather than in an ad hoc, reactive manner.

The London Tree Woodland Framework helped to inform the Mayor of London's supplementary planning guidance (SPG) covering green infrastructure and the open environment. This SPG is in four parts:

A – All London Green Grid
B – Guidance on Open Space Strategies
C – Preparing Tree and Woodland Strategies
D – London's Foundations.

Section C, the guidance on preparing tree and woodland strategies, should assist LAs in producing their own comprehensive strategy, while at the same time, ensuring consistency in policy across borough boundaries and encouraging the mutualistic relationships that are required between private and public tree owners and managers (GLA, 2013). The guidance stresses the need for early engagement with local politicians and officers, to inform them of the importance of a strategy to manage trees and woodlands within the LA and to garner Cabinet or Committee backing for its production. Before any assumptions can be made regarding aims and objectives, in terms of canopy cover targets, tree management options, planting opportunities and so on, an assessment of the existing condition must be collated. Once a receptive environment has been created and the necessary stakeholders engaged, a quantitative and qualitative assessment of the existing tree and woodland stock should be conducted. Ideally, in line with most other infrastructure management plans, the data collected would be geo-referenced using GIS (Geographical Information Systems). From this initial baseline position, some strategic decisions can be made with regard to existing tree species diversity, potential tree planting opportunities and overall canopy cover objectives. In addition, and perhaps of equal importance, the baseline data can also be used to assess the asset value of the trees.

9.3   GREEN INFRASTRUCTURE (GI) VALUATION

There are two main reasons to provide a monetised value for trees and other green infrastructure, if compensation for tree loss is being sought or for calculating the asset value of tree stock. If trees are damaged or removed without permission, there needs to be some sound basis for compensation to be calculated that is sufficiently robust to be acceptable to the court. If damaged trees can be returned to their pre-damaged state through the application of appropriate treatment and care, then recovery of the cost of that treatment and care could be found to be a suitable solution. In some situations, the damage can be so severe that no amount of treatment, however extensive, will facilitate recovery. If tree removal is the only safe course of action, then a direct replacement tree of similar size may be appropriate, but often, when dealing with large mature trees that would be prohibitively expensive to replace, some method of calculating a replacement cost is the only option.

On the face of it, valuation systems should also be very useful tools for monetising tree benefits, which can provide asset value data for use within the political arena by tree managers. As is typical in other asset management spheres, the monetised value could be used to negotiate and secure sufficient asset management resources, based on a percentage of overall asset value. However, a reasonable and defensible valuation of large trees can be quite difficult to establish.

9.3.1 CTLA

The Council of Tree and Landscape Appraisers (CTLA) is a consortium made up of representatives from North American industry organisations, with an interest in the production, care and management of, and design with, trees and plants. CTLA produces the guidance document *The Guide for Plant Appraisal* (CTLA, 2000). The tenth edition is currently being reviewed and should be released at some point in 2017. The CTLA method provided the idea of calculating a surrogate value, for trees that are larger than available replacements, from the trunk dimensions, the *Trunk Formula Method* (TFM). The value calculated for a unit area of stem (in this case square inches) is based on the cost of the largest trees commonly available in regional nurseries. The value is then reduced by factors to represent species quality, tree condition and location within the landscape. The factors range from 0.0 to 1.0 for each. The appraised value is:

Trunk area (in^2) x basic price per area unit (in^2) x species x condition x location

The value provided is a depreciated replacement cost, a theoretical structural value based on the physical resource, and does not calculate the environmental or aesthetic benefits provided by the assessed trees.

9.3.2 CAVAT

CAVAT (Capital Asset Valuation for Amenity Trees) (LTOA, 2010) was developed in the UK by Chris Neilan as a way to assess not only the replacement value of a chosen tree, but also the public amenity contribution provided. The methodology is primarily intended for use by local authorities to enable them to provide a repeatable asset value for the tree stock in their control. The first stage of the process provides a basic tree replacement value based on its size alone. Using a similar methodology to the CTLA *Trunk Formula Method*, a unit value for each sq. cm of stem is calculated using the average planted cost of a basket of commonly used, container-grown, 12–14 cm girth, standard street trees. The stem area of the surveyed tree (in sq. cm) is simply multiplied by this unit value factor (UVF) to provide the basic replacement tree cost. This basic replacement cost is then modified according to its location, accessibility, functionality, specific amenity benefits and safe life expectancy by a series of adjustment factors. Unlike the CTLA methodology, these CAVAT adjustment factors can enhance the overall value as well as depreciate it.

The full CAVAT process follows five stages as outlined by Neilan (2010) and shown below:

- The basic replacement value is calculated by multiplying the area of the tree stem, at breast height, by the UVF. The UVF in May 2015 was £15.88 per sq. cm. The UVF combines the nursery gate price for a replacement tree with the delivery and planting costs, but does not include after-care.
- The basic value is then modified according to the local population density and how accessible and visible the tree is to that local population, collectively termed the Community Tree Index (CTI). This stage involves two separate operations. First,

the basic value is adjusted to represent the population that is able to benefit from the presence of the tree. This is calculated from Office of National Statistics population density figures and ranges from 100 per cent, for large parts of the country, to a maximum of 250 per cent for some high-density, inner-city areas. The second operation makes an allowance for how accessible and visible the tree is to the public. Fully accessible trees alongside public highways and in public parks or woodlands would typically score 100 per cent. Those in private gardens, building courtyards and sheltered housing units would score lower, down to a minimum of 40 per cent.

- A physical tree survey is used to determine the biological functionality of the tree. This is based on the overall tree health and density and completeness of crown, compared with what would be expected from a well-grown, healthy tree of the same species and DBH. No assessment would be made for structural condition at this stage, unless the functional status of the tree was affected. The functionality factor modifies the CTI value above. Crown size may be modified by pruning, disease or damage. Crown condition may reflect pests and disease, root disorders and so on. Dead trees or those requiring urgent removal would score 0 per cent, and so, have a value of £0.

- An adjustment is made to reflect *special* amenity benefits such as proximity to a particular building or location, context or setting, local designation, rarity, distinctive visual qualities, specific biodiversity value and so on. Up to four of these special factors may score 10 per cent each, up to a combined maximum of 40 per cent. Veteran and ancient trees would score 30 per cent. Likewise, inappropriate species or location, disruptive root growth or path obstruction provides a negative factor and again, a maximum of four factors may score –10 per cent each, up to a combined maximum of –40 per cent.

- Finally, an adjustment is made to reflect the safe life expectancy (SLE). This is based on the SULE (Barrell, 1993) methodology and requires an estimate of present age of the tree, the average lifespan of the species and an assessment of the local environmental conditions that may affect that lifespan. This is then modified further by considering the biological health of the tree, its structural integrity, size and its location, in terms of proximity to number and quality of targets. Trees with an SLE greater than 80 years would retain 100 per cent of their value. Those with an SLE less than 5 years would have their value reduced to 5 per cent.

The final appraised value is the product of all of these stages multiplied together:

Basic value × CTI value x functional value × special amenity factor value × safe life expectancy

Some local authorities and Transport for London (TfL) are using CAVAT as a tool to value their tree stock, in much the same way as other public-owned assets are valued. However, there is no provision for calculating the actual ecosystem services provision of the tree stock assessed.

9.3.3   Helliwell

The Helliwell visual amenity assessment system used today is based on proposals devised by Rodney Helliwell and which were first published in the *Arboricultural Association Journal* (now the *Arboricultural Journal*) (Helliwell, 1967). The method was adopted by the Tree Council and published in 1974 as a leaflet. The Arboricultural Association revised the information and re-published the leaflet in 1984. A modified version suitable for the valuation of woodlands was published by the Arboricultural Association in 1986. The system requires values to be assigned to a number of different amenity factors determined by trained surveyors. These are then multiplied together to provide an overall score to which a monetary value can be assigned. The main difference between the Helliwell system and others is that it is deliberately independent of the production costs and replacement value of the assessed tree. Helliwell argues that replacement value is not a good indicator of the visual amenity qualities provided by a particular tree, growing in a particular location. A self-sown seedling may mature to become a magnificent landscape tree of great beauty and amenity value. Whereas, a very expensive tree may be planted in completely the wrong location, making it an ugly feature, of little landscape merit (Helliwell, 2008a). If used in cases where a compensation payment for a tree maliciously or accidentally damaged or removed is being assessed, the compensation figure should be calculated using either the loss of amenity or the cost of replacement and not both (Helliwell, 2008b).

The valuation method follows three steps. First, the tree is scored according to six amenity factors:

- Size is calculated as the area of the tree when viewed from the side. An average value can be applied if the area varies between viewpoints. The overall tree height is multiplied by the crown diameter and scored on a scale from 0 to 8, with 0 assigned to trees less than 2 sq. m and 8 assigned to those in excess of 200 sq. m.

- Expected duration or SULE is assessed taking into consideration the typical biological lifespan of the species, its current age and modifying factors that can either increase or decrease its life expectancy. Common oak, sweet chestnut, London plane and limes have much greater life expectancy than rowan, apples, cherries and birches, so would score higher. Some assessment should be made of the structural integrity and the number and quality of targets present. The tree is scored on a scale from 0 to 4, with a SULE less than 2 years scoring 0 and a SULE in excess of 100 years scoring 4.

- The visual prominence or importance of position within the landscape is assessed according to the visual amenity value provided to society as a whole. The more prominent and accessible the tree, the higher the assigned value. The tree is scored on a scale from 0 to 4, with 0 being assigned to those that cannot be seen from any normal vantage point, and so, considered of no importance. Whereas those considered of great importance and that provide the principle landscape feature of a public space would attain a score of 4.

- An assessment is made of the abundance of other trees within the locality. If one tree were to be lost within a landscape full of trees, it could be considered less important than a similar single, dominant tree, where few others are present. Helliwell points out that in some heavily wooded areas, selective tree removals could be advantageous to visual amenity. Here, the tree is scored on a scale from 0.5 to 4, where 0.5 is scored if other trees cover more than 70 per cent of the *visual area*, and 4 is scored if no other trees are present. The visual area needs some explanation. Many urban locations are bounded by tall buildings, which define the *visual area,* but some situations are unlikely to be so neatly determined. Helliwell suggests that an area of 50 ha is assessed where no clear boundary exists and recommends the use of aerial images to determine the area of ground covered by tree canopy.

- An assessment is made of the tree in relation to its setting. This factor considers how appropriate the tree appears within its location and how much the tree and site complement each other. This can be quite subjective, and Helliwell provides some guidance for the surveyor. For instance, large trees in tight sites can appear too cramped and overwhelming. A small tree in a large site can appear insignificant. Some careful consideration should be given to trees within formal groups or clumps. This factor is again scored from 0 to 4, with 0 representing a tree that is unsuitable for its location and where the landscape would be improved were the tree to be removed. A score of 4 would be assigned to trees that are considered to be especially suitable to their location and make a significant contribution to the landscape character.
- The final assessment is made on the tree form in terms of its aesthetic qualities. Here, the assessment can become very subjective, but Helliwell again provides some guidance. The scoring for this assessment ranges from 0.5 to 2.0, with very poor specimens scoring 0.5 and very good specimens scoring 2.0. Helliwell points out that most trees will attract an average rating of 1, unless there is something particularly aesthetically significant visible.

Once the six factors have been multiplied together, a unit monetary value is then assigned to the total point score attributed to the tree or trees. The total appraised value is:

Size x expected duration x landscape importance x other tree cover x suitability to setting x form x unit value.

The monetary value is assessed against the monetary benefit provided by the tree, in terms of property prices, tourism and so on and the appropriate expenditure incurred in retaining, planting and managing trees. The actual value is determined through consultation with 'a range of informed people', from which a consensus is taken (Helliwell, 2008). The point value at 1 January 2016 is set at £31.15 per point for individual trees (Arboricultural Association, 2016). The figure is adjusted in line with the Retail Prices Index and an annually updated value is available through the Arboricultural Association website.

The maximum achievable score for any tree is 4096 points (8 × 4 × 4 × 4 × 4 × 2). Therefore, the maximum attainable value for any tree is 4096 × £31.15 = £127,590.40 at January 2016 value.

The Helliwell system relies heavily on the expertise and experience of the tree appraiser, but still requires some quite subjective assessments to be made. As with the CAVAT method, the multiplicative nature of the arithmetic makes it prone to large variations in calculated value between different appraisers appraising the same tree (Watson, 2002; Price, 2003). However, Helliwell points out that when Anne Bary-Lenger and Jean-Paul Nebout compared six different tree valuation methods (2002), including the Helliwell system, the valuations 'were all remarkably consistent' (Helliwell, 2008).

9.3.4   i-Tree

i-Tree is a suite of software tools, developed by the USDA Forest Service, that provide analysis of the environmental benefits provided by the urban forest (i-Tree). The software is in the public domain and freely available, although data processing currently must be conducted by the USDA Forest Service. i-Tree Eco is one of the software applications and is designed to use field data either from a complete tree inventory or from randomly located plots within the survey area. It provides a snapshot of the structure of the urban forest, an analysis of the environmental benefits provided by that urban forest and a value for those environmental benefits. i-Tree Eco grew from an earlier Urban Forest Effects (UFORE) model, which was developed through a public–private co-operative formed from US Forest Service, The Davey Tree Expert Company and SUNY College of Environmental Science and Forestry in Syracuse, New York. Although predominantly used in North America, studies have also been conducted in Meso and South America, Australia, China and South Asia and several European cities.

For large, city-wide projects, a number of random sample plots of 0.04 ha are surveyed to save on resources and time, but still retain an acceptable error factor. A typical i-Tree Eco survey would use approximately 200 randomised plots. This is suggested to be a suitable number of plots for a survey crew of two people to complete in a summer, for a project area where the existing tree cover is approximately 20 per cent. The London i-Tree project gathered data from 721 random plots. For smaller projects, such as the

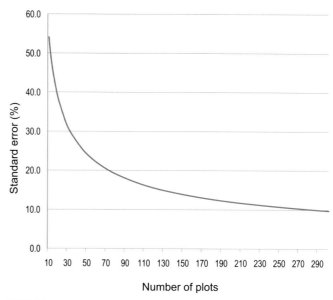

Figure 9.1
200 plots will yield a standard error of approximately 10 per cent for an estimate of the larger survey area. As the number of plots increases, the smaller the standard error will be, leading to greater confidence in the estimate for the population as a whole.

Victoria BID project, entire tree inventories can be conducted. The main advantage for conducting a complete inventory is that i-Tree Eco can calculate values for each individual tree, rather than only for the total population as a whole, with an estimate of error provided.

Tree data are collected and entered into a computer, running the i-Tree Eco software. Here the tree data are merged with local hourly meteorological and air pollution concentration data, from which it is possible to quantify structural and functional information of the urban forest, using the software's algorithms. The parameters currently calculated by the Eco model and for which accurate estimates are provided are as follows:

- Structure – Species composition, number of trees, tree cover, tree density, tree health (crown dieback, tree damage), leaf area, leaf biomass and assessment of shrub and ground covers.
- Air quality – Hourly removal of ozone, sulphur dioxide, nitrogen dioxide, carbon monoxide, $PM_{2.5}$ and PM_{10} particulate matter and related reductions in public health incidents due to air quality improvements. i-Tree Eco uses the hourly pollution and meteorology data to create a model that can simulate how pollutants interact with leaf surfaces via deposition and gas exchange. The model also allows for the negative effects caused by biogenic volatile organic compound (BVOC) emissions from the trees and provides a tree pollen allergenicity index.
- Carbon – Effects of trees on building energy use related to CO_2 emissions due to summer cooling and winter heating requirements, total carbon stored in biomass and net annual carbon sequestration.
- Surface water run-off – Annual interception of rainfall by the trees (volume of surface water run-off avoided).

- Pests and diseases – A risk analysis based on host susceptibility, pest and disease range and tree structural value.

It would appear to be common sense that without sufficient investment in maintenance, an asset will inevitably deteriorate, and unless the situation is improved, it will eventually fail. In asset management circles, maintenance ratio is the age of an asset value, which must be reinvested in the asset to prevent or postpone deterioration. In building asset management, such a percentage is typically between 0.75 per cent and 2 per cent per year (Levitt, 2009). Most LA tree maintenance budgets are simply determined from previous years' spending. If the tree baseline data is subjected to a recognised tree valuation methodology, an ecosystem services provision and a monetary value of the entire tree resource can be estimated. From this, an annual maintenance budget that is more closely related to other infrastructure management principles can be provided for meaningful negotiation.

This ecosystem services provision and monetary assessment approach has been taken in the two GI valuation studies that follow. These two GI studies share similarities: both employed the i-Tree Eco methodology to determine a value for the ecosystem services provision of the tree population and the CAVAT methodology to provide an assessment of the amenity value provided.

9.3.5 Green benefits in Victoria Business Improvement District

The Victoria Business Improvement District (BID) GI valuation project followed on from a GI audit, which initially set out to investigate ways to increase the amount of green space available as a way to combat summer overheating and to address an ongoing surface water flooding issue that was causing the occasional closure of Victoria station. As Victoria is a major transport hub and tourist destination, both of these issues were having significant impacts on local business and commerce. Both are also likely to become more frequent and more severe under predicted climate change patterns. The Victoria BID partners raised their own capital and also managed to unlock and secure funding from GLA, and the London Climate Change Partnership, to enable the GI audit and the GI valuation study to be commissioned through external consultants.

The GI valuation study was carried out by trained tree and GI surveyors, assisted by volunteers from the Trees for Cities project, during the summer of 2011 (Rogers, Jaluzot & Neilan, 2012). All trees, both in private and public ownership were field surveyed and their details recorded, unless access was not possible. The survey identified the following:

- A total of 1,225 trees within the BID area of approximately 126 ha provided 8.8 per cent canopy cover. This is consistent with those figures shown in Trees in Towns II (Britt & Johnston).
- The tree population is highly diverse for a relatively small inner city location, with 139 different species being recorded. Half of the tree population was represented by only six species with London plane alone representing 29 per cent. London plane was by far the most dominant species, providing more than twice the leaf area of all other tree species combined. Most of the planes are mature trees, representing 57 per cent of those trees with a stem diameter in excess of 61 cm.
- The Victoria BID area relies quite heavily on the London plane population to provide the bulk of ecosystem services, and with the majority of these trees being of a similar age and with a significant number of them most likely sourced from a small number

of clones, they are vulnerable to attack from pests and diseases. If the plane population were to be lost due to infection from plane wilt (*Ceratocystis fimbriata* f. *platani*), the cost to replace the trees would be approximately £22.3 million (as calculated using the CAVAT (LTOA, 2010) valuation).

- Consistent with the findings of the GLA in *Chainsaw Massacre* (Chainsaw, 2007) and by Britt and Johnson in Trees in Towns II (2008), interrogation of the stem diameter distribution would appear to indicate that there is an overall lack of large canopy tree species being planted. There certainly are few new plantings of London plane. This lack of large canopy succession will ultimately lead to a reduction in the overall canopy cover unless other large canopy trees are used to replace the dominant plane. Both European and small-leaved lime (*Tilia* x *europaea* and *T. cordata*, respectively) are present in the species mix, and although they collectively make up a fairly modest proportion of the overall population, it would appear that both are represented by a fairly healthy size class diversity.

9.3.6 *Valuing London's urban forest – Results of the London i-Tree Eco project*

The London i-Tree project covered all thirty-two boroughs and the City of London and was the largest urban forest survey in the world that used citizen science, in the form of 200 trained, volunteer surveyors (Rogers, Sacre, Goodenough & Doick, 2015). The project was led by the RE:LEAF partnership, and publication of the final report was funded by Unilever. The main aims were:

- Promote the ecosystem services and amenity value benefits provided by London's urban forest and to provide verifiable monetary values for those benefits.
- Establish a set of verifiable tree asset values that show parity with other infrastructure asset and risk-management protocols.
- Provide accurate metrics for London's tree and woodland cover.
- Engage with a body of volunteers through citizen science to develop tree surveying skills, to provide that body of volunteers with the necessary tools to enable them to promote the benefits of trees and to seek opportunities for tree planting and management.

Rather than field survey all the trees of Greater London, 721 randomly located plots of a consistent area were identified to provide a statistically relevant, representative sample. From this, an overall assessment could be extrapolated. The plots were surveyed during September and October 2014, using a mixture of guided volunteers and professional survey teams.

The results provided some interesting reading:

- The total tree canopy cover would appear to be significantly less than earlier tree canopy surveys that used aerial imagery rather than field measurements. The reduction from approximately 20 per cent (21.9 per cent in LTOA survey of 2012 and 19.5 per cent in GLA survey of 2013) to 13.6 per cent could partly be explained by the fact that, as this was a field survey, it enabled the separation of shrub canopy cover from tree canopy cover. The use of aerial imagery does not lend itself to making such a judgement.

- A total of 126 different tree species was recorded, making the tree species diversity for Greater London the largest for any UK city so far surveyed using i-Tree. However, approximately 21 per cent of the tree population comprises a range of clonal selections. Being genetically identical, and so lacking diversity, these can be susceptible to pest and disease outbreaks. Localised areas where a limited variety of species make up the tree cover, streets lined with London plane trees (*Platanus* x *hispanica*), for instance, are considered to be particularly vulnerable. In some of these situations, the trees were all planted at the same time, meaning that they are all of the same age, and in addition, are quite likely to be from clonal stock. Although plane makes up only 1.43 per cent of the total tree population, the canopy cover amounts to a significant 11.4 per cent. If this population were to be lost to infection from plane wilt, the effects would be quite devastating and could cost approximately £3.5 billion to replace (as calculated using the CAVAT (LTOA, 2010) valuation).

- The estimated tree population for the Greater London area is 8.4 million, which approximately equates to one tree for each London resident. Fifty-seven per cent of these trees are privately owned, with the remaining 43 per cent being in public ownership. More of these publicly owned trees are mature and with large canopies than the smaller private trees. As a consequence, they contribute approximately 60 per cent of the ecosystem services provided by the Greater London tree population. The proportion of trees in outer London that are in private ownership is 81 per cent, which is fairly consistent with the results from Trees in Towns and Trees in Towns 2. This further reinforces the need for tree strategies to fully encompass trees in private ownership as well as those owned by the local authority.

- Stem diameter is typically used as a surrogate for age, and size class distribution. These figures, therefore, provide information that informs age distribution of the tree population. Diversity in age distribution is considered to be important for a resilient population, although there is some debate over what is an 'ideal' distribution. Richards proposed some 'approximate guidelines' using data from long-lived species in Syracuse, New York: '. . . about 40 per cent trees under 20 cm diameter, 30 per cent 20–40 cm trees in the early functional stage, 20 per cent 40–60 cm functionally mature trees and 10 per cent older trees with most of their functional life behind them' (Richards, 1983). Millward and Sabir revised Richards' distribution goals so that: '40 per cent of a tree population fall within a DBH class of 0–15 cm (Group I), 30 per cent from 15–60 cm (Group II), 25 per cent in class 60–90 cm (Group III), and 5 per cent classified as 90 cm and above (Group IV)' (Millward & Sabir, 2010). The distribution of tree size classes for Greater London, like many other urban tree populations, shows a less than 'ideal' proportion of trees within the 40–60 cm range. Somewhat surprisingly, there also appears to be shortfall in the 0–15 cm range for trees planted in outer London, whereas the figures for inner London exceed the 'ideal'. A tree population is a dynamic collection of different age classes. As older trees die or are removed, they are steadily replaced with younger specimens. As the younger trees grow, they need to be replaced with new trees. A low figure within the 0–15 cm class suggests that replacement planting may not be sufficient to keep up with tree loss, and this could cause concern, if maintenance of tree canopy cover is the aim.

9.4 INCORPORATING TREES IN OTHER POLICY AREAS

One of the greatest challenges facing urban living is likely to be the effect of climate change, and in response, our commitment to trees needs to be bold and strategic. As urban trees can help local authorities achieve a wide range of their social and environmental objectives, they need to be considered during any high-level, strategic decision-making process. Unfortunately, tree managers and their teams tend not to be especially prominent within the LA hierarchy, making it difficult for their voices to be heard at high, strategic levels within their organisations. However, some encouraging developments have been observed through the use of the advisory materials produced by the Trees and Design Action Group (TDAG), such as *Trees in the Townscape: A Guide for Decision Makers* (2012) and *Trees in Hard Landscape: A Guide for Delivery* (2014). *Trees in the Townscape* is especially relevant to LA policy-makers and elected members. It sets out twelve principles of best practice to ensure that those involved in making or influencing decisions give an appropriate degree of consideration to the trees that can make and shape our urban landscapes. *Trees in Hard Landscape* is a companion to and follows on from *Trees in the Townscape*. Starting from where the policy decision has been made to either protect an existing tree or plant new ones, the guide provides a roadmap for successful delivery, using case studies to illustrate key points.

With careful planning, it is possible to ensure that the requirements of trees are met within our urban development policies in such a way that we can ensure their establishment and long-term survival. If managed correctly, the urban forest resource can be a highly cost-effective approach to delivering sustainable and multifunctional environmental improvements.

9.4.1 *Climate change adaptation and mitigation*

The Climate Change Act 2008 put in place a policy framework to promote and assess adaptation actions, in response to climate change. It required the UK government to assess the risks for the UK of both the current and predicted impact of climate change and lay these before Parliament (HM Govt, 2008). From this, the government carried out its *UK Climate Change Risk Assessment* (Defra, 2012a), which identified over 700 potential climate change impacts within the UK, across eleven key sectors. A more manageable list of approximately 100 risks was selected, following an assessment of magnitude and likelihood of risks, along with an appraisal of confidence in the evidence base and the perceived urgency of adaptation action. The findings were published in the *UK Climate Change Risk Assessment: Government Report* (Defra, 2012c). The risk assessment acknowledged the mitigation effects provided by green infrastructure in terms of its cooling and shading potential and the flood resilience provided, when used within Sustainable Drainage Systems (SuDS) (Defra, 2012b). It also identified the risk that the overall effectiveness of green infrastructure will be quite severely reduced by an increase in prolonged, dry, warm periods, as a consequence of climate change. It is projected that this reduction in GI effectiveness could reach 15 per cent by the 2050s and in excess of 30 per cent by the 2080s, under the medium emissions scenario (Defra, 2012b). This statistic is quite alarming.

Under its medium emissions scenario, the UK Meteorological Office predicts a mean summer temperature rise of 3.7°C and a maximum rise of 4.8°C by the 2080s (UKCP, 2009). With current urban heat island effects already typically adding 4°C to air temperatures within London (Graves, Watkins, Westbury & Littlefair, 2001; Wilby, 2003), compared with outlying rural areas, urban centres are especially vulnerable to the predicted effects of climate change temperature rise. Trees must be viewed as long-term landscape elements to enable them to perform as functional assets, and as such, will very likely be exposed to changes in climate during their expected lifespans. Selecting trees that show signs of being able to adapt to changing environmental conditions would appear to be a sensible policy and those responsible for the implementation and management of urban forests and other green infrastructure will need to factor climate change into species selection. The UK Climate Change Risk Assessment specifically identifies vulnerable locations such as hospitals, care homes and socially disadvantaged areas, with little access to urban green space, as requiring particular consideration (Defra, 2012b).

9.4.2 Planning

The UK Climate Change Risk Assessment acknowledges the importance of developing GI within and between urban areas as an effective and sustainable adaptation strategy. Such an approach may manifest in increased tree planting, habitat creation and green approaches to surface water run-off, such as SuDS (Defra, 2012b). This type of approach is supported in the *National Planning Policy Framework* (NPPF). Local plans need to consider the long-term impacts of climate change such as 'flood risk, coastal change, water supply and changes to biodiversity and landscape' (DCLG, 2012). Development proposals should avoid vulnerability to climate change impacts, and any risks should be managed through suitable adaptation measures, such as planned, multi-functional green infrastructure (DCLG, 2012). Defra's Final Report from the Tree Health and Plant Biosecurity Expert Taskforce (Defra, 2013b) and its *Tree Health and Plant Biosecurity Evidence Plan* (Defra, 2013a) also recognise the importance of both rural and urban trees in helping to mitigate the effects of climate change.

As overall GI and especially the quantum of tree cover increases, summer temperatures rise and rainfall becomes more erratic, there is the possibility that localised drying of soils will become more prevalent. This could be especially problematic on the shrinkable clay soils in London and the south-east. A conflict is likely to exist, therefore, between insurers wishing to remove trees to reduce subsidence risk and a desire for increased GI as part of any climate change adaptation strategy. The Association of British Insurers does provide advice and guidance on future tree root implicated subsidence and many insurers do provide compensatory planting. Local planning authorities with their knowledge of local soil conditions and any history of subsidence claims are probably best placed to guide right tree – right place planting, through a tree strategy, in such locations. It should be remembered that with any replacement planting, there is likely to be a significant time-lag between planting and a state of maturity where meaningful ecosystem services are provided.

Tree strategies must not be developed in isolation, but must be compatible with, and complementary to, other local planning policy areas, so that they can be adopted and embedded at appropriate points within local plans. Embedding a right tree – right place approach to tree planting within local authority climate change adaptation strategies, for instance, is likely to gain favour with politicians, as it offers an evidence-based, cost-effective and sustainable response. Trees have consistently been shown to deliver enormous benefits when provided with the right resources to enable them to reach productive maturity, while at the same time, providing a significant return on investment. There are compelling reasons to raise the priority of urban trees when making and shaping policy decisions. Indeed, the NPPF suggests that local planning authorities should 'set out a strategic approach in their Local Plans, planning positively for the creation, protection, enhancement and management of networks of biodiversity and green infrastructure' (DCLG, 2012). Planning proposals should then include an appropriate green infrastructure response that satisfies local and neighbourhood plan policies concerning tree and green infrastructure strategies. Tree planting proposals are frequently dealt with as a condition or as a reserved matter, attached to a planning permission, rather than being considered a requirement or a constraint. Too often, large canopy trees are removed to ease construction, only to be replaced with small canopy, shorter-lived varieties. The detailed provision of new trees is often included within the soft landscape package, which is typically let after the engineering and construction detail has already been designed and fixed. As a consequence, trees are essentially retro-fitted into an existing development scheme, with no scope to influence the location of other infrastructures and with little opportunity to ensure there is sufficient rooting volume. Trees must be considered at the conceptual and design development stages to ensure that they are adequately resourced, if the opportunities to deliver the ecosystem services they are capable of are to be maximised. Planning obligations (s. 106) or Community Infrastructure Levy (under s. 216 of the Planning Act 2008) may also be suitable mechanisms for securing funding for tree planting, maintenance and management and other GI provision (DCLG, 2016).

9.4.3 An example of where it can work

Phase 1 of the Poundbury urban extension to the Dorset market town of Dorchester is 20 years old. The site of Poundbury farm, owned by the Duchy of Cornwall, was selected in 1987 by West Dorset District Council as suitable for accommodating the future expansion of Dorchester. Prince Charles took the opportunity to work with the council to create a model urban extension that could be designed according to architectural and urban planning principles described by the Prince in his book *A Vision of Britain* (HRH the Prince of Wales, 1989). The Prince appointed the architect and urban planner Leon Krier to provide an overall concept master plan that was sensitive to the Prince's vision. This was exhibited in Dorchester for public consultation the following year and the revised master plan was submitted for planning. Permission was granted and construction began on the first of the four phases in 1993.

As each of the areas is developed in detail, the line and level information for the road network, indicative tree positions and locations for shared utility corridors are first determined

Figure 9.2
Tree selection according to location, right tree – right place, at Poundbury, Dorset. London planes are the avenue trees of choice where the roads are wide enough to accommodate the trees at maturity (left). A rowan is a more appropriate choice along one of the pedestrian alleyways (right).

and the master plan is then passed to the landscape architects, who confirm positions for trees and select species according to location, on a right tree - right place basis. The plan is then passed to the street lighting engineers who co-ordinate the lighting arrangement with the tree layout. Where unavoidable clashes do arise, the trees are either relocated or removed as appropriate. The strong commitment to street tree planting is evident everywhere one walks within the town. Perhaps, this is not altogether unsurprising given that the development is overseen by the Duchy of Cornwall and who provide an incredible £4,500 per tree to cover the cost of preparing each tree planting site and to maintain the tree afterwards (James, 2015).

9.5 DIVERSITY, RESILIENCE AND THE NATIVE OR EXOTIC DEBATE

Native environmental conditions no longer exist in our paved urban centres. As we have seen, the surfaces of paved urban sites tend to be sealed with impermeable materials, making access to water by tree roots uncertain. These sites are difficult for trees, where they are typically exposed to high extremes of temperature, low air humidity, high pH, limited soil volumes and water stress. All these stress features make tree species that are not well-adapted to growing in such hostile conditions much more susceptible to pests and diseases (Sæbø, Benedikz & Randrup, 2003; Tello et al., 2005). The predicted effects of climate change can only make matters worse (Roloff, Korn & Gillner, 2009). To adopt a 'native is good, exotic is bad' approach in urban landscapes seems to miss the point of what is required. Surely, it is better to select tree species that can establish and survive well in harsh urban conditions and deliver the ecosystem services required, rather than restrict oneself to natives only.

Resilience is defined as 'the capacity to recover quickly from difficulties; toughness' (Oxford Dictionaries, 2016). The link between diversity and resilience is recognised in the financial sector. Patrick Reinmoeller and Nicole van Baardwijk analysed the performance of Dutch companies listed on the Amsterdam Stock Exchange over the period 1983 to 2002. Their research shows that the most resilient of companies employ a dynamic balance of differing innovation strategies to ensure diversity (Reinmoeller & van Baardwijk, 2005). Likewise, diversity is considered essential in populations, to reduce the risk of pest and disease epidemics and ensure resilience in the supply of ecosystem services. Diversity then is essential if resilience is our aim, and to increase diversity, there has been widespread acceptance of Santamour's 10/20/30 rule (1990) (as discussed in Chapter 4), which states that no more than 10 per cent of any one species, no more than 20 per cent from any one genus and no more than 30 per cent from any one family should be contained in any urban tree population. If we were to be restricted to planting natives only, this rule would be almost impossible to apply while still maintaining the health and resilience of the tree population (Johnston, Nail & James, 2011).

The GLA's Tree and Woodland Framework acknowledges the importance of non-native trees and woodland for increasing biodiversity in the wider landscape. It also advocates a right tree – right place approach. The most successful method for selecting appropriate tree species is to match their requirements to the conditions and constraints of the site, following a thorough site assessment, as discussed in Chapter 4.

9.6 THE FUTURE?

So what of the future? Species diversity and increases in overall canopy cover are areas that certainly need to be addressed, especially with the spectre of climate change hanging over us.

More trees planted from a more diverse species palette. Is that enough? More fundamental than that, trees must be brought into the debate earlier. They need to be discussed at national government level with one government department taking overall responsibility for national green infrastructure policy. Raising the profile of the ecosystem services debate appears to be working; certainly, more people now recognise that trees can bring a range of benefits beyond the aesthetic, than they did a decade ago. That recognition still needs to be converted into more universal best practice and that best practice needs to become 'business as usual'.

There have been many bold claims regarding large-scale tree planting initiatives around the world. In 2006, the Mayor of Los Angeles, California, Antonio Villaraigosa, promised to plant 1 million trees as one of his campaign pledges. That same year, John Hickenlooper, the Mayor of Denver, Colorado, made a similar pledge in his State of the City address, to plant 1 million trees within metropolitan Denver by 2025 (The Mile High Million). In 2007, NY Mayor, Michael Bloomberg, promised to plant 1 million trees over the following 10 years. On 20 November 2015, the 1 millionth tree was planted at Joyce Kilmer Park in the Bronx (Million Trees NYC, 2015). These bold initiatives have been followed by many others. However, without careful planning, such schemes may not be able to match the intentions, in terms of the benefits they are able to deliver (Watson & Koeser, 2008).

With a greater emphasis placed upon site evaluation and a recognition and understanding of the opportunities and limits of site manipulation, it is hoped that a right tree – right place approach will become the norm. Only then can the trees that form the key component of urban green infrastructure mature into the productive, ecosystem services-providing assets that we need them to be. Much of the onus needs to be with the landscape architects, urban designers and the other land planning disciplines to ensure that the advantages attached to strategically located urban trees are communicated to developers and the public at large. It is this strategic approach, carried out thoughtfully and with care, that is important.

REFERENCES

Arboricultural Association (4 February 2016). What is the Helliwell system and how much is a 'point'? Retrieved 27 April 2016 from The Arboricultural Association: www.trees.org.uk/Help-Advice/Public/What-is-the-Helliwell-system-and-how-much-is-a-po.

Barrell, J. (1993). Pre-planning tree surveys: Safe useful life expectancy (SULE) is the natural progression. *Arboricultural Journal, 17*(1), 33–46. doi:10.1080/03071375.1993.9746943

Bary-Lenger, A. & Nebout, J.-P. (2002). *Evaluation financière des arbres d'agrément et de production: en ville, à la campagne, en forêt.* Paris: Tec & Doc-Lavoisier.

Britt, C. & Johnston, M. (2008). *Trees in Towns II – A New Survey of Urban Trees in England and their Condition and Management.* London: Department of Communities and Local Government.

CTLA (2000). *Guide for Plant Appraisal* (9th edn). Champaign, IL: International Society of Arboriculture.

DCLG (2012). *National Planning Policy Framework.* London: Department for Communities and Local Government. Retrieved from http://planningguidance.communities.gov.uk/wp-content/themes/planning-guidance/assets/NPPF.pdf.

DCLG (11 February 2016). *Planning Practice Guidance – Natural Environment: Green Infrastructure*, Paragraph: 032 Reference ID: 8-032-2160211. Retrieved 4 May 2016 from Department for Communities & Local Government: planningguidance.communities.gov.uk/blog/guidance/natural-environment/green-infrastructure/.

Defra (2012a). *Science and Research Projects: CCRA – UK Climate Change Risk Assessment 2012 – GA0204.* Retrieved 20 April 2016 from Department for Environment, Food and Rural Affairs: http://randd.defra.gov.uk/Default.aspx?Menu=Menu&Module=More&Location=None&Completed=0&ProjectID=15747#RelatedDocuments.

Defra (2012b). *The UK Climate Change Risk Assessment 2012 Evidence Report.* Department for Environment, Food and Rural Affairs. London: HMSO. Retrieved from http://randd.defra.gov.uk/Document.aspx?Document=10067_CCRA EvidenceReport16July2012.pdf.

Defra (2012c). *UK Climate Change Risk Assessment: Government Report.* HM Government, Department of Environment, Food and Rural Affairs. London: The Stationery Office. Retrieved from www.gov.uk/government/publications/uk-climate-change-risk-assessment-government-report.

Defra (2013a). *Tree Health and Plant Biosecurity Evidence Plan*. London: Department for Environment, Food and Rural Affairs. Retrieved from www.gov.uk/government/uploads/system/uploads/attachment_data/file/181846/pb13929-evidenceplan-tree-health-plantbiosecurity.pdf.

Defra (2013b). *Tree Health and Plant Biosecurity Expert Taskforce: Final Report*. London: Department for Environment, Food and Rural Affairs. Retrieved from www.gov.uk/government/publications/tree-health-and-plant-biosecurity-expert-taskforce-final-report.

DoE (1993). *Trees in Towns: A Survey of Trees in 66 Towns and Villages in England*. London: HMSO.

GLA (2005). Connecting Londoners with Trees and Woodlands: *A Tree and Woodland Framework for London*, London: Greater London Authority.

GLA (2007). *Chainsaw Massacre: A Review of London's Street Trees*. London: Greater London Authority.

GLA (2013). *Green Infrastructure & Open Environments: Preparing Borough Tree and Woodland Strategies*. London: Greater London Authority. Retrieved from www.london.gov.uk/what-we-do/planning/implementing-london-plan/supplementary-planning-guidance/tree-and-woodland.

Graves, H., Watkins, R., Westbury, P. & Littlefair, P. (2001). *Cooling Buildings in London: Overcoming the Heat Island*. London: Construction Research Communications. Retrieved from www.brebookshop.com/details.jsp?id=324608.

Helliwell, D. (1967). The amenity value of trees and woodlands. *Arboricultural Association Journal*, 1(5), 128–31.

Helliwell, D. R. (2008a). Amenity valuation of trees and woodlands. *Arboricultural Journal, 31*(3), 161–8. doi:10.1080/03071375.2008.9747532.

Helliwell, D. R. (2008b). *Visual Amenity Valuation of Trees and Woodlands (The Helliwell System) Arboricultural Association Guidance Note 4*. Romsey: The Arboricultural Association.

HM Govt (2008). Climate Change Act 2008: Part 4 – National Reports and Programmes. London: HMSO. Retrieved from www.legislation.gov.uk/ukpga/2008/27/part/4.

HRH the Prince of Wales (1989). *A Vision of Britain: A Personal View of Architecture* (1st edn). London: Doubleday.

i-Tree, n.d. i-Tree Eco. [Online] Available at: http://www.itreetools.org/eco/ [Accessed 11 August 2015].James, P. (2015). Personal communication, 4 August 2015.

Johnston, M. (2010). Trees in Towns II and the contribution of arboriculture. *Arboricultural Journal*, 33(1) 27–41.

Johnston, M., Nail, S. & James, S. (2011). 'Natives versus aliens': The relevance of the debate to urban forest management in Britain. In M. Johnston & G. Percival (eds), *Trees, People and the Built Environment: Preceedings of the Urban Trees Research Conference, 13–14 April 2011* (pp. 181–91). Edinburgh: Forestry Commission. Retrieved from www.forestry.gov.uk/pdf/FCRP017.pdf/$FILE/FCRP017.pdf.

Levitt, J. (2009). *The Handbook of Maintenance Management* (2nd edn). New York: Industrial Press.

LTOA (2010, September). Capital Asset Value for Amenity Trees. Retrieved 12 April 2016 from the London Tree Officers' Association: www.ltoa.org.uk/component/docman/cat_view/98-capital-asset-value-for-amenity-trees-cavat.

Million Trees NYC (2015). Million Trees NYC. Retrieved 18 July 2016 from Million Trees NYC: A PlaNYC initiative with NYC Parks and New York Restoration Project: www.milliontreesnyc.org/html/home/home.shtml.

Millward, A. A. & Sabir, S. (2010). Structure of a forested urban park: Implications for strategic management. *Journal of Environmental Management, 91*(11), 2215–24. doi:10.1016/j.jenvman.2010.06.006

Neilan, C. (2010). *CAVAT (Capital Asset Value for Amenity Trees) Full Method: User's Guide*. London: London Tree Officers Association. Retrieved from www.ltoa.org.uk/documents/doc_download/139-cavat-full-method-user-guide-updated-september-2010.

Oxford Dictionaries (2016). *Oxford Dictionaries – Language Matters*. Retrieved 5 August 2016 from www.oxford dictionaries.com/definition/english/resilience.

Price, C. (2003). Quantifying the aesthetic benefits of urban forestry. *Urban Forestry & Urban Greening, 1*(3), 123–33. doi:10.1078/1618-8667-00013

Reinmoeller, P. & van Baardwijk, N. (2005). The link between diversity and resilience. *MIT Sloan Management Review*, 61–5.

Richards, N. A. (1983). Diversity and stability in a street tree population. *Urban Ecology, 7*, 159–71.

Rogers, K., Jaluzot, A. & Neilan, C. (2012). Green Benefits in Victoria Business Improvement District: An analysis of the benefits of trees and other green assets in the Victoria Business Improvement District. London: Victoria Business Improvement District. Retrieved from www.victoriabid.co.uk/wp-content/uploads/2015/02/VBID_i-Tree_Report_2012.pdf.

Rogers, K., Sacre, K., Goodenough, J. & Doick, K. (2015). *Valuing London's Urban Forest: Results of the London i-Tree Eco Project*. London: Treeconomics. Retrieved from www.forestry.gov.uk/pdf/2890-Forest_Report_Pages.pdf/$FILE/2890-Forest_Report_Pages.pdf.

Roloff, A., Korn, S. & Gillner, S. (2009). The Climate-Species-Matrix to select tree species fo rurban habitats considering climate change. *Urban Forestry and Urban Greening, 8*, 295–308.

Sæbø, A., Benedikz, T. & Randrup, T. B. (2003). Selection of trees for urban forestry in the Nordic countries. *Urban Forestry and Urban Greening, 2*(2), 101–14. doi:10.1078/1618-8667-00027

Santamour, F. S., Jr (11–12 June 1990). Trees for urban planting: Diversity, uniformity and common sense. *Proceedings of the 7th METRIA Conference, 11–12 June 1990, Lisle, IL*, pp. 57–65.

Schwab, J. C. (2009). *Planning the Urban Forest: Ecology, Economy, and Community Development.* Chicago, IL: The American Planning Association. Retrieved from www.na.fs.fed.us/urban/planning_uf_apa.pdf.

TDAG (2012). *Trees in the Townscape: A Guide for Decision Makers*, London: Trees and Design Action Group.

TDAG (2014). *Trees in the Hard Landscape: A Guide for Delivery.* London: Trees and Design Action Group. Retrieved from www.tdag.org.uk/uploads/4/2/8/0/4280686/tdag_trees-in-hard-landscapes_september_2014_colour.pdf.

Tello, M.-L., Tomalak, M., Siwecki, R., Gáper, J., Motta, E. & Mateo-Sagasta, E. (2005). Biotic urban growing condition – threats, pests and diseases. In C. C. Konijnendijk, K. Nilsson, T. B. Randrup & J. Schipperijn (eds), *Urban Forests and Trees* (pp. 325–65). Berlin: Springer.

The Mile High Million, n.d. The Mile High Million – who we are. [Online] Available at: http://milehighmillion.org/pages/section/who-we-are [Accessed 18 July 2016].

UKCP (2009). UK Climate Projections User Interface (Online). Retrieved 23 December 2015 from http://ukclimate projections.metoffice.gov.uk/.

Watson, G. W. (2002). Comparing formula methods of tree appraisal. *Journal of Arboriculture, 28*(1), 11–18. Retrieved from http://joa.isa-arbor.com/request.asp?JournalID=1&ArticleID=21&Type=2.

Watson, G. W. & Koeser, A. (2008). The Landscape Below Ground III.Researcher Summit.White Paper. In G. W. Watson, L. Costello, B. Scharenbroch & E. Gilman (eds), *The Landscape Below Ground III* (pp. 389–96). Champaign, IL: International Society of Arboriculture.

Wilby, R. L. (2003). Past and projected trends in London's urban heat island. *Weather, 58*(7), 251–60. doi:10.1256/wea.183.02

Appendix 1: Specifications for engineered rooting substrates

SAND-BASED MEDIA

Heicom Tree Sand

Parameter	Unit	Result
Texture		
Clay (less than 0.002 mm)	% (by weight)	1
Silt (0.002 0.63 mm)	% (by weight)	3
Sand (0.05–2.0 mm)	% (by weight)	96
Textural class		Sandy loam
Very fine sand (0.05–0.15 mm)	% (by weight)	3
Fine sand (0.15–0.25 mm)	% (by weight)	31
Medium sand (0.25–0.50 mm)	% (by weight)	48
Coarse sand (0.50–1.0 mm)	% (by weight)	12
Very coarse sand (1.0–2.0 mm)	% (by weight)	2
Stones (2–20 mm)	% (by weight)	0
Stones (20–50 mm)	% (by weight)	0
Stones (greater than 50 mm)	% (by weight)	0
Organic matter (lost on ignition)	% (by weight)	5.9
pH		7.8
Exchangeable sodium percentage	%	5
Available nutrients		
Nitrogen	mgl^{-1}	0.24
Phosphorus	mgl^{-1}	65
Potassium	mgl^{-1}	690
Magnesium	mgl^{-1}	107
Carbon:nitrogen ratio	14:1	
Additional analysis		
Electrical conductivity	µScm^{-1}	797
Saturated hydraulic conductivity	mmhr^{-1}	77

Bourne Amenity Structural Tree Sand

Parameter	Unit	Result
Texture		
Clay (less than 0.002 mm)	% (by weight)	6
Silt (0.002–0.63 mm)	% (by weight)	4
Sand (0.05–2.0 mm)	% (by weight)	90
Textural class		Sandy loam
Very fine sand (0.05–0.15 mm)	% (by weight)	4
Fine sand (0.15–0.25 mm)	% (by weight)	15
Medium sand (0.25–0.50 mm)	% (by weight)	51
Coarse sand (0.50–1.0 mm)	% (by weight)	18
Very coarse sand (1.0–2.0 mm)	% (by weight)	2
Stones (2–20 mm)	% (by weight)	4
Stones (20–50 mm)	% (by weight)	0
Stones (greater than 50 mm)	% (by weight)	0
Organic matter (lost on ignition)	% (by weight)	3.0
pH		7.8
Exchangeable sodium percentage	%	5
Available nutrients		
Nitrogen	$mgkg^{-1}$	0.13
Phosphorus	$mgkg^{-1}$	52
Potassium	$mgkg^{-1}$	628
Magnesium	$mgkg^{-1}$	83
Carbon:Nitrogen ratio		13:1
Additional analysis		
Electrical conductivity (1:2.5 water extract)	μScm^{-1}	859
Electrical conductivity (1:2 $CaSO_4$ extract)	μScm^{-1}	2,917
Permeability (2.5 kg rammer)	$mmhr^{-1}$	26
Permeability (light compaction)	$mmhr^{-1}$	253
Total porosity	%	39
Moisture content	%	10
Mean CBR value		5.2

CONTAMINANTS

	Unit	Guidelines	Value	Result	Compliance
Phytotoxic contaminants					
Total zinc	mgkg^{-1}			n/a	
Total copper	mgkg^{-1}			n/a	
Total nickel	mgkg^{-1}			n/a	
Heavy metals and hydrocarbons					
Total arsenic (As)	mgkg^{-1}	Soil Guideline Values CLEA 2009 (SGV)	< 32	9.6	Yes
Total cadmium (Cd)	mgkg^{-1}	SGV	< 10	< 0.1	Yes
Total chromium (Cr)	mgkg^{-1}	SGV	< 130	31.7	Yes
Complex cyanide	mgkg^{-1}	Dutch Action Value (DAV)	n/a	< 1.0	n/a
Free cyanide	mgkg^{-1}	Dutch Action Value (DAV)	n/a	< 1.0	n/a
Total cyanide (Cn)	mgkg^{-1}	Dutch Action Value (DAV)	< 20	< 1.0	Yes
Total lead (Pb)	mgkg^{-1}	SGV	< 450	5.3	Yes
Total mercury (Hg)	mgkg^{-1}	SGV	< 170	< 0.02	Yes
Total (mono) phenols	mgkg^{-1}	SGV	< 420	< 1.0	Yes
Total selenium	mgkg^{-1}	SGV	< 350	0.16	Yes
Thiocyanate	mgkg^{-1}	SGV	n/a	< 5.0	n/a
Acenaphthylene	mgkg^{-1}	LQM	< 400	< 0.05	Yes
Acenaphthene	mgkg^{-1}	LQM	< 480	< 0.05	Yes
Anthracene	mgkg^{-1}	LQM	< 4,900	< 0.05	Yes
Benzo(a)anthracene	mgkg^{-1}	LQM	< 4.7	< 0.1	Yes
Benzo(b)fluoranthene	mgkg^{-1}	LQM	< 6.5	< 0.1	Yes
Benzo(g, h, i)perylene	mgkg^{-1}	LQM	< 46	0.2	Yes
Benzo(k)fluoranthene	mgkg^{-1}	LQM	< 9.6	< 0.1	Yes
Chrysene	mgkg^{-1}	LQM	< 8.0	< 0.1	Yes
Dibenzo(a, h) anthracene	mgkg^{-1}	LQM	< 0.86	0.1	Yes
Fluoranthene	mgkg^{-1}	LQM	< 460	< 0.1	Yes
Fluorene	mgkg^{-1}	LQM	< 380	< 0.05	Yes
Indeno(1,2,3-cd)pyrene	mgkg^{-1}	LQM	< 3.9	0.2	Yes
Naphthalene	mgkg^{-1}	LQM	< 3.7	< 0.05	Yes
Phenanthrene	mgkg^{-1}	LQM	n/a	< 0.1	n/a
Pyrene	mgkg^{-1}	LQM	< 1,000	< 0.1	Yes
Coronene	mgkg^{-1}	LQM	n/a	< 0.1	n/a
Asbestos		Control of Asbestos Regulations 2006	Absent	Absent	Yes

CU STRUCTURAL SOIL

In North America, CU-Soil® must be purchased through a licensed supplier to ensure quality control of the material.

The material is a uniform blend of crushed stone, clay loam and hydrogel, mixed to the following proportions:

- crushed stone: 800 kg dry weight
- clay loam: 200 kg dry weight
- water-retentive copolymer (hydrogel): 0.3 kg dry weight per 1,000 kg crushed stone.

Crushed stone

Angular crushed granite, limestone or other similar rock. The stone used will have an effect on pH of the mix. Appropriate plants will need to be selected accordingly.

Particle size distribution

Sieve size	Per cent passing by mass
40 mm	90–100
28 mm	20–55
20 mm	10

- The ratio of nominal maximum to nominal minimum particle size of 2 is required.
- Acceptable aggregate dimensions will not exceed 2.5:1.0 for any two dimensions chosen.
- Minimum 90 per cent with one fractured face, minimum 75 per cent with two or more fractured faces.
- Magnesium sulphate soundness test < 18 per cent.
- Resistance to fragmentation (LA abrasion test): < 40 per cent.

Clay loam soil

Clay loam based on the USDA soil classification as determined by mechanical analysis, of uniform composition without admixture of subsoil. It must be free of stones greater than 12.5 mm, lumps, plants, roots, debris and other extraneous matter. It must not contain substances harmful to plant growth or human health.

Particle size distribution

Gravel (> 2 mm)	< 5%
Sand (0.063–2 mm)	20–45%
Silt (0.002–0.063 mm)	20–50%
Clay (< 0.002 mm)	20–40%

CHEMICAL ANALYSIS

- pH: 6.0–7.8
- organic matter: 2–5 per cent by dry weight
- nutrient levels: As required by the testing laboratory recommendations for the type of plants to be grown
- electrical conductivity (1:2.5 water extract): 1,500 μS/cm (max)
- electrical conductivity ($CaSO_4$ extract): 2,800 μS/cm (max).

Copolymer hydrogel

The water-retentive polymer shall be a potassium propenoate-propenamide copolymer (hydrogel).

Mixing

The soil should be mixed using suitable equipment to ensure a consistent and uniform material. If using a loading shovel, mixing should be carried out on a flat paved surface.

- Spread a 200–300 mm layer of crushed stone.
- Spread evenly over the stone the specified amount of dry hydrogel.
- Spread over the dry hydrogel and crushed stone a proportional amount of clay loam.
- Blend the entire amount by turning, using a loading shovel or other suitable equipment until a consistent blend is produced.
- Add moisture gradually and evenly during the blending and turning operation as required, to achieve the required moisture content. Delay applications of moisture for 10 minutes prior to successive applications. Once established, mixing should produce a material within 1 per cent of the optimum moisture level for compaction.

Appendix 2: The collection and analysis of soil samples

INTRODUCTION

Soil in urban locations can be highly heterogeneous, and collecting sufficient information to enable an assessment at a site scale can be problematic. If soil analysis results are to be of value, it is important that the samples submitted for analysis are representative of the area from which they are taken. These guidance notes are issued to assist those without a soil science background, in taking representative samples.

TAKING A REPRESENTATIVE SAMPLE

For site-wide testing, where the soil is fairly uniform, it is typical for at least ten, but preferably twenty, samples to be collected. Do not skimp on the number of samples taken. Bear in mind that 1 ha of land is equivalent to about 1,300 t of soil for each 10 cm of depth. Each collected sample may be only one-thousand-millionth at that.

The individual samples should be well mixed and sub-divided by quartering to provide a composite sample of not less that 1 kg, or 2 kg if the soil is particularly stony. This composite sample should be placed in a clean, stout polythene bag. Sample bags are often available from the analysis laboratory for this purpose. One such composite sample may represent up to 1 ha of land, provided that there is no marked change in soil type (colour, texture, stoniness, consistency) or change in management.

It may be preferential to divide large areas into smaller, uniform sections for sampling, based on topography, vegetation type, plant vigour, soil texture or colour, drainage status, land use and so on. Sometimes, geotechnical investigations can help in determining how areas may be divided. Each area should be identified on a plan and marked onsite. Each composite sample from each area will require individual testing, but the cost is modest when compared to the overall cost of the pre-construction survey works required.

Separate samples may also be required for areas that have been, or are intended to be, used for different end-uses or planting schemes.

- Samples should be taken at regular intervals, either along a series of zigzag lines or based upon a rectilinear grid, covering the area under investigation. Sampling points should be marked on the site plan.
- Samples are best taken using a soil auger, but a spade or trowel can be used to take samples when neither a core sampler nor an auger is available. Dig a hole to the required depth and sample a 10-mm thick slice from the side of the hole.

- Try to restrict damage and compaction to the soil sample during collection and delivery.
- Record the depth of sampling.
- Do not mix topsoil (darker surface layer) with the underlying subsoil in the sample. If deeper sampling is needed, keep different soil layers separate from each other.
- Do not sample in small areas of soil that are obviously very different from the general area being sampled. Soils of different types should never be mixed to form a composite sample; these areas should be identified on the plan and separate samples taken as required.
- When sampling, stones should be included as these form part of the soil. A full analysis would be incomplete without assessing the stone content.

Sampling should not be taken after recent fertiliser applications or heavy rain. If residues of slow or controlled-release fertilisers are present, they may give falsely high values for soil nutrient content. It is also best to avoid sampling from frozen ground.

TOPSOIL SAMPLING DEPTHS

Turfed areas: Samples should normally be taken from the top 100 mm of the soil.

Shrub or tree beds: Samples should normally be taken from the top 200 mm. Note that backfill in tree pits may differ from *in situ* soil.

In situ *soils to be stripped:* Full depth of topsoil (usually 200–300 mm deep).

Stockpiled material: One composite soil sample should be taken from approximately each 1,000 cu. m. Sample from the full depth of the heap as well as the surface.

ANALYSIS OF SOIL SAMPLES

Once the samples have been collected and bagged, they should be submitted for analysis to a suitable qualified, quality-assured laboratory, which has MCERTS accreditation for all the parameters requested. UKAS is the national accreditation body in the UK, which ensures that all certification, testing, inspection and calibration services comply with agreed international standards such as ISO 17025. Typically, the following parameters, as listed in the topsoil specification, are analysed:

1 visual examination (soil structure, texture, compaction, consistency, Munsell colour, deleterious materials and so on)
2 particle size analysis (clay, silt, five sand fractions)
3 stone content (2–20 mm, 20–50 mm, > 50 mm)
4 pH value (soil/water extract)
5 electrical conductivity (soil/water extract)
6 electrical conductivity (soil/$CaSO_4$ extract)
7 exchangeable sodium percentage
8 total nitrogen
9 extractable phosphorus, potassium and magnesium

10   organic matter content
11   carbon:nitrogen ratio (by calculation)
12   moisture content
13   Atterberg limits (if appropriate).

The results from testing the samples against these parameters would be presented in a Certificate of Analysis by the laboratory. This will enable easy comparison to be made against the contract specification. The test certificates should also be accompanied by an interpretive report, which will comment on the horticultural quality of each sample and its suitability for the use identified. Where any deficiencies are identified, recommendations for treatments and/or additives should be included.

If there is a danger that contamination materials may be present, it is recommended that advice is sought from an appropriate specialist. In any event, an additional suite of tests would be applied to the submitted soil samples. Typically, the following parameters would be tested:

1   heavy metals
2   soluble sulphate
3   elemental sulphur
4   acid-volatile sulphide
5   total cyanide
6   total (mono) phenols
7   total petroleum hydrocarbons (PHC) (C10–C40)
8   speciated polycyclic aromatic hydrocarbons (PAHs) (US EPA 16 suite)

As above, the results would be presented in a Certificate of Analysis, and any recommendations for treatment would be included in the interpretive report.

A typical Certificate of Analysis would look something like the following.

CERTIFICATE OF ANALYSIS

Client: _____	Date received: _____
Site details: _____	Sample Reference: _____
Depth sample taken: _____	Test suite ID: _____
Date sample taken: _____	Date analysis complete: _____
	Sampled by: _____

Particle size distribution

Clay (< 0.002 mm)	_____ %
Silt (0.002–0.05 mm)	_____ %
Very fine sand (0.05–0.15 mm)	_____ %
Fine sand (0.15–0.25 mm)	_____ %
Medium sand (0.25–0.5 mm)	_____ %
Coarse sand (0.5–1 mm)	_____ %
Very coarse sand (1–2 mm)	_____ %
Texture class (UK classification)	_____ *

Stone content (Dry weight basis)

Stones (2–20 mm)	_____ %w/w
Stones (20–50 mm)	_____ %w/w
Stones (> 50 mm)	_____ %w/w

Soil reaction and soluble salts

pH value (1:2.5 water extract)	_____ units
Electrical conductivity (1:2.5 water extract)	_____ µS/cm
Electrical conductivity (1:2 $CaSO_4$ extract)	_____ µS/cm

Organic matter and nutrient status

Organic matter (Walkley Black)	_____ %
Total nitrogen (Dumas)	_____ %
C:N ratio	_____
Extractable phosphorus	_____ mg/l
Extractable potassium	_____ mg/l
Extractable magnesium	_____ mg/l

UK soil texture classification

C	Clay	ZC	Silty clay
SC	Sandy clay	ZCL	Silty clay loam
CL	Clay loam	SZL	Sandy silt loam
SL	Sandy loam	ZL	Silt loam
SCL	Sandy clay loam	S	Sand
LS	Loamy sand		

POTENTIAL CONTAMINANTS	
Metals	
Total arsenic (As)	_____ mg/kg
Boron-water soluble (B)	_____ mg/kg
Total cadmium (Cd)	_____ mg/kg
Total chromium (Cr)	_____ mg/kg
Hexavalent chromium	_____ mg/kg
Total copper (Cu)	_____ mg/kg
Total lead (Pb)	_____ mg/kg
Total mercury (Hg)	_____ mg/kg
Total nickel (Ni)	_____ mg/kg
Total selenium (Se)	_____ mg/kg
Total zinc (Zn)	_____ mg/kg
Inorganics	
Total cyanide (CN)	_____ mg/kg
Elemental sulphur (S)	_____ mg/kg
Acid-volatile sulphide (S)	_____ mg/kg
Water-soluble sulphate (SO_4)	_____ g/l
Organics	
Naphthalene	_____ mg/kg
Acenaphthylene	_____ mg/kg
Acenaphthene	_____ mg/kg
Fluorene	_____ mg/kg
Phenanthrene	_____ mg/kg
Anthracene	_____ mg/kg
Fluoranthene	_____ mg/kg
Pyrene	_____ mg/kg
Benzo(a)anthracene	_____ mg/kg
Chrysene	_____ mg/kg
Benzo(b)fluoranthene	_____ mg/kg
Benzo(k)fluoranthene	_____ mg/kg
Benzo(a)pyrene	_____ mg/kg
Indeno(1,2,3-cd)pyrene	_____ mg/kg
Dibenzo(a,h)anthracene	_____ mg/kg
Benzo(g,h,i)perylene	_____ mg/kg
TPH by GC-FID (C10-C40)	_____ mg/kg
Total PAHs (sum USEPA16)	_____ mg/kg
Total (mono) phenols	_____ mg/kg

Appendix 3: Tree inspection checklist

DEFINITIONS

- Origin and provenance have the meaning given in NPS
- Name, forms, dimensions and other criteria: As scheduled and defined in NPS

ALL PLANTS SHALL BE

Condition
- Materially undamaged, sturdy, healthy and vigorous

Appearance
- Of good shape and without elongated shoots
- Plants shall also be free from disfiguring knots, abrasions of the bark, wind or freezing injury or other disfigurements and shall bear evidence of proper pruning.

Hardiness
- Grown in a suitable environment and hardened-off

Health
- Free from pests, diseases, discolouration, weeds and physiological disorders

Root system and condition
- Balanced with branch system and good, fibrous root systems, through having been regularly transplanted in the nursery according to the needs of the species

Species
- True to name, consistent in species, cultivar and clone

Origin/provenance
- Grown in Great Britain for at least two growing seasons, prior to dispatch, unless otherwise approved

CHECKLIST	
Take a digital photograph, with date recorded on the image.	
Define shape of the canopy.	
Age, condition, X transplanted.	
Measure stem girth (cm) at 1 m above the soil level.	
Measure the overall tree height from soil level to top of crown.	
Measure the height of clear stem from top of soil to lowest branch.	
Determine root treatment (bare-root = BR, root ball = RB, container-grown = C).	
Determine the size of root spread, root ball or container (diameter, depth, volume).	
Determine the number of stems (for multi-stemmed) or branches (for standard).	
Note the condition of root system, if possible. Record if not possible.	
Inspect bark and note condition (abrasions, knocks, constrictions, marks, unhealed or large pruning scars).	
Inspect leaves, branches and stem for signs of pests and/or diseases.	
Inspect for signs of stress such as pale or wilting leaves.	
Fix plastic security tag with dedicated number code.	
Record security tag number, nursery reference number and location on inspection sheet.	

MATERIALS REQUIRED
• Digital camera with date-insert capability
• Tags – own tags such as coloured and numbered cable (zip) ties, loosely tied, are best to ensure that they are not removed
• Soft measuring tape or girth tape
• Measuring rods/canes

Appendix 4: Simple field test (ADAS method)

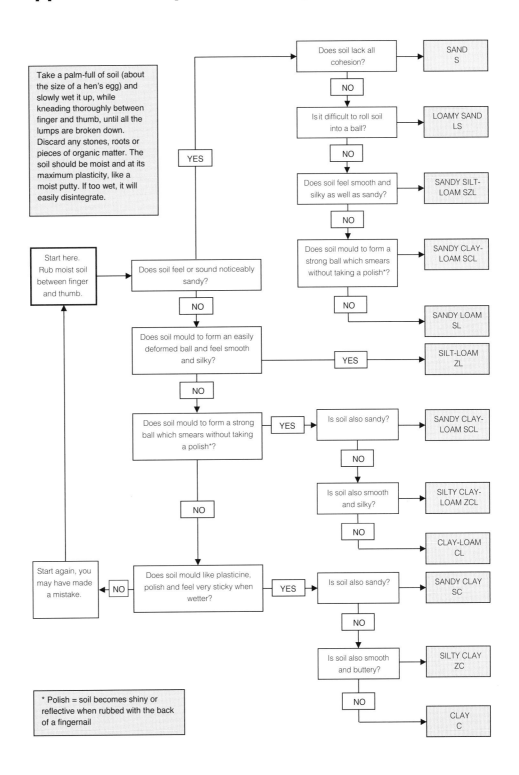

Take a palm-full of soil (about the size of a hen's egg) and slowly wet it up, while kneading thoroughly between finger and thumb, until all the lumps are broken down. Discard any stones, roots or pieces of organic matter. The soil should be moist and at its maximum plasticity, like a moist putty. If too wet, it will easily disintegrate.

Start here. Rub moist soil between finger and thumb.

Does soil feel or sound noticeably sandy?

NO

Does soil mould to form an easily deformed ball and feel smooth and silky?

NO

Does soil mould to form a strong ball which smears without taking a polish*?

NO

Start again, you may have made a mistake.

NO

Does soil mould like plasticine, polish and feel very sticky when wetter?

YES

YES

YES

Does soil lack all cohesion? → SAND S

NO

Is it difficult to roll soil into a ball? → LOAMY SAND LS

NO

Does soil feel smooth and silky as well as sandy? → SANDY SILT-LOAM SZL

NO

Does soil mould to form a strong ball which smears without taking a polish*? → SANDY CLAY-LOAM SCL

NO

SANDY LOAM SL

SILT-LOAM ZL

Is soil also sandy? → SANDY CLAY-LOAM SCL

NO

Is soil also smooth and silky? → SILTY CLAY-LOAM ZCL

NO

CLAY-LOAM CL

Is soil also sandy? → SANDY CLAY SC

NO

Is soil also smooth and buttery? → SILTY CLAY ZC

NO

CLAY C

* Polish = soil becomes shiny or reflective when rubbed with the back of a fingernail

Index

Note: *italics* denote figures; **bold** denotes tables.